THE ORGANIZATION
OF ACADEMIC WORK

THE ORGANIZATION
OF ACADEMIC WORK

PETER M. BLAU

A WILEY-INTERSCIENCE PUBLICATION

JOHN WILEY & SONS
New York • London • Sydney • Toronto

Library of Congress Cataloging in Publication Data

Blau, Peter Michael.
    The organization of academic work.

    "A Wiley-Interscience publication."
    Includes bibliographical references.
        1. Universities and Colleges—United States—
Administration. I. Title.

LB2341.B54   378.73   73-6992
ISBN 0-471-08025-X

Printed in the United States of America

10 9 8 7 6 5 4 3 2 1

To

PAMELA LISA BLAU

PREFACE

Do universities and colleges have essentially the same administrative structures as government bureaus and private firms? Is the oft-voiced criticism of large multiuniversities that they are more bureaucratic than small colleges valid or is it a misleading stereotype? Are bureaucratic tendencies of academic institutions more detrimental for teaching or for research? How significant are economic resources for academic pursuits? Does the research of faculty members depend only on their individual qualities or is it also affected by the colleague climate in a university? What conditions in institutions of higher education influence faculty authority? Which ones have an impact on student dropout and continuation rates? Which ones affect academic innovation? Why does academic life pose various dilemmas? What characterizes the academic stratification system?

Answers to these questions and related ones are suggested in the study presented of American universities and colleges, based on empirical data from a sample of 115 of them. The system of higher education in the United States is far too large and complex to be analyzed in all its ramifications in a single inquiry. Many hundreds of books on academic life and institutions have been written in recent decades. The feature of modern higher education on which attention is centered here is that it is carried out in formal organizations, in contrast to such other endeavors as art and literature or, for that matter, higher education in previous eras. At the same time, teaching and scholarship are in important respects more akin to art and literature than to the responsibilities of most other kinds of work organizations. They need freedom to explore, do not lend themselves to routinization, and cannot easily be regulated by administrative procedures. To perform activities of this nature within an administrative framework entails conflicts and strains, and these and how they are resolved are major themes of this book. Thus, the focus is on the administrative structure of universities and colleges and its implications for academic pursuits—put briefly, on bureaucracy and scholarship.

The subject matter and approach of this inquiry represent an intersection of my professional interests as a sociologist, including my personal interest as a faculty member who has spent his entire career, nearly a quarter of a century, in academic institutions. The substantive specialty in which I have done most work is the study of formal organizations. My early research consisted of case studies of organizations and emphasized the informal relations and practices that develop in work groups. In the last decade I have turned to the investigation of the formal structure of organizations using the comparative approach, by which I mean that organizations rather than their individual members are the units of analysis, that data are obtained from a sample of organizations large enough to permit quantitative analysis, and that the variables being analyzed refer to characteristics of organizations, not of persons, for instance, the division of labor or the authority structure. This comparative approach is adopted in the present study of academic institutions, with the aim of analyzing the direct and indirect relationships between various institutional attributes. At certain points, the effects of structural characteristics on individual faculty members are examined, refining the procedure for tracing structural effects that I developed earlier. Another substantive field in which I have an interest of long standing is social stratification, and this interest is reflected in the recurrent discussions of the academic stratification system.

Regardless of my specialized substantive concerns and of the fact that most of my work involves empirical research, I consider myself a social theorist and have a strong interest in the development of theory in sociology. But my assumptions about both the fundamental conceptual framework in sociology and the criteria for judging theories have undergone alterations over the years. My earlier conception of social structure was sociopsychological. I believed that a theory of social structure must be rooted in and derived from investigations of interpersonal relations and the sociopsychological processes governing them. This is the orientation in my theoretical analysis of social exchange, and some ideas developed there about exchange and power and about the significance of dilemmas for the dynamics of social structures are utilized in this book. In recent years I have moved away from a sociopsychological toward a macrosociological conception of social structure. My view now is that a systematic theory of social structure requires a conceptual framework that is confined to macrosociological properties—characteristics of organizations or societies or other collectivities—and excludes from consideration psychological and interpersonal factors, just as it excludes physiological ones. Everything cannot be questioned simultaneously, and a theory must take many aspects of reality as given while abstracting others to be taken into account. The implication is that a consistent theory to explain the complex interrelations among characteristics of social structures cannot be developed unless it is confined to this task and does not also try to account for the behavior of individuals and their interpersonal relations. In conformity with this conception, the study of universities analyzes the characteristics of these organized collectivities and not, except in a few instances, those of their individual members.

Concurrent with this change in my conception of social structure has been a change in my thinking about constructing and judging social theory. According to my previous perspective of theorizing, which rested largely on Weber's principle of *Verstehen*, social theories are built by discovering interpretations of empirical observations and social processes that are meaningful in terms of human experience, and the criterion for judging them is the profound understanding of social life they furnish. But I have become increasingly convinced that theories in sociology, like those in other sciences, should consist of deductive systems of propositions that are derived from systematic empirical research. Deductive theories are built by inferring from empirically established relationships, with the aid of theoretical concepts, generalizations from which these relationships can be logically deduced. The criterion for judging the theoretical generalizations in a deductive system is not the empathic understanding they evoke but the fact that they logically imply, in addition to the empirical propositions from which they were derived, a variety of new empirical predictions that defy falsification in subsequent research. Constructing deductive theories is an arduous task. Much of the research reported in this book is exploratory and merely provides building stones for systematic social theory. Some of it, however, involves testing a deductive theory of the structure of organizations, which was developed on the basis of an earlier study of government bureaus, in the entirely different context of academic institutions.

I must acknowledge numerous debts for assistance without which this project could not have been completed. Above all, I am grateful to the administrators of the universities and colleges in the sample who gave up some of their valuable time to be interviewed at considerable length. Information was obtained from every single case selected, which indicates how cooperative these administrators were. I also owe thanks to Talcott Parsons and Gerald M. Platt for letting me use their data on individual faculty members. The study was supported by grants GS-1528, GS-27073, and GS-28646X, of the National Science Foundation, as part of its continuing support for the Comparative Organization Research Program, which is gratefully acknowledged. (This book is C.O.R.P. Report No. 17.)

Several graduate students have earned my gratitude for their devoted work as research assistants on the project. Serena P. Laskin cheerfully assumed much responsibility during the early phases of the study, including data collection, processing, and preliminary analysis, and R. Danforth Ross and Ellen L. Slaughter participated extensively in this work. During the later stages of the analysis, I was assisted by Andrew A. Karmen, Adair T. Lummis, Horst H. Stipp, and Phelps K. Tracy. Valuable help with statistical procedures and computer programming was provided by Francis Kinley Larntz, Nadim R. Habra, and particularly Robert Fay. I also am grateful for advice on methodological problems to my colleagues, Otis Dudley Duncan, John L. Hammond, Jonathan L. Kelley, and William H. Kruskal, who must, of course, not be blamed for the shortcomings of this book owing to my limited knowledge of quantitative methods. Karlyn B. Ritchie did an admirable job typing hundreds of pages. Finally, I am greatly indebted to three of my colleagues for extensive helpful comments on the entire first draft of the book, Donald J. Treiman, Herbert J. Gans, and Judith R. Blau, the last of whom also patiently supplied sustenance and comfort to a husband immersed for months in his manuscript.

PETER M. BLAU

Columbia University
New York, New York
Spring 1973

CONTENTS

TABLES

FIGURES

THE ORGANIZATION
OF ACADEMIC WORK

CHAPTER ONE

BUREAUCRACY AND
SCHOLARSHIP

Academe, the grove where Plato developed his influential philosophy in discourse with disciples, continues to provide not only the label but also the romantic ideal of academic work. The image of such a small community of scholars in spontaneous intellectual intercourse without need for any administrative framework, however, is not an accurate reflection of the realities of contemporary academic life in the United States. How could it be?

Millions of young Americans are interested in pursuing higher education, and the country's economy demands millions of college-educated men and women. To satisfy these interests and meet these demands requires numerous large institutions of higher education. Much modern scholarship entails large-scale research necessitating abundant economic and human resources. This too requires large institutions, the only ones capable of supplying the needed resources.

For hundreds or thousands of people to be engaged in a common enterprise—an academic no less than any other enterprise—explicit procedures are needed for organizing and coordinating their activities, which is not necessary in small groups. Universities and colleges, like other organizations, therefore develop administrative machineries to organize and coordinate the academic work of students and faculty. Since the smallest American colleges have hundreds of students and dozens of faculty mem-

1

bers, even they are beyond the range of a small group in which regular direct contacts among all members obviate the need for explicit administrative mechanisms.

Administrative machineries and procedures tend to bureaucratize an organization and the performance of tasks in it. But bureaucratic rigidity and discipline are incompatible with scholarship, which requires a flexible, imaginative approach to teaching that stimulates student interests and the freedom to explore original ideas and depart from established practices in the pursuit of knowledge. A basic question raised in this book is how academic institutions cope with the dilemma posed by the incompatibility of bureaucracy and scholarship. We shall seek answers to this question on the basis of an analysis of various conditions in a sample of American universities and colleges.

THE GROWTH OF SCIENCE AND EDUCATION

The increasing rationalization of modern life is a main theme of Max Weber's theoretical analysis. In the half-century since his death, we have witnessed a continuation of this trend in the United States as well as in the rest of the world.

The growth of science has been so rapid that, as Price points out, "80 to 90 percent of all the scientists that have ever lived are alive now."[1] Science has expanded at an exponential rate, although this tremendous rate of growth has recently tapered off, with the exponential curve turning into a logistic curve, an inevitable transformation of all exponential growth curves as saturation levels are reached.[2] Nevertheless, scientific expansion continues at a very rapid rate. The number of scientific journals has doubled every 15 years ever since they were established three centuries ago, and so has the number of scientific abstracts. The number of living scientists has also doubled every 15 years, which implies that the number of scientists active today is about seven times the number of the entire population of scientists working in all the centuries before Weber's death 50 years ago.[3]

This striking proliferation of scientific manpower and accomplishments has been accompanied by great advances in technology. One measure of

[1] Derek DeS. Price, *Little Science, Big Science,* New York: Columbia University Press, 1956, p. 1.
[2] *Ibid.,* pp. 20–32.
[3] *Ibid.,* pp. 6–11.

the state of a country's technology is the machine horsepower utilized in manufacturing industries. In the first half of this century (specifically, from 1899 to 1954), horsepower per production worker in manufacturing increased fourfold in the United States, from 2.2 to 8.8.[4] These improvements in technology have raised worker productivity. Value added by manufacture per production worker increased in the same period from $1000 to $9700,[5] about three times as fast as the decline in the purchasing power of the dollar. Data reported by Mclman reveal a parallel trend: output per production worker man-hour, in international units, increased from 0.38 in 1899 to 1.43 in 1947.[6]

Changes in the economy and in the occupational structure resulted from these advances in technology and productive efficiency. The manpower required to produce food and other basic necessities steadily decreased. The most dramatic evidence of this change is the decline in American farmworkers from 11.5 million or 27 per cent of the labor force in 1920 to 3.1 million or 4 per cent of the labor force in 1970. As manpower was freed from having to supply the basic necessities of life, an increasing proportion of the labor force entered occupations that provide professional and technical services and that require a relatively high level of training and skills. The number of professional and technical workers quadrupled in the United States between 1920 and 1970, from 2.3 to 11.1 million, and their proportion of the total labor force nearly tripled in this period, from 5.4 to 14.2 per cent.[7]

A concurrent trend has been the growth of large—sometimes gigantic —organizations; most workers now are employed in such organizations, which dominate the economy. Weber considered the development of large organizations administered through impersonal criteria of efficiency to be part of the general tendency toward the rationalization of ever wider areas of social life. The large stream of migrants from small farms to cities, where most of them became employed in large factories, has contributed to this growth of organizations. The average size of manufac-

[4] Computed from U.S. Bureau of the Census, *Census of Manufacturers,* Vol. 4, Washington: U.S.G.P.O., 1968, p. 7.

[5] Computed from *Census of Manufacturers, op. cit.* Other indicators show similar patterns; see, for example, U.S. Bureau of the Census, *Historical Statistics of the United States,* Washington: U.S.G.P.O., 1960, p. 414.

[6] Seymour Melman, *Dynamic Factors in Industrial Production,* Oxford: Blackwell, 1956, pp. 113–115.

[7] Computed from *Historical Statistics of the United States, op. cit.,* p. 74, and from U.S. Bureau of the Census, *Statistical Abstracts of the United States,* Washington: U.S.G.P.O., 1971, p. 222.

turing concerns has nearly doubled in the last 50 years and is now more than 60 employees.[8] But this average is misleading, since it includes many small firms, whereas most persons work in large firms. Specifically, three-quarters of the employees in manufacturing work in establishments with more than 100 employees; even in retail trades, the bulwark of small business, more than one-fifth of all employees work in firms that large. General Motors employs ¾ million workers, and the International Telephone and Telegraph Corporation, which "in the past 10 years has acquired 101 corporations in the United States and 67 foreign countries,"[9] employs more than ½ million. There are other giant concerns of similar size.

Not the least important of the historical developments that have occurred in this century is the remarkable expansion of education. Improvements in technology and productivity have made it possible for young people to remain in school longer, as well as for old ones to retire earlier, since the number of years of productive labor needed to support the population has been reduced and, indeed, more goods and services are now produced in a shorter working day. A high level of education in a society depends on freeing people's time from economic activities and giving them the opportunity to pursue learning. Hutchins notes that the superior education in ancient Athens, which was confined to an elite, "was made possible by slavery." And he continues: "Machines can do for every modern man what slavery did for the fortunate few in Athens."[10]

As the efficiency of modern technology makes more years of schooling for more people possible, the greater complexity and skill requirements of many jobs in today's economy make formal education necessary. Professional and technical workers, whose proportion in the labor force has increased at a rapid rate, need much training. In addition, virtually all jobs today necessitate a fairly high level of literacy, which was not true at the beginning of the century, when a third of the labor force worked on farms. Literacy is essential not only in the economic arena but also in the political one in a modern democracy, because the electorate cannot make informed decisions without it. Finally, the popular demand for more education has increased with the rising levels of occupational expectations and aspirations, which have been stimulated by increases in productivity and in the standard of living and by the expansion of high-status occupations that require considerable schooling.

---

[8] Computed from U.S. Bureau of the Census, *Census of Manufacturing*, Vol. 1, Washington, U.S.G.P.O., 1971, p. 26.
[9] *The New York Times*, 26 March 1972, Section E, p. 4.
[10] Robert M. Hutchins, *The Learning Society*, New York: Praeger, 1968, p. 135.

The rise in the educational level of the American population has been spectacular. At the beginning of the century, less than one-tenth of the age cohort having reached 17 years graduated from high school; 50 years ago, one-sixth did; by 1940, it was the majority; and today, about two-thirds are high school graduates.[11] The median years of schooling completed by the age cohort remained between eight and nine years from the end of the last century until 50 years ago, but it then rose rapidly to more than 12 years by 1940, and it has kept on rising, though at a somewhat slower pace.[12] Fewer than 50,000 young men and women received college degrees fifty years ago, whereas more than 500,000 do so today,[13] a tenfold increase, while the population only doubled. The superior education of the young raised the average level of schooling of the entire population. In 1940, when one-half of the youngsters graduated from high school, the median years of schooling of all Americans 25 years of age or over was still only 8.6; by 1970, it had risen to 12.2.[14]

American education is often disparaged for being more superficial and less academically oriented than education in Europe. But this criticism, even if granted, ignores the important fact that more years of schooling are provided for more young persons in the United States than in any other country. Although European educational systems may prepare the elite better than the American system does, education beyond the eighth grade is furnished to more people in the United States than in Europe.

The various trends that have been discussed converge in institutions of higher education, where most scientific work is carried out, where most professionals and technicians are trained, and where more and more young men and women go to complete their formal education. As a result, American higher education has expanded greatly. Enrollment in colleges and universities has doubled every 15 years between 1870 and 1950 and has grown at a still faster rate since then, as Ben-David, quoting Ashby, notes.[15] The number of undergraduates has increased from less than 600,000 to nearly 6,500,000 in the last 50 years. This tenfold increase of undergraduates is greatly exceeded by a no less than fiftyfold increase in graduate students, from 15,600 in 1920 to 826,000 in 1970.[16] Similarly, whereas the number of college degrees earned increased tenfold, from

[11] *Historical Statistics of the United States, op. cit.,* p. 207.
[12] *Ibid.,* p. 214.
[13] U.S. Office of Education, *Digest of Educational Statistics,* Washington: U.S.G.P.O., 1970, p. 78.
[14] *Statistical Abstract of the United States, op. cit.,* p. 110.
[15] Joseph Ben-David, *American Higher Education,* New York: McGraw-Hill, 1972, p. 1.
[16] Otis A. Singletary, *American Universities and Colleges,* Washington: American Council of Education, 1968, p. 20.

50,000 to 500,000, in that period, as mentioned, the number of doctor's degrees increased thirtyfold, from 615 in 1920 to 18,237 in 1966.[17] Although the growth rate of all students in institutions of higher education has been less rapid in this country (7 per cent per annum between 1930 and 1959) than in the rest of the world (10 per cent per annum), the reason is that other countries had many fewer students than the United States in the earlier period. The number of students of higher education per 1000 inhabitants is still larger in the United States than in any other country; it is 1.7 here, with the second highest ratio being Russia's of 1.0 (in 1955–59).[18]

As student enrollment has increased, so has the number of faculty members and the number of institutions of higher education. Between 1920 and 1966, the number of faculty members has grown from 50,000 to 600,000, and the number of institutions from 1041 to 2230.[19] The rate of increase of faculty members has kept pace with that of students; that of institutions has not, but institutions of higher education have become larger.

Colleges and universities have increased in size just as other organizations have. In 1920, the average American institution of higher education had 50 faculty members and 500 students; by 1966, these averages had risen to 270 faculty members and 2500 students. As institutions have grown larger, the number of those remaining small has declined, their proportion has declined at a faster rate, and the proportion of students attending them has declined at a still faster rate. Between 1938 and 1968, the number of institutions with less than 250 students decreased from 724 to 292; the proportion of all institutions with so few students diminished from 43 to 12 per cent; and the proportion of all students going to colleges with an enrollment of less than 250 declined from 6 to about $\frac{1}{2}$ per cent. In the same period, the proportion of institutions with an enrollment of at least 2500 increased from 6 to 26 per cent, and the proportion of all students in these large institutions increased from 49 to 79 per cent.[20]

The extreme result of this growth of academic institutions is the modern multiuniversity, as Kerr calls it, with tens of thousands of students,

[17] *Digest of Educational Statistics, op. cit.*

[18] UNESCO, *World Survey of Education,* Vol. 4, Paris: UNESCO, 1965, pp. 65, 67.

[19] *Digest of Educational Statistics, op. cit.*

[20] Donald J. Reichard, *Campus Size,* Atlanta: *Southern Regional Education Board,* 1971, pp. 1, 3. Data in this source and the others cited in the last paragraphs include junior colleges and specialized ones, such as teachers colleges, whereas only colleges and universities granting four-year degrees in liberal arts are included in the research reported in this book.

thousands of faculty members, hundreds of administrators, scores of schools and colleges. A polar example is the University of California. Kerr describes the immense scope it had already in 1963 in the following words:[21]

The University of California last year had operating expenditures from all sources of nearly half a billion dollars, with nearly another 100 million for construction; a total employment of over 40,000 people, more than IBM and in a far greater variety of endeavors; operations in over a hundred locations, counting campuses, experiment stations, agricultural and urban extension centers, and projects abroad in more than fifty countries; nearly 10,000 courses in its catalogues; some form of contact with nearly every industry, nearly every level of government, nearly every person in its region. . . . It will soon have 100,000 students—30,000 of them at the graduate level; yet much less than one third of its expenditures are directly related to teaching.

It is often assumed that the rapid growth in the quantity of American higher education has produced a deterioration of its quality, but Ben-David points out that the evidence does not support this assumption: "The scientific reputation of American institutions of higher education rose all the time. Their share in the world production of scientific papers, or in such honors as Nobel prizes, reached an all-time high after World War II." He goes on to show, citing evidence from a variety of sources, that teaching effectiveness has not declined either, and concludes "that increased emphasis on research, whatever effects it may have had on other aspects of college life, did not lead to a decline in the effectiveness of college study. If anything, the change has probably been for the better."[22] Historically, then, the increasing emphasis on research has not adversely affected college teaching, according to Ben-David, and we shall have an opportunity to examine whether the same is true when academic institutions are compared, that is, whether an emphasis on research is inversely related to the quality of college teaching.

Large academic institutions, no less than other large organizations, require and acquire a complex administrative apparatus, and administrative concerns with budgets and regular procedures can easily endanger academic pursuits. For good teaching and scholarship involve creative imagination, which cannot be harnessed by bureaucratic discipline. What makes the problem worse is that the most advanced training and research, which depends most on freedom from bureaucratic restraints, tends to be carried out in large multiuniversities, whose size and complexity make

[21] Clark Kerr, *The Uses of the University,* Cambridge: Harvard University Press, 1964, pp. 7–8.
[22] Ben-David, *op. cit.,* pp. 2–3.

them most susceptible to bureaucratization. But are large universities actually most bureaucratic? In which respects are they and in which respects are they not? What aspects of bureaucratization are found in academic institutions, and which ones are most detrimental for education and research?

ADMINISTRATIVE STRUCTURE AND ACADEMIC WORK

The basic problem under investigation is how the organization of an academic enterprise affects academic work. We wish to examine how the administrative structure established to organize the many students and faculty members in a university or college influences academic pursuits.

In short, the issue posed refers to the relationship between bureaucracy and scholarship. To study this issue, it is necessary to ascertain what conditions govern the development of differentiated and complex administrative structures and to examine whether these bureaucratic developments in academic institutions are similar to those in other types of organizations. Another general question pertaining to this issue is how the economic and human resources of an academic institution and the way they are organized by its administrative structure affect several factors that have indirect bearing on academic performance, for example, recruitment of faculty and students, the academic climate in the institution, and the prevailing orientation to teaching and research. To clarify the implications of bureaucracy for scholarship, it is important to analyze the impact various conditions in universities and colleges have on decentralization of authority, institutional innovation, and, especially, academic performance itself. Three recurrent themes of the analysis are the significance of differentiation and specialization, the roots of the academic stratification system, and dilemmas of academic life, including that posed by the need for and the adverse consequences of bureaucratic structures in academia today.

The large university frequently is criticized for being bureaucratic, and its large size often is held responsible for making it a poor learning environment for students.[23] Three well-known critics of American higher education are Veblen, Goodman, and Hutchins. Veblen is rightfully scornful of the business mentality that pervades so much of higher

---

[23] See, for example, Herbert Stroup, *Bureaucracy in Higher Education*, New York: Free Press, 1966; Arthur W. Chickering, *Education and Identity*, San Francisco: Jossey-Bass, 1969, esp. pp. 185–195; and J. Douglas Brown, *The Liberal University*, New York: McGraw-Hill, 1969.

education in the United States, in our days no less than in his.[24] Goodman castigates the emphasis of college administrators on efficient management to the detriment of scholarship—indeed, not only that of administrators. "The community of scholars is replaced by a community of administrators and scholars with administrative mentalities, company men and time-servers among the teachers, grade-seekers and time-servers among the students."[25]

Hutchins too attacks the emphasis on technology and efficiency in American higher education, and he generally condemns the prevailing preoccupation with marketable skills, practical training, and giving students information and answers rather than stimulating in them a deeper understanding of scholarship. He stresses that "the benefits of education are indirect. The mind is not a receptacle; information is not education. Education is what remains after the information that has been taught has been forgotten. Ideas, methods, habits of mind are the radioactive deposits left by education."[26] He advocates a liberal education with theoretical emphasis as more practical than practical training in a rapidly changing society like ours, in which practical information soon becomes obsolete. "It now seems safe to say that the most practical education is the most theoretical one."[27] Such general education is not the privilege of an aristocratic elite. "Liberal education should not be condemned because it was once limited to rulers or to those who had the leisure to be human. Now that all men are rulers and all will have some leisure, liberal education can be extended to all."[28]

This ideal of a liberal education that enlarges the mind for all citizens, which the efficiency of modern technology has brought within reach, is appealing in a democratic society. Many of the criticisms made of contemporary higher education seem well justified—the business mentality so often found in it, the tendency to judge its accomplishments in terms of short-run efficiency, and the narrow focus on vocational skills frequently manifest. But the remedy proposed is questionable. Hutchins implies that a university must remain small lest it become transformed from an intellectual community of scholars into a bureaucratic knowledge factory.[29] Goodman also advocates that the community of scholars should be "quite moderate in size; historically, except in exceptional

[24] Thorstein Veblen, *The Higher Learning in America*, New York: Viking Press, 1918, pp. 200–210.
[25] Paul Goodman, *The Community of Scholars*, New York: Random House, 1962, p. 74.
[26] Hutchins, *op. cit.*, p. 38; see also pp. 74–77, 132.
[27] *Ibid.*, p. 8.
[28] *Ibid.*, p. 32.
[29] *Ibid.*, pp. 105–118.

cases, the number has hovered between 500 and 1,000, and sometimes we shall speak of celebrated universities that numbered 100 people!"[30] Both implicitly assume that the large size of modern universities is responsible for the proliferation of bureaucratic machinery and the administrative centralization that they criticize. But have large universities in fact proportionately more administrative personnel and a more centralized authority structure than small colleges? These are empirical questions, which must be answered on the basis of research before one can meaningfully evaluate the significance of institutional size for higher education.

A romantic pleading for a return to small communities of scholars fails to take into account the demands made on higher education in modern society.[31] It overlooks the need for many large universities and colleges to meet the demands of millions of young men and women for education beyond high school in order to attain upward mobility or retain the social level of their parents, since superior occupational achievement has increasingly become dependent on at least some college education. Many large academic institutions are also needed to meet the demands of the modern economy for large numbers of college-trained persons. The two sets of demands are connected, of course, inasmuch as the economic demands for highly educated labor greatly strengthen the motivation of young people to demand a college education and enable many of them to achieve upward mobility by going to college. These considerations imply that the practical consequences of higher education must not be ignored. One may agree with Hutchins that academic studies should include a liberal education designed to broaden the mind, but this must not prevent us from realizing that colleges—unless restricted to a small elite—must also provide students with training they can use in their occupational life.

To enhance our understanding of today's large academic institutions requires more than exhortations against the evils of large size and bureaucracy. It requires conceptual clarification of the terms used, and it requires systematic analysis of the conditions in universities and colleges and their influences on academic work; this is a prerequisite for developing theories that can explain these conditions and policies that can improve them. Most of this book is devoted to such an analysis of American universities and colleges. At this point, let us examine two basic concepts—bureaucracy and professionalism. Both reflect frequent

---

[30] Goodman, op. cit., p. 5.
[31] As a matter of fact, Joseph Ben-David asserts that universities were already quite large in the late middle ages. "A university consisted of several thousands of students, 6,000 in Paris in 1300—and, at times, hundreds of masters . . ." "The Scientific Role," *Minerva* 4 (1) (1965–66), p. 19.

criticisms of academic institutions, specifically, their tendency to become bureaucratized and the danger that scholarship may become submerged by professional concerns.

The first question is whether it is correct to consider academic institutions bureaucracies. This question has no straightforward answer. The term "bureaucracy" is usually used loosely, and even when it is rigorously defined at great length, as in Weber's analysis, it encompasses many different elements. Such a broad concept tends to be misleading, because it invites indiscriminate application. I may call a union bureaucratic because of the centralized leadership's *preoccupation with* administrative *efficiency,* and I may call a government agency bureaucratic because of the prevailing rigid conformity with rules in *disregard of* considerations of *efficiency.* To be useful in systematic analysis, broad concepts must be dissected into their elements. Universities and colleges have some bureaucratic characteristics, such as a formal division of labor, an administrative hierarchy, and a clerical apparatus. But they do not have other bureaucratic attributes; for example, there is no direct supervision of the work of the major group of employees, the faculty, and there are no detailed operating rules governing the performance of academic responsibilities. With respect to many bureaucratic characteristics, there is much variation among academic institutions; the degree of administrative centralization of authority is a typical example. A major problem under investigation is how different bureaucratic traits affect academic life, and the variations in these traits among institutions make it possible to analyze this problem.

A second question is whether academics are professionals. There is some disagreement among social scientists on this subject. Both Ben-David and Goode consider university faculty members the prototype of professionals.[32] On the other hand, Hughes draws a contrast between scientists and professionals, the distinguishing criterion being that scientists do not have clients and professionals do,[33] which implies that academics in their role as scientists and scholars are not professionals. The reason for the existence of such differences is that "professionalism," just as "bureaucracy," is a broad term encompassing many elements, and not all investigators focus on the same ones. Nevertheless, there is general agreement, as Goode notes, "that the two central generating qualities [of professionalism] are (1) a basic body of abstract knowledge, and

[32] Joseph Ben-David, "Science as a Profession and Scientific Professionalism," in R. C. Baum et al., *Explorations in General Theory in the Social Sciences,* New York: Free Press (in press); and William J. Goode, "The Theoretical Limits of Professionalization," in Amitai Etzioni, *The Semi-Professions and Their Organization,* New York: Free Press, 1969, pp. 266–313, esp. p. 267.

[33] Everett C. Hughes, *Men and Their Work,* Glencoe, Ill.: Free Press, 1958, pp. 139–144.

(2) the ideal of service."[34] Other characteristics of professions he lists are: "high income, prestige, and influence; high educational requirements; professional autonomy; licensure; commitment of members to the profession. . . ."[35]

Many of these characteristics of professionals are shared by academics. They have high social status, high educational requirements, and strong commitments to their work, for instance. In regard to Goode's two central criteria of professionalism, however, the case is not unequivocal. To be sure, academic work is probably the polar case of work being based on an abstract body of knowledge, but different academic disciplines are based on different bodies of knowledge. The concept of profession implies a unified body of knowledge, as in medicine; although one can specialize in one aspect of medicine, one can also be a general practitioner; the same is true for law and for the ministry. But one cannot be a general practitioner in "academicology." As a a matter of fact, there is no such word, because there is no such discipline. (The liberal arts are not a discipline and do not have general practitioners.) In terms of this criterion, though different academic disciplines may be considered professions, the entire academic community cannot be so considered.

In terms of the second criterion, the exact opposite is the case. The service ideal implies that professionals are practitioners who serve the needs of clients. In their roles as scientists and scholars in different disciplines, academics have no clients, as Hughes emphasizes, and thus are not professionals. In their role as teachers, which the academics in the various disciplines share, they have students whose needs they are expected to serve, and in this common role they accordingly may be considered professionals by the second criterion, though not by the first. Moreover, university students, particularly advanced students, are not really clients, and university faculties are experts in their various disciplines and not in teaching, which finds institutionalized expression in the fact that they are neither trained nor licensed to teach. If scholarship is the aim, the relation is not that between practitioner and client but between scholar and student who is being socialized to become a fellow expert, whereas professionals do not seek to transform their best clients into colleagues.

Academics differ in several respects from professionals, though there are also a number of similarities between the two. Probably the most important similarity for a study of academic institutions is the significance of professional and academic autonomy and self-regulation. Since

---

[34] Goode, *op. cit.*, p. 277.
[35] *Ibid.*, p. 276.

the work of specialized experts is too complicated to be accurately judged by laymen, fellow specialists are the only ones qualified to evaluate it. This principle has become institutionalized in professional associations that claim sole jurisdiction over licensing professionals and judging their work, and in university faculties that demand freedom from administrative interference in evaluating academic work and making faculty appointments. Such authority of professionals, including now academics, which rests on institutionally recognized expert knowledge, conflicts with administrative authority, which is based on official positions in a bureaucratic hierarchy. Hence administrative and faculty expectations tend to come into conflict. Other sources of strain are the competing demands made by research and teaching, which may put students and faculty on opposite sides, and which found expression in student uprisings in the last decade, and the problem of mobilizing sufficient economic resources for academic pursuits, in which governing boards and the university community represent contrasting interests, and which is reflected in the current financial crisis of academic institutions. One objective of this inquiry is to ascertain how these conflicts are resolved and what conditions determine how they are resolved.

PROBLEMS UNDER INVESTIGATION

Academic institutions differ in many fundamental respects from such organizations as government bureaus or private firms. The first question to be raised is whether they and other organizations are nevertheless homologous, that is, exhibit essential similarities in their administrative structures. Of particular interest are some consistent empirical regularities in the relationship of size, differentiation in the structure, and administrative apparatus exhibited by government bureaus. A theory to explain these relationships has been advanced. The study of academic institutions provides an opportunity to test the theoretical assumptions and examine whether the same empirical patterns are found in this entirely different organizational setting. If so, it would indicate that the formal structure of academic institutions does not differ from that of other bureaucracies, though it would not mean that there are no important differences or that universities are bureaucratic in most respects.

Research on other kinds of organizations reveals that size exerts a pervasive influence on organizational characteristics. We shall see that this is also the case in academic institutions. One may well ask, however, whether multiuniversities and small colleges are not entirely different types of institutions and whether these differences in type rather than size itself are responsible for the great differences in characteristics. To be sure, Harvard University and Paine College in Georgia, for example, basically differ in many more ways than merely their size. The solution to this problem is not to make variations in size a criterion for differences in type, because the cutting points would necessarily be arbitrary and other important distinctions would be ignored. The solution adopted is rather to ascertain what influences size has when other differences are controlled and what influences other conditions have independent of size or mediating indirect effects of size.

Institutions are not engaged in work; only individuals are. The quality of an academic institution and of the academic work performed in it depends on the qualifications and abilities of its faculty and students. But institutional conditions determine the capability of a university or college to recruit good students and faculty. A number of problems pertaining to this issue will be examined. How is faculty recruitment affected by extrinsic rewards, notably salaries, and by intrinsic rewards of the job itself? Do bureaucratic features of a university interfere with its recruitment of promising students and faculty members? Do recruitment patterns reveal personal preferences unrelated to economic rewards and academic work, such as preferences for particular locations? Impressionistically, for instance, it seems that Southern universities and colleges have greater difficulties in recruitment than Northern ones, and it is of interest to ascertain whether this is actually the case.

The influence of the size of academic institutions on recruitment poses a paradox. The multiuniversity is often unfavorably compared with the less impersonal small institution in academic circles. Yet the best faculty members and students, who have more freedom of choice in deciding where to go, are found in disproportionate numbers in large universities. To cite only one illustrative empirical result: the survey of nearly 2500 social scientists in 165 universities and colleges by Lazarsfeld and Thielens shows that two-thirds of those in very large institutions (more than 9000 students) but less than one-third of those in small institutions (less than 2500 students) scored high on the index of scholarly productivity.[36] Does large size make an academic institution more or less attractive to faculty and students? Generally, do the same conditions that facilitate recruitment of able faculty also improve recruitment of able students, or are the conditions that attract good students different from those attracting good faculty? In analyzing recruitment, another problem of interest is whether there is any class bias. Looking at this problem from another

[36] Paul F. Lazarsfeld and Wagner Thielens, Jr., *The Academic Mind*, Glencoe, Ill.: Free Press, 1958, p. 23; for sample and index, see pp. 3–8.

perspective, what academic institutions are main avenues of upward mobility?

The orientation of faculty members toward academic work has much bearing on how they perform their roles and what endeavors receive most of their attention. A major issue already mentioned is the extent to which the faculty concentrates on research and teaching, respectively. In exploring this issue, several influences on the orientations of faculty members must be analytically separated. As we shall see, the differences among academic institutions in the average qualifications of their faculties are reflected in differences in the prevailing orientation to research. The question arises how much of this results from the influence of the individual's own qualifications on his attitude toward research and how much of it is indicative of what I have called a structural effect, that is, the influence of the academic climate created by many highly qualified colleagues on a person's orientation to and involvement in research, independent of his own qualifications. Further clarification requires that the influence on faculty research of administrative demands for publications be distinguished from the influences of both the academic climate among colleagues and the individual's own training and background. We must also consider whether the faculty's involvement in research helps or hinders the recruitment of students with high ability and how the faculty's academic orientation affects contacts with undergraduates.

The orientation of faculty members to their local institution as well as their orientation to academic work is of interest. Gouldner, applying Merton's concepts to a study of the members of a college faculty, distinguishes between cosmopolitans, who are primarily oriented to colleagues in their discipline outside the college, and locals, whose basic orientation is to their own college.[37] We shall try to determine the conditions that promote a cosmopolitan perspective and discourage allegiance to the local institution among faculty members and those that foster a cosmopolitan interest in recruiting outside faculty among administrators. It will be shown that characteristics of faculty members have, strange though it seems, opposite effects on their own and on their colleagues' loyalty to the local institution. Characteristics associated with high academic status make those possessing them more cosmopolitan and less loyal to their institution but simultaneously make the institution a more desirable place and thus enhance the loyalty of colleagues to it.

The study of the degree to which authority over various kinds of deci-

[37] Alvin W. Gouldner, "Cosmopolitans and Locals," *Administrative Science Quarterly* 2 (1957–58), 281–306, 444–480.

sions is centralized in the hands of administrators rather than being decentralized to the faculty is of special importance for understanding one aspect of bureaucratization of academic institutions. It is generally acknowledged that the best academic institutions tend to be more decentralized than others. If this is the case, we shall want to know what about them sustains faculty influence. Outstanding academic institutions typically are wealthy, have superior faculties, and have good students. Can one discern whether decentralization results from the institution's own academic standing or the superior academic status of its faculty members? Is decentralization a form of *noblesse oblige* in affluent institutions, owing to their lesser need to maintain tight control of the purse strings? Insofar as superior faculties promote decentralization, we shall want to know the specific attributes of good faculties that are responsible for this effect. Is decentralization affected primarily by the faculty's formal qualifications, academic performance, or opportunities to obtain positions elsewhere? Does faculty influence become institutionalized? What significance does the formally instituted faculty government have for the actual decision-making power of the faculty?

The pressure of a large number of managerial decisions fosters delegation of responsibilities to middle management in large government agencies. Are large academic institutions more decentralized than small ones, corresponding to the situation in other types of organizations, or are large universities more centralized, in accordance with the bureaucratic stereotype? If the presidents of large academic institutions make fewer decisions than do the presidents of small ones, does this merely mean that in large institutions more authority is vested in deans and other administrators, which would parallel delegation to middle management in government agencies, or is there also more decentralization to the faculty in large academic institutions? Since larger institutions have better faculties, it will be necessary to separate the influences on decentralization of size as such from those of the conditions associated with size, like faculty quality. A final illustration of the questions the inquiry poses in this area is what effect presidential turnover has on the authority of the president. The answer is not as obvious as it may seem.

It is essential for academic institutions to keep up with the developments in various fields, especially in the rapidly changing scientific fields. This raises the problem of how academic progress can be institutionalized. Of course, individual faculty members, not institutions, are the ones who must keep informed about new developments in their disciplines, but the conditions in academic institutions either facilitate or impede the endeavors of individuals to remain abreast of scientific advances. One such condition is the faculty teaching load. Another is the departmental structure, specifically, how many departments in new fields the institution includes. The establishment of new departments is an institutional innovation that facilitates innovative academic work, because it brings together academics with common intellectual interests, crystallizes new academic roles for them (transforming biologists with specialized interests into microbiologists, for instance), and helps to channel their scientific work in new directions.

We shall investigate the conditions that lead to the creation of new departments. Does an academic tradition further or hinder such innovation? Faculty members often are accused of being conservative with respect to internal matters of their own institution and resisting change, regardless of how progressive their political opinions may be. This would imply that administrative initiative is necessary to establish new departments and that the faculty does not favor but opposes such innovations. We shall see whether the evidence supports this common assumption. Another question is whether managerial succession fosters innovation in academic institutions, as it has been found to do in other kinds of organizations. One may also ask whether students, though they have little power in colleges and universities, indirectly influence the tendency to innovate and to keep up with new scientific developments.

After having discussed the various conditions in academic institutions and their interdependence, we shall consider how these conditions affect academic performance. The basic responsibilties of universities and colleges are education and scholarly research, and the effects of various conditions on both of them will be examined. The two indications of educational performance are college dropouts and the inclination of graduates to continue their education and go to graduate school, on the assumption that successful education promotes the pursuit of further education. Another assumption is that the performance of students is also indicative of the effectiveness of the faculty's performance of educational duties, provided that the ability of entering students is controlled. A fundamental issue is whether the emphasis on research and advanced training in major universities infringes upon faculty responsibilities for undergraduate education. Do many graduate students, for example, preempt faculty attention and time and consequently have detrimental effects on undergraduate education? Does frequent faculty contact with undergraduates improve their educational progress, as is often alleged? Does the prevalence of highly qualified faculty members, most of whom are engaged in research, make undergraduate education less effective than it is when faculty members are not so highly qualified but are more concerned with teaching?

Finally, we turn to the faculty's published research and scholarship. A most pertinent question is whether research productivity benefits most from a centralized authority structure, though it gives faculty members less freedom, or from decentralized responsibilities, though they put more administrative burdens on faculty members. Other institutional conditions affecting publications will be examined as well. For example, is research output higher in universities than in colleges even when quality of personnel input is controlled? Does institutional size have independent effects on research and publications? The qualifications of the faculty must be controlled to determine what institutional conditions improve scholarly performance. Attempts will also be made to infer *how* various institutional conditions affect academic performance, whether by selecting faculty members who perform well or by stimulating their performance once they are there.

THE ROLE OF RESEARCH

My goal is to develop a theory that explains the structure of academic institutions and that of other organizations, and my ultimate aim is to contribute to a general theory of social structure. Indeed, I consider advancing theory the sole objective of science. Although research may have many objectives—policy formation, advancing the revolution, selling cars—the one I am interested in is its contribution to theory. Here two roles of research can be distinguished. Once a rigorous theoretical formulation has been developed, research is essential to try to falsify the theory and thereby to test it.[38] But there is little rigorous theory in sociology. At the present stage, the role of research largely is different: research must provide information in systematic form suitable for constructing theory, which is another way of saying that at the present stage of sociology research is largely exploratory, though not without theoretical focus.

Empirical answers to questions like those raised in the preceding section are needed to start building a theory of the organization of academic work. For a theory is designed to improve our understanding of empirical reality by explaining it,[39] and before we can explain something we must know what it is like. It does not make sense to try to explain why large universities have disproportionately many administrators, for example, unless we know that they in fact do. To be sure, conceptual frameworks

[38] On the importance of unsuccessful attempts to falsify a theory for testing it, see Karl R. Popper, *The Logic of Scientific Discovery*, New York: Basic Books, 1961, esp. pp. 40–42, 78–92.
[39] Richard B. Braithwaite, *Scientific Explanation*, Cambridge (England): University Press.

and theoretical conjectures derived from previous research will shape the research design and the interpretation of empirical results. Depending on the theoretical framework and assumptions, the research findings will be fruitful for developing systematic theories or sterile or perhaps even misleading. The conceptual framework may neglect the most relevant conditions, and the assumptions about causal sequence may be defective. These problems reflect the complex interdependence between theory and research. Ideally, we should have one before undertaking the other. Unfortunately, this is not possible, though a resemblance of it results from the development side by side of social theories, often based on merely impressionistic empirical information, and social research, often without theoretical focus.

Social research should be guided by a theoretical framework and focus, in my opinion, but the systematic analysis of empirical data is a prerequisite for constructing systematic social theories. Accordingly, most of this book presents an analysis of empirical data on universities and colleges in the United States. Before turning to this analysis, the research procedures must be described.

CHAPTER TWO

THE COMPARATIVE STUDY
OF AMERICAN UNIVERSITIES
AND COLLEGES

In the comparative approach to the study of social structure the units of analysis are organized collectivities, be they academic institutions, political or economic organizations, or entire societies. Most social research, in contrast, treats human beings as the units of analysis. The variables under investigation in comparative studies are characteristics of organized collectivities, such as their size, the division of labor, and the decentralization of authority, not attitudes and behavior characterizing individual persons, as is the case in conventional surveys. The term "comparative study" usually is employed for international comparisons, but research on different nations is essential only if the units of analysis are societies. If they are academic institutions, as here, or other organizations, the comparison can be confined to those in a single country.

The general question raised in conventional surveys is how social conditions affect the attitudes and conduct of individuals, for example, how the socioeconomic conditions in which individuals find themselves influence their political behavior. In such investigations social conditions are taken as given, that is, they are exogenous variables that are used to explain the opinions and activities of individuals but that are not themselves being explained. The basic issue posed by sociological theorists, however, is precisely how to explain why various social conditions develop, which means that they treat characteristics of societies or other organized collectivities as the endogenous variables to be explained. For instance, Durkheim asked why the division of labor develops, Marx analyzed the factors governing the class structure, and Weber sought to explain the rise of modern capitalism. The comparative approach formulates problems of inquiry in the same way sociological theory does and considers the social conditions in organized collectivities not as given exogenous factors but as the subject matter to be explained. For this purpose, the interdependence among various social conditions is analyzed. Such an analysis of the characteristics of American universities and colleges will be presented.

This chapter deals with the research procedures employed. The sample of academic institutions used, the sources from which data were obtained, and how the data were collected are described. Operational measures of characteristics of academic institutions are discussed, and so are the results of a reliability check. The regression procedures utilized and the assumptions made in them are explicated in general terms and on the basis of a substantive example, namely, how various conditions influence faculty salaries.

DATA COLLECTION

Data were collected on 115 universities and colleges, which constitute a representative sample of all four-year institutions granting liberal arts degrees in the United States in the mid-1960s. Excluded are junior colleges, teachers colleges, and other specialized colleges such as music schools and seminaries. A specific academic institution, not a university system, is defined as a case. Thus the University of California is not considered a single academic institution, but its Berkeley campus is one of the cases in the sample, as is its Riverside campus. The most recently established colleges and universities are also excluded, since the sample was selected from a 1964 list of American universities and colleges.[1] In 1964 there were just over 1000 institutions meeting the criteria, although when the data were collected in 1968 the number had risen to about 1150, as some new colleges had been created and some junior and teachers colleges had been transformed into four-year institutions in the liberal arts. There is some advantage in not including in the analysis the newest colleges still in the process of developing their curriculum, personnel, and organization.

[1] Allan M. Cartter, *American Universities and Colleges*, Washington: American Council of Education, 1964.

Information was obtained from three types of sources. First, in the spring of 1968, personal visits were made to all 115 campuses by research assistants who interviewed two members of the central administration and questioned additional officials if necessary to complete the information called for by the interview schedules. There were no refusals (after a few initial refusals had been persuaded to change their mind by a telephone call of the author). One interview was held with the president or his representative; it was the president himself in 44 cases, the academic vice-president or provost in 51, and another vice-president or official in a similar position in the remaining 20. The second person interviewed was an assistant to the president who was familiar with administrative procedures and had access to the institution's records. Self-administered questionnaires were distributed to deans, who were asked to mail them back.

One purpose of the interview was to obtain information on the administrative structure, for example, the number of administrative levels, counting all faculty except chairmen as the lowest level and the president as the highest; the number of officials reporting to the president and the number on the next level reporting to them; the number of nonclerical administrators and the number of clerical personnel. Examples of the large amount of other data obtained in the interviews are the following: the number of student applications, student admissions, faculty appointments, and appointed faculty members with degrees from this institution, all for the academic years 1967–68; the departments that had been recently created and those that had been recently abolished; and a variety of indications of the authority exercised by the president and by others in several areas.

Published compilations of quantitative information on the academic institutions in the United States constitute the second source of data. The publication utilized most extensively is the tenth edition of the American Council of Education's *American Universities and Colleges.*[2] Among the data abstracted from this source are information on revenue; number of faculty members, enrolled students, and degrees awarded; mean SAT (Scholastic Aptitude Test) scores of entering students; and proportion of college graduates expected to continue in graduate or professional schools.

A number of other publications yielded additional data. Thus information on faculty salaries was supplied by a survey conducted by the

[2] Otis A. Singletary, *American Universities and Colleges,* Washington: American Council of Education, 1968.

American Association of University Professors.[3] An index of the institution's reputation among outstanding students is based on a score constructed by Astin.[4] Other data, used either as indicators of different institutional characteristics or to check the reliability of the information from one source with that from a second, were derived from the academic institution's own publications (faculty handbook, student handbook, catalogue), those by the U. S. Office of Education on academic personnel, and one by the National Science Foundation on federal support. Whenever possible, information for the academic year 1967–68 is used, though in some cases that for an earlier year had to suffice.

The third source of data is a survey of a sample of 2577 faculty members drawn from the same 115 academic institutions. This questionnaire survey was conducted by the Survey Research Center at the University of Michigan in 1967 for a study by Talcott Parsons and Gerald M. Platt, who kindly made their data available. Since one of the 115 institutions in the sample did not participate in the faculty survey, responses are available from faculty members in 114 of the 115 academic institutions under study, an average of 23 per institution. (A larger proportion of individuals in small than in large institutions was sampled.) These responses from faculty members are of great value in the present study for several reasons, even though the focus here is on the characteristics of academic institutions rather than those of individual members.

Many conditions in universities and colleges cannot be reliably reported by top administrators but require information from a sample of faculty members. (Still other conditions would require information from a sample of students, and the meager data from students, confined to those in published sources, limits the scope of the study, excluding from it an extensive analysis of student life.) For example, only faculty responses can provide valid indicators of the prevailing orientation to research and to teaching, or of the extent of influence the faculty has over decisions in various areas. Many characteristics of universities and colleges that are of interest are, in the terms of Lazarsfeld and Menzel,[5] not global properties describing the institution as whole, such as its age, but analytical properties referring to aggregate attributes of its

[3] American Association of University Professors, "The Annual Report on the Economic Status of the Profession, 1967–68," *AAUP Bulletin* 54 (1968), 208–241.

[4] Alexander W. Astin, *Who Goes Where to College?* Chicago: Science Research Associates, 1965, pp. 25, 55, 57–83.

[5] Paul F. Lazarsfeld and Herbert Menzel, "On the Relation Between Individual and Collective Properties," in Amitai Etzioni, *A Sociological Reader in Organizations*, New York: Holt, Rinehart and Winston, 1969, pp. 503–507.

personnel, such as proportion of faculty members whose fathers were college graduates, or average frequency of faculty-student contacts. The inclusion of aggregate or analytical characteristics of institutions in the study depends on information from its individual members or a sample of them. Information on individuals is also necessary to investigate the structural effects of the research climate among colleagues in an institution, that is, to differentiate the effects on faculty members of their colleagues' qualifications and academic orientations from those of their own corresponding characteristics. Finally, the examination of the influence of institutional conditions on faculty research productivity is possible only on the basis of the reports of faculty members on their publications.[6]

To take advantage of the opportunity to use the survey of faculty members, the same sample had to be employed in the study of the administrative structure of academic institutions. A stratified sample had been selected from the universe of 1006 academic institutions, which comprises all listed in the ninth (1964) edition of *American Universities and Colleges*[7] except those that do not offer four-year programs in the liberal arts. The universe of these institutions was divided into three size categories and along a second dimension into three categories roughly representing quality, the criterion being based on the average of three measures, faculty-student ratio, proportion of faculty members with Ph.D's, and educational and general expenditures per student. (It should be noted that these three measures were combind for sampling only; similar measures are used separately in the analysis.) Unequal proportions of academic institutions in the nine cells generated by the three size and the three "quality" categories were selected for the sample. Thus the major academic institutions, which, although few, are large and occupy a commanding position in the academic system, are assured representation. In a random sample of the same size, no more than one or two of the major

---

[6] Another indication of the quality of the academic staff is the proportion (or number) of departments that are included among the top 20 in the ratings obtained by Allan M. Cartter, *An Assessment of Quality in Graduate Education*, Washington: American Council of Education, 1966. But these best departments are so concentrated in major universities that their distribution is highly skewed and strongly correlated with size and affluence, with the result that these correlations obliterate all other influences, which robs the ratings of interest in a study encompassing colleges of all kinds as well as universities.

[7] Cartter, *American Universities and Colleges, op. cit.*

universities would be included. Of the 13 large universities of high quality, 11 were selected for the sample, in contrast to only 16 of the 473 small colleges of low quality. The sample includes nearly one-half (46 of 99) of the large academic institutions, 16 per cent (33 of 206) of the medium-sized, and only 5 per cent (36 of 701) of those that are small.

A weighting procedure had to be devised to compensate for the unequal sampling ratios in the nine cells and make the results of the analysis representative of the universe of American academic institutions providing at least four years of liberal education. This was done by a statistical consultant, and a computer program incorporating the weighting formula was used to generate means, standard deviations, and correlation coefficients, from which regression equations and coefficients of various kinds could be derived. The sampling procedure and weighting formula are presented in Appendix A.

Reliance on a sample in which some categories are much less well represented than others and on a complex weighting procedure to compensate for these differences raises the question of how reliable the estimates produced are: are the statistical parameters of the universe of academic institutions correctly estimated by the sample and weighting formula? As a reliability check, some estimates obtained are compared with the corresponding figures computed from data on the entire universe of academic institutions. Since it is impossible to match exactly the universe of four-year institutions in the liberal arts, the figures cannot be expected to be identical.

Let us first examine the regional distribution of institutions of higher education. According to the sample, 29 per cent are in the Northeast, 33 in the North Central region, 27 in the South, and 11 in the West. The file of academic institutions of the American Council of Education contains 1151 that meet the sampling criteria,[8] and of these there were in 1967–68 28 per cent in the Northeast, 30 in the North Central region, 25 in the South, and 18 in the West. The sample underestimates the proportion of academic institutions in the West, but since it is based on the 1963–64 distribution of institutions, this may well reflect the situation then, on the assumption that in recent years more colleges have been established in the West than in other parts of the country. Indeed, of the 969 academic institutions meeting the criteria in an Office of Education report for the year 1965–66,[9] only 12 per cent were in the West, but 35

[8] John A. Creager and Charles L. Sell, *The Institutional Domain of Higher Education*, Washington: *ACE Research Report*, Vol. 4, No. 6, 1969, pp. 31–32.
[9] U.S. Office of Education, *Digest of Educational Statistics*, Washington: U.S.G.P.O., 1966, p. 78.

per cent were in the South, which implies that the sample somewhat underestimates Southern institutions.

"The percentages of institutions in public and in private control show virtually no change in proportion since 1941," states Hodgkinson, and he adds that the "proportion of sectarian vs. nonsectarian type of control [sic] is the same today as it was in 1941" as well.[10] This makes it possible to compare the figures based on sample estimates for the distribution in 1963–64 with those derived from the ACE file for the entire universe of 1151 institutions four years later. The comparison shows that the proportion of public institutions is virtually identical—29 per cent according to the estimate, 31 according to ACE data. But the estimate of 21 per cent of private secular institutions is slightly too low (ACE figure, 25 per cent) and that of 49 per cent religious institutions is somewhat too high (44 per cent). These differences are not large, however, and they may well result from differences in the rate of expansion in recent years or from variations in the criteria used for classifying institutions as four-year liberal arts colleges.

Academic institutions have expanded rapidly in this century—at a rate of doubling their size every 20 to 25 years—so that comparisons of size are not likely to reveal the same figure unless they refer to the same year and the criteria for type of institution included and type of member included are exactly the same. Since institutions are classified in different ways in various sources, they cannot be compared exactly—for instance, liberal arts colleges are usually not distinguished from specialized colleges—and the criteria for defining faculty and full-time students are seldom specified and frequently ambiguous.

The sample estimate indicates that in 1968 the average academic institution had 304 faculty members, of whom 223 were full-time, and 4913 students. (Although the distribution of institutions by region or by control type pertain to 1963–64, the characteristics of institutions, such as their size, refer to 1967–68, the academic year in which the data were collected.) The figures based on the ACE file are lower: the mean for the "generated staff total," presumably referring to full-time equivalents, was 244 and total student enrollment was 3774 in 1967. One reason for the difference is that the ACE file includes the newest colleges, which are in all probability smaller on the average than older ones. In fact, the correlation between age and faculty size is .23, even when the newest colleges are excluded. Changes in definition may also play a role, particularly since many teachers colleges have recently become, at least in name,

[10] Harold H. Hodgkinson, *Institutions in Transition*, New York: McGraw-Hill, 1971, pp. 8, 9.

general colleges in the liberal arts. Reports of the Office of Education[11] require much guesswork in modifying their categories of the universe of academic institutions in order to approximate the universe of liberal arts institutions used for sampling. Doing so yields figures for total faculty, full-tme faculty, and student enrollment that are closer to the sampling estimates than are figurcs from the ACE file.

In any case, the sampling estimates apparently overrepresent large universities, thus inadvertently anticipating the expansion that has occurred since 1968. Major correlates of the size of academic institutions are also somewhat overestimated by the sample. For instance, the proportion of graduate students in the average academic institution is 11 per cent according to the sample, whereas the ACE file of 1151 institutions yields a figurc of 8 pcr cent. Total revenue is estimated as more than 11 million dollars by the sample; on the basis of the ACE data it is just over 9 million dollars. At least parts of these differences reflect probably again the elimination from the sample of the newest colleges, which are likely to have fewer graduate students and economic resources. Among the academic institutions represented in the sample, age is correlated with the proportion of graduate students .20 and with total revenue .26.

The average faculty salary paid by academic institutions in 1967–68 is only slightly overestimated by the sample. The mean it provides is $10,720, and a report by the National Education Association gives an average for the entire universe that year of $10,235, a difference of less than 5 per cent.[12] Still more accurate is the sampling estimate of the proportion of faculty members with Ph.D.'s or professional degrees. It is 38.4 per cent in the average academic institution, with the corresponding ACE figure for the universe being 38.0 per cent. Many more of these degrees are Ph.D.'s (34.1 per cent) than professional degrees (3.9 per cent). The proportion of faculty members who have completed advanced training seems small, particularly since teaching assistants and graduate students who are also lecturers are not included in the faculty. Actually, two-thirds of all faculty members have advanced degrees, but the proportion in the average institution is much lower, because the many small colleges with few faculty members who have completed advanced training exert a strong influence on the institutional average, an influence that is proportionate to the number of small *institutions* but disproportionately great in terms of the number of *faculty members* in them.

[11] U.S. Office of Education, *op. cit.*; *Opening Fall Enrollment in Higher Education*, Washington, U.S.G.P.O., 1965 and 1967; and *Numbers of Characteristics of Employees in Higher Education*, Washington: U.S.G.P.O., 1969.
[12] National Educational Association, *Salaries in Higher Education*, 1967–68, NEA Research Report, 1968-R7.

The conclusion to which these reliability tests point is that the stratified sample estimates the characteristics of the universe of four-year institutions offering liberal arts programs fairly accurately, though not perfectly. The major discrepancies are that the size of academic institutions and those of their characteristics that are strongly correlated with size are overestimated by the sample and the weighting procedure used.

VARIABLES

The operational definitions of the variables used are presented in Appendix B, together with the source from which each variable was derived, the number of cases on which information is available, the mean, and the standard deviation. Most of the measures are straightforward and do not require further explication. It is plausible, for example, to measure the relative size of the administrative apparatus in an academic institution by the ratio of administrators to faculty and, as a second index, the ratio of clerical personnel to faculty. Some of the decisions to use a certain operational indicator for an underlying concept should be explained, however.

The size of an academic institution may be measured by its revenue or expenditures, its student enrollment, its full-time faculty, or its total faculty, to mention only the most conspicuous indications of the scope of its operations. In a study of social structure, a measure of size based on people who occupy positions in the structure is preferable to one based on dollars or some other units. When one speaks of the size of a university or college, the reference is usually to student enrollment. But there are two reasons number of faculty members is used here to indicate the size of an academic institution. Most of the analysis of academic work pertains to that of the faculty, and using employees of the academic institution as the measure of size improves comparability with other types of organizations, in which size is also measured by number of employees. Although such comparability would be enhanced if other employees were combined with faculty members in the index of size, doing so would make the analysis of the relationship of size and academic work much less meaningful. Whether to use total or only full-time faculty is a more arbitrary decision. An advantage of the former is that many part-time faculty members in some institutions teach what is elsewhere considered a full-time load and many others, for instance in medical schools, are important components of the teaching staff. In any case, the various measures of size are highly correlated.

The indicator of size selected is total number of faculty members. It exhibits a correlation with full-time faculty of .92 and one with student enrollment of .85, which is raised to .94 if both variables are logarithmically transformed. To take account of the size of the student body, the student-faculty ratio is used as an additional variable (the mean is 17). In some instances, the number of faculty members (size) and the student-faculty ratio have additive effects on a dependent variable, which implies that the underlying factor is number of students (enrollment, which is the product of number of faculty and student-faculty ratio). Student enrollment will therefore be substituted for both faculty size and student-faculty ratio in these cases.

The high correlations of size with many other factors that are conceptually distinct from it prompted the decision to use ratios or percentages as measures of these factors in some cases. Since size and total revenue are correlated .85, for example, revenue per student is used as the index of the institution's affluence (mean, $2000 in 1968). Similarly, the correlation of .74 between size and number of departments in new fields makes it advisable to use the ratio rather than the number of such innovative departments. Several indicators based on percentages or ratios have already been mentioned, and illustrations of others are the percentage of the faculty oriented to research, expressing firm allegiance to their institution, and having frequent contacts with students.

Straightforward indicators are preferred to more subtle and less clear ones generally and particularly for the formal structure of official positions and roles, which is of special concern in this inquiry. The measure of the formal division of academic labor is the number of departments in an institution, which averages 25. The index of vertical differentiation is the number of hierarchical levels (with a mean of 4.3), and that of horizontal differentiation is the number of schools and colleges (mean, 3.1), supplemented by the span of control of the president, including heads of administrative divisions as well as deans of schools and colleges (7.6), and the mean span of control of administrators below the president (6.0). Two indications of the administrative apparatus are the ratio of administrators to faculty (mean, 1:3) and the clerical-faculty ratio (4:3). It should be noted that some of these measures have distributions that are by no means normal and that make the apparently continuous variable for practical purposes a categorical one. Thus the majority of small academic institutions have only one college, and most large ones have more than the three schools and colleges indicated by the somewhat misleading mean. Most academic institutions have either four levels—faculty, chairmen, deans and vice-presidents, whatever their title, and president—or three, there being no level of deans and vice-presidents, since a single provost or academic dean is not counted as a level (the operational definition of level requires two or more positions, except in the case of the president). Numerous institutions have five levels, usually because there are separate levels of vice-presidents and deans. Very few have more than five or fewer than three levels.

Only crude operational measures could be devised for some concepts of interest. For example, the sole indication of faculty inbreeding is the proportion of faculty members appointed *in the last academic year* who have any degree from the same institution. To study the significance of democratic participation in an institutionalized faculty government, two rough indicators must suffice: the proportion of the faculty on the senate, and the proportion of elected faculty members on the most important committee. The measures of academic performance are also rather crude. College dropout is measured ideally by ascertaining the proportion of a cohort of freshmen who have not graduated after a certain number of years, whereas we must be satisfied with the ratio of graduates to student body in a given year, controlling for expansion, as a rough indication of dropout. The second measure of educational performance, the proportion of graduates expected to continue in graduate school, is merely an estimate made by administrators, who have a good basis for making correct estimates, however, since students applying to graduate or professional schools must request transcripts of their college records. Two limitations of the index of faculty research productivity are that it is based on reports from faculty members themselves, which may be biased, and that it is confined to quantity of publications and ignores qualitative differences.

Although some variables are merely rough indicators of the underlying concepts, they make it possible to analyze problems of substantive interest that would otherwise have to be ignored, owing to the lack of better indicators. The analysis can be refined by controlling relevant conditions. For example, since a smaller proportion of the faculty tends to participate in the deliberations of the faculty senate in large than in small academic institutions (where senate meetings often include the entire faculty), controlling size makes the proportion of senators a more valid index of faculty government by preventing it from simply reflecting small institutional size. Another illustration is that the investigation of the influences of institutional conditions on educational performance or output must control input, as Astin has emphasized, lest differences in achievements resulting from variations in the abilities of incoming students be erroneously attributed to the quality of the college education they have received.[13] Faculty qualifications as well as student abilities will

[13] Alexander W. Astin, "The Methodology of Research on College Impact," *Sociology of Education* 43 (1970), 223–254.

be controlled in the analysis of the effects of institutional conditions on academic performance. Weaknesses in measures generally can be compensated for by executing proper controls in the analysis, because a poor measure is usually one that reflects not only the underlying concept under investigation but also other factors, and controlling these rectifies much of what is wrong with the measure.

Two issues of great importance for understanding academic institutions are the orientation to teaching and research and the degree of decentralization of authority and influence. Therefore, much information on these two areas was collected. Responses of faculty members and administrators to more than 50 questions pertaining to research and teaching and more than 100 pertaining to decentralization were examined. As an initial step to bring some order into this large body of empirical data, two factor analyses were performed, one with each of the two sets of items. (The unweighted sample was used, because it was not practicable to apply the weighting procedure to the nearly 600 variables still under consideration at this early stage.)

Preliminary regression analysis was carried out with three types of measures in either case (employing now the weighted sample) : factor scores; arbitrary summary scores based on items with high factor loadings; and single items, selected on the basis of high factor loadings and theoretical interest. The results obtained when using these three types of operational variables were essentially similar, though of course not identical. To avoid repetition, the type of variable to utilize in the final presentation had to be selected. The disadvantages of factor scores are that they are unstable, can be affected in strange ways by items with small loadings, and have no unambiguous substantive meaning. Scores based on several items are arbitrary and also do not have unambiguous meaning. Subtle conceptual differences between similar items are taken into account if they are kept distinct rather than combined into one score.[14] (Table 9.3 provides a good illustration.) For these reasons, single items are used here as variables, but every major dimension is represented by several items analyzed as separate variables. In short, the factor analy-

[14] On the advantages the use of multiple indicators has over combining them into a composite index, see Richard F. Curtis and Elton F. Jackson, "Multiple Indicators in Survey Research," *American Journal of Sociology* 68 (1962), 195–204. See also Herbert L. Costner, "Theory, Deduction, and Rules of Correspondence," *American Journal of Sociology* 75 (1969), 245–263; and the comments by Hubert M. Blalock, Jr., "Multiple Indicators and the Causal Approach to Measurement Error," *ibid.,* pp. 264–272.

ses were used only as general guides to identify underlying dimensions and help select variables.

At the outset of this study the orientation to teaching and the orientation to research were expected to be independent of one another. Contrary to this expectation, which implies that the two are independent dimensions (factors), the factor analysis based on responses pertaining to both yielded one dominant factor, accounting for three-fifths of the common variance, on which items referring to research and publishing had high loadings and those referring to teaching had low ones. This implies that for institutions, though not necessarily for individuals, much emphasis on teaching reduces concern with research. The item with the highest loading (.92) is used to represent this factor, supplemented by that with the highest negative loading (−.84). The item with highest loading is that faculty members at this institution are obligated to publish research, according to faculty responses, and the one with highest negative loading is that teaching ability is extremely important for senior appointments, again according to faculty. In the average institution, one-quarter of the faculty members sampled affirmed the first statement and three-fifths the second, and similar differences indicative of more emphasis on teaching than research in most colleges are revealed by directly comparable responses. Four additional items of interest in this area will also be examined (research involvement of faculty members, weight of research for senior appointments, and faculty contacts with undergraduates and with graduate students).

The items on decentralization refer to the influences over several kinds of decisions of trustees, administrators in various positions, faculty members in various ranks and groupings (departments, committees), and students. In this case, the factor analysis yielded six factors. The two strongest, accounting for one-quarter and one-fifth of the common variance, respectively, are also substantively of most interest: centralization of decisions on educational matters and centralization of faculty appointment decisions. The items with the highest loadings on these two factors and on one other were selected for analysis, as were other items for substantive reasons. The item with the highest loading on the first factor (.68) is that the board of trustees has much influence over general educational policy, according to faculty responses. The second factor is represented by the item with the highest (.72) and the one with the highest negative loading (−.69) on it: the administration exerts much influence over faculty appointments, and senior faculty members make the formal decisions concerning faculty appointments, both according to faculty responses. A third factor, referring to the president's discretionary authority over funds, is indicated by the item with the highest loading (.71), namely, his discretion over unexpended funds for tenure faculty, according to his own (or his representative's) statement. Two other items pertaining to the president's authority are his influence over faculty appointments and faculty raises, as reported by himself or his deputy.

Another problem of great interest is the significance of the colleague climate in an academic institution. It is a basic sociological assumption that the social environment influences the attitudes and activities of individuals. An implication of this assumption is that the composition of the colleague group in a university or college has structural effects on the academic orientation and work of individuals, for example, on their concern with research. If faculty members with superior qualifications are more interested in research than are others, the colleague climate in a faculty with superior qualifications is expected to enhance the research interests of individuals beyond the degree of interest their own qualifications would engender in another environment. A test of this hypothesis requires that the effects of one's colleagues' and one's own qualifications on research involvement be analytically separated.

The procedure previously suggested for this purpose[15]—using contingency tables to separate the influences of an individual's own and his colleagues' traits on a dependent variable—has been justly criticized on two grounds. If characteristics of individuals that are continuous variables are held constant in contingency tables using two or three categories, they are in fact not effectively held constant, and what appears in the tables as an effect of the characteristics of others in one's environment may actually be an effect of one's own characteristics that have not been fully controlled.[16] Besides, even assuming that characteristics that are unquestionably the independent variable, such as sex, are adequately controlled for individuals, the finding that their prevalence in a group is related to certain attitudes does not demonstrate a structural effect of these characteristics in the social environment on these attitudes, because other factors correlated with their prevalence may have produced the effect.[17]

The method used in the analysis to be presented provides an opportunity to meet both those criticisms and to show how structural effects can be discerned. First, the regression procedures to be employed, in contrast to contingency tables, effectively control all other independent

[15] Peter M. Blau, "Structural Effects," *American Sociological Review* **25** (1960), 178–193.
[16] Arnold S. Tannenbaum and Jerald G. Bachman, "Structural Versus Individual Effects," *American Journal of Sociology* **69** (1964), 585–595.
[17] Robert M. Hauser, "Context and Consex," *American Journal of Sociology* **75** (1970), 645–664.

variables in the equation as partial coefficients reveal the relationship between any one and the dependent variable. Second, most of the conditions in universities and colleges affecting a given dependent variable will already have been ascertained before the structural effects of the colleague climate are examined. By controlling the conditions known to account for one-half or more of the variation in a dependent variable among academic institutions when analyzing the effects of the colleague climate, the likelihood that its observed effects are really due to unknown correlates of it is greatly diminished. To be sure, it is still possible that an imputed structural effect is actually spurious, owing to other correlated factors that have been neglected, but the same is true for relationships of individual attributes based on survey data.[18] Structural effects of the colleague climate on orientation to and involvement in research as well as on orientation to the local institution will be investigated.

REGRESSION ANALYSIS

The two basic substantive questions we want answered for any given characteristic of academic institutions are (1) what conditions influence it and (2) how are these influences exerted, through which mediating processes. These two questions raise two more. Which associations are spurious, resulting from the effects of common antecedents, and therefore do not reflect influences exerted on the dependent variable? And which intervening factors can be discovered that mediate the effect of an antecedent on a consequence, thereby transforming a direct into an indirect effect and simultaneously supplying clues for explaining the process of influence?

Regression analysis can help answer these questions. The standardized regression coefficient or beta weight is indicative of the direct effect of each independent on the dependent variable, controlling the other variables in the regression equation. Differences between the beta weight (which is a partial coefficient) and the corresponding zero-order correla-

[18] The importance of controlling other factors in multivariate analysis when investigating structural effects is noted in the critical comments on Hauser's article by Allen H. Barton, *American Journal of Sociology* **76** (1970), 515–517. Hauser's main criticism of structural or contextual effects (repeated in his reply to Barton, *ibid.*, p. 519) that they may be spurious due to unknown correlates is meaningless without specifying what the correlates might be, because any empirical finding not based on a controlled experiment can be similarly dismissed by saying that it may have been produced by some unknown correlates.

tion (which is equivalent to the zero-order standardized regression coefficient, without controls) are the result of either one of two different situations, or a combination of both. The first is that common antecedents have produced a spurious zero-order correlation, or possibly suppressed an actual nexus between variables in their zero-order correlation. The second is that the influence of the independent on the dependent variable is mediated by some intervening variable or variables included in the regression analysis. Which of the two alternatives accounts for the observed difference, or the extent to which either does, depends on assumptions about the causal order among the variables and cannot be derived from the statistical analysis. As a matter of fact, such sequence assumptions are also necessary for the earlier decision on which conditions to include as independent variables in the investigation of a certain dependent variable.

To utilize regression procedures to best advantage in deriving meaningful interpretation and ultimately theories from empirical findings requires explicit assumptions about the causal sequence of variables, though not about their causal *influences,* of course, which are revealed by the empirical results, given the assumptions about their *sequence.* But this requirement is not a limitation of the statistical method. All theorizing and all interpreting of empirical data involve, at least implicitly, assumptions about causal sequence. There is an advantage in putting one's cards on the table by making these assumptions explicit and letting others challenge them. To be sure, many conditions in academic institutions and other complex social structures are mutually dependent and exert reciprocal influences on one another. Hence the assumptions made about causal direction are sometimes arbitrary, and they may be wrong. Nevertheless, no meaningful analysis of social structures is possible if the investigator always vacillates, attributes any concomitant variation of conditions to reciprocal influences, and refuses to commit himself to a predominant causal direction. Every major social theory makes such a commitment. Weber emphasized that the Protestant Ethic brought about the development of modern capitalism, and the significance of his theory rests on this thesis, though he acknowledged reciprocal influences of economic on religious developments. Marx stressed that a society's economic organization determines its class structure and its other characteristics. Durkheim held that advances in the division of labor change the nature of social solidarity, and not vice versa.

Conditions in social structures not only exert reciprocal influences but also exhibit complex feedback patterns and causal loops, which further confound assumptions about their causal sequence. Factor A may influence B and C, which in turn influence D, but D may have an effect on A.

Some feedback effects will be discussed in the text, but no attempts will be made to incorporate them in the statistical analysis. It would be tempting to treat some factors as both independent variables that influence earlier conditions and dependent variables that are affected by later conditions, but doing so simply introduces inconsistencies into the exposition and is not an adequate method for including feedback processes in the statistical analysis.[19] A commitment to an order among the variables that reflects the assumed predominant flow of influences must be made for the sake of consistency, though it is fully recognized that there are influences in the opposite direction, which make the assumed sequence necessarily incorrect in some respects.

It cannot be stressed enough that the assumptions about causal order to be made are highly tenuous and tentative. There simply is not enough systematic theory and research to provide a firm basis for deciding on the causal precedence among various social conditions in academic institutions or in other social structures. The causal sequence rests on mere assumptions, to be tested, like all assumptions introduced in making theoretical interpretations, in future research. A complete matrix of simple correlations between all pairs of variables is presented in Appendix C, which, together with the means and standard deviations in Appendix B, make it possible to reanalyze the data using different assumptions.

One principle on which the assumptions about the causal ordering of variables is based is that characteristics over which academic institutions have no control may affect but cannot be affected by those they can control, and the same principle applies, though less rigorously, to the difference between character-defining traits that cannot be easily altered and other factors that are more easily changed. Universities and colleges have no power to alter the existential conditions in which they find themselves such as the region in which they are located and their age. Though not impossible, it is difficult and rare for an academic institution to change the control it is under—public, private, secular, or religious. These external conditions are therefore given priority in the causal sequence.

The economic and human resources of a university or college cannot

19 For a discussion of the complex procedures and assumptions required in the quantitative analysis of feedback, see Hubert M. Blalock, Jr., *Theory Construction*, Englewood Cliffs, N.J.: Prentice-Hall, 1969, pp. 21–26, 60–69, and *passim*.

be greatly changed in the short run either, and they are of fundamental importance in determining its structure and its other characteristics. Accordingly, affluence and size of personnel are assumed to precede structural and other institutional attributes. To be sure, superior academic quality enables an institution to attract more students, more faculty, and more financial resources, and hence to grow in size as well as affluence. But expansion can be distinguished from size and treated separately, and major *differences* in size among institutions are character-defining traits that do not change readily. Whereas most American academic institutions have expanded in recent times, the differences in size among them have not been drastically altered. Reed and Swarthmore, despite their outstanding reputations, have not surpassed New York University and the University of Minnesota in size.

Other traits that define the nature of an academic institution are the extent to which it concentrates on graduate training, as indicated by the proportion of graduate students and by its being a university granting Ph.D.'s, and the student-faculty ratio. One may question the placement of these variables so early in the causal sequence; for example, one may ask whether superior faculty qualifications and publications are not what attracts many graduate students. It seems most plausible, however, to assume that the extent of graduate training in the institution governs the kind of faculty that will be recruited. Indeed, a doctorate is often a prerequisite for teaching graduate students but not for teaching undergraduates. Another factor assumed to be an antecedent rather than a consequence of the internal conditions in the academic institution is the average faculty salary, and still another is whether salary raises are standardized, since both are indications of the way resources are utilized.

The administrative structure—that is, the distribution of official positions and roles—is considered to be the basic framework within which academic work is carried out and which influences by what personnel and how it is carried out. In accordance with Durkheim's theory, the fundamental structural attribute is assumed to be the formal division of academic labor, as indicated by the number of departments. The division of labor probably antecedes and possibly affects other forms of differentiation in the structure—the number of administrative divisions under deans, the number of levels in the hierarchy, and the span of control of the president and of the other top administrators. Structural differentiation creates administrative problems of coordination and hence is held to precede the size of the administrative apparatus (the ratio of administrators to faculty and the clerical-faculty ratio).

The recruitment of faculty and students is assumed to depend on the formal structure, which circumscribes the positions to be filled, as well as on resources and how they are utilized and on existential conditions, because they define the nature of the academic institution and are largely beyond its control. Indications of success in recruitment are the qualifications of an institution's faculty and its attraction to outstanding students. Two other aspects of recruitment are faculty inbreeding and class origins.

Recruitment governs the intellectual resources for performing academic work existing in an institution. Thus the academic orientations that prevail in a university or college are assumed to be contingent on the nature of the personnel that has been recruited. No assumptions about the order among the variables within this group are made. They include the emphasis on teaching and that on research and publications; the localism-cosmopolitanism of both faculty and administration; the mobilization of outside support for academic pursuits, as reflected in the proportion of revenue from federal sources; and the salience of traditional liberal arts, as indicated by the proportion of revenue spent on books. Since people's orientations influence their conduct, academic orientations are assumed to precede academic practices and their results, including the selectivity of admission policies, the ability of incoming freshmen,[20] and the frequency of faculty contacts with graduate students and with undergraduates.

A number of institutionalized procedures and a few other factors require no more specific assumption about their place in the causal sequence than that they are antecedents of the distribution of influence and authority as well as academic performance. This is the case for the use of computers for administrative purposes, utilization of mechanical teaching aids, and the two aspects of an institutionalized faculty government previously described. It is also the case for recent expansion in size and for the length of tenure of the president's predecessor and his own.

The degree to which decision making is administratively centralized or decentralized to the faculty—there is little decentralization to students so far—is assumed to change more often than preceding conditions and hence is placed after them in the sequence, and no assumptions are made with respect to the internal order of the seven measures of various aspects of centralization. The two last places in the causal sequence are assigned to institutional innovation (departments in new fields, recent creation of

---

[20] Not all decisions concerning the causal sequence are unequivocal—a point that bears repeating—and some are primarily based on heuristic considerations. Of two closely related factors—the institution's reputation among highly able college applicants and the abilities of entering freshmen $(r=.77)$, one is placed before and the other after the indications of faculty background and orientations in the causal sequence, which makes it possible to examine influences in both directions.

new departments, and recent discontinuation of departments) and to academic performance (college dropout, rates of continuing beyond college, and faculty research productivity). Undoubtedly, the quality of academic performance not only is influenced by but also influences a number of the factors assumed to precede it in the sequence, and the same may be true for academic innovation. The placement of academic innovation and performance at the end of the causal sequence is admittedly somewhat arbitrary, and it it justified only by the fact that the basic substantive problem under consideration is how the administrative structure and institutional conditions in universities and colleges affect academic work.

An overview of the assumed causal order can be obtained in Appendices B and C, in which the variables are presented in this order. It should be noted, however, that not every difference in the rank order between two variables entails an assumption about causal sequence. In very many cases, no such assumptions are necessary, because two variables are unrelated or their correlation proves to be spurious under controls. It is only for the empirical relationships actually observed that sequence assumptions must be made. Even in these cases, it will sometimes be noted in the text that a given relationship probably reflects partly or wholly the opposite influence from that initially assumed. And still readers undoubtedly will often consider different causal assumptions more plausible than those made here, which reflects the fact, to reiterate once more, that numerous sequence assumptions rest on weak grounds. But making these assumptions explicit is what enables others to criticize, test, and alter them.[21]

Aside from these causal assumptions, regression analysis entails statistical assumptions which require some comments. It must be acknowledged at the outset that the ideal assumptions of regression analysis are not met by the data.[22] Although many variables are in continuous form, many others are not interval scales but represent ordinal scales consisting of a few categories, and some are dichotomous (dummy) variables,

---

[21] The order of discussion in the book will follow the assumed causal sequence, as will the listing of independent variables in the tables.

[22] A number of methodologists have noted in recent years that data that do not fully conform to the assumptions of regression analysis can be used without distorting results. See, for example, Edgar F. Borgatta, "My Student the Purist," *Sociological Quarterly* 9 (1968), 29–34; Jacob Cohen, *Bulletin* 70 (1968), 426–443; and Richard P. Boyle, "Path Analysis and Ordinal Data," *American Journal of Sociology* 75 (1970), 461–480.

though these are used only as independent and not as dependent variables. Moreover, several distributions are not normal and include extreme values, a polar example being that of size. But the extreme cases do not seem to distort the correlations obtained, as shown by the fact that they change little when the two largest academic institutions are excluded.[23] Transformations of variables designed to make their distributions normal have the disadvantage that they obscure the meaning of the variables and an understanding of their relationships. Hence a variable is transformed only if its strong curvilinear relationship with another necessitates transformation, and then only in one way, using its logarithm to the base 10, the criterion being that the transformation increases the correlation by at least .05.

Strong associations between some conditions in academic institutions raise the problem of multicollinearity when the effects of both on a dependent variable are under study, that is, their effects cannot reliably be distinguished. The general procedure adopted is not to use independent variables simultaneously in a regression problem if their correlation is .70 or higher. But overriding substantive interests led to violation of this principle in five instances, the two extreme cases being size and number of departments (correlated .83) and size and number of schools and colleges (.81). Finally, the analysis ignores interaction effects, that is, the possibility that the effect of one independent on the dependent variable may be contingent on differences in another. A limited search for interaction effects by using product terms in the regression analysis yielded none that are substantial or require modification of the other findings. Whereas this does not mean that further investigation would not reveal interaction effects, it does imply that an analysis that ignores them is not fundamentally misleading.

The procedure used for decomposing the simple correlations between each independent and the dependent variable in a regression problem is designed to show to what extent the association is spurious, whether there is a direct effect, and what other factors mediate indirect effects, if any. This procedure is a simplified version of path analysis. Instead of presenting path diagrams, which do not clarify the lines of influence but create a confusing picture when more than a half dozen independent variables are considered, and instead of indicating every path coefficient, this information is summarized by the procedure used to give a simple answer to the substantive question asked for any indirect link between

[23] Deleting the two largest cases makes a difference of less than .05 in all but one of the more than 1500 correlations in Appendix C. The correlation between size and creation of last new department is the one changed most, from .18 to .23, by deleting the two largest cases.

an independent and the dependent variable: which other variable or few variables are primarily responsible?

The direct effect of an independent on the dependent variable is indicated by its beta weight or standardized regression coefficient, as already noted. The indirect connections between any independent and the dependent variable, which account for the difference between their simple correlation (r) and beta weight (b^*), are necessarily due to the other independent variables in the regression problem. Each indirect connection between an independent variable, x, and the dependent variable, y, resulting from a single other independent variable, i, is produced by the correlation between the independent variable under consideration and the other variable (r_{ix}) and the other's direct effect on the dependent variable (b^*_{yi}). The product of these two values $(r_{ix} b^*_{yi})$ indicates the strength of the indirect connection. The sum of all indirect connections between x and y, so computed, and the direct effect of x on y, represented by the beta weight, equals their zero-order correlation. The assumptions about causal order among independent variables are required to decide which indirect connections are spurious and which are indirect effects. The part of the correlation between x and y produced by i's assumed to precede x is spurious, whereas the part mediated by i's assumed to follow x in the causal sequence is indicative of indirect effects.[24]

To illustrate this decomposition procedure, the conditions in academic institutions that influence average faculty salaries are discussed. The dependent variable in Table 2.1 is mean faculty salary in 1967–68 (for

[24] Full path analysis decomposes correlations completely and gives more detailed information, whereas the abbreviated version described summarizes this information by decomposing only partially, which is its purpose but also its limitation. Let us assume there are four independent variables in a regression problem—1, 2, 3, and 4—and we are now concerned with the effect of 1 on y. The abbreviated version would indicate to what extent the simple correlation between 1 and y is a direct effect, and to what extent it is mediated by 2, by 3, and by 4. For example, it may show that .30 of the correlation of .35 is an indirect effect of 1 on y mediated by 4. Full path analysis would provide more complete information instead, specifically, which part of it is due to each of the following chains: 1–2–3–4–y, 1-3-4-y, and 1-4-y. The abbreviated procedure is designed to obviate the need to add this detailed information for every indirect link in one's head and to reveal directly that 4 is the major intervening variable in this case. The limitation of failing to decompose the association between 1 and 4 further is that the abbreviated procedure does not tell us whether this association is spurious, owing to effects of common antecedents on 1 and 4. But this simply means that the use of the abbreviated procedure presupposes that any intervening variable in a given regression analysis has been previously analyzed as a dependent variable and that the knowledge about spurious associations obtained in the earlier analysis is taken into account when interpreting later statistical results. Since variables are analyzed in sequence in this book, this is easily done.

which information on only 88 cases is available). In the upper part, which has the same format as most other tables in the book, the independent variables are ordered in their assumed causal sequence, and for each the beta weight and the simple correlation with salaries are shown. Correlations revealed to be spurious in preliminary analysis (given the causal assumptions) have been excluded from the final regression equation presented, in other tables as well as here. Beta weights that are less than twice their standard error are considered to indicate no appreciable effect.

The lower part of Table 2.1 is a matrix of decomposition coefficients with the same variables in corresponding rows and columns, designed to explicate the procedure, and a similar matrix will not be included in other tables. The beta weights, which are also shown in the upper part, are in the diagonal of the matrix. The value in every cell outside the diagonal represents the indirect connection between the variable in the row, x, and faculty salaries, y, produced by the variable in the column, i, and the value is obtained by multiplying r_{ix} by b_{yi}^{*}. The sum of the values in every row is, except for rounding errors, identical with the simple correlation between x and y shown in the upper part of the table. Since the variables are ordered in the assumed causal sequence, the values to the left of the diagonal reveal the amount of spurious association between x and y produced by common antecedents, the i's in the columns; and the values to the right of the diagonal reveal indirect effects of x on y mediated by intervening variables, the i's in these columns. (Decomposition coefficients of less than .10 are not worth mentioning, but their values within a row may be added.) The direct effect of x on y indicated by the beta weight depends on the other variables being considered and would differ if additional relevant variables were included.

Southern academic institutions pay lower salaries to their faculties than those in other regions of the country, as the first row in Table 2.1 shows, possibly because of the lower cost of living in the South. Their lower salaries would lead one to expect that universities and colleges in the South have difficulties in recruiting well-qualified faculties, and we shall ascertain in Chapter Four whether this is actually so. Since regional location is assumed to precede the other factors in the causal sequence, no part of its correlation with faculty salaries can be spurious, though some of it could result from indirect effects. Actually, however, all the decomposition coefficients to the right of the diagonal in row 1 of the matrix are trivial, and the beta weight is identical with the zero-order

Table 2.1   Average Faculty Salaries[a]

	Beta Weight	Simple Correlation
1. South	−.17*	−.17
2. Age	.21**	.37
3. Private secular	.15*	.34
4. Affluence	.37**	.60
5. Size	.41**	.60

$R^2 = .62$ $(\hat{R}^2 = .60)$; [b]$n = 88$

	Variables				
	1	2	3	4	5
1. South	−.17	.04	−.02	.00	−.03
2. Age	−.03	.21	−.00	.10	.09
3. Private secular	.02	−.00	.15	.12	.06
4. Affluence	−.00	.06	.05	.37	.13
5. Size	.01	.05	.02	.11	.41

* More than twice its standard error.
** More than three times its standard error.
[a] The title in the table always refers to the dependent and the row stubs to the independent variables in the regression analysis.
[b] In parenthesis, the R^2 corrected for degrees of freedom is provided, using the formula, $\hat{R}^2 = 1 - (1 - R^2)(n-1)/(n-k-1)$, where n is the number of cases and k the number of independent variables.

correlation. The entire negative effect of Southern location on faculty salaries is direct, which simply means that we have no data that would help explain it, but which also shows that independent of financial resources, which are controlled, Southern academic institutions offer lower faculty salaries than others.

Older academic institutions pay their faculties higher salaries than newer ones. Part of this effect of institutional age is indirect, as the coefficients to the right of the diagonal in the second row of the matrix indicate. One reason why older universities and colleges pay higher faculty salaries than others is that they have greater financial resources for doing so. (The mediating influences of affluence per student and size may be combined in this case and considered a reflection of economic resources; see the discussion below.) But this is not the only reason, as indicated by the direct effect of age on faculty salaries, manifest in the beta weight. It may well be that an academic tradition that has developed over many years finds expression in the tendency to devote more economic resources to strictly academic pursuits, such as recruiting better faculty by offering higher salaries to improve or maintain academic standing. The interpretation implies that older universities and colleges also spend more of their resources on other academic matters, for example, their libraries. Indeed, age has a positive effect on proportion of revenue spent on books when affluence is controlled ($b^* = .20$, which exceeds twice its standard error).

If a strong concern with strictly academic affairs is reflected in high faculty salaries, as the interpretation assumes, one would expect high salaries in private secular institutions, which tend to have the best academic reputations,[25] and in which such concern is less likely to be diluted than in either religious institutions, owing to spiritual interests, or in public ones, owing to their obligation to provide some useful training to large numbers from less advantaged homes. Alternatively, one might think that the playboy element in many private secular institutions makes faculty qualifications less important and lowers salaries. The data in Table 2.1 confirm the first expectation. The dummy variable, private secular, is correlated with average faculty salaries .34, as shown in the table's upper part. Virtually none of the correlation is spurious, as indicated by the first two entries in the third row of the matrix; about one-half of it represents an indirect effect (last two columns, third row) and slightly less a direct one (diagonal). Private secular universities and colleges pay their faculties more than other institutions partly because they have superior resources for doing so, but partly independent of their resources, which presumably reflects a greater emphasis on academic quality, in accord with the interpretation suggested for the association between age and faculty salaries.

The two conditions in academic institutions that exert the strongest influence on faculty salaries are their affluence and their size. The high correlation of either with salaries—which happens to be the same (.60) in both cases—is partly spurious (see the first three columns in the last two rows), but most of it is not. The ability of affluent institutions to offer higher salaries is plausible and requires no explanation. But why does large institutional size also raise faculty salaries? The measure of affluence is revenue per student, which means that the institution's economic resources depend on its size as well as on this measure of resources per student. Thus available resources, as reflected in these two variables together, greatly affect faculty salaries, which is not surprising. Since the

25 The dummy variable, private secular, exhibits a correlation of .30 with the measure of reputation.

index of affluence is revenue per student, it may seem preferable to use student enrollment instead of faculty size as the supplementary index of economic resources. Doing so alters the pattern of observed effects little.[26]

But why not substitute total revenue as the indicator of economic resources for both size and revenue per student? If this is done, the empirical results are somewhat changed, though not greatly. The beta weight for the South is essentially the same ($-.18$); those for age and private secular increase (to .28 and .27, respectively); that for total revenue is .50 ($r=.61$); and the amount of variation in salaries among institutions accounted for (R^2) is reduced from 62 to 53 per cent (corrected, from 60 to 51 per cent). A feedback effect excluded here that affects the results in Table 2.1 may be responsible for this reduction. Whereas an academic institution's economic resources limit the salaries it can offer to faculty members, poor salaries probably restrict the number of faculty members willing to accept a job, particularly the number with superior qualifications, and thus also the number of students interested in admission. Faculty salaries consequently would affect the institution's size. Regardless of such a feedback effect, the main conclusions of the analysis remain the same. The salaries paid to faculty members depend not only on the institution's economic resources but also on other conditions, notably an academic tradition that places much emphasis on academic standing.

THE ROLE OF THEORY

A formal theory from which empirical predictions can be logically deduced plays the dominant role in research that is designed to test the predictions and thereby indirectly the theory. Some empirical tests of the implications of a fairly systematic set of theoretical assumptions will be presented. Since there is little rigorous theory as yet in sociology, however, the typical role of theoretical conceptions and principles nowadays is to provide a guiding framework for largely exploratory research, as noted at the end of the first chapter. A few remarks are in order about the specific differences a theoretical approach, as distinguished from a rigorous theory, makes for research.

A favorite term of opprobrium of social research is that it is a "fishing expedition." But how does a fishing expedition differ from exploratory

[26] The beta weights of the variables in Table 2.1, presented in the same order, except that student enrollment is substituted for faculty size, are: $-.16$, .23, .16, .46, and .39. The simple correlation for enrollment is .47; $R^2=.62$ (.60).

research, which includes most current social research? Surely, the investigator hopes not merely to demonstrate once more what is already known but also to discover quite unanticipated patterns, as Merton has emphasized in his discussion of the significance of serendipity for the development of social theory.[27] To realize this hope, the investigator must keep looking for unexpected findings, which involves him in a fishing expedition. Although the inferences made to explain a serendipity finding are not validated by it, of course, the same is true for all interpretations of empirical data that do not rest on a systematic theory formulated in advance. In regression analysis using computers, a matrix of simple correlations between all pairs of variables under consideration is prepared. It would hardly make sense not to look at this matrix or not to pay attention to unanticipated correlations observable in it. As a matter of fact, ignoring empirical associations that do not fit into the analyst's preconceived interpretative scheme, far from being required for theoretically oriented research, is illegitimate on theoretical grounds. For it creates the virtually unavoidable danger of reporting only findings that fit into the theoretical scheme and not those inconsistent with it. The decision made here is to report all substantial associations observed, except those that proved to be spurious, including those for which no good interpretation came to mind.[28]

Two specific roles a theoretical framework plays in exploratory research, aside from providing general guidelines for the inquiry, deserve to be stressed. The first is that it determines the concepts to be used, because of their significance in the theoretical scheme, to account for differences in the empirical characteristics of, in our case, academic institutions. The objective is not simply to maximize prediction or the amount of variation accounted for in the dependent variable (indicated by R^2, the coefficient of determination),[29] which frequently can be done without improving theoretical understanding, for instance, by adding independent variables closely related to the dependent variable (last year's income to predict this year's). The objective is rather to analyze

[27] Robert K. Merton, *Social Theory and Social Structure*, New York: Free Press, 1968, pp. 157–162. Merton's titles of this chapter and the one preceding it in his book suggested the subheads chosen for the last sections of the first two chapters in this monograph.

[28] Indirect effects of region, control (public, private secular, or religious), and affluence are reported only if they are of substantive interest; that is, otherwise these variables were excluded from the regression analysis presented.

[29] This point is made in Joseph Berger et al., "Where Is the Gap Between Theory and Research?" paper delivered at the meetings of the American Sociological Association, 1971.

how conditions selected in terms of the theoretical scheme affect various factors directly and indirectly. Explaining much of the variation in dependent variables within such a framework assumes new significance, because it provides a pragmatic test of the conceptual scheme.

The second important role of a theoretical orientation in exploratory research, which is not unrelated to the first, is to indicate an order of priority among the factors that are being investigated. Tenuous as these assumptions about causal sequence may have to be—and they must ultimately be empirically tested, of course, like all theoretical assumptions— research is theoretically meaningless without them. The worst offense in this respect is the use of stepwise regression programs, which lets the computer decide the order of independent variables on the basis of their effective prediction of the dependent variable. The result is that several measures of the same underlying concept may be selected, and factors that exert only indirect effects on the dependent variables are excluded, since they do not improve prediction. (Thus, if annual incomes for several years are part of the data, a stepwise regression program would probably not include education and occupation as factors influencing current income, because their influences are likely to be obliterated by those of the incomes in preceding years.)

To exclude conceptually significant factors because they have only indirect effects on a dependent variable defeats the very purpose of a theoretically oriented analysis of empirical data. Theoretical interest in the study of a given social characteristic is not confined to those of its antecedents that have independent effects on it. Quite the contrary, the theoretical focus is on the most fundamental conditions that affect it, and the aim of the analysis is not to preserve but to diminish the statistical relationships between these causes and their effect by introducing intervening variables that mediate their influences, for doing so provides the clues that lead to theoretical explanations of the influences.

CHAPTER THREE

ADMINISTRATIVE STRUCTURE

Professionals tend to view their vocations as utterly incomparable with work in factories or government offices, and they may not even use the same language when speaking of their occupations and of others. We in academia have the same tendencies. Other people do plain work; professionals call what they do practice, and we speak of discharging our academic responsibilities. We do not refer to getting hired and fired but to being appointed to academic positions and having contracts not renewed. Academic institutions are places to teach and carry out research, not usually spoken of as organizations, which are the places where other people are employed to do work. Universities and colleges are organizations, however, though they are unquestionably different in many ways from most work organizations. There is no eight-hour working day for faculty, no direct supervision, no unambiguous measure of efficiency, and there are many other differences. Not the least important of these are distinctive characteristics of the administrative structure.

Although faculty members vary in rank and influence over academic affairs, they are not organized into a hierarchy of supervisors and subordinates, but all constitute the operating personnel, the bottom level in terms of formal authority of the administrative hierarchy comprising chairmen, deans and other administrators, vice-presidents, and the president. Another difference is that the specialists on the faculty perform the

major line functions of teaching and research, and administrators provide most of the supportive staff services in academic institutions, whereas
in the typical work organization professional specialists are the staff and
the managerial hierarchy has line functions, as Etzioni has noted.[1] However, this difference does not extend to senior administrators, whose
basic management functions of mobilizing and distributing resources for
the effective achievement of objectives[2] are essentially the same in academic institutions and other organizations, albeit the ways to execute
these responsibilities successfully are not the same.

The first question to be raised in this inquiry is whether the administrative structure of universities and colleges is fundamentally homologous
to that of other types of organizations, notwithstanding the important
differences that have just been illustrated. Several consistent empirical
regularities in the formal structure were discovered in a study of the 53
headquarters and 1201 local offices of all employment security agencies
in this country,[3] and subsequent research on other kinds of organizations
revealed parallel regularities. An attempt was made to construct a theory
of the structure of organizations that encompasses these empirical findings and can account for them.

The administrative structure of American academic institutions is
analyzed from the perspective of these results of previous research and
the theoretical inferences drawn from them. Are the same empirical regularities observed in the structure of government bureaus (as well as that
of other organizations) also observable in universities and colleges, thus
indicating a significant homology among otherwise contrasting types? A
positive answer would imply that universities and colleges are in crucial,
though not necessarily in all, respects similar to other bureaucracies. At
the same time, the theoretical assumptions made to explain the earlier
findings can be tested in an entirely different setting, and the theory can
be explicated, revised, or refined in accordance with the results.

DIFFERENTIATION

Two basic theorems derived from the research on government bureaus
are: (1) increasing organizational size is accompanied by increasing dif-

---

[1] Amitai Etzioni, "Authority Structure and Organizational Effectiveness," *Administrative Science Quarterly* **4** (1959), 43–67.
[2] Jacques Barzun, *The American University*, New York: Harper and Row, 1968, p. 95.
[3] Peter M. Blau and Richard A. Schoenherr, *The Structure of Organizations*, New
York: Basic Books, 1971, pp. 62–97, 183–204, 297–344.

ferentiation along several lines; and (2) these increases in differentiation occur at decelerating rates with increasing size. As the size of government bureaus increases, the differentiation in their structure does too, at a rapid rate with initial and at a slower rate with subsequent increases in size. This is the case whether one examines the division of labor, horizontal differentiation into functional divisions or their subunits, vertical differentiation into hierarchical levels, or geographical differentiation into local branches.

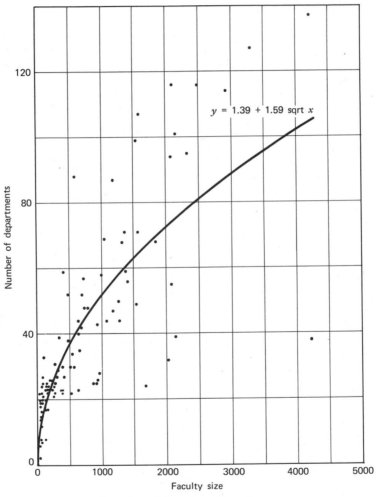

Figure 3.1.   Regression of number of departments on size.

Three measures of differentiation in academic institutions are available to test these two theorems. The index of the formally instituted academic division of labor is the number of departments. Horizontal differentiation into the major academic subunits, corresponding to the major divisions with different functions in government bureaus, is indicated by the number of schools and colleges in an institution. Vertical differentiation in the hierarchy is measured by the number of administrative levels, counting all faculty except chairmen as the lowest and the president as the highest level. Each of the three measures refers to the number of subunits into which the institution is differentiated in a given dimension.

The size of an academic institution is highly correlated with all three aspects of its differentiation. It exhibits a correlaton of .83 with the academic division of labor, one of .80 with the number of schools and colleges, and one of .37 with the number of hierarchical levels, which is raised to .51 when size is logarithmically transformed. (Such a transformation is indicated by the criterion adopted in the last case but not in the other two.) The correlation of size and the division of labor in academic institutions is virtually identical with that in employment security agencies (.78), though its correlation with horizontal differentiation is higher and that with vertical differentiation is lower in academic institutions than in these government agencies (in which the former is .54 and the latter .72, using size in logarithmic transformation). Despite some differences in the magnitude of two of the associations, the data on institutions of higher education clearly confirm the first theorem.

Large universities and colleges have a more differentiated, and thus a more complex, administrative structure than small ones, just like other large bureaucracies, but do the increases in differentiation with increasing size also occur at decelerating rates in academic institutions? To answer this question, scatter diagrams have been prepared, and a curve has been drawn in each indicating the relationship between size, on the horizontal axis, and the measure of differentiation, on the vertical axis. These scatter diagrams (Figures 3.1, 3.2 and 3.3) are of course based only on the cases in the sample, and large institutions are consequently overrepresented on them, which compensates for their small number.[4]

----

[4] The correlations of size in the unweighted sample are .76 with number of departments, .82 with number of schools and colleges, and .36 with number of levels (raised to .55 if size is logarithmically transformed). The curves were drawn by obtaining predicted points from the equations shown in the figures. Whether the logarithmic or square root equation was used (in these three figures as well as in Figure 3.4 below) was determined by goodness of fit, the criterion being the proportion of the variation in y accounted for. All predictions are improvements over those of the linear equations.

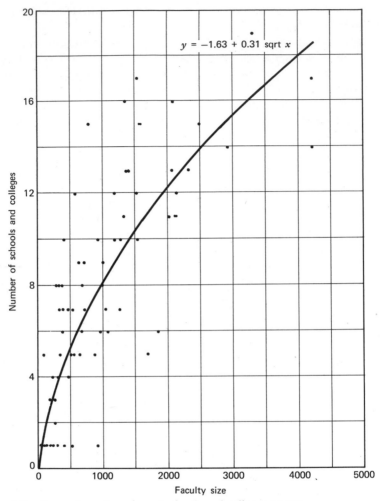

Figure 3.2.   Regression of number of schools and colleges on size.

Although there is much scatter among the observed points, the relation-ship between the two variables, which is pronounced, is best represented not by a straight line but by a concave curve in all three diagrams, the curvature being only slight in the case of departments and that of schools and colleges but pronounced in that of levels. As the size of academic institutions increases, the differentiation in their structure along three dimensions—all that have been examined—increased at decelerating rates, in accordance with the second theorem.

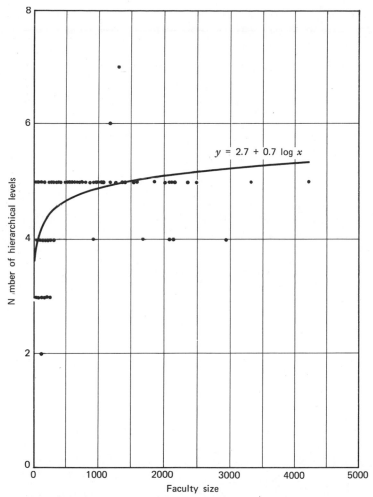

Figure 3.3   Regression of number of hierarchical levels on size.

Let us now determine what antecedents in addition to size influence the administrative structure of universities and colleges and examine how the three aspects of differentiation are interrelated. Table 3.1 presents the results of the regression analysis of the conditions that affect the formal division of academic labor, indicated by the number of departments in an institution. A pronounced division of labor means that academic departments are more specialized—anthropology and sociology are not combined but in separate departments, for example—and that

Table 3.1   Number of Departments (Division of Labor)

	Beta Weight	Simple Correlation
1. Affluence	.00	.29
2. Size	.70**	.83
3. University	.21**	.64
$R^2 = .73$ ($\hat{R}^2 = .72$); $n = 113$		

** More than three times its standard error.

some specialties, such as astronomy, are not taught. Whereas specialized scholarly endeavors can be carried out by individuals located in departments representing broad disciplines, only specialized departments provide the institutional conditions that encourage specialized academic work by having the appropriate course offerings and degree programs, thus furnishing to each specialist a social environment of students and colleagues with similar specialized interests.

Universities have a more specialized departmental structure than colleges not granting Ph.D.'s, and although much of the high correlation between university status and number of departments is spurious, owing to the influence of size, the beta weight in the table's last row shows that part of it persists when other conditions are controlled. The complex responsibilities of universities promote specialization, and this effect is independent of the large size of most universities. The second row in the table indicates the dominant influence of large size on specialization, which accounts for two-thirds of the variation in number of departments. An academic institution must be large to have many diverse departments and thereby foster specialized academic work. Most of the influence of size on departmental specialization is direct, though some of it results from the fact that more large than small institutions are universities (the decomposition coefficient is .13). Affluent academic institutions have more specialized departments than do poor institutions, but the entire effect of economic resources is indirect, mostly mediated by the large size of affluent institutions (.22).

The number of schools and colleges in an academic institution depends primarily on two conditions besides their size, university status and number of departments, as Table 3.2 shows. Universities granting Ph.D.'s have more schools and colleges than other institutions, which may consist of only one college (see Figure 3.2). Whereas the strong correlation

Table 3.2   Number of Schools and Colleges
            (Horizontal Differentiation)

	Beta Weight	Simple Correlation
1. Size	.38**	.81
2. University	.31**	.72
3. Departments	.28**	.80
$R^2 = .76$ $(\hat{R}^2 = .75)$; $n = 115$		

** More than three times its standard error.

between university status and number of schools and colleges is partly
due to the two other factors in the regression equation, a considerable
beta weight remains when these are controlled, indicating a direct connection between advanced training and separate schools and colleges.
The strong association between number of departments and number of
schools and colleges also persists under controls in an attenuated form,
but the direction of influence is not entirely clear.

The initial assumption was that the division of labor is more fundamental than horizontal differentiation into major administrative subunits, which implies that an increasing number of departments in an
academic institution leads to their being organized into several colleges
and schools. Professional schools, such as medical schools, usually do not
develop in this manner, however. Some of the observed relationship may
reflect a feedback effect on the number of departments of the existence
of professional schools, many of which have their own departments,
sometimes even duplicating similar departments in other parts of the
university.

The regression analysis in Table 3.2 helps explain why large academic
institutions are much more differentiated into schools and colleges than
are small ones. It is partly because large institutions are more often universities (.19) and have more departments (.24), but it is partly
independent of these conditions, as the substantial beta weight (.38)
indicates.[5]

Vertical differentiation into a multilevel hierarchy is more prevalent

[5] If many departments are primarily a consequence rather than an antecedent of many
schools and colleges, it would not alter the gross effect of size on number of schools
and colleges, but eliminating number of departments as an independent variable
would increase the beta weight indicating the net effect of size (to .58).

in universities than in colleges as well as in large than in small institutions. Three antecedents exerting independent positive effects on the number of administrative levels could be identified: size (in logarithmic transformation to correct for the pronounced curvature shown in Figure 3.3) ; student-faculty ratio; and university status. As pointed out in Chapter Two, if number of faculty (size) and student-faculty ratio have cumulative effects on a variable, then number of students (enrollment) , the product of the two, probably is the underlying cause and should be substituted for both. If this is done (Table 3.3) , the variation in hierarchical levels accounted for remains the same, with the influences of both faculty size and student-faculty ratio now being subsumed by the influence of student enrollment.

Apparently the size of the student body as well as that of the faculty governs the administrative work and personnel required in an academic institution—an inference that, though plausible, will be presently tested —and thus the degree of differentiation in the administrative hierarchy.[6] The number of students, since it is much larger than the number of faculty members, supplies better evidence of this impact of the academic community's total size on the administrative hierarchy.[7] The large size of an academic institution promotes vertical differentiation into a multilevel hierarchy, and university status exerts an additional influence on such differentiation. The complex responsibilities of universities are reflected in a complex structure that is more differentiated along all

[6] These considerations may seem to make it preferable to assume that the administrative ratio affects rather than depends on the hierarchical structure, but this would make it impossible to examine the hypothesis of theoretical interest concerning the opposite influences of size and structural differentiation on the administrative ratio.
[7] Problems of multicollinearity make it inadvisable to examine the effects of both number of students and number of faculty members on the administrative hierarchy in a regression analysis, since the correlation between them (using log) is .94.

Table 3.3   Number of Hierarchical Levels (Vertical Differentiation)

	Beta Weight	Simple Correlation
1. Enrollment (log)	.48**	.59
2. University	.19*	.47
$R^2 = .37$ $(\hat{R}^2 = .36)$; $n = 115$		

* More than twice its standard error.
** More than three times its standard error.

three lines examined than that of colleges, and these effects are parallel to, though independent of, those of large size.[8]

In government bureaus, vertical differentiation into multiple levels and horizontal differentiation into major administrative divisions with different functions, which both increase with size, are inversely related to each other when size is controlled. The interpretation that has been advanced for this finding is that many division heads who report to the top executive widen his span of control and overburden him with supervisory duties, infringing on other managerial responsibilities. An excessive span of control of top management—or, for that matter, of managers on lower levels—can be narrowed to reduce the load of administrative detail of managers only by extending the number of levels in the hierarchy. Is the same inverse relationship between vertical levels and major horizontal administrative subdivisions, with size controlled, also observable in universities and colleges?

If number of levels is added to the three other independent variables considered in Table 3.2, its beta weight does not reveal an inverse relationship between number of levels and number of schools and colleges in an academic institution but an insignificant positive one (.09), in contrast to the strong negative relationship observed in employment security agencies.[9] A possible reason for the difference is that the number of schools and colleges does not encompass all major subunits for which the president is responsible in an academic institution, inasmuch as this number excludes administrative divisions.

The president's total span of control, including the number of administrative as well as academic major subunits in the structure, is indeed inversely related to the number of hierarchical levels in academic institutions (see Table 3.4), just as in government bureaus. Large size increases and multiple levels decrease the top executive's span of control in both kinds of organizations. A difference in findings is that the positive direct effect of size in academic institutions is weaker and obliterated by its indirect effect mediated by multiple levels, so that the zero-order correlation reveals little if any overall effect of size, whereas the stronger

[8] The number of departments has no effect on the number of levels, their correlation being the spurious result of the effects of size and university status on both.
[9] In the regression analysis of number of divisions there, the beta weight of number of levels is $-.45$ and that of size (log) is .88 (Blau and Schoenherr, *op. cit.*, p. 75). Since this finding has been replicated in a number of studies, it is unlikely that it is an artifact produced by multicollinearity.

Table 3.4   President's Span of Control

	Beta Weight	Simple Correlation
1. Size (log)	.40**	.11
2. Levels	−.56**	−.35
$R^2 = .24$ $(\hat{R}^2 = .23)$; $n = 115$		

** More than three times its standard error.

effect of size in employment security agencies overcomes the counteracting effect of levels and is manifect in a substantial zero-order correlation.[10]
Notwithstanding this difference, the basic pattern is essentially the same. Moreover, the average span of control of vice-presidents and other officials on the level immediately below the president's reveals the same pattern of relationships, a positive one with size and a negative one with hierarchical levels, as the beta weights in Table 3.5 indicate.[11] Thus the large size of an academic institution widens the span of control of its administrators in the two top ranks, independent of the hierarchical structure, but the multilevel hierarchies that prevail in large organizations narrow the span of control of administrators, largely compensating for the effect size otherwise would have (see the very small simple correlation in the first rows of Tables 3.4 and 3.5).

Vertical differentiation into hierarchical levels is inversely related to horizontal differentiation into functional subunits (if administrative units are included) in academic institutions, just as in other organizations. This inverse relationship indicates that administrative structures vary in shape from a squat pyramid—short, with an obtuse angle at the apex—to one that is relatively tall and slim. Although large size expands the pyramid in both dimensions, there are variations in shape within a given size. What conditions affect these variations? One factor found to do so in government bureaus is the technology employed, specifically, the use of computers, presumably because such automation serves as an impersonal mechanism of control, substituting in part for managerial

[10] Size has been logarithmically transformed in Table 3.4 to take account of its curvilinear relationship with levels (see Figure 3.3) and to match the regression analysis of the data on employment security agencies, though the criterion noted in Chapter Two for making such a transformation is not met. With size in raw form, the pattern is similar to that in Table 3.4; the beta weights are smaller (.27 for size, −.44 for levels) but still exceed twice their standard errors.
[11] Size has been logarithmically transformed in Table 3.5, and the same considerations noted in footnote 10 apply here.

Table 3.5   Mean Span of Control of Officials Reporting
to the President

	Beta Weight	Simple Correlation
1. Size (log)	.29*	.03
2. Levels	−.51**	−.36
$R^2=.19$ $(\hat{R}^2=.17)$; $n=107$		

* More than twice its standard error.
** More than three times its standard error.

directives and therefore making the problems of communication that arise in multilevel hierarchies less of an impediment for management. Whereas managerial supervision plays a much smaller role in universities and colleges than in government bureaus, its role in the administrative divisions of academic institutions, as distinguished from their colleges and schools, is not fundamentally different from that in other organizations.

Since it is of interest to ascertain whether the automation of administrative matters has the same effect on the hierarchical structure in academic institutions as in public bureaucracies, a score of the extent of administrative use of computers, excluding their use by faculty and students for research and training, is introduced as an independent variable into the regression analysis of number of levels. Doing so admittedly is contrary to the most plausible causal order, which would place the use of computers by academic administrators later in the sequence of variables, but it is justified by the attempt to replicate a previous analysis in a different type of organization.

The administrative use of computers is reflected in a multilevel hierarchy in academic institutions, resembling its effect in government bureaus. If the score of administrative computer use is added as the third to the two independent variables shown in Table 3.3, its beta weight is .21, which is more than twice the standard error. Large academic institutions are more likely than small ones to use computers for administrative purposes, and part of the strong zero-order correlation between computer use and levels (.50) is spurious, mostly owing to size, that is, enrollment (.22). The beta weights in Table 3.3 are reduced in the regression analysis in which computer use is included as a third independent variable (to .37 for enrollment and .16 for university status), because the latter now mediates some of the influences of enrollment and university status on levels. There is little point in pursuing the interpretation of these data, however, inasmuch as it is predicated on the assumption that the use of computers by academic administrators affects the hierarchy, which is questionable. The alternative assumption that the hierarchical structure precedes computer use in the causal sequence does not alter the interpretation much. It would imply that the administrative problems that arise in multilevel hierarchies encourage academic administrators to use computers extensively.[12]

The main conclusion remains the same, whichever sequence assumption is correct. In an academic institution both a complex technology, as indicated by extensive administrative use of computers, and complex responsibilities, as indicated by university programs leading to the Ph.D., are more compatible with a complex hierarchical structure than with a simple hierarchy consisting of only a few levels.

ADMINISTRATION

The data analyzed so far reveal striking parallels in administrative structure between academic institutions and government bureaus. Increases in the size of either are accompanied by initially rapid and gradually declining increases in differentiation along varous lines of the formal structure. Vertical differentiation into hierarchical levels and horizontal differentiation into major functional subunits are inversely related when size is held constant in both cases. A complex technology manifest in the use of computers is associated with vertical differentiation creating a steeper hierarchy in academic institutions as well as government bureaus. Whereas complex responsibilities in academic institutions exert an independent effect on the various aspects of differentiation that make the administrative structure more complex, perhaps this was not observed in employment security agencies simply because no corresponding measure of the nature of responsibilities was available in the research on these agencies.

Does this homology extend to the size of the administrative component, whose role in universities and colleges is in many ways different from that of the managerial component in most work organizations? Interestingly enough, the relative size of either component is the same. The ratio

---

[12] In the regression analysis of administrative use of computers, using the only three conditions identified that affect it as independent variables, the beta weight of levels is .34; that of size (log), .25; and that of religious affiliation, −.24; all three exceed twice their standard errors.

of administrators to faculty members in the average American academic institution is one to four, or 20:80, and the mean of the percentage of managers and supervisors in the 53 employment security agencies in this country is 19. The close match of these figures may well be fortuitous, inasmuch as many administrators devote their time to student affairs rather than faculty matters. Of greater concern than these averages are the conditions on which differences in the administrative ratio depend and, particularly, the similarity of these influences on the administrative ratio in academic institutions and in government bureaus. The empirical data on employment security agencies indicate that size and structural differentiation (in both main dimensions, vertical into levels and horizontal into subunits), although strongly related, have opposite effects on the administrative ratio, whether its measure is the proportion of managers and supervisors or that of staff (rather than line) personnel, and whether the structure of the 53 agency headquarters or that of the 1201 local branches is under investigation.[13]

The larger the size of an employment security agency or of one of its local branches, the lower is the administrative ratio in it. These government bureaus exhibit an economy of scale in administration. Contrary to the common stereotype, there is no proliferation of the administrative apparatus in large bureaucracies. The opposite is true. Large government bureaus have substantially smaller proportions of administrative personnel than do small bureaus. Much of the reduction of the percentage of managers and supervisors in large organizations results from the wider span of control of first-line supervisors. Since academic administrators do not include first-line supervisors of faculty members, one may wonder whether a similar inverse relationship between size and administrative ratio can be expected in universities and colleges. Moreover, some critics of the extensive administrative machinery in modern universities attribute this machinery to the universities' large size. Goodman clearly implies that small academic institutions require fewer administrators—presumably, proportionately fewer—than large ones; Hutchins implies the same less directly.[14] Before turning to the empirical evidence to ascertain whether these critics are right or whether the relationship between size and administrative component in academic institutions is similar to that in other organizations, let us examine how this component is affected by differentiation in government bureaus.

Structural differentiation enlarges the administrative component in

[13] Blau and Schoenherr, op. cit., pp. 90–92, 195–197.
[14] Paul Goodman, The Community of Scholars, New York: Random House, 1962, p. 5; Robert M. Hutchins, The Learning Society, New York: Praeger, 1968, p. 118.

employment security agencies. Vertical differentiation into multiple levels and horizontal differentiation into major divisions and their subunits have independent positive effects on the proportion of administrative personnel, though these effects are apparent only when size is controlled. A differentiated structure engenders problems of coordination and communication in government bureaus, which demand administrative attention and thus require additional administrative personnel. Since large employment security agencies have a more differentiated structure than small agencies, large size has an indirect effect, mediated by differentiation, that increases the administrative ratio as well as a direct effect that decreases it, but since the direct is stronger than the indirect effect, the overall impact of large size is to reduce the administrative ratio substantially, producing the economy of scale in administration. Yet the growing differentiation that accompanies expanding size weakens the influence of large-scale operations on administrative economies, which is reflected in the finding that the administrative ratio decreases *at a declining rate* with increasing size in employment security agencies. Is this intricate pattern of influences on administrative personnel also characteristic of academic institutions, even though their schools and colleges tend to be less interdependent and need less continual coordination than the functional subdivisions of government bureaus?

The ratio of administrators to faculty members is *lower* in large universities than in small colleges, which contradicts the implicit assumption of critics that keeping academic institutions small reduces the proportion of administrators, and which conforms to the relationship observed in government bureaus. Whereas the negative correlation between size and administrative ratio is not as strong in academic institutions as in employment security agencies ($-.45$ with proportion of managerial and $-.60$ with proportion of staff personnel), it is not negligible ($-.28$, using the logarithm of size in all three cases). As a matter of fact, the analysis in Table 3.6 reveals that the administrative economies effected by the large size of academic institutions are greater than this correlation indicates. Moreover, the decrease in the administration-faculty ratio with increasing institutional size occurs at a declining rate, as Figure 3.4 shows, disclosing another parallel with the pattern in public bureaucracies. This finding that the impact of size on the administration-faculty ratio diminishes with increasing size suggests that an opposing effect of the differentiated structure of large academic institutions may be operative, as is the case in employment security agencies.

A large number of students per faculty member exerts an independent influence on the administrative ratio, reinforcing that of large faculty size

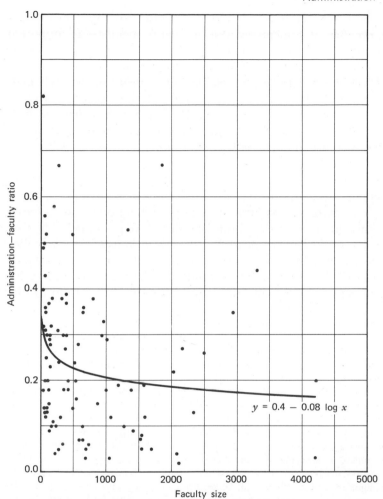

Figure 3.4.   Regression of Administration–Faculty ratio on size.

on it and further decreasing the ratio.[15] This counterintuitive empirical result that proportionately fewer administrators suffice for a large student body constitutes a dramatic indication of the administrative economies of scale observable in universities and colleges, just as in other organiza-

[15] In the regression analysis of administrative ratio with four independent variables, the beta weight of student faculty ratio is   .37; the three other beta weights are: size (log), −.53; schools and colleges, .17; and levels, .25.

tions. The earlier inference that the administrative component depends on the number of students as well as faculty members is supported by these findings, though in an unexpected way. The procedure previously adopted when number of faculty and student-faculty ratio have cumulative effects on a dependent variable is to substitute for both of them number of students, which is the product of the two and encompasses both (see the discussion of Table 3.3).[16] Doing so also has the methodological advantage that the measure of size, student enrollment, is not the same as the denominator in the administration-faculty ratio.

Table 3.6 shows that both horizontal differentiation into numerous schools and colleges and vertical differentiation into multiple hierarchical levels enlarge the administration-faculty ratio in academic institutions.[17] A complex administrative structure highly differentiated in its two main dimensions expands the size of the administrative personnel. The division of labor has no such effect on administration in universities and colleges,[18] nor does it in employment security agencies. When structural complexity is controlled, the large size of an academic institution is seen to have a strong direct effect reducing the administration-faculty ratio (indicated

---

[16] Faculty size, not student enrollment, is used in Figure 3.4, as in the scatter diagrams presented earlier, to make them comparable. In the scatter diagram using enrollment instead, the administration-faculty ratio reveals a similar curve. (In the unweighted sample, the correlation of raw size with their administrative ratio is $-.12$ and that of the logarithm of size is $-.23$.)

[17] There remains the methodological problem that the number of administrators in an organization has a mathematical nexus with the number of levels (more hierarchical ranks cannot exist without administrators occupying them) and, to a lesser extent, with number of schools and colleges (each has at least one dean). To control for this in the study of government bureaus, it was shown that the effects of differentiation on the span of control of supervisors (which has no mathematical connection with differentiation measures) correspond to its effects on the ratio of administrative personnel, reversing sign, of course (Blau and Schoenherr, op. cit., pp. 195–197, 282–284, 335). Whereas no data on supervisory span of control are available for academic institutions, the finding that several hierarchical levels have parallel effects on the spans of control of two ranks of administrators (Tables 3.4 and 3.5) as on the ratio of all administrators, reversing signs again, provides similar support for the assumption that the observed relationship between differentiation and administrative ratio is not due merely to the mathematical nexus between the measures but reflects actual influence. [If number of schools and colleges is added as a third to the two independent variables in Table 3.5, its beta weight is also negative ($-.25$), like that of levels, but less than twice the standard error (.15). It cannot be added as an independent variable in Table 3.4, because it is part of the dependent variable—the president's span of control.]

[18] If number of departments is added as a fourth to the three independent variables shown in Table 3.6 in a regression analysis of administrative ratio, its beta weight is negative ($-.22$) but less than twice the standard error (.14).

Table 3.6   Administration-Faculty Ratio

	Beta Weight	Simple Correlation
1. Enrollment (log)	−.75**	−.37
2. Schools and Colleges	.30*	−.14
3. Levels	.26*	−.04
$R^2=.22$ $(\hat{R}^2=.20)$; $n=103$		

* More than twice its standard error.
** More than three times its standard error.

by enrollment's beta weight of −.75) . This pronounced economy of scale in administration is greatly diminished, however, by the complex structure of most large academic institutions, specifically, by the positive indirect effects of large size on the administrative component mediated by the number of schools and colleges (.23) and that of levels (.15) . Nevertheless, a substantial negative gross effect of large size persists, as indicated by the simple correlation (−.37) , which means that most large academic institutions, despite their complex structure, have proportionately fewer administrators than do small institutions.

The complicated pattern of influences of size and differentiation on the administrative component is essentially the same in universities and colleges as in government bureaus. This further evidence of homology in formal structure between academic institutions and other organizations is particularly impressive in view of the important differences in goals and other characteristics, including some directly pertaining to administration. The roles and responsibilities of academic administrators differ in many respects from those of the managerial personnel in most work organizations. The need for administrative coordination is in all likelihood not as great for the academic work carried out in various schools and colleges as for the operations performed in the usually more highly interdependent subdivisions of the typical work organization. And the goals of government bureaus—for instance, administering unemployment insurance and providing employment service—are, of course, different from the academic goals of universities and colleges and require different practices to implement them. Notwithstanding these differences in function, there is a basic equivalence in structure.

As a result of this homology, the theorems derived from the research on employment security agencies are supported by the empirical findings on universities and colleges. Two of these have been discussed earlier in this chapter. Four additional theorems follow:

1. Large organizational size reduces the proportion of administrative personnel.
2. Differentiation increases the proportion of administrative personnel.
3. Large size has opposite influences on the administrative ratio, indirectly increasing it, owing to the greater structural differentiation of large organizations, as well as directly reducing it.
4. The influence of expanding size on reductions in the administrative ratio is increasingly weakened by its counteracting indirect influence mediated by differentiation, so that these reductions occur at a declining rate.

The data on American universities and colleges conform to all these propositions.

TESTING THEORETICAL ASSUMPTIONS

Several theoretical assumptions were advanced to explain the consistent empirical regularities observed in the formal structure of employment security agencies and other work organizations.[19] The data on universities and colleges provide an opportunity for testing some of the implications of these assumptions.

The division of labor is assumed to have compelling instrumental advantages in work organizations that create strong pressures fostering its development to the limits that the organization's size permits. It makes the work of subunits as well as individuals in the organization more homogeneous, thereby facilitating and improving performance. The subdivision of work segregates tasks into relatively homogeneous functions of subunits and jobs of individuals, which usually range from routine to very difficult duties. For example, the progressing division of labor in hospitals replaces many registered nurses and general practitioners with nurses' aides and with surgeons and other specialists, respectively. The double advantage of the division of labor for the organization is that it makes it possible to accomplish many jobs with less skilled personnel and to recruit specialized experts for the most difficult jobs, so that more complex work can be performed better and with fewer highly trained

[19] Peter M. Blau, "Interdependence and Hierarchy in Organizations," *Social Science Research* 1 (1972), 1–24. Although some data on universities and colleges are included in the tables in this paper, their implications for the theory are not analyzed there.

employees to boot. The subdivision of work among organizational seg-ments with comparatively homogeneous functions has similar instru-mental advantages, as does the subdivision of administrative responsibili-ties among staff units and among managers on different hierarchical levels, which also preserves top management's ultimate authority resting on its command over resources. The instrumental advantages of the differentiation of work along various lines exert imperative constraints on the management of an organization, since it is interested in effective operations, to make the decisions required to promote differentiation. Given these conditions, the development of differentiation tends to be largely limited by the organization's size, lest work become so fragmented that individuals are deprived of colleagues and effectual coordination is no longer possible.

These theoretical conjectures can explain the strong impact of an or-ganization's size on the differentiation of work along various lines in it, but they raise questions, and the data on academic institutions help answer some of these. One question is whether the organizational devel-opment of the division of labor occurs partly because it results in greater specialized expertness of some jobs and not exclusively because it results in the routinization of others. The assumption has been that the division of labor has *two* instrumental advantages that foster its development— that more complex work can be performed better in the more specialized positions *and* that less training and skills are needed for the more routine jobs. But is not the routinizing effect alone, because it reduces labor cost, accountable for the progressive subdivision of work in organizations? A related question is whether the concern with measurable short-run effi-ciency that prevails in most work organizations is the driving force behind the development of the division of labor. Both questions raise the issue of whether its economic benefits account for the development of the division of labor in organizations. Durkheim argues that this is not the case for the division of labor in entire societies,[20] but formal organi-zations differ from societies. Another assumption that may be questioned is that the advancing division of labor depends on the intervention of the organization's management, which has an interest in operating efficiency.

The empirical findings on universities and colleges give a negative answer to the first two questions and thus support the theoretical assump-tions made. First, the academic division of labor does not make work more routine but more specialized and generally enhances the skills and

---

[20] Emile Durkheim, *The Division of Labor in Society*, Glencoe, Ill.: Free Press, 1947, pp. 233–263.

training required to perform it (compare the expert knowledge of an archaeologist with that of a sociologist teaching a course in anthropology with a lecture on archaeology). But the division of labor is more advanced in large academic institutions, whose size places less restrictions on its development, than in small ones, just as is the case for the division of labor in other work organizations, where it largely routinizes jobs. Second, the short-run efficiency of academic work cannot be measured in comparable units that permit regular computation of profit or loss, quite aside from the fact that concern with efficiency is disavowed by academics and academic administrators, particularly in the major universities in which work is most specialized. Since the division of labor develops readily in academic institutions, as well as in other organizations, a concern with immediate efficiency measurable in dollars and cents cannot be at the roots of its development. These inferences from the data support Durkheim's argument that the division of labor cannot be explained simply by the economic benefits it produces. We have not yet examined the role of administrators of universities or colleges in decision making and, specifically, in institutionalizing the academic division of labor, and the discussion of the assumption that managerial intervention is essential for the organizational development of the division of labor must be postponed until we have done so.

The major theoretical principle assumed to explain the observed direct and indirect influences of size on the administrative component is that organizing the work of others—which, in its broadest sense, is what is meant by administration—entails investments of time and effort that do not directly depend on the volume of work being organized. The efforts involved in designing a procedure for performing a certain job depend little on whether only one or several hundred employees carry out this job, or on whether they do so merely for a brief period or for a long time. Once a computer program has been perfected, it can be used to produce a few tabulations or many thousands of a similar kind. The same time is required to recruit a clerk who is needed for a month and one who is hired for several years (except that turnover does increase recruitment efforts). The larger the volume of productive work and of the number of persons engaged in it, the smaller is the proportion of administrative personnel needed, because the administrative investments in organizing the work can be amortized, as it were, over a larger volume of work.

The differentiation of responsibilities in an organization changes the situation, however, since the foregoing considerations apply to relatively homogeneous work. Inasmuch as it increases the heterogeneity of the work among various subunits and individuals (in the process of reducing *internal* heterogeneity), differentiation enlarges the administrative investments needed for organizing and coordinating the work and thus leads to an expansion of the administrative component, whose responsibility is organizing and coordinating operations.

These theoretical assumptions are intended to explain why the large size of work organizations decreases the administrative ratio, why differentiation increases it, and why the indirect effect of large size, mediated by the pronounced differentiation in most large organizations, also increases it. A question that arises is whether these effects are the result of the fragmentation of work into mostly very simple jobs—the assembly line being an extreme illustration. The reasoning is that many similar simple jobs can be supervised by a small number of administrative personnel (the number of keypunch operators per supervisor is twice that of more skilled workers in employment security agencies, for example) but that the many different interdependent jobs require much administrative coordination. The data on universities and colleges indicate that the effects on the administrative ratio just noted are not confined to organizations in which responsibilities are fragmented into simple operations that are highly interdependent. The academic division of labor does not make the duties of faculty members more similar and simpler but more diverse and requiring more specialized skills, and the work in one school or college depends relatively little on that carried out in others, yet the effects of size and differentiation on the administrative ratio are the same in academic institutions as in other organizations.

A final assumption is that the administrative problems engendered by a differentiated structure in an organization find expression in resistance to further differentiation and in adjustments to the existing complexity of the structure. The adjustments to the problems of coordination and communication arising in a differentiated structure take the form of enlarging the administrative personnel responsible for dealing with these problems, as indicated by the positive effect of differentiation on the administrative component. Since expanding organizational size reduces the proportion of administrative personnel, the additions to such personnel made to adjust to the growing differentiation accompanying growing size increasingly counteract reductions in the administrative ratio; this is reflected in a declining rate of the reductions in the administrative ratio effected by expanding size. In similar fashion, the effect of expanding size on differentiation encounters increasing resistance from the differentiation already produced and hence becomes weaker as size, and with it differentiation, increase; this is reflected in the declining rate of the growth of differentiation with expanding size.

The declining rate of the increases in the number of subunits into which organizations become differentiated as their total size increases necessarily implies that the average size of subunits, as well as their number, is greater in large than in small organizations. Large subunits are indicative of large amounts of relatively homogeneous work, just as differentiated subunits are indicative of heterogeneity in work among them. Consequently, the assumption that the administrative problems resulting from differentiation create resistance to it not only can account for the declining rate of increases in differentiation with increasing size, but it also helps explain why large organizations have relatively small administrative components, that is, the economy of scale in administration. For the resistance to differentiation is responsible for the larger subunits, within which work is comparatively homogeneous, in large than in small organizations, and according to a previous assumption, much homogeneous work reduces the proportion of administrative personnel needed.

Here again a question arises on which the data on academic institutions can throw some light. The larger size of subunits in large organizations implies that supervisors, on the average, have a wider span of control in large than in small organizations; the research on employment security agencies furnishes direct evidence of such correlation between organizational size and mean span of control of supervisors on different levels and in various functional divisions.[21] The question is whether the savings in administrative personnel accruing to large organizations are not simply due to more efficient supervision and better utilization of supervisory personnel. But there is little direct supervision of faculty members in universities and colleges, and whatever there is—for instance, sitting in on classes—is carried out by department chairmen or senior faculty, not by administrators. Yet academic institutions also exhibit an economy of scale in administration, which therefore cannot be attributed solely to more efficient utilization of supervisors. Moreover, academic institutions reveal the same *declining rates* of the increases in differentiation that occur with increasing size as do other organizations; this implies a growing resistance to differentiation and an expansion of subunit size as the size of the total institution becomes larger. In fact, the total size of an academic institution is correlated .77 with the average size of its departments and .32 (.41 if total size is logarithmically transformed) with the average size of its schools and colleges.

[21] Blau and Schoenherr, *op. cit.*, pp. 195, 221–223, 283–288.

Large academic institutions have larger as well as more diverse departments than do small institutions. Although this merely confirms what one would have impressionistically concluded anyway, this fact does not explain it. Specialization has important advantages, but so do large subunits, even when economies in supervision are not relevant for their existence. A very small department that does not comprise a critical mass of colleagues provides little opportunity for social integration, for consultation with fellow specialists in a variety of subspecialties, and for academic stimulation. Small colleges are doubly disadvantaged by being restricted not only to fewer, less specialized departments but also to smaller ones. The many diverse departments in large academic institutions are sufficiently specialized to permit a slower pace of further specialization in order to enlarge departments and thereby to improve the academic programs they offer students and the academic environment they furnish faculty members.

The theoretical assumption that academic institutions, like other organizations, require administrative investments manifest in opposite effects of size and differentiation on administration can be subjected to another test by analyzing the clerical-faculty ratio (including among clerks all ancillary personnel except administrators). Whereas clerks in government agencies cannot be considered part of the administrative apparatus, since many of them are line personnel (not supportive staff) and provide basic services such as unemployment insurance services, clerks in universities and colleges are part of the administrative apparatus, furnishing support for and not being themselves engaged in academic work. The simple correlation between size and the clerical ratio is .30, which apparently contradicts the prediction that large size reduces the clerical staff. But the results of regression analysis alter this conclusion. In discussing these results, influences of conditions other than size on the clerical ratio are examined first.

The larger the number of departments in an academic institution, the higher is the proportion of clerks to faculty members (last row of Table 3.7). This relationship concretely illustrates how differentiation enlarges the administrative personnel. Even quite small academic departments usually have a departmental secretary. Large departments may have several secretaries, but their ratio to faculty tends to be lower than that in small departments. The situation is analogous to that of work groups in other organizations, which have a supervisor whether they are small or large, though an assistant supervisor is sometimes appointed in very large

Table 3.7   Clerical-Faculty Ratio

	Beta Weight	Simple Correlation
1. Affluence	.36**	.46
2. Size	−.32*	.30
3. University	.11	.38
4. Departments	.53**	.44

$R^2 = .35$ $(\hat{R}^2 = .32)$; $n = 98$

* More than twice its standard error.
** More than three times its standard error.

groups. Besides, the existence of many academic departments undoubtedly increases administrative work in the central administration, enlarging the clerical and other support personnel there too. If both number of schools and colleges and number of hierarchical levels are substituted for the single variable, number of departments, in a regression analysis of the clerical ratio with the same other three independent variables, the total variation accounted for is reduced (from 35 to 29 per cent; corrected, from 32 to 25 per cent); the beta weight of schools and colleges (.29) is much smaller than that of departments (.53); and the beta weight of levels is in effect nil (−.03). The regression analysis in the table is preferable to that one.

Differentiation along all three lines examined seems to increase the need for administrative personnel, but substructural differentiation into many departments enlarges primarily the clerical staff, whereas differentiation in the two main dimensions of the formal structure—into schools and colleges and into levels—enlarges primarily the staff of senior administrators, as we saw in Table 3.6. This difference suggests that the degree of differentiation into major components of the administrative structure makes demands on senior administrative personnel, whereas further differentiation within these major components makes demands that can be satisfied with less skilled, clerical personnel. The reason may be that departmental differentiation raises problems of communication, which require more clerks, but it raises less serious problems of integration and resource allocation than the differentiation of major structural components, which therefore requires more senior administrative personnel.

Universities have proportionately more clerks than do colleges, as the simple correlation in the third row of Table 3.7 indicates, largely because they have more departments (the decomposition coefficient is .34). The complex departmental structure of universities accounts for their higher clerical-faculty ratio. There is little difference in this ratio between universities and colleges when number of departments is controlled, and the beta weight fails to exceed twice its standard error. The first row in the table reveals that the affluence of an academic institution raises the number of clerks per faculty member, an influence that persists in slightly reduced form if other conditions are held constant. Superior economic resources make more clerical assistance available to faculty members and senior administrators, relieving them of administrative detail.

The major reason why large academic institutions have more clerks than small ones, proportionately as well as in absolute numbers, is that they have more departments (the decomposition coefficient is .44). The greater affluence of large academic institutions and their greater likelihood of being universities contribute further to the positive association between size and clerical ratio (.11 and .07, respectively). When these conditions are controlled, however, size as such is seen to reduce the ratio of clerks to faculty members, as the negative beta weight in the table's second row shows.[22]

Thus the large size of academic institutions has two opposite effects on the clerical ratio, a direct one reducing it and an indirect one mediated by differentiation increasing it, in accordance with theoretical expectations. These effects of size parallel its effects on academic administrators and its effects on the managerial component and on the staff component in other kinds of organizations. But there are some differences. Whereas the negative direct effect of size is stronger than its positive indirect effect in the other cases, with the result that the gross effect of large size reduces these administrative ratios, the situation is reversed in the case of the clerical ratio. Here the negative direct effect of size is *weaker* than its positive indirect effect, so that the gross effect of large size raises the clerical ratio. Since there is no overall decrease in the clerical ratio with increasing size, no declining rate of such a decrease can be observed, as it is for other administrative ratios. Furthermore, it is departmental differentiation that mediates the positive indirect effect of size on the clerical ratio, whereas other aspects of differentiation account for its positive indirect effects on the ratios of administrators.

The main difference is that large academic institutions have disproportionately many clerks, though they, as well as other large organiza-

---

[22] If student enrollment is substituted for faculty size in a regression analysis that includes otherwise the same variables as that presented in Table 3.7, the pattern is little changed. But both the simple correlation (.22) and the beta weight ($-.21$) of enrollment with the clerical ratio are weaker than those of size (the b^* is less than twice its standard error), which reduces the total variation accounted for slightly (to .33; corrected, to .30).

tions, have disproportionately few administrators. It may be that both associations, despite their opposite signs, reflect the better utilization of manpower in large organizations, which have sufficient administrative responsibilities of various kinds to occupy their complements of high-paid administrators fully, and which have enough routine work in various parts to substitute low-cost clerks for higher-paid personnel. There may also be less resistance to the expansion of clerical staff than to that of senior administrators, not only because the labor cost of clerks is lower, but also because they are subordinates whose assistance is welcome and not persons in positions of authority who may infringe on the authority of other administrators and restrict the freedom of the faculty. Whatever the correct interpretation of this difference turns out to be, the conclusion of primary interest is that the underlying pattern of influences of size and differentiation on the clerical ratio supports the theoretical assumptions.

IMPLICATIONS

The administrative structure of academic institutions exhibits a remarkable homology with that of other organizations. The strong dependence of differentiation on size, the inverse relationship between the two main dimensions of differentiation in the structure, the interlaced influences of size and a complex differentiated structure on the administrative apparatus—all these are in principle the same in academic institutions and public bureaucracies. To be sure, there are differences in detail—the strength of various influences, and therefore sometimes the direction of their combined influence. Yet the overwhelming impression is one of homology, since even when differences are initially observed refined analysis tends to uncover underlying similarities. This does not mean that universities and colleges are just as bureaucratic as government agencies, a description that is in need of refinement in any case. Small colleges and small government bureaus are less bureaucratic than their large counterparts if we refer to the complexity of the formal structure, but they are more bureaucratic if we refer to the relative size of the administrative machinery. Many academic practices differ from bureaucratic procedures—those governing faculty appointments are a good example—and the practices in the largest universities usually are furthest removed from bureaucratic ones, as we shall see. The different aspects of bureaucratization do not necessarily vary together. What the findings presented so far do show is that variations in the formal structure of academic institutions closely parallel those in government bureaus.

The distinctive nature of academic work makes it possible to take advantage of these parallels, as well as of the differences observed, to clarify some implications of the theoretical assumptions made to explain the empirical regularities in government agencies. The differentiation of work among subunits and individuals tends to advance as far as size permits because it has two important advantages for the organization according to the theory. An intensive division of labor makes some jobs more routine and others more specialized, enabling an organization to discharge more complex responsibilities requiring specialized expertness with a smaller proportion of costly skilled personnel. The implication is that specialization suffices for the division of labor to expand in large organizations and that this expansion is not solely due to the reduced labor cost of routine jobs. Since the academic division of labor makes the work of faculty members more specialized, not more routine, without reducing labor costs, it provides a test case for this implication, and its strong association with the size of academic institutions supports the theoretical inference.

Another assumption made is that the administrative investments required for organizing work reduce the proportion of administrative personnel needed as the volume of homogeneous work increases, and they enlarge this proportion as work becomes more differentiated and heterogeneous. The assumption is designed to explain the negative effects of size and the positive effects of differentiation on administrative ratios. One may suspect that these influences are confined to organizations in which work is highly fragmented, inasmuch as many simple operations can be supervised by one foreman but a large number of interdependent jobs demand much coordination by managerial personnel. This is not so, however. The same pattern of influences is observed in universities and colleges, where academic duties are not highly fragmented into simple routines that are directly interdependent, regardless of the extent of the academic division of labor. The theoretical assumption concerning administrative investments apparently applies to quite different kinds of organizations.

To explain the declining rates of both the increases in differentiation and the decreases in administrative ratios that occur with increasing organizational size, it has been assumed that feedback processes modify the influences of size on differentiation and administration. The specific assumptions are that the administrative problems arising in differentiated structures lead to resistance to further differentiation, on the one hand, and to adjustments to these problems by adding administrative personnel, on the other. The resistance to differentiation diminishes the positive effect of size on differentiation, and the additions to administrative personnel diminish the negative effect of size on the administrative ratio, as size, and with it differentiation, increase. Since a declining rate of differentiation necessarily implies an increase in average subunit size with increasing organizational size, the assumption that a feedback effect creates resistance to and slows the pace of differentiation also explains why large organizations tend to have larger subunits than small organizations.

In most work organizations, the savings in supervisory manpower resulting from large subunits and wide spans of controls of supervisors may be the underlying factor producing feedback processes from differentiation that slow its continuing pace, but this cannot be the only factor generating resistance to differentiation. For declining rates of differentiation reflecting such resistance and consequent increases in average departmental size also accompany the expanding size of academic institutions, though larger academic departments hardly save supervisory manpower. The size of a department limits the courses it can offer, the variety of views it can represent, and the intellectual stimulation it can provide for students and faculty (and similar considerations apply to the size of schools and colleges). The limitations of small size create pressures to expand departments, which increasingly counteract the pressures promoting specialization as the departments in an institution have already become highly differentiated and specialized.

What are the implications of the differences found between academic institutions and government bureaus? No attempt is made to interpret variations in the strength of similar influences. Some differences in simple correlations revealed upon closer analysis similar underlying influences, though of varying strength, accounting for the difference. One example is the effect of size on top executive's span of control, which becomes apparent in academic institutions only when vertical differentiation is controlled. Similarly, the negative effect of size on the clerical ratio in academic institutions, disclosed by the regression analysis, is concealed in a positive zero-order correlation, owing to the counteracting indirect influence of size mediated by departmental differentiation. An important advantage of regression procedures is their ability to uncover such latent patterns.

The research indicated only two substantive differences in administrative structure between academic institutions and employment security agencies (excluding variations in strength of influences), and at least one of these probably reflects a methodological rather than a substantive difference. Differentiation in all three dimensions is more pronounced in universities granting Ph.D.'s than in colleges that do not, independent of their size. Complex responsibilities of academic institutions find expression in complex formal structures. The same may well be true for other organizations, but it could not be observed in employment security agencies, since no measure of the nature of responsibilities existed. In the analysis of the local branches of these agencies, the more complex work in employment service offices could be distinguished from the simpler duties in unemployment insurance offices. More complex responsibilities, so measured, promote differentiation in these government offices, though their influence is much weaker than that of university status on differentiation.[23]

The academic division of labor, as indicated by number of departments, is positively related to horizontal differentiation into schools and colleges when size and university status are controlled in academic institutions. A corresponding relationship between division of labor and horizontal differentiation into major subdivisions is not observable under controls in large government bureaus, only in small ones.[24] The average size of academic institutions is not so small to account for this difference. But the difference may be a methodological artifact resulting from the measures of the division of labor used. In academic institutions, the measure is the number of departments, which are structural components of the institution; in government bureaus, it is the number of job titles or occupational positions, which are not. There may also be a substantive difference, however. The colleges and, particularly, the professional schools in a university are likely to be more independent than the functional divisions in a government bureau, with each having considerable influence in deciding on its own complement of departments or internal division of labor. As the number of schools and colleges in an academic institution increases, therefore, so does the total number of departments.

[23] Blau and Schoenherr, op. cit., p. 214.
[24] Ibid., pp. 75, 187, 341–344. The last reference is to an analysis of the data on a second type of government bureau—finance departments of American state and local governments—and shows how the independent influence of the division of labor on structural differentiation becomes suppressed by the counteracting influence of the combination of large size and the division of labor (using a product term) with increasing organizational size.

CHAPTER FOUR

RECRUITMENT

Academic institutions provide important, though largely indirect, services to society. The liberal education they offer to increasing numbers of young people creates the enlightened citizenry that is essential for democracy. The scientific knowledge originating in them improves the technology and makes possible rising standards of health and living. The contributions to the arts and the humanities their scholars make enrich the culture. The advanced technical training received in them supplies a professional labor force. Some students of academic affairs, like Hutchins, emphasize the pursuit of knowledge as an end in itself and lament the encroachments on liberal education of practical training and research oriented to industrial problems.[1] Others, like Ben-David, conclude that the strong concern with professional training and applied research in American higher education has furthered purely scientific progress and strictly academic developments.[2]

This issue poses a dilemma for higher education. Ben-David is probably right in saying that society's support for academic institutions, which permits the pursuit of science and scholarship in their own right, depends on the practical contributions of immediate benefit that higher

[1] Robert M. Hutchins, *The Learning Society*, New York: Praeger, 1968, pp. 37–38, 96, and *passim*.
[2] Joseph Ben-David, "The Universities and the Growth of Science in Germany and the United States," *Minerva* **7** (2) (1968–69), 1–35, esp. pp. 12–13, 21–24, 29–30.

education makes. Yet one cannot dismiss Hutchins' insistence that the benefits of a genuine education are necessarily indirect and that an interest in knowledge for its own sake is worth stimulating and deserves being protected from attack. If the claim is justified that the pursuit of science and scholarship as ends in themselves makes long-range contributions to society that are not readily discernible, there is a need to defend such an approach to academic work against the recurrent attacks from various quarters that want institutions of higher education to serve ends of more immediate value.

The alternative objective against which the freedom to pursue an interest in knowledge as such must be defended has varied widely in history. It was to strengthen religious institutions in the early colleges here and in Europe. It was to contribute to the greater glory of the Third Reich for a short period in Germany. It has frequently been to supply a trained labor force and useful information to business and industry in the United States. It may serve a good cause, like curing cancer. Most recently, it has been to furnish action programs relevant for dealing with the serious social problems of society and for transforming outmoded institutions. Yet regardless of one's agreement with the urgent need to change existing institutions to enable them to cope with new social problems and improve the common welfare, a commitment to scholarship requires that universities be protected against demands to subordinate all else to serving this need and be preserved as ivory towers in which theoretical understanding is an ultimate end, not a means to solve practical problems, urgent though they may be. For a concern with knowledge and understanding in their own right makes important contributions to the commonweal in the long run.

The quality of an academic institution and its contributions to knowledge and to society depend on the quality of its faculty and students. Naturally only people and not institutions perform academic work, and how good it is hinges on these people. But this does not mean that institutional characteristics are irrelevant for academic quality, because the conditions in an academic institution determine the quality of the faculty and students it is able to recruit. This chapter deals with the conditions in universities and colleges that affect the recruitment of well-qualified faculty and capable students, and it also raises the question of whether there is any class bias in faculty recruitment.

RECRUITING QUALIFIED FACULTY

The measure of faculty qualifications is the proportion of faculty members in an academic institution who have Ph.D.'s or professional degrees.

Although the measure is based on all faculty members in the institution, not merely the sample interviewed, excludes students who also teach, and includes professional degrees as well as Ph.D.'s, it is a crude indication of academic quality, as Orlans warns.[3] It refers only to completion of advanced training and fails to take into account the quality of the higher education received as well as differences in abilities that are independent of graduate training. But it is not intended as an overall index of academic quality (which will be further analyzed), merely as an indicator of formal qualifications, in order to investigate what conditions in academic institutions govern their success in recruiting faculty members who have at least completed advanced training.

Academic positions, like other jobs, provide both extrinsic rewards, in the form of salaries and other material benefits, and intrinsic ones derived from the work itself. The intrinsic gratifications of academic work are undoubtedly greater than those in most other jobs, and many if not most academics think of themselves as being more influenced by these than by material rewards. A curious anomaly concerning the relative significance of extrinsic and intrinsic rewards in the thinking of academics is revealed in a study by Caplow and McGee, based on interviews with departmental chairmen and colleagues in 10 universities concerning positions recently vacated by one faculty member who was replaced by another. "The departure of the replacements from their former place of employment is attributed in good part to the prestige advantages of the new position and thus reflects credit on the reporting department. The attraction of positions elsewhere for men who were lured away from the department are all objective—salary, duties, location. There is very little perception of prestige advantages in the new position. . . ."[4]

In short, why colleagues leave a department tends to be explained by those who remain in terms of material benefits, but why others join is usually explained in terms of the department's intrinsic advantages. The authors interpret these findings as resulting from the inflated image academics frequently have of the prestige of their own department. In defense of this image, the department's intrinsic characteristics are perceived to be responsible only for movements into it but not for movements out of it, which are attributed to extrinsic factors. Given these misperceptions, the significance of salaries for faculty members cannot be determined by asking them but must be inferred by ascertaining how

---

[3] Harold Orlans, *The Effects of Federal Programs on Higher Education,* Washington: Brookings Institution, 1962, pp. 16–17. The measure he discusses does not include professional degrees, but the basic point applies nevertheless.

[4] Theodore Caplow and Reece J. McGee, *The Academic Marketplace,* New York: Basic Books, 1958, p. 57.

much salary differences influence the jobs of those whose superior qualifications give them more choice than others have over their careers.

The average salaries in academic institutions exert more influence than anything else on the formal qualifications of their faculties. The zero-order correlation in row 7 of Table 4.1 shows that no less than one-half of the variation among institutions in the proportion of faculty members with advanced degrees is accounted for by salary differences alone.[5] The beta weight indicates that the influence of salaries on qualifications remains pronounced when eight other conditions in academic institutions are controlled. This finding strongly supports the assumption made in Chapter Two that poor salaries are a major impediment to effectual faculty recruitment. It does not mean, however, that financial rewards override all other considerations in the job choices of academics, nor that most would accept otherwise quite unsatisfactory jobs simply because higher salaries are offered. They are rarely confronted with extreme choices of this kind, since their academic reputations govern how many academic institutions with desirable working conditions are interested in them and thus the salary they can command. As a result, faculty members with superior reputations can get higher salaries without having to sacrifice the intrinsic advantages of positions in good universities or colleges, whereas those whose achievements are not widely recognized, whether justly or not, are often doubly penalized by having to work in less desirable places and for lower salaries to boot.

Salaries are important for faculty recruitment because they frequently make the marginal difference between more or less equally attractive academic positions. Hence how well qualified a faculty an academic institution can recruit depends on its economic resources. Its affluence exerts a strong influence on the formal qualifications of its faculty, as indicated by the pronounced simple correlation (.52) in row 3 of the table, hardly any of which is spurious (.06). But the trivial beta weight reveals that the entire influence of affluence is indirect, most of it resulting from the better salaries affluent institutions can offer (the decomposition coefficient is .35). Although sufficient financial resources to pay relatively high faculty salaries are important for recruitment, they are not the sole attribute of academic positions that faculty members consider. As a matter of fact, an empirical study by Marsh and Stafford finds that the job choices of academics are less responsive to salary differences than those of persons in the same specialties in other employment—that the

[5] Hardly any of this zero-order correlation of .73 is spurious, owing to common antecedents (.02). Salaries cannot be expected to account for as much of the variation in qualifications among individuals, since aggregating data—in this case, by institutions—tends to increase the correlation between variables.

Table 4.1   Formal Qualifications of Faculty

	Beta Weight	Simple Correlation
1. South	.17*	.06
2. Age	.24**	.53
3. Affluence	.04	.52
4. Size	−.30*	.44
5. Percentage of graduate students	.23**	.43
6. University	.08	.44
7. Salaries	.58**	.73
8. Departments	.31*	.45
9. Levels	−.17*	.05

$R^2 = .71$ ($\hat{R}^2 = .68$); $n = 104$

* More than twice its standard error.
** More than three times its standard error.

supply of academic labor is comparatively inelastic, in the terminology of economics.[6]

These research results imply that the employment decisions of faculty members are more highly influenced by intrinsic rewards—as well as nonmonetary extrinsic ones, such as location—than are those of other people. Why then do we find that salaries exert the strongest influence on the recruitment of faculties with superior qualifications? The reason may well be that the significance of intrinsic rewards is more variable and more dependent on personal considerations than the significance of the generalized extrinsic reward of income. Let us assume that the job choices of individual faculty members are primarily influenced by intrinsic rewards but that those of *different* individuals are most affected by *different* features of the job—graduate teaching for some, specialized research for others, and geographical location for still others—while the choices of all are considerably affected by salaries. Under this assumption, although individual choices are less strongly influenced by salaries than by other factors, the influence of salaries, being less variable, would be more manifest in the "ecological correlations" between institutional conditions here examined. But this is not a methodological error, since "ecological" rather than individual relationships are the relevant ones for the problem under consideration, namely, what conditions influence an academic institution's faculty recruitment, not what governs the employment deci-

[6] John F. Marsh, Jr., and Frank P. Stafford, "The Effects of Values on Pecuniary Behavior," *American Sociological Review* 32 (1967), 740–754.

sions of individuals. The salaries offered are the most important factor determining the chances of academic institutions to recruit faculties with advanced degrees. Several intrinsic characteristics of academic jobs also influence faculty recruitment, however.

The more specialized and the more advanced the academic work in an institution of higher education is, the better are the formal qualifications of its faculty. The beta weight in row 8 of Table 4.1 shows that many departments, which are indicative of institutionalized specialization, increase the proportion of faculty members who have Ph.D.'s or professional degrees, regardless of other conditions in the academic institution. Many graduate students have the same effect, as the beta weight in row 5 reveals. And the second measure of advanced academic work—that the institution is a university granting Ph.D.'s—also raises faculty qualifications, though in this case only indirectly (see the substantial simple correlation, which is not spurious, and the insignificant beta weight in row 6).

A plausible reason for these influences is that graduate training as well as specialized academic work requires higher academic qualifications than teaching undergraduates and performing less highly specialized academic responsibilities. To meet these requirements, however, a university must offer sufficient salaries to recruit well-qualified faculty members. The interpretation consequently implies that at least part of the reason for the better formal qualifications of faculties in institutions in which academic work is more advanced and specialized is that these institutions pay higher salaries than others. Indeed, the decomposition coefficients reveal that some of the influences of advanced and specialized academic work in an institution on faculty qualifications are due to better salaries (for percentage of graduate students, .20; for university status, .27; and for specialized departments, .31), because large and affluent institutions offer more advanced and specialized academic work and pay better salaries.[7] But a large proportion of graduate students and many specialized

---

[7] Analysis not presented shows that the pronounced relationships of salaries with percentage of graduate students ($r = .34$), university status (.46), and departments (.53) are spurious and disappear when size and affluence are controlled (which is why the first two have not been included in the regression analysis of salaries in Table 2.1 and why salaries have not been included in that of departments in Table 3.1). Such information about spurious associations between independent variables must be supplied and taken into account in interpreting the decomposition coefficients, because the statistical procedure employed indicates only whether the correlation between every independent and the dependent variable is spurious, given the causal assumptions, and not whether the correlations between pairs of independent variables are, as mentioned in footnote 24 of Chapter Two. Table 4.1 is the only one of 30 regression problems presented in which the abbreviated decomposition procedure produces misleading results that falsely indicate indirect effects and that must be corrected by knowledge derived from other tabulations about spurious associations among independent variables.

departments also have direct effects on faculty qualifications when salaries and other conditions in the academic institution are controlled (as
the beta weights in rows 5 and 8 show), and university status too affects
qualifications regardless of salaries, though indirectly, owing to the
greater departmental specialization in universities (.20).

Apparently, both advanced and specialized academic work raise the
formal qualifications of the faculty *independent* of the salaries and other
conditions in an academic institution. The inference is that working
with graduate students and working in specialized fields make the job
intrinsically more attractive to qualified faculty members and therefore
enable an academic institution to recruit more of them than its salary
schedule would otherwise make possible. The superior training and
competence required for advanced specialized academic work enhance
the prestige as well as the salary it commands, and its higher prestige
contributes to the intrinsic satisfaction it gives and reduces the extrinsic
rewards necessary to recruit personnel to carry out such work. Reciprocal
influences may also be operative here, inasmuch as faculties with superior
qualifications attract more graduate students to a university and perhaps
also stimulate the development of more specialized departments.[8]

The older a university or college is, the larger is the proportion of its
faculty with full academic credentials, as row 2 of Table 4.1 indicates.
Part of this influence of age on faculty qualifications is the result of the
better faculty salaries in older than in more recently established academic
institutions (.21), but part of it is direct (see the beta weight). The
stronger academic tradition developed over many decades, which is
reflected in the greater share of the older institution's resources devoted
to recruiting faculty (by offering better salaries), may well also find
expression in greater concerns with faculty welfare in other respects and
in more scholarly climates that attract academics to older institutions.
The special aura a position in one of the venerable old universities has
perhaps further facilitates recruitment of qualified faculty members.

Regional preferences influence the career decisions of faculty members
in unexpected ways. A person who has spent his academic life in the
North, as the author has, gets the impression that Southern universities
and colleges must find it difficult to recruit qualified faculties, because so
many students completing Ph.D.'s, as well as colleagues, are reluctant to

[8] The analysis in Chapter Eight will make it possible to test whether superior faculty
qualifications actually promote the development of specialized departments.

accept academic positions in the South. But this impression is false, created by the prevailing anti-Southern bias among Northern academics. Faculty qualifications in Southern academic institutions, despite their lower salaries, are not inferior to those in the rest of the country, as the simple correlation in row 1 of Table 4.1 shows. For a Southern location makes it easier, not more difficult, to recruit qualified faculty (see the beta weight indicative of a positive direct effect). It may well be that the anti-Southern preferences of many Northerners not only are mirrored in but further strengthen the pro-Southern preferences of many white Southerners, who are the minority in the nation and faced by the majority's anti-Southern attitudes in the North. The conjecture that Southern academics have particularly strong regional loyalties is supported by findings of a study by Brown. The responses from several thousand faculty members who have recently moved show that, although those from all regions tend to return to the region where they were educated, the tendency "is strongest in the Southeast where, for all categories, over 63 per cent return."[9] The strong regional loyalties of Southerners help Southern universities and colleges to recruit qualified faculties.

The discussion of the complicated influences of an academic institution's size on the formal qualifications of its faculty has been reserved to the end of the analysis of Table 4.1.[10] The simple correlation in row 4 indicates that the larger an academic institution is, the higher is the proportion of its faculty who have completed advanced training. One might speculate that this may be because large universities produce more academics, whose loyalty to their alma mater makes it easy to recruit them; or because it requires a critical mass of scholars to attract others who are well-qualified; or perhaps even because the better football teams of many large universities make them better known. The analysis reveals, however, that all these speculations are wrong and that the superior faculty qualifications in large academic institutions are entirely accounted for by three specific conditions.

Large academic institutions succeed in recruiting better qualified faculties than small ones because they pay higher salaries (.35), have more specialized departments (.26), and concentrate more on graduate training (percentage of graduate students and university status together, .15).

---

[9] David G. Brown, *The Mobile Professors*, Washington: American Council on Education, 1968, p. 88. Southeast comprises two of the three regions in the South.

[10] The reverse causal sequence that faculties with superior qualifications attract more colleagues and thus expand the institution's size can hardly account for differences in total faculty size among institutions, inasmuch as these differences depend on resources and scope of academic responsibilities. Hence the causal assumption is that institutional size influences faculty qualifications.

When these conditions that make positions in large universities attractive are controlled, it becomes evident (in the beta weight) that large size as such reduces the proportion of the faculty with advanced degrees. Institutional size has a positive gross but a negative net effect on faculty qualifications. If otherwise similar academic institutions are compared, the faculties of large are not as good as those of small institutions, but conditions in large universities are generally different and more favorable for obtaining good faculties, though this is not always the case. Illustrations of exceptions are large municipal colleges, where poor academic conditions impede faculty recruitment despite high salaries, and the best liberal arts colleges, whose academic prestige and atmosphere attract good faculty despite low salaries.

The findings imply that academics prefer small to large institutions, other conditions being equal, but that the more attractive conditions usually existing in large universities override these preferences and incline candidates who have alternatives to choose positions in large institutions. (The assumption is that the presence of better qualified faculty members, whose options are greatest, is indicative of preferences.) What makes large size itself an impediment for recruiting qualified faculty may be the impersonality and bureaucratization for which multiuniversities are often criticized. Whereas the interpretation of the positive gross effect of large institutional size on faculty qualifications is based on the empirical analysis, which reveals what the intervening factors are, the data do not supply evidence for the interpretation of its negative net effect (or for that of any direct effect). But there is some indirect evidence for the interpretation suggested. If the bureaucratization that prevails in large academic institutions is what makes them encounter difficulties in recruiting qualified faculty, indicators of bureaucratization itself must have the same effect. One such indicator is a multilevel bureaucratic hierarchy. The number of hierarchical levels does indeed also reduce the proportion of the faculty with advanced degrees, as the beta weight in the last row of Table 4.1 shows, supporting the interpretation.

ATTRACTING GOOD STUDENTS

An explicit measure of the preferences of able students for various colleges at the time they apply for admission is available, whereas the attraction of qualified faculty members to different academic institutions could only be inferred from their presence. The expressed preferences of outstanding prospective students are good indications of which academic institutions attract them, but not of the institutions in which they will be found the following fall, since where they actually go also depends on differences in tuition and scholarships. Variations in student abilities among colleges will be analyzed in Chapter Six, permitting comparison with the preferences analyzed here. The measure is the number of choices received by an academic institution from semifinalists and recipients of letters of recommendation in the National Merit Scholarship program, relative to the size of the college's freshmen class. It has been developed by Astin on the basic of responses to the question which two colleges the student would most like to attend.[11] The use of the measure as dependent variable here indicates what conditions attract highly able students to a college. Its use as an independent variable later when analyzing other influences makes it possible to control the institution's reputation, as reflected in the preferences of intelligent young people greatly interested in making informed choices.

The last row in Table 4.2 shows that good faculties attract good students, which is hardly surprising. If anything is surprising, it is the small size of the beta weight, particularly in view of the fact that faculty qualifications undoubtedly not only influence an institution's reputation among able students but are influenced in turn by this reputation. An explanation for the failure of these reciprocal influences to be manifest in a larger beta weight will be suggested shortly. The simple correlation is so much larger than the beta weight because a number of conditions in academic institutions affect faculty qualifications and student preferences in parallel ways, spuriously raising the association between the two variables. The underlying processes of these influences are not always the same for students and faculty, however.

Two aspects of differentiation in an academic institution have opposite effects on both faculty qualifications and student preferences. A multilevel hierarchy, which has been considered indicative of a bureaucratic structure, makes an academic institution less attractive to good students (see row 8 in the table),[12] just as it makes qualified faculty members less inclined to accept positions there. A bureaucratic hierarchy separates faculty and students from the president and his academic deputy, whatever the title, by interposing administrative levels, which reduce social access and create red tape by leading to the substitution of lengthy forms

---

[11] Alexander W. Astin, *Who Goes Where To College?* Chicago: Science Research Associates, 1965, pp. 25, 52–53, 55.

[12] We shall examine in Chapter Nine whether the dislikes of entering students for institutions with bureaucratic hierarchies is realistic, that is, whether such hierarchies adversely affect undergraduate education.

Table 4.2   Reputation Among Able Students

	Beta Weight	Simple Correlation
1. Northeast	.35**	.39
2. South	−.15*	−.41
3. Religious	.26**	−.03
4. Affluence	.15*	.51
5. Size	−.31**	.26
6. Salaries	.46**	.65
7. Departments	.37**	.28
8. Levels	−.28**	−.16
9. Faculty qualifications	.20*	.58

$R^2 = .75$ $(\hat{R}^2 = .73)$; $n = 108$

* More than twice its standard error.
** More than three times its standard error.

and formal memoranda for personal contacts. This situation is detrimental for the free communication in an academic community and makes it less attractive. Differentiation into many departments, on the other hand, attracts outstanding students to an academic institution (row 7), corresponding to its effect on well-qualified faculty members, though in this case the process of influence may well be different. The variety of departmental programs and the diversity of the academic environment probably appeal most to able students, whereas the greater opportunity to engage in specialized academic work if departments are subdivided is likely to be the factor that interests qualified faculty members most. In any case, however, the preferences of both students and faculty for much departmental and little hierarchical differentiation make incompatible demands, since the two forms of differentiation tend to develop together with the increasing size of academic institutions.

High faculty salaries also attract good students (row 6 in Table 4.2) as well as good faculty to academic institutions. Only a small part of the strong influence of salaries on student preferences results from the larger proportion of faculty members with advanced degrees that higher salaries attract (.14). Most of the effect is direct, as the beta weight indicates. Why do students prefer institutions that pay better salaries to faculty members? A class bias may be operative, and faculty members whose salaries enable them to maintain the style of life of the upper middle class may raise a college's value in the eyes of students. But another factor is in all likelihood more important. High salaries reflect superior academic standing of the institution and, particularly, superior abilities of its faculty, even when the proportion who have completed advanced training is controlled. Young faculty members who are highly recommended and older ones who are reputed scholars command higher salaries than others who also have advanced degrees. Faculty quality exerts more influence on student preferences than the small beta weight of the merely formal qualifications of the faculty seems to imply, because its influence is also reflected in the beta weight of salaries. There may also be some feedback, since the ability to attract good students might raise the resources available to recruit better faculty.

Students of high caliber are more attracted to affluent institutions than to poor ones, as row 4 in Table 4.2 shows. The major reason is that affluent institutions pay higher salaries, which enable them to recruit better faculties (the decomposition coefficient for salaries and qualifications together is .38). As just mentioned, some of this may result from a feedback effect that raises the resources for faculty recruitment of institutions with superior reputations among outstanding students. The beta weight indicates that affluence also has some direct effect on student preferences, independent of other conditions. A possible interpretation of this net effect is that the superior facilities and better fellowships in affluent institutions attract bright students, although the possibility that wealth as such and its symbolic value make an institution preferable cannot be excluded.

Large academic institutions are preferred by able students because they can afford better faculties and have more diverse departments than small institutions, but large size itself, independent of these attractive conditions usually associated with it, detracts from the appeal of an institution of higher education to students. In other words, size has a positive gross and a negative net effect on capable students (see row 5, Table 4.2), furnishing another parallel with the pattern of influences on qualified faculty. The processes mediating the indirect effects of size are similar but not identical, partly because faculty qualifications are the dependent variable in one but an intervening variable in the other case.[13] Bright students are attracted to large academic institutions by their many diverse departments (.31) and by the superior faculties that their higher salaries recruit (salaries and qualifications together, .37). These attractions tend to overcome the preferences of good students for small, less impersonal

---

[13] In purely statistical terms, the two intervening variables responsible for most of the positive indirect effect of size in Table 4.2 are salaries (.28) and departments (.31), just as is the case for Table 4.1 (.35 and .26, respectively). But the substantive implications are not the same.

colleges if conditions were the same (indicated by the negative beta weight) and make large academic institutions more popular among them (indicated by the positive simple correlation).

Most of the characteristics of academic institutions that attract qualified faculty, as inferred from their presence, attract able students as well, as revealed by their stated preferences. These parallels have methodological and substantive implications. Methodologically, the assumption that the attractiveness of institutional conditions may be inferred from their influences on the proportion of better qualified faculty members receives some support from the findings that the explicit preferences of outstanding students also indicate the attractiveness of these conditions. Substantively, the parallels imply that outstanding high school seniors who plan to go to college are neither less informed about nor less sensitive to variations among academic institutions than are faculty members. There are some differences in influences on students and faculty, of course, since one can hardly expect all institutional attributes to have the same significance for students seeking a college education and for faculty members engaged in teaching and research.

The college preferences of exceptional entering students are hardly affected by whether an institution is a university granting Ph.D.'s or by the proportion of graduate students in it,[14] whereas these two factors have a substantial influence on qualified faculty, as we have seen. The greater prestige and challenge of working with advanced students seem to make qualified faculty members interested in moving to universities with many graduate students. But the very interest of university faculties in graduate education may deprive undergraduates of faculty attention, neutralizing any advantages the better faculties and more diverse departmental offerings in universities have for them. As a result of these compensating disadvantages and advantages, the degree of concentration on graduate work in an academic institution makes no appreciable difference for the college preferences of good incoming students. How realistic it is for these student preferences to discount the advantages of universities depends on whether concentration on graduate work actually has disadvantages for undergraduates, such as reducing the faculty attention they receive and impeding their educational progress. These problems will be examined in Chapters Six and Nine, respectively.[15]

[14] The small correlations with reputation among able students of university status (.15) and percentage of graduate students (.21) are spurious, which is why these variables are not included in the regression analysis presented in Table 4.2.

[15] Although age and student preferences are correlated (.22), their association is the result of the better salaries and faculties in older institutions. This does not make the correlation spurious in terms of the causal assumptions, but it is of little substantive interest, which is why age has been excluded from the regression analysis presented in Table 4.2.

The religious affiliation of an academic institution exerts no independent influence on faculty qualifications,[16] but it does play a role in the preferences of able students. Although the simple correlation in the third row of Table 4.2, which is close to nil, indicates that there is no difference in these preferences between religious and other colleges, this lack of difference conceals two effects in opposite directions. The lower salaries and the consequently less well-trained faculties in religious academic institutions exert a negative influence on the preferences of outstanding students (decomposition coefficient of salaries and qualifications together, $-.21$). But when the conditions that make religious institutions less attractive are controlled, disproportionate numbers of outstanding students are seen to prefer religious colleges, as the positive beta weight shows.

Jencks and Riesman note that religious commitments provide pools of students for Protestant and Catholic colleges, despite their usually inferior quality. They warn, however, that increasing numbers of the best students go to secular academic institutions, citing data to the effect that fewer than one-half of the National Merit Scholars who are Catholics choose Catholic colleges.[17] Nevertheless, the findings here reveal that the number of these highly able students who prefer denominational colleges, undoubtedly owing to their religious commitments, is sufficient to counteract the preferences of others for better secular colleges, so that religious academic institutions, though their quality is inferior, attract as many bright students as other institutions.

Regional loyalties influence the academic choices of students as well as those of faculty members, but not in the same way; at least, the end product is not the same. Able students are more attracted to colleges in the Northeast and less to Southern colleges than to those in the rest of the country (see first two rows in Table 4.2), in contrast to the positive attraction to Southern academic institutions of faculty members that their location implies.[18] Does this mean that the regional loyalties of Southern students are weaker than those of students elsewhere, whereas Southern faculty members have particularly strong regional loyalties? Not necessarily. The local allegiances of Southern students may well be

[16] The small negative correlation between religious affiliation and faculty qualifications $(-.19)$ is essentially the result of the lower salaries in religious institutions. If the dummy variable, religious affiliation, is added to the independent variables in Table 4.1, its beta weight is .09, less than twice the standard error.

[17] Christopher Jencks and David Riesman, *The Academic Revolution*, New York: Doubleday Anchor, 1969, pp. 312–405, esp. pp. 333, 387–388.

[18] The dummy variable, Northeast, has no effect on faculty qualifications $(r=.04$; if added in a regression analysis to the variables in Table 4.1, $b^*=.10$, less than twice its standard error).

at least as strong as those of students elsewhere.[19] These regional preferences of *individual* students would still produce proportionately few preferences for Southern colleges if one assumes that disproportionately few of the National Merit Scholars making the choices are from the South. This is a very reasonable assumption, since educational attainments of all kinds are lower in the South than in other regions.[20] The excess of preferences for Northeastern colleges cannot be interpreted in the same terms, inasmuch as educational attainments are highest in the West, not in the Northeast. The high prestige of the Ivy League may be responsible for the attraction of Eastern colleges.

CHANNELS OF UPWARD MOBILITY

In the average academic institution, about three-quarters of the faculty members interviewed report that their fathers had not graduated from college. This reveals much upward social mobility, even taking into consideration the general increase in education during the last generation, though it also indicates that academics come from better educated homes than the population at large. Academia is an avenue of social mobility for many Americans, but not all universities and colleges are equally good channels of mobility. By analyzing faculty social origins, we can ascertain which academic institutions provide the best opportunities for upward mobility and simultaneously infer which ones seem to exhibit a class bias in faculty recruitment.

The proportion of faculty members in an academic institution who have advanced degrees must be controlled in this analysis, lest the expected association between father's and son's or daughter's educational attainments leads to misleading conclusions. The percentage of the faculty with advanced degrees and the percentage whose fathers graduated from college in an academic institution are correlated .38. Strangely enough, however, an analysis of the 2540 individuals from whom these institutional proportions are derived reveals a correlation of only .08 between the faculty member's having an advanced degree and his fa-

[19] The proportion of students attending institutions of higher education *in their home state* is very slightly higher in the South (85 per cent) than in the rest of the country (82 per cent). Computed from 1968 data in U. S. Office of Education, *Digest of Educational Statistics,* Washington: U.S.G.P.O., 1970, p. 69.

[20] Indeed, the number of winners of National Merit Scholarships among eleventh graders in the participating schools is 16 per 1000 in the South but 26 per 1000 in the rest of the country. Computed from Robert C. Nichols, "Participants in the 1965 NMSQT," *NMSC Research Reports* 2 (1) (1966), Table 1.

ther's having a college degree. This finding raises two questions. First, why is the correlation between own and father's educational attainments so much lower for academics than for the American population, for which it is .45 (males 20–64 years old) ? Second, what produces the correlation between the proportion of an institution's faculty members with advanced degrees and the proportion whose fathers had college degrees, given that it does not simply reflect a similar correlation for individual faculty members?

With respect to the first question, one reason that the association between the amount of education of faculty members and that of their fathers is so much lower than the corresponding association for other people is that a ceiling effect depresses it. Since all academics are highly educated, the education of their fathers can vary, with rare exceptions, only in one direction from their own, in contrast to an entire population distribution of educational attainments, from which father's education is free to vary in both directions. In addition, the indicators for education in the faculty sample are not scales, as they are in the population sample, but dichotomies—whether or not the son has an advanced degree, and whether or not his father had a baccalaureate. Dichotomous variables tend to restrict the size of a correlation coefficient and make it dependent on the distributions of the two variables.[21] Hence it is quite possible that the observed difference in educational inheritance between the general population and faculty members is a methodological artifact. But there may also be a substantive reason for this difference: perhaps once a person has gone to college and moved up some distance from his social origins further advancements depend on social origins much less than do occupational achievements generally. This interpretation accords with the theoretical model of quasi-perfect mobility developed by Goodman.[22]

The second question raised is why there is a substantial correlation for academic *institutions* between proportion of faculty members with advanced degrees and proportion with college-educated fathers, in the absence of an equally strong correlation between these two variables for the same *individual* faculty members. The reason again may be method-

[21] The correlation of .08 between the two dummy variables indicating faculty member's educational qualifications and his father's education is not increased if a score of father's education is substituted for the latter; it is then .07.

[22] Leo Goodman, "On the Statistical Analysis of Mobility Tables," *American Journal of Sociology* **70** (1965), 564–585. The underlying assumption of Goodman's model may be described by saying that family background affects social mobility not like a rubber band, making further movements away increasingly difficult, but like an umbilical cord, a strong bond resisting detachment but losing its hold once severed.

ological. It is known that aggregating variables into groups—in this case, academic institutions—increases their correlations over that between them if they are not aggregated. To inquire whether this fact is responsible for the considerable difference between the institutional and the individual correlation, a regression analysis of father's education of 2540 individual faculty members was performed, with two independent variables, whether the individual has a Ph.D. or professional degree, and the proportion in his institution who do so.[23] The proportion of colleagues with advanced degrees in the institution is related to the individual faculty member's social origin (father's education) even when his own education is controlled ($b^* = .12$, which is small but still five times its standard error in this large sample; $r = .13$). In contrast, individual's own education is unrelated to his or her father's if the education of colleagues in the institution is controlled ($b^* = .02$, which is less than one standard error; $r = .07$).[24] These findings imply that the social origins, measured by father's education, and the educational qualifications of the faculty in an institution have a connection that is independent of the association between individual's origin and his or her own education, whatever the effect of aggregating may be.

It is the reputation of an academic institution that produces this connection between the educational qualifications and social origins of its faculty members. We have seen in Table 4.2 that superior qualifications of the faculty in an academic institution are associated with its reputation, as indicated by the preferences of outstanding students. And the last row in Table 4.3 shows that the reputation of a university or college has a pronounced effect on the social origins of its faculty, that is, the proportion with college-educated fathers. The beta weight in row 6 of the table reveals that the substantial association between faculty's educational qualifications and social origins is reduced to an insignificant relationship under controls, and decomposition discloses that the institution's reputation is responsible for this reduction (.29).

Why do universities and colleges with superior reputations recruit faculties with high social origins? Perhaps the reason is that high social origins are indicative of greater academic abilities, independent of formal qualifications. Men and women raised by well–educated parents in

[23] Father's education is used as the dependent variable because it is a score, whereas faculty member's own educational qualifications are a dummy variable, whether or not graduate education has been completed.

[24] If other conditions in an academic institution that affect the social origins of faculty members are controlled, the beta weight of colleague's educational qualifications is reduced (.06) but remains more than twice its standard error, and that of own educational qualifications is the same (.02).

Table 4.3   Social Origins of Faculty (Father's Education)

	Beta Weight	Simple Correlation
1. Northeast	.13	.35
2. Religious	−.36**	−.39
3. Affluence	.07	.42
4. Student-faculty ratio	−.20*	−.36
5. Salaries	−.25*	.41
6. Faculty qualifications	.12	.38
7. Reputation	.50**	.55

$R^2 = .51$ ($\hat{R}^2 = .48$); $n = 114$

* More than twice its standard error.
** More than three times its standard error.

middle-class homes have economic and psychological advantages that others lack. They may have gone to better universities and may be better scholars. One way to check on this is to ascertain whether father's education and research productivity are correlated. They are for institutions (.38) but not for individuals (.02), and the relationship for institutions also disappears under controls.[25] This indicates that scholarly productivity cannot account for the higher social origins of the faculties in the best academic institutions.

The findings suggest that academic institutions with superior reputations exhibit some class bias in faculty recruitment. One reason for such bias is that elite universities recruit their faculties primarily from graduates of elite universities, as a number of studies have shown, and middle-class students have a better chance to go to elite universities than others. Berelson, for example, notes that 85 per cent of the faculties of the top 12 American universities received their highest degree from these 12 elite universities.[26] More direct evidence of class bias is provided in Crane's

[25] If faculty research productivity is added to the independent variables in Table 4.3 in a regression analysis, its beta weight is only .03 (less than one standard error), with reputation being primarily responsible (.26) for the difference between it and the simple correlation. Paul F. Lazarsfeld and Wagner Thielens, Jr., however, report that socioeconomic background is positively related to research productivity (using different measures) for individual faculty members in their sample, the average difference in three age groups being 9 per cent; *The Academic Mind*, Glencoe, Ill.: Free Press, 1958, p. 10.

[26] Bernard Berelson, *Graduate Education in the United States*, New York: McGraw-Hill, 1960, p. 118. See also Mark J. Oromaner, "A Note on Analytical Properties and Prestige of Sociology Departments," *American Sociologist* 5 (1970), 243.

secondary analysis of data collected by Berelson on two samples of faculty members—a sample of the graduate faculty in 92 universities and a national sample of recent recipients of doctorates. She finds that class background—whether measured by father's education or father's occupation makes little difference—affects the quality of the undergraduate and of the graduate degrees in both groups and consequently the likelihood of having a position at a major university. Moreover, even if quality of doctorate is controlled, superior social origins improve the chances of obtaining a job in a major university for the younger group fresh out of graduate school, though not significantly for the older group of graduate faculty members.[27] The influence of family background on academic careers apparently becomes attenuated with increasing experience and age, as is also the case for other occupational careers.[28] Crane's findings clearly support—without conclusively proving, to be sure—the inferences derived from the analysis here that faculty recruitment in the best academic institutions reveals a bias in favor of candidates with middle-class origins.

Table 4.3 supplies additional indications of the significance of an academic institution's prestige for the class composition of its faculty, and of the career handicaps of academics who have moved up from lower social origins. The high prestige of many Eastern universities and colleges is reflected in disproportionate numbers of middle-class faculty members in them, and the difference in faculty composition between them and institutions in other regions is reduced to insignificance when reputation is controlled (see row 1; the decomposition coefficient for reputation is .19). Affluent academic institutions have more middle-class faculty members than poor ones also primarily because they have superior reputations (row 3; the decomposition coefficient for reputation is .25). Thus many upwardly mobile academics work in universities and colleges that have insufficient economic resources to facilitate the work of their faculties. Whereas this influence of affluence is indirect, a high student-faculty ratio in an institution exerts a direct negative influence on the proportion of faculty members with middle-class backgrounds (beta weight, row 4). This implies that disproportionate numbers of upwardly mobile

[27] Diana Crane, "Social Class Origin and Academic Success," *Sociology of Education* **42** (1969), 1–17, esp. pp. 8–12. She finds no relationship between social origins and research productivity (p. 8), which conforms to the findings here and differs from those of Lazarsfeld and Thielens cited in footnote 25.

[28] Peter M. Blau and Otis D. Duncan, *The American Occupational Structure*, New York: Wiley, 1967, pp. 182–187.

academics are located in institutions where high teaching loads and large class sizes leave them little time for scholarship and research, thereby handicapping their further careers.

Upwardly mobile faculty members have current as well as future economic disadvantages, inasmuch as excess numbers of them are in academic institutions that have low salary scales. The higher the salaries in an academic institution, the larger is the proportion of its faculty with college-educated fathers, as the simple correlation in row 5 of Table 4.3 indicates. The main reason is that institutions with superior academic reputations tend to pay higher salaries and to have more middle-class faculties (decomposition coefficient for reputation, .33). When reputation and other conditions are controlled, however, the beta weight reveals a *negative* relationship between salaries and proportion of faculty with high social origins. Disregarding other conditions, therefore, upwardly mobile academics tend to be in institutions that pay relatively good salaries. The finding suggests that financial rewards are particularly important for upwardly mobile faculty members, who have special difficulties getting jobs that are intrinsically rewarding, and many of whom have experienced economic hardships. Yet despite the greater attraction better salaries seem to have for academics from lower social origins, their salaries tend to be inferior to those of academics from higher social origins, who are more often employed in institutions with higher pay scales, partly owing to their superior academic preparation, but probably in part owing to discrimination.

Religious academic institutions have faculties with comparatively low class origins. The difference between them and secular institutions in this respect is substantial and persists under controls, as row 2 in Table 4.3 shows. Denominational colleges and universities, particularly Catholic ones, are channels of upward mobility, as research by Slaughter based on these data indicates.[29] Jencks and Riesman stress the importance of Catholic educational institutions as vehicles for the Americanization and upward mobility of the children of large waves of immigrants.[30] The significance of Catholic institutions for social mobility extends to faculty as well as students, and that of Protestant institutions is not much less.

[29] In the unweighted sample, the average Catholic academic institution has 87 per cent faculty members whose fathers had not graduated from college; the corresponding percentages are 75 for Protestant, 74 for public, and 63 for private secular institutions. Among religious institutions, the dummy variable, Catholic versus Protestant, has a simple correlation of .39 with the percentage of faculty members whose fathers had *no* college degrees. See Ellen L. Slaughter, "The Comparative Study of Religious and Non-Affiliated Institutions of Higher Education," M.A. thesis, University of Chicago, 1972.

[30] Jencks and Riesman, *op. cit.*, pp. 341–342.

This tolerant acceptance of men and women from humble social origins is rooted in discrimination along other lines. Brown presents data that show that Protestant colleges discriminate in faculty recruitment against non-Protestants, and Catholic colleges discriminate still more against non-Catholics.[31] The religious preferences for the ingroup of denominational academic institutions probably override other considerations and lead to greater acceptance of lower-class persons of the same faith, making these institutions important avenues of upward mobility.[32]

Let us reexamine in conclusion how good the evidence concerning class bias in academic recruitment is; specifically, reference is to preferences for candidates from middle-class families not attributable to their greater academic abilities. Such a bias has not been unequivocally demonstrated, inasmuch as not all possible differences in academic abilities have been controlled, or could be in any research other than a controlled experiment. However, we have seen that class differences in faculty composition remain after several aspects of academic abilities have been held constant—not only the formal qualifications of the faculty but also the additional differences in academic abilities reflected in salaries and in research productivity. The reasonable inference is that these persisting differences result from class bias in faculty recruitment. Elite universities and generally academic institutions with superior reputations and working conditions, such as light teaching loads, have disproportionate numbers of middle-class faculty members not only because they usually have the best academic preparations but also because recruitment in all probability discriminates against candidates of lower social origins. Why do the best universities exhibit most class bias in recruitment? The most likely reason is that they can afford to do so, whereas the smaller pools of available candidates in less attractive institutions restrict their freedom of choice in making appointments.[33]

[31] The ratio of the percentage of faculty members appointed who are of the institution's own faith and the percentage expected if there were no discrimination and only publications and chance would govern appointments is 75:54 for Protestant and 67:15 for Catholic academic institutions; Brown, op. cit., p. 83. Standardized, the discrimination score for Catholic institutions is 450 (per 100) or three times that of Protestant institutions of 150.

[32] Size is not included in the regression analysis in Table 4.3 because its correlation with faculty social origins (.26) is spurious and disappears when Northeast and affluence are controlled ($b^* = .12$, less than twice its standard error).

[33] This interpretation implies that elite universities also discriminate in other ways, not only on the basis of class origins. Indeed, Brown finds that the top 10 per cent of academic institutions in terms of prestige discriminate most against women; op cit., p. 79.

The main channels of upward mobility are universities and colleges of low academic standing, since the weaker academic preparations of academics reared in working-class homes are presumably reinforced by discrimination against them in the best academic institutions. Thus upwardly mobile faculty members work predominantly in institutions that have meager economic resources, pay low salaries, have high student-faculty ratios, and employ less qualified faculties. Lack of stimulating colleagues, heavy student loads, and insufficient resources and facilities discourage research and scholarship in such an environment. Religious institutions also are major channels of upward mobility, as they have been for many centuries. But since religious colleges and universities tend to have low academic prestige, their role as an avenue of mobility merely reinforces the prevailing tendency of most opportunity for upward mobility into academic positions to be provided by the less desirable institutions.

THE DILEMMA OF SIZE

Students as well as faculty often criticize the large modern university and compare it unfavorably with the less impersonal and less bureaucratic small college. Yet the best faculty and students, who have most freedom of choice, tend to be attracted to and located in large academic institutions. The academic conditions that qualified faculty members and able students value are most frequently found in large universities, because the resources of a large institution are required to create these conditions. It takes the economic and intellectual resources of a large academic enterprise to offer high salaries and to provide much advanced and highly specialized academic work, which furnish both the extrinsic and intrinsic rewards that facilitate recruiting qualified faculty. And the resulting better faculties combined with the more diverse departmental programs in large academic institutions make them attractive to good students. The influences reinforce one another, as the better students make teaching more gratifying for the faculty, and the better faculties attract more advanced as well as better students to the university. But the large size of an academic institution itself and the bureaucratic hierarchical structure that typically accompanies it reduce its attraction for both faculty and students.

The findings summarized here reflect the dilemma posed by the size of an academic institution. The ability of a university or college to recruit good faculty and good students and to attain and maintain a high academic reputation depends on conditions that in turn depend to a considerable extent on the large scope of the academic enterprise. High academic standing requires specialized academic pursuits in a large number of diverse fields, which simply cannot be developed in a small college. It also requires competing with other institutions for the best faculty and the best students, and the financial resources for doing so can rarely be mobilized by a small academic institution. Once a top reputation has been achieved, it attracts financial contributions, outstanding students, and great scientists and scholars, helping to sustain the elite standing of the academic institution, and at the same time fostering further growth.

The large size of a university, necessary as it is for excellent academic work in a variety of disciplines, simultaneously has consequences that endanger the quality of academic work. It inevitably makes the academic institution more impersonal and engenders bureaucratic developments in it, both of which reduce its attraction for the best students and faculty members. The establishment of cluster colleges—small, semiautonomous units within larger universities—is an attempt to relieve these problems.[34] The problems are not so easily disposed of, however, and they are intensified by the expanding size of academic institutions to meet the increasing demand for higher education. One symptom of these problems is the occurrence of student uprisings in the last decade in many large universities, and primarily in large universities, as a number of studies have shown.[35] Although often prompted by external political events and revealing the special sensitivity of college students to the nation's political life, the preponderance of these student rebellions in large universities with bureaucratic tendencies cannot be dismissed as accidental and must be considered a sign of the underlying stresses large size generates in an academic community. The point here is not to blame students for these disruptions of academic work but, quite the contrary, to emphasize that these student uprisings are merely symptomatic of the stresses and strains generated by the large size of a university that threaten its quality by making it a less desirable place for the most academically committed students and faculty members.

That is the dilemma. Large size is essential for the superior quality of a university, of its personnel, and of the academic work performed in it, yet it has deleterious consequences that make the university a poorer environment for performing academic work, alienate the best faculty and students, and endanger the institution's academic standing.

[34] Donald J. Reichard, *Campus Size,* Atlanta: Southern Regional Conference Board, 1971, pp. 23–28.
[35] See, for example, Joseph W. Scott and Mohamed El-Assal, "Multiuniversity, University Size, University Quality and Student Protest," *American Sociological Review* **34** (1969), 702–709; and Peter M. Blau and Ellen Slaughter, "Institutional Conditions and Student Demonstrations," *Social Problems* **18** (1971), 475–487.

CHAPTER FIVE

ORIENTATIONS TO ACADEMIC
WORK AND INSTITUTION

The relative emphasis on the two main academic responsibilities—educating students and advancing knowledge through research—differs widely among academic institutions. There is much dispute over the proper balance between them, and the insufficient concern with one or the other is often criticized. Many young instructors, steeped in research in graduate school and eager to pursue it further, find themselves frustrated in their first jobs by heavy teaching loads and a lack of interest in scholarship of administrators and senior colleagues. Many outstanding and admired teachers, on the other hand, feel that they are unjustly deprived of recognition for their successful educational endeavors by their colleagues in the wider discipline, because research commands most esteem. Since most academics work in institutions where teaching responsibilities predominate and research must be carried out on the side, at some sacrifice, the greater prestige of research causes much resentment.

The disputes over this issue are brought out in a study by Lipset and Ladd based on questionnaire responses from 58,000 faculty members in American colleges and universities:[1]

---

[1] Seymour M. Lipset and Everett C. Ladd, Jr., "The Divided Professoriate," *Change* **3** (3), (1971) 58.

The professoriate, then, is divided sharply as to what its functions should be, as to whether the present allocation of the time of academics approaches what it should be. Fifty-seven per cent of the respondents in our Carnegie faculty survey agreed that "big contract research has become more a source of money and prestige for researchers than an effective way of advancing knowledge." One in four among the entire faculty, and one in three among professors 35 and younger found their fields too research oriented. About 57 per cent maintained that undergraduate education would be improved if there were less emphasis on "specialized training" and more on "broad liberal education" (code words for rejecting research), and nearly half (48 per cent) accepted the charge that "many of the highest paid university professors get where they are by being 'operators'." Thirty-six per cent of the entire sample believed that the concentration of research grants in the major universities was "corruptive" of the schools getting them—and this includes 35 per cent of those at big grant-getting institutions.

It is important to note that Lipset and Ladd direct attention to the disagreements among academics about the role of research reflected in these figures, not to a widespread condemnation of research, which the figures do not indicate. Only between one-quarter and about one-third of the faculty members directly state that there is too much emphasis on research. Even the euphemism that "broad liberal education" would be improved if less emphasis were placed on "specialized training," which many scholars committed to research would grant, was agreed upon by less than three-fifths of the respondents. Criticisms of "operators" and "big contract research" do not imply wholesale condemnations of research itself, after all, only of certain types of research and researchers. Yet these conflicting attitudes toward research, which indicate lack of value consensus, raise a theoretical question: Why does research play a dominant role in the academic prestige system? The analysis in this chapter may help to shed some light on this question.

The first topic to be discussed is the conditions in academic institutions that influence the orientations of faculty members to research and teaching and their actual involvement in research. Of special interest is the analysis of the structural effects of the colleague climate in an academic institution, that is, the effects of the characteristics of the rest of the faculty on the academic work of individuals, *independent* of the influences of their own corresponding characteristics. For this purpose, the more than 2500 individual faculty members sampled in the academic institutions under consideration are the units of analysis in the second section of the chapter (whereas institutions, of course, are the units of analysis in most of the rest of the book). This investigation makes it possible to distinguish the influences on research attitudes and practices apparently exerted by administrative procedures governing personnel selection, by colleague pressures and stimulations, and by the individual's own background.

In the third section, we turn from the study of orientations to academic work to that of orientations to academic institutions, specifically, the strength of allegiance of faculty members to their own university or college. Implicit in this discussion is the difference stressed by Gouldner between "locals" with firm loyalties to the academic institution in which they have appointments and "cosmopolitans" oriented primarily to reference groups in their discipline outside the institution.[2] After comparing academic institutions with respect to this difference in orientation as exhibited by both administrators and faculty, the focus of the analysis shifts back to the sample of individual faculty members to discern whether the characteristics of a person's colleagues influence allegiance to the local institution differently from his or her own characteristics.

RESEARCH AND TEACHING

"Publish or perish" is the derogatory slogan readily voiced by those who are critical of too much emphasis on publishing research and too little on teaching in the major academic institutions, as if there were something despicable about the demand that scholars and scientists endeavor to advance knowledge and make the results of their endeavors public. But even Jencks and Riesman, convinced as they are of the need for improving teaching in American higher education, denigrate this view. "Publication is the only way a man can communicate with a significant number of colleagues or other adults. Those who do not publish usually feel they have not learned anything worth communicating to adults. This means that they have not learned much worth communicating to the young either. There are, of course, exceptions: men who keep learning but cannot bring themselves to write. . . . Still, these are exceptions."[3] Publications make the results of research generally available, to be challenged and improved by other experts in the field, and to be utilized in social action and policy. Secrecy is incompatible with scholarship. Disparaging references to "publish or perish" are an academic form of restriction of output, equivalent to such other verbal sanctions as "rate buster" among factory workers and "curve bender" among students.

[2] Alvin W. Gouldner, "Cosmopolitans and Locals," *Administrative Science Quarterly* **2** (1957–58). 281–306, 444–80.
[3] Christopher Jencks and David Riesman, *The Academic Revolution*, Garden City, N.Y.: Doubleday Anchor, 1969, p. 532.

This is not to say that a misplaced emphasis on publication records has no deleterious consequences, however. As a matter of fact, good research as well as good teaching is likely to be adversely affected by a concern with the number and bulk of publications on the part of administrators and personnel committees, whose lack of expert knowledge in the various specialized disciplines creates a strong temptation to judge on the basis of mere output quantity instead of scholarly quality. Ludicrous practices may develop as a result; for example, the names of all members of a research team may appear on every publication though only one or two worked on each, to raise the publication records of all; the same research findings, with minor modifications, may be published in two or more journals. What is of greater significance, the pressure to publish diverts attention from more important research problems to those promising to yield quick results. The consequence is that scholarship suffers, and many articles in learned journals "resemble finger exercises on the piano . . . [and are little concerned] with answering real questions or solving important problems," in the words of Jencks and Riesman.[4]

The pressure to publish tends to be especially detrimental to the quality of teaching, since it discourages faculty members from devoting much effort to teaching, as these authors also note. Whereas research interests in principle make teachers more stimulating, "many potentially competent teachers do a conspicuously bad job in the classroom because they know that bad teaching is not penalized in any formal way."[5] Educating students and engaging in research are not inherently incompatible. On the contrary, teaching—particularly though not only teaching graduate students—is improved by and in turn contributes to the faculty member's scholarship. But teaching and research do make conflicting demands on the time of faculty members, and fostering the two makes conflicting demands on the incentive systems of academic institutions.

Given the significance of the issue of teaching and research, much information pertaining to both activities was collected. A variety of questions about research emphasis and practices and about teaching emphasis and practices were asked of faculty members and of administrators, and distributions of personnel and expenditures for research were ascertained. A factor analysis on these 58 items yielded one dominant factor, reflecting a positive emphasis on research and a negative one on teaching, as noted in Chapter Two, and it was used as a general guide for selecting variables to represent this dimension. A detailed analysis is presented of the item with the highest factor loading—the proportion of faculty mem-

4 *Ibid.*, p. 533.
5 *Ibid.*, p. 532.

bers in an institution who state that publishing research is a faculty obligation there. Since the regression analysis of the main teaching item (with the highest negative loading) produced results largely similar to those obtained with the main research item,[6] it is not presented in full, but discrepancies in results are discussed. The conditions affecting three different aspects of research emphasis—weight of research for promotions, faculty obligation to publish, and individual's actual involvement in research—will be compared in the next section, devoting particular attention to the influences of the colleague climate. Two indicators of teaching emphasis—specifically, of faculty-student contacts—will be analyzed in Chapter Six.

The findings of the preliminary analysis imply that academic institutions that emphasize research tend to place relatively little emphasis on teaching and vice versa. Although teaching and research are not intrinsically incompatible and many an outstanding scholar is also a great teacher, in an academic institution where administrative procedures and personnel practices stress one the other is deemphasized. These contrasting incentive systems are manifest in two of the preliminary findings mentioned: First, an emphasis on teaching and one on research are not independent dimensions but opposite poles of the same factor. Second, using different measures for the two that are not mathematically related, those conditions in academic institutions that influence an emphasis on publishing research tend to have the opposite influence on an emphasis on teaching.[7]

The better the formal qualifications of the faculty in an academic institution are, the stronger is the orientation toward publishing research, as row 6 in Table 5.1 shows. Part of the simple correlation between faculty qualifications and research orientation is spurious, resulting from the better qualifications and stronger research orientations in large universities than in small colleges (size and university status together, .26), but there is also a substantial direct effect. This is not unexpected. Notwithstanding notable exceptions, completion of advanced training tends to be a prerequisite for scholarly research. The finding also implies that superior formal training makes faculty members more interested in re-

[6] The correlations between these two items is − .59.
[7] The negative correlation between the research and the teaching measure (−.59) is not so large to make such opposite effects inevitable. Indeed, there is one major exception of substantive interest, as we shall see, one condition that has parallel effects on these two variables.

search and possibly less interested in teaching.[8] Both these interpretations assume that individuals with better qualifications are more highly oriented to research than others; this assumption, though plausible, is not demonstrated by the finding that academic institutions with more qualified faculty members also have more research-oriented ones than do other institutions, because the two groups may not include the same persons. For example, this ecological correlation may have been produced by the fact that academic institutions that have the highest reputations have the best qualified faculties and emphasize research publications most. If we check on this, however, we find that it is not the case. Reputation makes no difference for the emphasis on research in an institution when other conditions are controlled, and controlling it does not lessen the influence of faculty qualifications on this emphasis.[9] But the finding raises another question: Is the association between faculty qualifications and research orientations exclusively the result of the greater concern of better trained *individuals* with research, and thus probably attributable to personnel selection, or is it partly produced by peer group pressures that strengthen or weaken the individual's involvement in research, depending on the colleague environment? We shall return to this question presently.

The data indicate that it is unlikely for the obligation to publish research to be prevalent among its faculty unless an institution offers sufficiently high salaries to attract well-qualified faculty members. Row 5 in Table 5.1 indicates that high salaries, though strongly correlated with an emphasis on publications, have no *direct* positive effect on it. Part of the simple correlation is spurious, resulting from the difference between large universities and small colleges (size and university status together, .32) , and the rest is an indirect effect mediated by faculty qualifications (.25) . Adequate salaries are required for an institution to be able to recruit a faculty qualified to assume obligations for research that is publishable. Faculty salaries in turn depend on financial resources. There is more emphasis on research and publications in affluent than in poor academic institutions. Comparison of the simple correlation and the beta weight in the table's first row shows that the influence of economic resources on the role of research is largely indirect. Affluent institutions stress research more than poor institutions because disproportionate

[8] In the regression analysis of teaching emphasis, with the same independent variables, the beta weight of faculty qualifications is $-.19$ $(r=-.43)$, which is just short of two standard errors.

[9] If institution's reputation among able students is added to the independent variables in Table 5.1, its beta weight is negative $(-.07$, less than one standard error), and the other beta weights are little changed. The correlation between reputation and research emphasis (.29) is spurious, mostly owing to faculty qualifications (.21).

Table 5.1   Faculty Obligations to Publish Research

	Beta Weight	Simple Correlation
1. Affluence	.09	.42
2. Size	.30**	.63
3. Percentage of graduate students	.04	.38
4. University	.30**	.64
5. Salaries	.08	.56
6. Faculty qualifications	.34**	.61

$R^2 = .60$ $(\hat{R}^2 = .58)$; $n = 114$

** More than three times its standard error.

numbers of the former are large universities (together, .19) and because they can afford higher salaries, thus attracting faculties with superior formal qualifications (.17).

Universities that concentrate on graduate education exhibit more emphasis on publishable research than colleges that do not. Scholarly research is important for training advanced students. The proportion of graduate students has a substantial zero-order correlation with publication emphasis, and the status of an institution as a Ph.D.-granting university has a still stronger correlation with it, as rows 3 and 4 in Table 5.1 show.[10] Part of both correlations are spurious. The proportion of graduate students exerts some indirect effect on research orientation, mediated by faculty qualifications (.14), however, and so does university status (.15), which has in addition a substantial direct effect on this orientation (see the beta weight in row 4). There may be some reciprocal influences, resulting from the attraction a qualified and research-oriented faculty exerts on graduate students and from the interest of such a faculty in establishing Ph.D. programs, but these are unlikely to account for the pronounced direct relationship between university status and publication emphasis when faculty qualifications and other conditions are controlled.

These findings suggest that teaching graduate students, in any case, is compatible with an orientation toward research and publications. Indeed,

[10] The correlation between the dummy variable, university status, and the proportion of graduate students is only .26, and it disappears when size is controlled ($b^* = .06$, less than one standard error), which means that the effects of these two variables are largely independent of each other. The reason must be that many colleges, which may call themselves universities, do not grant Ph.D.'s but have large numbers of M.A. students.

the proportion of graduate students in an institution has a positive direct effect on teaching emphasis[11] as well as the positive indirect effect on research emphasis just noted, and it is the only antecedent that has parallel effects on both, whereas all others that increase concern with research decrease concern with teaching. Training many graduate students requires a faculty qualified for and interested in scholarly research, and it also requires that teaching responsibilities be emphasized. This double focus, which is otherwise rare, is facilitated by the complementarity of faculty research and graduate training. The research training and guidance given to graduate students (who are appropriately called "research students" in Britain) is better and requires less effort if faculty members are themselves engaged in research; furthermore, work with graduate students often stimulates and aids rather than interrupts the faculty member's research. The larger the proportion of graduate students in an institution is, the smaller is the proportion of its undergraduates. The findings imply, therefore, that teaching as well as research suffers in purely undergraduate colleges. The fact that it is easy to think of exceptions—excellent undergraduate colleges—does not negate this implied hypothesis, and we shall have an opportunity to test it with indicators of actual educational performance, instead of simply emphasis on teaching, in Chapter Nine.

Universities granting Ph.D.'s emphasize teaching much less ($b^* = -.38$) and research much more (.30) than colleges, *independent* of the faculty's formal qualifications and other conditions. This pattern of influence differs from that of percentage of graduate students, which affects teaching and research concerns in parallel, not opposite, ways, and which affects research concerns only indirectly, through faculty qualifications. What accounts for the distinctive direct effects of university status on the prevailing orientation to academic work? Two possible answers come to mind. First, the colleague groups in universities, who tend to be better trained for research than those in colleges, may create an academic environment that intensifies concerns with research at the expense of concerns with teaching through more or less subtle peer group pressures. Second, different administrative practices, which make promotions dependent primarily on publications in universities and on teaching in colleges, may be

---

[11] In the regression analysis of teaching emphasis, with the same independent variables as in Table 5.1, the beta weight of proportion graduate students is .20* ($r = -.12$). The other beta weights (with the simple correlations in parentheses) are: affluence, $-.12$ ($-.39$); size, $-.34^{**}$ ($-.58$); university, $-.38^{**}$ ($-.64$); salaries, .04 ($-.48$); faculty qualifications, $-.19$ ($-.45$). One asterisk refers to a value twice, and two to one three times, its standard error. $R^2 = .53$ (.50).

responsible for the stronger obligations to publish research expressed by faculty members in universities. It will be of interest to see whether further analysis supports either or both of these interpretations.

Finally, there is more emphasis on research (and less on teaching) in large than in small academic institutions. Although some of the pronounced effect of large institutional size on faculty obligations to publish research is indirect, because large institutions are more often universities (.18) and have better faculties (.15) than small ones, there is also a substantial direct effect (row 2 in Table 5.1). It is somewhat puzzling that the large size of an academic institution, independent of whether it is a university and the qualifications of its faculty, promotes more emphasis on research. Administrative differences in personnel practice might be responsible, on the assumption that large size as such, not the conditions associated with it, makes appointments and promotions more dependent on publications, though why this should be the case is not clear. An alternative interpretation rests on the assumption that colleagues in one's own field, rather than colleagues in other disciplines, or students, are more important internal reference groups the larger the institution is, because there are not enough specialists in each field in small institutions. (It may be remembered from Chapter Three that institutional size and average size of departments are highly correlated; $r = .77$.) Inasmuch as colleagues in the same field share interests in scholarly research, whereas colleagues in diverse subjects share mostly teaching concerns, the greater significance of the former as reference groups in large than in small academic institutions stimulates increasing interest in research, according to this reasoning, and thus accounts for the direct effect of size on research orientation.

STRUCTURAL EFFECTS OF COLLEAGUE CLIMATE

The foregoing analysis raised a number of questions that cannot be answered without investigating individual differences in qualifications for, orientations to, and involvements in research. The first of these is whether the observed relationship between the faculty's formal qualifications and emphasis on research is entirely the result of the influence of the individual's qualifications on his own research orientation or is partly produced by the influences of better qualified colleagues who stimulate the individual's research interests. Other questions are whether the direct effects of size and of university status on research orientation persist when the individual's own formal qualifications as well as those of his colleagues in the institution are controlled, and whether the analysis of individual differences makes it possible to discriminate between the alternative interpretations of these direct effects suggested. In addition, the concept of research emphasis should be refined to distinguish the obligations faculty members experience to engage in research and publish it (the variable analyzed in the preceding section) from their actual involvement in research, on the one hand, and from the weight research has in the institution's appointment procedures, on the other.

To isolate the structural effect on research orientations of the colleague climate, a regression analysis of the research orientations of the 2500 *individual* faculty members sampled is performed, introducing as independent variables *both* the proportion of faculty respondents in each individual's institution who have advanced degrees and whether the individual himself or herself has one. Three regression analyses are presented, one for a person's actual *involvement* in research, one for the *obligation* to publish research, and one for the *weight* research has for promotions to tenure positions at the institution, in all three cases as reported by faculty respondents.[12] Other institutional conditions affecting research orientations are included as independent variables in the regression analyses,[13] and so is a person's broad discipline (whether or not it is a natural science). The purpose of this analysis of individuals is to clarify the substantive questions raised by the analysis of academic institutions, not to predict individual variations in research interests and practices. At the same time, the analysis is intended to meet criticisms raised against cruder procedures used earlier for identifying structural effects.[14] As noted in Chapter Two, the objection that contingency tables do not effectively control independent variables does not apply to regres-

[12] The three measures are as follows. (1) Involvement: five-point score, with one point each for the answers to the questions whether the respondent is engaged in research, whether he is engaged in research or creative activity, whether he has received research support in the last three years, and whether he expects to publish (used only for individuals). (2) Obligation: in a list of what *"are* faculty obligations at your institution," the item "to publish my research" (five-point score for individuals; percentage agreeing for institution). (3) Weight: "At this institution it is very difficult for a man to achieve tenure if he is not engaged in research." (Five-point score for individuals; percentage agreeing for institution.) Although the number of faculty respondents per institution is small (the average is 23), this is not a serious problem, since all individuals from various institutions with similar characteristics are considered together in the regression analysis. Faculty members from institutions with superior academic standing are overrepresented in the sample.

[13] The only independent variable in Table 5.1 not included in the regression analyses of individuals is affluence, since it neither has a direct effect nor raises any substantive questions. Adding it does not alter the other coefficients appreciably from those shown in Table 5.2. Affluence has no direct effects on involvement and on obligations and only a trivial one on weight ($b^* = .05$).

[14] Peter M. Blau, "Structural Effects," *American Sociological Review* **25** (1960), 178–193.

sion analysis, in which variables are effectively controlled. Another objection that has been raised is that effects attributed to a given structural difference—in the case at hand, differences in the proportion of the faculty with advanced degrees—may actually be the result of entirely different factors correlated with these differences. But since two-thirds of the variation among institutions in faculty qualifications (Table 4.1) and three-fifths of those in research orientations (Table 5.1) can be accounted for by known antecedents, it seems not very likely that some undiscovered institutional correlate of faculty qualifications really is responsible for the observed effects of colleague qualifications on research orientations.

The results of all three regression analyses are presented in Table 5.2 side by side to facilitate comparison. Variable definitions, basic statistics, and a matrix of simple correlations appear in Appendix D. Very small beta weights are more than twice their standard error, because the number of cases is so large, and those that are less than .10, though they will be mentioned, should be considered trivial. The last row of the table illustrates such trivial effects. Natural scientists put slightly more emphasis on research, in all three respects, than faculty members in other disciplines. It is surprising that natural scientists are only a little more involved in research than scholars in other disciplines once the greater proportion of natural scientists with advanced degrees ($r = .22$) is controlled. The slim difference in research activities (column 1) is reflected in a similar difference in research obligations (column 3), and promotions also seem to depend slightly more on research in the natural sciences than in other fields (column 5).

Faculty members who have advanced degrees are actively involved in research substantially more often than those who do not, but they are no more likely to report that research is given much weight in promotions to tenure in their institution (columns 1 and 5, row 6, Table 5.2). This is precisely the difference one would anticipate on the assumption that respondents accurately report the weight research has in their institution, which should not be affected by their own training, and that their reports of their own research activities are also fairly accurate, since better trained persons are expected to be more involved in research than others. Hence the findings help validate the measures used. Research obligations are influenced by the individual's own training, but only to a small degree (column 3), which suggests that research obligations reflect primarily institutional personnel practices rather than the individual's training for and interest in research. Indeed, the individual's obligations have a considerably higher correlation with the weight research has in the institution (.63)—and his own statement what this weight is (.62)—than with his research involvement (.34). Yet a person's own training does color his response concerning obligations, though the question was worded as

Table 5.2   Three Measures of Research Emphasis of Individuals

	Research Involvement		Research Obligations		Research Weight for Tenure	
	1. Beta Weight	2. Simple Correlation	3. Beta Weight	4. Simple Correlation	5. Beta Weight	6. Simple Correlation
Institution						
1. Size	−.03		−.01		−.01	
		.28		.40		.44
2. Percentage of graduate students	−.06*		.12**		.14**	
		.28		.45		.51
3. University	.08**		.26**		.26**	
		.34		.51		.53
4. Salaries	.19**		.16**		.26**	
		.42		.50		.57
Colleague climate						
5. Percentage with advanced degrees[a]	.22**		.15**		.14**	
		.48		.52		.55
Individual						
6. Advanced degree	.26**		.07**		−.03	
		.42		.29		.22
7. Natural scientist	.04*		.05**		.04*	
		.16		.16		.14
	$R^2 = .30$;[b] $n = 2577$		$R^2 = .37$;[b] $n = 2399$		$R^2 = .43$;[b] $n = 2518$	

* More than twice its standard error.
** More than three times its standard error.
[a] The same variable termed "faculty qualifications" in other tables.
[b] The R^2 corrected for degrees of freedom ($\hat{R}^2$) is not different (if carried out to two decimals) from the uncorrected one, in any of these cases.

a factual statement (whether publishing their research *is* an obligation of faculty members at the institution), which indicates that the answers are not purely factual reports but to some degree express internalized feelings of obligations.

The colleague climate exerts a pronounced influence on the research involvement of individuals, independent of the individual's own training and of institutional conditions—an influence nearly as strong as that of his or her own training (column 1, row 5, Table 5.2). Since we just saw that faculty members who have advanced degrees are more involved in research than those who do not, the proportion with advanced degrees on the faculty, the measure of colleague climate, is indicative of prevalent research activities as well as qualifications. The colleague climate also influences research obligations and the weight research has for promotions, but not so much (columns 3 and 5). Unless many faculty members have the advanced training that promotes research interests and activities, administrators and personnel committees are unlikely to give much weight to research in promotions, and faculty members are unlikely to experience strong obligations to publish research. (The emphasis on research in an academic institution probably has a reciprocal effect on qualifications, attracting more faculty members whose advanced training makes them interested in research.) Although these promotion policies and obligations undoubtedly influence the degree of actual involvement in research, they do not account for the influence of the colleague climate on this involvement. For adding measures of research weight and obligations to the independent variables in column 1 virtually does not reduce the direct effect of colleague climate on research involvement ($b^* = .21$, compared to the original .22).

Whether a faculty member's research interests are stimulated or stifled in an academic institution depends on his colleagues, on how many of them have completed graduate education, which has socialized as well as trained them for research, and which makes it probable that they are actually engaged in research. The discussions of such colleagues about their research experiences—the problems encountered and the exciting discoveries made—with those who share research interests, and primarily with them, are incentives likely to activate any latent interest in research a person may have. To become a genuine member of a colleague group of this kind, one must be involved in research and thus be able to participate fully in the discussions about research. Colleagues with research skills facilitate one's own research by tending to give advice when needed, since being asked for advice is a welcome sign of respect for their superior skills, and they make working on research more gratifying by furnishing attentive listeners interested in hearing about promising leads and suggestive results. These processes of social exchange[15] are a continual source of rewards for scholarly endeavors and create group pressures to engage in scholarly research by depriving those failing to do so of social rewards.

---

[15] See George C. Homans, *Social Behavior*, New York: Harcourt, Brace and World, 1961.

In colleague groups whose members are not identified by their training and experience with research, opposite normative pressures tend to stifle the individual's research interests; here the often arduous process of scholarship is not rewarded with social approval but frequently ridiculed with such phrases as "publish or perish."

Higher salaries in academic institutions promote greater emphasis on research, in all three respects considered. They have a direct effect on each of the three expressions of the importance of research, which is stronger on the weight of research in promotions than on research obligations and involvements, as row 4 in Table 5.2 shows (and which for some unknown reason is not evident in the analysis of institutions in Table 5.1). This direct effect is complemented by an indirect one mediated in all three cases mostly by the proportion of faculty members with advanced degrees (decomposition coefficient: for weight, .10; for obligation, .11; for involvement, .16). The indirect effects are readily explained: the faculties with better research qualifications recruited with higher salaries make it possible to give research more weight in promotions, increase research obligations, and produce a colleague climate that fosters active involvement in research. [Twice as much of the influence of salaries on research involvement is mediated by the climate of qualified colleagues (.16) as by the individual's own qualifications (.08), and the differences are still more pronounced for weight and for obligations.]

But what accounts for the direct effect of salaries on the three manifestations of research emphasis? It may well be the greater research abilities that are reflected in higher salaries even when formal qualifications are controlled, as noted in the discussion of the direct effect of salaries on institution's reputation among able students in Chapter Four. On this assumption, the direct effects of salaries on research orientations can be explained in the same terms as their indirect effects mediated by formal qualifications. The productive scientists and scholars who command better salaries encourage making tenure appointments dependent on research, strengthen research obligations, and promote active involvement in research. The influence of a climate of superior colleagues on the individual's tendency to be engaged in research is greater than the direct effect of colleague climate in row 5 (of column 1) implies, inasmuch as the direct effect of salaries in row 4 as well as their indirect effect mediated by colleague climate (together, .35) also partly reflect this influence.[16] High salaries have a "snowball effect" on scholarly research in an

[16] Whereas the beta weights and the decomposition coefficients pertaining to the same independent and dependent variable in a regression analysis can be added (and must sum to their simple correlation), the beta weights of different independent variables (those in different rows) must not be added, although they do indicate independent influences that together are greater than either.

academic institution, because they not only attract more productive scholars and scientists but consequently create a colleague climate that further stimulates scholarly activity.

The extent of graduate training in an academic institution influences the various aspects of research emphasis in ways that are complementary to the influences of an individual's own advanced training. The fact that an institution is a university granting Ph.D.'s has a pronounced direct effect, regardless of other conditions, on the weight research has for promotions and on the faculty's research obligations, and the proportion of graduate students has independent direct effects further increasing the weight of research and research obligations. (See the beta weights in rows 3 and 2, columns 5 and 3, of Table 5.2.) These direct effects are supplemented by indirect effects of both university status and percentage of graduate students on both weight of research for tenure and research obligations, which are mediated by higher salaries and the better qualified faculties they attract. (The decomposition coefficients of salaries and qualifications together are similar in the four cases, varying only between .19 and .25.) In contrast, the research involvement of individuals is mostly indirectly and hardly directly affected by their being in universities with many graduate students. When other conditions are controlled, the remaining positive relationship of research involvement with university status is small and that with percentage of graduate students has even turned into a slight negative relationship (column 1). The pattern of influence of universities with much graduate work is the reverse of that of the individual's own advanced training, which has direct effects increasing research involvement substantially but research obligations little and weight of research in appointments not at all, as we have seen (compare the three beta weights in row 6 with those in rows 2 and 3).

The question raised earlier of whether the stronger orientation to research in universities with many graduate students is attributable to a more stimulating academic environment or to different administrative practices can now be answered. The direct effects clearly indicate that universities granting Ph.D.'s, and to a lesser extent all institutions with many graduate students, have personnel practices that differ from those in undergraduate colleges, giving more weight to research in faculty appointments and obligating their faculties to publish research. When other conditions are controlled, university status and proportion of graduate students hardly affect the extent to which faculty members are actually engaged in research, which seems to imply that the differences in personnel policies do not create an academic environment more conducive to research in institutions concentrating on graduate work than in undergraduate colleges. This is not correct, however, since it ignores indirect effects. Both university status and percentage of graduate students indirectly promote research involvement, as the considerable simple correlations in column 2, which are not spurious, show. Individual faculty members in universities with many graduate students are more likely to be engaged in research than are those in undergraduate colleges because they themselves are better trained (.07 and .06 for university and graduate students, respectively) and particularly because their academic environment consists of more stimulating colleagues, who are better trained (.13 and .12) and command higher salaries (.10 and .13).

A similar question was raised in the preceding section concerning the direct effect (in Table 5.1) of size on research orientations in academic institutions, that is, whether differences in colleague environments or in administrative practices between large and small institutions are responsible. In this case the answer the data give is different. No such direct effect of size on research orientations is any longer evident when individual's own training as well as that of his colleagues is controlled, as row 1 in Table 5.2 indicates. Although the simple correlations show that large academic institutions exhibit substantially more research emphasis in all three respects, the beta weights reveal that size itself makes no difference in any of them once other conditions are controlled. Large institutions are more likely than small ones to be universities and have more graduate students, which partly accounts for the greater weight of research for tenure appointments and for the greater research obligations in them (together, .22 in both cases), and *individuals* in them are more likely to have advanced degrees, which accounts for a slight part of the influence of size on research involvement (.06). The major reason for the more pronounced research orientations in large academic institutions, however, is the superior colleague environment, as indicated by the formal qualifications of colleagues and the salaries they command (together, .23 for weight; .27 for obligations; .23 for involvement).[17]

Faculty members generally have both more and better qualified colleagues in their own field in large than in small academic institutions. The small number of members in most departments in a small institution means that most social contacts on the job are with colleagues in other departments, who cannot provide the same stimulation and social support for research as can colleagues in one's specialty. The number of colleagues in the same discipline who are trained and interested in research tends

---

[17] Since individual's own salary is not controlled, these figures somewhat overestimate the three mediating effects of colleague climate.

to be sufficiently large in large academic institutions to stimulate specialized scholarly interests and thereby increase active involvement of faculty
members in research as well as their obligations to publish and the weight
they give to research in promotions. Whereas the comparatively strong
research emphasis in universities concentrating on graduate work results
in good part from distinctive administrative policies in universities, that
produced by large size does not result from different administrative policies in large and small institutions. This is implied by the finding that
size, in contrast to both university status and percentage graduate students, has no direct effect on the weight of research in tenure appointments. The *indirect* effect large size, independent of extent of graduate
training, does have on the weight of research in tenure decisions seems
to be due primarily to the greater commitment to research of faculty
members in large institutions, which presumably affects their personnel
recommendations. These greater research commitments in turn are apparently attributable to the stronger peer group pressures exerted by the
larger and better qualified colleague groups that share specialized interests in large academic institutions.

Before concluding this section, let us examine briefly how the weight
of research in an institution influences faculty obligations to publish and
how both affect actual involvements in research, assuming that the causal
sequence is weight—obligations—involvement.[18] The weight of research
in senior appointments (if added to the independent variables in Table
5.2 in a regression analysis of obligations) exerts the dominant influence
on the obligations of faculty members to publish research ($b* = .48$;
$r = .63$).[19] The importance of research for tenure appointments in an
institution is the main immediate determinant of faculty research obligations—though this finding does not indicate whether incentives or

[18] Weight is measured by aggregate faculty responses in an institution, whereas obligations are measured by individual responses, for a substantive and a methodological
reason. Substantively, the weight of research for promotions is an institutional characteristic but obligations are experienced by individuals. Methodologically, the high
zero-order correlation between the aggregate responses concerning weight and obligations (.94) creates problems of multicollinearity making it inadvisable to use both as
independent variables in a regression analysis. The correlation between weight defined
by aggregate responses and obligations defined by individual responses is considerably
lower (.63). The difference is of some substantive interest, indicating that the basic
influence on publishing obligations is the weight of research in the institution and
that individual variations in feelings of obligations tend to cancel one another when
the answers of the various individuals in an institution are aggregated.
[19] The beta weights of the other independent variables are: size, .01; percentage of
graduate students, .05*; university, .10**; salaries, −.08*; colleague climate, .10**;
individual's degree, .07**; natural scientist, .05**. The R^2 is .42.

selection are responsible—and it mediates some of the other influences on obligations.

Faculties of · universities concentrating on graduate work express stronger obligations to publish than those of undergraduate colleges largely because research has greater weight in university appointments (decomposition coefficient for university status, .34; for percentage of graduate students, .32), which supports the interpretation that these effects represent differences in personnel policies between universities and undergraduate colleges. The influence of salaries on research obligations is also primarily accounted for by the greater weight of research in the appointment decisions of institutions paying better salaries (.39), and the beta coefficient of salaries becomes actually negative (−.08) when weight as well as other conditions are controlled. The main reason that salaries and research obligations are associated is that institutions paying higher salaries have more stringent research requirements for appointments. The negative beta weight might reflect a lesser concern with salaries of the individuals most committed to research, though this is sheer speculation.

A faculty member's active involvement in research is affected only indirectly by the weight of research in promotions, not directly as would be expected if incentives were operative. This conclusion is based on a regression analysis of involvement with weight and obligations included as independent variables together with those in Table 5.2. The direct effect of the weight of research in promotions on research involvement is close to zero ($b^* = .04$), though it has indirect effects ($r = .42$). The importance of research for an institution's tenure appointments increases the research activities of faculty members primarily because it raises their own research qualifications (.08) and because it furnishes them with more research-oriented colleagues, as indicated by their better qualifications (.15) and the better salaries they command (.13). The individual's research obligations have some direct effect on his or her research involvement ($b^* = .06$), but most of the association between the two ($r = .34$) is indirect, resulting in smaller part from the individual's own training (.07) and in larger part from the colleague climate (.11 for colleague training and .08 for salaries). None of the direct effects of the other independent variables, shown in column 1 of Table 5.2, is altered by more than .03,[20] which means that the interpretations suggested need not be modified.

[20] All the beta weights in this regression equation are: size, −.02; percentage of graduate students, −.07**; university, .05*; salaries, .17**; colleague climate, .21**; individual's degree, .25**; natural scientist, .05*; weight of research, .04; research obligations, .06*. The R^2 is .31.

The findings imply that an academic institution's personnel policies affect the research activities of faculty members in two ways but not in a third. The dependence of promotions on research does not appear to motivate individuals who are not already inclined to engage in research. Appointments based on research raise research involvements by governing the selection of persons committed to research and by consequently providing a colleague climate that stimulates research interests. Indications are that the academic qualifications of a faculty member's colleagues influence his research involvement no less than his own.

ALLEGIANCE TO LOCAL INSTITUTION

Although the comment is often made that faculty members today have little loyalty to their university or college,[21] three-fifths of those interviewed agree with the statement, "My allegiance to my present *institution* is very strong." The proportion expressing allegiance in the average academic institution is still somewhat higher (70 per cent). This reveals considerable institutional loyalty, granting that it is easier to express loyalty verbally than in action. Not all universities and colleges command the same allegiance, of course. The findings suggest that faculty attitudes to their own institution depend not alone on its attraction but also on the extent to which these attitudes are diverted by a cosmopolitan orientation to outside reference groups. The results of the regression analysis of the proportion of faculty members interviewed who express allegiance to their local institution are shown in Table 5.3.

[21] See, for example, Jencks and Riesman, *op. cit.*, p. 14.

Table 5.3   Allegiance to Local Institution

	Beta Weight	Simple Correlation
1. Northeast	−.34**	−.36
2. Public	−.29**	−.37
3. Size (log)	−.28**	−.56
4. Faculty qualifications	−.20*	−.34
$R^2 = .46$ ($\hat{R}^2 = .44$); $n = 114$		

* More than twice its standard error.
** More than three times its standard error.

Universities and colleges in the Northeast command less loyalty from their faculties than those in other parts of the country, as the first row of Table 5.3 shows. This can hardly be attributed to the lesser attraction of jobs in Eastern academic institutions, which tend to have high prestige, attract the best students, and recruit more faculty members with middle-class backgrounds, as we saw in Chapter Four. The proverbial cosmopolitanism of Easterners may be responsible for their weaker commitments to the local institution. Row 2 indicates that faculty members express less allegiance to public academic institutions than to private ones, be they religious or secular. The religious ties of many faculty members to denominational colleges and universities may account for their stronger allegiance, but religion cannot account for the similar difference in allegiance between private secular and public institutions.[22] The impersonal conditions in public academic institutions do not invite strong personal commitments to them. This conjecture is supported by the finding in row 3 that large academic institutions command less loyalty of their faculties than small ones, independent of other conditions, inasmuch as large size also implies greater impersonality. The stronger personal bonds among faculty members in a small college strengthen local attachments. The impersonality of large places, universities no less than cities, weakens local bonds and fosters cosmopolitan perspectives.

The better the formal qualifications of the faculty in an academic institution, the less likely are faculty members to express allegiance to it (row 4 in Table 5.3). Faculty members who have completed advanced training are more imbued than others with the academic norms that demand a cosmopolitan orientation to outside reference groups of colleagues in one's discipline instead of a narrower commitment to one's local colleagues. Superior qualifications in one's field make contacts with colleagues in the same field from other institutions more rewarding by lessening the danger of unfavorable comparisons, and hence they encourage outside contacts. Maintaining such contacts at professional meetings and elsewhere helps one keep up with developments in one's discipline and improves research and scholarship. Although these improvements in faculty performance resulting from a cosmopolitan interest in communication with colleagues outside benefit the academic institution, the weaker loyalty of the better qualified faculty members harms it. For this difference in allegiance threatens to create a process of negative selection,

---

[22] Although the dummy variable of private secular institution has a negative simple correlation with allegiance ($-.11$), it has a positive direct effect ($b^* = .29$) supplementing that of religious institution ($b^* = .31$; $r = .43$) if both are used in a regression analysis instead of the dichotomy public-private; since the two have parallel effects, the dichotomy public-private, which combines them, is used instead.

as the best faculty members, whose local commitments are weaker, leave
and the least qualified ones, who have stronger local ties, remain behind.
The interpretations advanced throughout this paragraph have implicitly
assumed that the inverse ecological correlation between the proportion
of better qualified and the proportion of loyal faculty members in an
institution results from a similar inverse correlation between individual
qualifications and local commitments. This must be checked by examining data on individual faculty members, which will be done after looking
at indications of cosmopolitanism among administrators.

   The president or his deputy in each academic institution was asked
how important it is to attract faculty from other institutions (with the
answers constituting a five-point score). The expectation was that weak
faculties would induce administrators to look for outside replacements,
but the facts of the case are the opposite. The better qualified the faculty
is, the more importance do administrators attach to recruiting established
faculty members from other institutions. One might start interpreting
this paradoxical finding by noting that not all universities and colleges
compete in the same market for faculty. Whereas there are no sharp
dividing lines, the national—indeed, international—market in which the
major universities compete for the most promising scholars and scientists
is not within the reach of the economic and intellectual resources of
most small colleges. For the weakest institutions, even competition in
regional labor markets is hazardous. The poorer the faculty's qualifications, which usually also implies that the institution cannot afford high
salaries, the worse are the chances of success in the competition for faculty, creating tendencies to avoid vigorous outside recruitments, especially of senior faculty, lest repeated rejections of offers puncture the
prevailing inflated images of institutional and departmental prestige.
Academic institutions with well-qualified faculties, which tend to pay
higher salaries as well, court less danger by competing with other institutions for faculty, and they must do so to maintain their quality. An
academic administrator's interest in strengthening the faculty by recruiting outsiders does not reflect a weak faculty in his or her institution but
a cosmopolitan orientation to outside reference groups made possible by
and needed to sustain the faculty's strength.
   The data in Table 5.4 show that three of the four conditions that
foster a cosmopolitan orientation among faculty members, as implied by
a *negative* influence on their allegiance to the local institution, also promote a cosmopolitan orientation among administrators, as implied by a

Table 5.4   Importance of Attracting Outside Faculty

	Beta Weight	Simple Correlation
1. Public	.32**	.36
2. Size (log)	−.28	.39
3. University	.17	.50
4. Schools and colleges	.31*	.44
5. Faculty qualifications	.37**	.45

$R^2 = .40 \ (\hat{R}^2 = .37); \ n = 112$

* More than twice its standard error.
** More than three times its standard error.

positive influence on interest in faculty from other institutions. The simple correlations in rows 1, 2, and 5 show that top administrators of public and of large academic institutions as well as of those with better qualified faculties exhibit such a cosmopolitan interest in outside faculty, just as faculty members in institutions with these three characteristics manifest a cosmopolitan orientation, implicit in their low allegiance to their own institution. The positive influences of the public nature of the institution and of high faculty qualifications on the administrator's orientation to outside reference groups for faculty appointments persist when other conditions are controlled (see the beta weights in rows 1 and 5), though that of size does not. Before discussing size further, let us examine other influences on the interests of administrators in outside faculty.

The larger the number of schools and colleges in an academic institution, the more prone is its president to want to attract outsiders to its faculty, independent of other conditions (see row 4). In an institution with many schools and colleges the central administration is removed from faculty and students, who are under the jurisdiction of separate deans. Without social distance from the faculty, it is not easy for the president to maintain an interest in appointing outsiders instead of promoting insiders, advantageous as doing so may be for the institution, because his or her social ties with faculty members discourage a disloyal preference for outsiders. (How influential top administrators actually are in faculty appointments will be discussed in Chapter Seven.) This finding illustrates that a weakening of ingroup loyalties—here produced by social distance—is at the roots of a cosmopolitan orientation to outsiders.

The administrators of large universities express more interest in recruiting faculty from other institutions than those of small colleges, as the simple correlationse in rows 2 and 3 of Table 5.4 indicate. University status as well as large size increases concern with outside faculty; the beta weights show that both positive effects are indirect; and decomposition reveals that both indirect effects are mediated by number of schools and colleges (.34 for university status; .26 for size) and, to a lesser extent, by faculty qualifications (.16 for university status; .15 for size). University presidents are more eager than presidents of small colleges to attract faculty members from other institutions because the deans of the various schools and colleges in large universities remove the president from faculty pressures and because the better qualified faculties in large universities are in need of outside replenishment to preserve their superior standing.

Size, in addition to sharing these indirect effects with university status, also directly affects recruitment of outsiders. When the conditions that promote interest in recruiting outsiders to the faculty in large institutions are controlled, large size itself is seen to have, if anything, the opposite effect of reducing interest in outside recruitment (the negative beta weight in row 2 is just short—by .01—of twice its standard error). The reason might be that competitive recruitment of outside faculty poses nearly unsurmountable problems for academic administrators if the faculty is large without being of high quality. Such a faculty is threatened by outsiders and strong enough to organize, formally or informally, to demand preferential treatment for insiders. Municipal colleges in New York and elsewhere are examples. Thus the large size of an academic institution, independent of conditions usually associated with it, discourages a cosmopolitan orientation to the larger academic community outside the local institution among administrators, whereas it has the opposite effect among faculty members, as we saw before.

We turn now to the analysis of the allegiance of 2552 *individual* faculty members to their local institution, using responses to the same question as in the institutional analysis in Table 5.3, except that the dependent variable here is the extent to which an individual expresses allegiance to his or her institution (on a five-point score) instead of the proportion in the institution expressing allegiance.[23] The discussion concentrates attention on the direct effects revealed by the beta weights in Table 5.5, and it should be kept in mind that the influences noted are independent of

[23] For variable definitions, basic statistics, and a matrix of simple correlations, see Appendix D.

Table 5.5   Allegiance to Local Institution of Individuals

	Beta Weight	Simple Correlation
Institution		
1. Northeast	−.02	−.02
2. Public	−.07**	−.13
3. Size (log)	−.16**	−.17
4. Inbreeding	.16**	.16
Colleague climate		
5. Percentage with advanced degrees	.08*	−.13
6. Percentage who emphasize teaching	−.14**	.13
Individual		
7. Advanced degree	−.06*	−.08
8. Emphasis on teaching	.21**	.28
9. Research involvement	−.10**	−.18
10. Undergraduate contacts	.08**	.15
11. Tenure position	.28**	.30
$R^2 = .21$ $(\hat{R}^2 = .21)$; $n = 2552$		

* More than twice its standard error.
** More than three times its standard error.

those of all other conditions included in the table. Three of the four findings in Table 5.3 are confirmed by those of the analysis of individuals in Table 5.5. Public academic institutions command less loyalty than private ones (row 2), large institutions less than small ones (row 3), and individuals with advanced degrees express less allegiance to their institution than those without (row 7). The finding that better qualified individuals exhibit slightly less local allegiance gives limited support to the earlier inference that superior academic qualifications promote a cosmopolitan orientation to outside reference groups, on the assumption that a local orientation is the inverse of a cosmopolitan one. The three beta weights in Table 5.5 are smaller than the corresponding coefficients in Table 5.3, owing to individual differences in allegiance within academic institutions, though additional reasons for the slight influence of individual's formal qualifications on allegiance will shortly become apparent.

Individual faculty members in the Northeast, however, do not express appreciably less loyalty to their academic institution than those in other parts of the country (row 1 in Table 5.5), contrary to the finding in Table 5.3. The great differences between institutional and individual analysis in both the simple correlation ($-.36$ versus $-.02$) and the beta weight ($-.34$ versus $-.02$) make it unlikely that individual variations within universities or colleges are entirely responsible. What accounts for the difference in findings is that the influence of region on local loyalties is contingent on the size of the academic institution. Small colleges in the East command less allegiance from their faculty members (63 per cent of 249 individuals express allegiance) than small colleges elsewhere (76 per cent of 460). But medium-sized and large academic institutions, with total faculties of more than 165 members, command as much allegiance in the East (58 per cent of 576) as in other regions (56 per cent of 1267). Since the many small colleges have much weight in the institutional analysis and the many individuals in large academic institutions have most weight in the individual analysis, the regional differences in local loyalties that are confined to small institutions are reflected in the institutional but hardly in the individual analysis. Only the generally stronger faculty loyalties in *small* colleges are attenuated by the cosmopolitan atmosphere on the Eastern seaboard.

The factor that exerts the strongest influence on a faculty member's loyalty to his academic institution is that he has a tenure appointment (row 11 in Table 5.5).[24] Until the university or college makes a commitment to an individual by giving him a tenure position, he is naturally hesitant to make a strong commitment to it. Dressel and his colleagues similarly find "that there is a progression from orientation to discipline to department to university as one rises in rank." They go on to explain:[25]

The younger assistant professor has few friends in his new job. . . . As he gets older he makes more friends; at first they come from his department and then from the larger university in which he works. As he publishes fewer papers than anticipated, and receives less acclaim from his discipline, he turns to others with whom he daily interacts for job-related rewards. Thus his attachment to the discipline weakens as he is pulled into the social web of the university.

Inbreeding promotes faculty loyalty, as row 4 in Table 5.5 indicates. The larger the proportion of recently appointed faculty members who

[24] Placing the dummy variable of whether the individual has a tenure position in the last row is not meant to imply that it necessarily follows orientations to academic work in a causal sequence. No causal assumptions about the individual characteristics in the last four rows in Table 5.5 are made.

[25] Paul L. Dressel et al., *The Confidence Crisis*, San Francisco: Jossey-Bass, 1970, p. 79.

have degrees from the same institution, the greater is the allegiance of faculty members to it. The finding presumably reflects the greater identification with a university or college of faculty members who received their education there. Unfortunately, this inference cannot be tested, since no information is available about where *individuals* obtained their degrees. The methodological question arises why this influence of an institutional characteristic—the prevalence of recent inbreeding—is not evident in the institutional analysis in Table 5.3. Actually, the effect on allegiance of inbreeding, if added to the variables in Table 5.3, is of nearly the same magnitude ($b^* = .12$; $r = .16$) as that shown in Table 5.5 ($b^* = .16$; $r = .16$), but the smaller number of cases in the institutional analysis make the former beta weight less than twice its standard error, which is why inbreeding has been excluded from that analysis.[26]

A faculty member's own academic qualifications and those of his colleagues have opposite effects on his local allegiance. It has already been mentioned that individuals who have completed advanced training express slightly less allegiance to their academic institution than those who have not (row 7 in Table 5.5). Moreover, a faculty member's involvement in research further reduces his commitment to his place of employment (row 9). One reason why the individual's formal qualifications have so small a *direct* negative effect on his local commitment in the table ($-.06$) is that part of their negative effect is *indirect*, mediated by the greater research involvement usually accompanying superior qualifications ($-.04$). These findings provide some additional support for the earlier assumption that the differences observed in Table 5.3 are produced by the individual's own qualifications on his allegiance. Well-qualified academics actively engaged in research tend to be enmeshed in the wider community of scientists or scholars in their discipline, and their cosmopolitan reference groups limit their local commitments.

The superior qualifications of a person's colleagues in the institution, on the other hand, strengthen his or her allegiance to the academic community (row 5). While his own superior qualifications make a person less dependent on the academic institution where he works, his colleagues' superior qualifications make it a more attractive place for him. The structural effect of superior faculty qualifications is the reverse of that of superior individual qualifications on allegiance. Although these opposite influences are small, other influences reveal the same kind of reversal in stronger form.

Individual faculty members who emphasize the importance of teaching

[26] Apparently, aggregating a variable does not always raise its correlation with another; in this case it does not.

are considerably more loyal to their local institution than those who do not (row 8 in Table 5.5). The frequency of a faculty member's contacts with undergraduates, which is another indication of his interest in teaching, further increases his loyalty to his university or college (row 10). Here we have the prototype of Gouldner's academic locals, who are much dedicated to undergraduate education and exhibit firm loyalties to their college.[27]

The more prevalent an emphasis on teaching is in an academic institution, by contrast, the less loyalty does it command from its faculty (row 6). For better or for worse, teaching does not have as high standing in academic circles as scholarly research, which puts teachers at a disadvantage in their relations with colleagues and which helps to account for the reverse structural effect of teaching concerns on allegiance. A predominant interest in teaching draws a faculty member closer to his academic institution, not only because he derives gratification from educating students there, but also because he probably fails to obtain gratifications in meetings with colleagues in the discipline outside, where his teaching quality is not known and his lack of published research makes him unknown. Since a teaching reputation is largely confined to the local scene, teachers tend to have stronger commitments to their local institution. Given the superior standing of research and researchers, however, a prevailing emphasis on teaching in the institution and among its faculty diminishes the attraction of the institution and of its members for most academics, who typically have internalized the academic norm of scholarly research and respect those who practice it even if they themselves do not. Widespread preoccupation with teaching accordingly tends to lower the value of an academic community in the eyes of most faculty members and reduce commitments to it.

Paradoxically, then, the very qualities of faculty members that make them attractive colleagues and enhance commitments to the institution where they work make them less committed to the institution, and the qualities that raise a faculty member's own loyalty to his college or university reduce that of his colleagues. The source of the paradox is the academic prestige system. Scholars and scientists whose accomplishments are well known in the wider academic discipline are respected colleagues, and their presence increases the allegiance of others to an institution, but they themselves are less dependent on and attached to their local institution. By the same token, faculty members whose limited academic reputation restricts their opportunities and strengthens their allegiance

[27] Gouldner, *op. cit.*, pp. 446–447.

to the local institution are less desirable colleagues, and large numbers of them weaken commitments to an academic community.

THE STATUS OF RESEARCH

Research has superior academic standing and earns a man or woman higher social status than teaching. Orientations to academic work and institutions reflect this in a number of ways. Fully trained faculty members are more interested and involved in research and emphasize teaching less than those who have not completed advanced training. Researchers command higher salaries than teachers. Affluent academic institutions tend to utilize their financial resources to recruit faculties predisposed to research, whereas poorer institutions stress the importance of teaching. Universities require evidence of research abilities, but little evidence of teaching abilities, at least of their graduate faculties, who train the most advanced students and have the highest prestige.

An academic institution's investment of economic resources in faculty members qualified for and interested in research has "snowball effects." Its direct effect on the amount of scholarly research in the institution is supplemented by indirect effects, for it not only increases the proportion of faculty members interested and actively engaged in research but by doing so creates an academic environment of research-oriented colleagues that further promotes research involvement. Whether an individual's research potentials become activated or suppressed depends in part on the colleague climate in his institution, specifically, on the prevalence of research skills and orientations among colleagues, which stimulates his own research interests and exerts group pressures on him to engage in research. The advanced training of the faculty in an institution has a structural effect on research, as well as an effect due to each individual's own training, because the better trained individuals who are more concerned with research create a structure of colleague relations that has an independent effect intensifying research concerns and activities. University policies that make appointments and promotions dependent on research have a catalytic effect similar to that of investments in faculty salaries. Although such personnel procedures do not seem to serve as incentives for individuals to engage in research but largely act as screening devices for selecting faculty members whose training predisposes them to research, they thereby produce a colleague climate in the university that provides additional inducements for becoming more involved in research.

There is much dispute over the dominant status of research in the academic stratification system, and the harmful effects on education resulting from the meager rewards for good teaching are often deplored, as noted at the beginning of this chapter. But is it not natural for contributions to knowledge to be more highly rewarded than the dissemination of this knowledge? Posing the issue in these terms surely oversimplifies it, however. Much research makes little if any original contribution to knowledge, and good education is not mere dissemination of knowledge, as Hutchins rightly emphasizes.[28] One may readily agree that the importance of educational responsibilities requires adequate incentives to meet these responsibilities and that good teaching is insufficiently rewarded at present. Yet it is not simple to decide what a just distribution of rewards is, a problem that has been debated for many centuries.

Instead of entering into this controversy, let us redefine the question and ask whether the existing differences in academic status and rewards between research and teaching are the result of emergent social forces or of deliberate institutional policies. Since differences in academic prestige are undoubtedly less subject to the direct control of academic institutions than differences in financial remuneration and in rank, the problem may be redefined once more by asking whether the wider reputation of researchers is what enables them to command higher salaries and achieve better positions, or whether their higher incomes and influential positions are responsible for their superior prestige. The findings supply some clues, though by no means clear-cut evidence, for answering this question.

Researchers are less committed than teachers to their local institution, probably because their wider reputation both sustains and is sustained by a cosmopolitan orientation to reference groups in the discipline at large. A wider reputation encourages cosmopolitan contacts with fellow specialists from other institutions by making these contacts gratifying sources of respect, the more so the greater the reputation is. At the same time, the researcher's reputation depends on his or her cosmopolitan interest in communicating with others outside the institution's boundaries, not only because outside contacts are necessary to keep up with developments in one's field, but also because it is only by communicating ideas and discoveries to wider circles, at meetings or through publications, that a reputation is built. A senior position at a major university undoubtedly often enhances a person's reputation beyond what his or her scholarly achievements deserve, by creating a presumption that this person's work must be good. It is unlikely, however, that most differences in scholarly reputations rest on such biased perspective, particularly in scientific

---

[28] Robert M. Hutchins, *The Learning Society*, New York, Praeger, 1968, pp. 33–38, 74–77.

fields with their unambiguous criteria for judging contributions. In any case, concern here is merely with the difference in reputations between researchers and teachers, not with that among researchers. The wider reputation researchers tend to acquire gives them better opportunities than teachers to obtain jobs elsewhere, which weakens the allegiance of researchers and strengthens that of teachers to their present institution.

The paradox the academic stratification system produces is that attributes associated with differences in reputation have opposite effects on the loyalty to the local institution of the faculty members possessing them and of their colleagues. The superior reputation of researchers reduces their commitment to their academic institution, for they are in demand elsewhere, and simultaneously increases the commitments of their colleagues, for their reputation raises the institution's and makes it a more desirable place. Similarly, the inferior reputation of teachers strengthens their allegiance to their university or college, since they have few alternative opportunities, and simultaneously weakens the allegiance of their colleagues, since their emphasis on teaching lessens the institution's attraction for academics. The underlying principle, which unquestionably also applies to the stratification systems outside academia, is that high-status attributes, virtually by definition, create a demand for a person in many places, thus diminishing that person's exclusive attachment to any one place but intensifying the attachments of others to the one where he or she is found.

A major university is constrained by the encompassing stratification system to allocate more resources to recruiting researchers than to recruiting teachers. Not only its academic standing but even the loyalty of its faculty depends on doing so, notwithstanding the tendency of researchers to have weaker local commitments than teachers have, inasmuch as the presence of many researchers raises and that of many teachers lowers faculty commitments. These inferences from the findings imply that the higher salaries and better positions of researchers, compared to those of teachers, result from the higher reputation research has in the academic community and do not produce this reputation, though position and salary often affect the reputation of *individual* researchers, but this is another matter. Academic institutions are not free to manipulate material rewards in order to alter the relative status of teaching and research. Profound changes in the academic stratification system would be necessary for this purpose.

CHAPTER SIX

STUDENTS

American higher education is a vast enterprise, and this book centers attention on only some aspects of it—the administrative structure of academic institutions and its influences on the work of the faculty. Little information on students is available. But since educating students comprises at least a good part of the work of the faculty, and in some colleges nearly all of it, three factors significant for the educational process are analyzed in this chapter. The first is student selectivity, that is, the ratio of rejections to admissions of applicants for entering college. The second question raised is what conditions influence the abilities of incoming freshmen, as reflected in their Scholastic Aptitude Tests, given by the College Entrance Examination Board and available for most though not all academic institutions. Whereas individual students may achieve quite different scores on the verbal and mathematical SAT tests, the average scores of the students a college admits are very similar on the two tests (the correlation for institutions is .95). Hence only one—the mean mathematical SAT score—is used as an index of the ability of entering freshmen. The third topic is the frequency of contacts of faculty members, based on reports by those interviewed, with undergraduates and with graduate students.

Matters pertaining to the process of education are analyzed in this chapter, whereas the inquiry into some outcomes of this process will be conducted in Chapter Nine. The reason for dividing the analysis of these two conceptually related problems is the assumption that the dependent variables here under consideration are indicative of the process of higher education but that the outcome of education may be affected by and provides criteria for judging all conditions in academic institutions, including those yet to be investigated, decentralization and innovation.

SELECTIVITY

The proportion of applicants for admission to a college who are not accepted is a straightforward indication of the degree of selectivity in undergraduate admissions, given the pool of applicants. (The measure is based on admissions in 1967–68, as reported by an assistant to the president.) On the average, a college accepts two-thirds and rejects one-third of its applicants. This rejection rate does not take into account differences in the quality of the applicants among academic institutions, which result, for example, from the known high standards of some colleges that discourage students with mediocre records from applying. The actual aptitudes of incoming freshmen must be separately analyzed, and this will be done in the next section.

An academic institution's reputation among outstanding prospective students, analyzed in Chapter Four, is called "Estimated Selectivity" by Astin, who developed this index.[1] The degree of selectivity among college applicants as indicated by the rejection rate does not seem to be influenced by this measure of reputation or estimated selectivity. Although the two are correlated (.41), the relationship is spurious and disappears when the measure is added to the independent variables shown in Table 6.1 ($b^* = .05$, less than one standard error). Which one of the two is the better index of selectivity depends on what one means by a college's selectivity. If the concept refers to a college's ability to recruit students with high aptitudes, Astin's index is the appropriate one. But if it refers to the actual degree of selectivity among a college's pool of applicants, and the aptitudes of freshmen are analyzed separately, the rejection rate is the appropriate indicator. By adopting the latter conception, it is possible to compare conditions on which an academic institution's attraction for able students depends (Table 4.2) and those on which its selectivity among applicants for admission depends (Table 6.1) with the conditions influencing the abilities of its actual undergraduates (Table 6.2).

---

[1] Alexander W. Astin, *Who Goes Where to College?* Chicago: Science Research Associates, 1965, p. 55.

It might be noted initially that several important differences among academic institutions do not affect their undergraduate selectivity manifest in the rate of rejections of applicants. Universities do not differ from colleges in their rejection rates $(r = -.02)$, the proportion of graduate students makes no difference in them (.02), and neither does the student-faculty ratio (.04). Nor do large academic institutions have significantly different rejection ratios from small ones (.12). The formal qualifications of the faculty are associated with the degree of selectivity among college applicants (.28), but this relationship too becomes insignificantly small when other conditions are controlled.[2] The same is the case for the correlation between an academic institution's reputation among able students and its selectivity, as already noted.

Eastern colleges are, on the average, much more selective than those in the rest of the nation, rejecting a larger proportion of their applicants for undergraduate admission, as row 1 in Table 6.1 shows. We saw earlier that academic institutions in the Northeast have superior reputations among outstanding students (Table 4.2), but this cannot be responsible for their greater selectivity, since controlling reputation does not appreciably reduce the influence of Northeastern location on selectivity $(b^* = .47)$. The superior abilities of students entering college in the East cannot be responsible either,[3] for superior aptitudes should make it less rather than more necessary to reject many applicants. Why academic institutions in the Northeast accept fewer students than those in other regions cannot be determined without comparing in detail places available, selection criteria, number of applications, and characteristics of applicants. One might surmise, however, that the stronger academic tradition of many Eastern colleges encourages maintaining high standards by means of more severe screening of applicants for admission. Other findings support this conjecture.

It was previously suggested that the longer an academic institution has been in existence, the stronger is the academic tradition that has developed and become institutionalized in it. The stronger academic tradition of older than newer universities and colleges was considered to account for the greater economic resources they devote to faculty recruitment

---

[2] If the variable, faculty qualifications, is added to those in Table 6.1 in a regression analysis of selectivity, its beta weight is .10, less than twice the standard error. The simple correlation of .28 is spurious, inasmuch as only .02 of it—that owing to the percentage of revenue spent on books—may be considered to result from intervening rather than antecedent variables.

[3] The dummy variable, Northeast, is correlated .41 with mean SAT scores. Although mean SAT scores here are the scores of admitted students, it is likely that similar, albeit less pronounced, differences exist among applicants.

Table 6.1   Selectivity (Ratio of Rejections to College Applications)

	Beta Weight	Simple Correlation
1. Northeast	.49**	.68
2. Age	.18*	.18
3. Private secular	.25**	.47
4. Inbreeding	−.17*	−.29
5. Revenue spent on books	.22**	.32

$R^2 = .60$ $(\hat{R}^2 = .58)$; $n = 113$

* More than twice its standard error.
** More than three times its standard error.

(Table 2.1) and for their greater success in recruiting qualified faculty even independent of the salaries offered (Table 4.1). If a strong academic tradition increases student selectivity, as assumed in the foregoing interpretation of the greater selectivity of Eastern colleges, and if older institutions have stronger academic traditions than more recently established ones, it follows that the age of an institution should increase its selectivity in admitting students. The second row in Table 6.1 indicates that this is the case. Older colleges are slightly more likely than newer ones to screen applicants thoroughly and reject greater numbers.

A well-established academic tradition apparently creates high standards of college admission. When the positive influence of institutional age on faculty salaries was interpreted in Chapter Two as resulting from the tendency to devote more resources to strictly academic matters in a university with a tradition of long standing, it was noted that the interpretation implies that an old academic tradition also leads to devoting more resources to other scholarly matters, such as books for the library. The implication was confirmed by the finding that older universities and colleges spend larger proportions of their revenues for books. This analysis has some bearing on that of selectivity. If the share of an institution's annual financial resources invested in replenishing the library is an indicator of strength of its academic tradition, this share can be used to test further the inferences that Northeastern colleges have stronger academic traditions than those elsewhere and that an academic tradition promotes selectivity in student admissions. The findings support both inferences. Eastern academic institutions spend a larger proportion of their revenues on books than do other institutions ($r = .30$). Moreover, this indicator of the strength of an institution's academic tradition is positively related to the stringency of selection standards in undergraduate admissions, as indicated by high rejection rates, even when the institution's Eastern location and age are controlled (row 5 in Table 6.1).

The table's third row shows that private secular universities and colleges are more selective than other institutions in student admissions. An academic tradition that makes scholarly matters the primary focus can explain this finding too. There are good reasons to expect private secular institutions to have higher academic standards and exhibit more concern with purely academic affairs than other institutions. Maintaining their superior reputation (correlation between private secular and reputation, .30) requires such high standards, and concern with scholarly affairs is not so likely to be diverted in private secular institutions either by religious commitments, as in denominational colleges and universities, or by the obligation to furnish vocational skills to large numbers, as in public institutions of higher education. In accordance with this expectation, we saw in Table 2.1 that private secular institutions pay higher faculty salaries than others not only because they are more affluent but also relative to their affluence, and we see in Table 6.1 that they have higher academic standards for student admission. The high rejection rates of private secular institutions reflect higher standards and not less qualified applicants, since their applicants are unlikely to have inferior aptitudes, given that the freshmen they admit have SAT scores considerably superior to those admitted to other institutions ($r = .30$). The long academic tradition that has developed over many generations cannot be responsible for the higher screening standards in private secular institutions either, because their average age (even though some are very old) is no greater than that of other academic institutions ($r = .01$). To be sure, disproportionate numbers of private secular colleges and universities are in the Northeast ($r = .44$), where academic traditions seem to be strongest, which accounts for part of the simple correlation between private secular control and selectivity (decomposition coefficient of Northeast, .21). Independent of the influence of the Eastern academic atmosphere, however, private secular colleges and universities are particularly selective and reject disproportionate numbers of their applicants, as the beta weight indicates.

The four conditions increasing selectivity discussed so far virtually spell Ivy League—Eastern location, established many years ago, well-maintained libraries, and private secular control. Contrast this with the Big Ten, for example, located in the Midwest, not so old, largely under public control, and better known for their football teams than their libraries (although they include excellent universities such as the University of Michigan and the University of Wisconsin). Indeed, colleges in the Ivy League are notorious for their high rejection rates of student applicants. The significance of the high rejection rates of the private colleges with the greatest prestige deserves brief comment. Jencks and Riesman discuss the strong emphasis on selectivity to improve student competence in private colleges, and they note in this connection that the dependence of these colleges on private donors makes it difficult to reject children of alumni.[4] A high rejection ratio, which implies that there are more qualified student applicants than a college needs, enables a private college to eat its cake and have it too—to use a proverbial phrase, which is often inverted, in its proper sequence.[5] For a large pool of applicants with good records and test scores permits a college to admit many children of alumni without sacrificing academic standards.

A final factor shown in Table 6.1 (row 4) to influence student selectivity, though not strongly, is faculty inbreeding. The greater the tendency in an academic institution to appoint its own graduates to the faculty, the less rigorous is the selection process of undergraduates and the fewer applicants are refused admission. Whereas the measure of inbreeding refers to the proportion of faculty members appointed in 1967–68 who had at least one degree from the academic institution appointing them (the average is 14 per cent), it is assumed that the degree of inbreeding then roughly reflects that in preceding years. Inbreeding reveals that merit criteria of faculty selection are compromised in an academic institution by particularistic preferences for individuals who have been educated there. The disposition in a university or college to be more or less selective is likely to find expression in its student admissions as well as in its faculty appointments. Since inbreeding introduces extraneous considerations into faculty recruitment, it may also lower academic standards in the institution, including those applied to the selection of students for admission, and it may reduce the pool of student applicants by lowering the quality of the institution's faculty, thus requiring fewer applicants to be rejected.

These conjectures raise two questions: what conditions in academic institutions affect inbreeding, and does inbreeding have adverse effects on faculty quality? With respect to the first question, it must be admitted that only few conditions influencing inbreeding were discovered, quite

[4] Christopher Jencks and David Riesman, *The Academic Revolution,* Garden City, N.Y.: Doubleday Anchor, 1969, pp. 281–286.
[5] See Wilson Follett, *Modern American Usage,* London: Longmans, 1966, p. 96.

possibly owing to the weakness of the measure that is restricted to inbred appointments during one year only. A difference that is revealed by the data is that between private academic institutions with and without religious affiliations. Faculty inbreeding is relatively prevalent in religious ($r=.25$) and rare in secular private institutions ($-.29$), with that in public ones being intermediate ($-.01$).[6] These differences are similar to complementary ones in student selectivity, which is lowest in religious ($r=-.33$) and highest in secular private colleges ($.47$), with public institutions again occupying an intermediate position ($-.06$). The stronger the tendency toward inbreeding, the worse seem to be its consequences for recruiting qualified faculty. In religious academic institutions, which are most inclined to appoint their own graduates to the faculty, inbreeding is inversely correlated with faculty qualifications ($-.28$), but in private secular institutions, which are least inclined to appoint their own graduates, inbreeding is positively correlated with faculty qualifications ($.46$).[7]

Does the last finding imply that among the best universities, which have the best graduates, inbreeding improves quality, inasmuch as private secular institutions include disproportionate numbers of outstanding universities? Berelson states that inbreeding in the top universities is "naturally high since they have been the major producers: the oldest and best institutions always have had more in-breeding than the others. This may place a new light on the concept that is usually given a negative connotation in academic circles."[8] His data show that better universities have larger proportions of faculty members whose highest degrees are from their present institution, but he presents no data to demonstrate that inbreeding helps maintain high quality, although he clearly implies it does. The data here, using an admittedly poor index of inbreeding, indicate that inbreeding has no beneficial effect on any indication of quality. Inbreeding is not positively correlated with an academic institution's reputation ($-.17$), with the qualifications of its faculty ($-.17$), with their research orientation ($-.05$), or with their research productivity ($-.09$). It might be objected that these associations for all academic

---

[6] These three correlations of inbreeding with the dummy variables indicative of control type are, of course, not independent of one another. Among religious colleges and universities, Catholic ones exhibit more inbreeding than Protestant institutions; see Ellen L. Slaughter, "The Comparative Study of Religious and Non-Affiliated Institutions of Higher Education," M.A. thesis, University of Chicago, 1972.

[7] *Ibid.* These correlations are based on the *unweighted* sample of institutions. In public institutions, the correlation between inbreeding and faculty qualifications is .12.

[8] Bernard Berelson, *Graduate Education in the United States*, New York: McGraw-Hill, 1960, p. 116.

institutions do not address themselves to the hypothesis that in the best universities, which produce the best graduates, inbreeding improves quality. A combination of longitudinal and cross-sectional data would be necessary to test this hypothesis adequately. But a very crude test can be performed by comparing the influence of inbreeding on indications of quality in the 11 universities defined as representing the biggest and best for sampling purposes and in the rest of the academic institutions (the eight cells in the sampling frame of smaller and less good institutions, using unweighted data). It cannot be stressed enough that the small number of cases, the questionable quality criteria used for sampling purposes only, and the weak measure of inbreeding make this a crude test indeed. Still, seven of the 11 universities singled out are among Berelson's top 12, and two more are in his second-ranking 10. In these 11 major universities, the correlation of inbreeding with reputation is $-.40$, and its correlation with faculty research productivity is $-.56$, the strongest negative correlation in any of the nine sampling groups.

At the best universities, inbreeding seems to be more harmful than at other academic institutions. Where inbreeding may improve quality is in the weakest large universities,[9] perhaps because their poor bargaining position for outside faculty makes their own best graduates, who have some allegiance to them, better candidates than they could otherwise obtain. This is not the case for the best universities, however, whose bargaining strength obviates the need for reliance on their own graduates and enables them to avert the narrowness of ingrown faculties. What promotes inbreeding in a major department in this country, with its many universities, is not that graduates of no other department are good enough but that the members of this department are unwilling to admit that they are. Inbreeding is likely to disturb the processes of selection best designed to maintain high quality in faculty recruitments as well as student admissions.

ABILITY OF FRESHMEN

The abilities of the students an institution of higher education attracts are as important for its success as the abilities of its faculty. What it can accomplish by educating students and deepening their understanding of

---

[9] Its correlation in the sampling cell consisting of the largest third and the lowest-quality third of academic institutions is .30 with reputation and .29 with faculty research productivity, each being the highest correlation in any of the nine cells.

various matters depends on their aptitudes and inclinations for learning. The accomplishments of a university or college tend to be judged by the achievements of its graduates, by the outstanding men and women in different fields that have received their education in it. If one finds many Harvard men in leading positions, one is impressed by the good education Harvard provides, typically without thinking of the differences in background and potentials between the students entering Harvard and those going to a municipal college in an urban slum. In an interesting paper, Astin shows that the very colleges whose education appears to be outstanding, on the basis of the high proportion of their graduates who later earn Ph.D.'s, prove to be the ones that produce, when the background and ability of their incoming students are taken into account, disproportionately few graduates who subsequently obtain Ph.D.'s. For example, several of the well-known men's colleges in the East, which have many graduates who get Ph.D.'s, have actually fewer of them than a number of municipal colleges in New York *relative* to the potentials of their respective students.[10] This does not mean that variations in conditions among colleges do not affect the education they furnish, only that differences in the abilities of entering students must be controlled to appraise the educational significance of varying conditions.

The aptitudes of the students in a college not only govern how much they profit from their higher education but also influence the role of the faculty and even the extent to which departments keep up with the developments of new academic specialties, as we shall see later. Now we turn to the analysis of conditions in an academic institution that affect the abilities of entering freshmen.

Good colleges attract good students, so that the quality of the academic institutions and that of its recruits reinforce each other. Row 6 in Table 6.2 shows that the factor that exerts the strongest influence on the aptitudes of freshmen, as revealed by their average score on the mathematical SAT, is a college's reputation among able students. This is hardly surprising. Yet its implications are not entirely without interest. What it implies is that an academic institution's reputation is a self-fulfilling prophecy, in Merton's terms,[11] since it attracts the highly able students whose successful education and subsequent careers give the institution a superior reputation. The qualifications of the faculty, as the beta weight in row 5 shows, exert an additional influence on the abilities of the undergraduates who enter a college. This direct nexus probably results

[10] Alexander W. Astin, "'Productivity' of Undergraduate Institutions," *Science* 136 (1962), 129–135.
[11] Robert K. Merton, *Social Theory and Social Structure*, New York: Free Press, 1968, pp. 475–490.

Table 6.2   Freshmen Aptitudes (Mean SAT-Mathematical Score)

	Beta Weight	Simple Correlation
1. South	−.20**	−.44
2. Affluence	.14*	.43
3. Size (log)	.44**	.45
4. Salaries	−.16	.59
5. Faculty qualifications	.33**	.52
6. Reputation	.52**	.77
7. Research emphasis	−.38**	.17

$R^2 = .76$ $(\hat{R}^2 = .74)$; $n = 81$

* More than twice its standard error.
** More than three times its standard error.

in part from a reciprocal effect the quality of the students in an institution has on the inclination of qualified faculty members to accept positions there. A further indication of this reciprocal effect of students on faculty will shortly become apparent.

The formal qualifications of the faculty also have indirect effects in opposite directions on the abilities of incoming students. Superior faculty qualifications attract better students to an institution not only directly (.33), as just noted, but indirecly as well by helping to raise its reputation (decomposition coefficient, .30). At the same time, however, the greater concern with publishing research exhibited by faculties with superior qualifications diminishes an institution's success in getting the best students (decomposition coefficient, −.24). For an emphasis on publishing research in an academic institution, independent of other conditions, reduces the quality of the undergraduates who go there to receive an education, as the beta weight in row 7 of Table 6.2 indicates.

To achieve a high reputation and attract the best students, it is important for an academic institution to recruit a well-qualified faculty. But institutions that appoint faculty members with superior qualifications tend to emphasize the obligation to publish, and faculty members with superior qualifications are themselves interested in carrying out research and publishing it, as the discussion in Chapter Five showed. This concern of faculty members with research and publications presumably diverts attention from undergraduate teaching and thus seems to discourage able undergraduates from going to a college. Although the best students are still found in the academic institutions with the best faculties (as the coefficients in row 5 reveal), the relationship between faculty and student quality is not as strong as it would be if the research orientations that prevail among better faculties had no adverse effects on teaching and on the tendencies of the most promising undergraduates to come to a college. One might suspect that an emphasis on teaching raises the abilities of entering freshmen, just as an emphasis on publishing research lowers it, but that is not the case. If anything, a teaching emphasis has a negative influence on the abilities of incoming freshmen.[12] The reason may be that a primary emphasis on teaching usually reflects a lack of scholarly interests that make a faculty less appealing to bright students, who prefer a scholarly faculty, though ideally one whose scholarly interests do not divert their efforts from undergraduate teaching to research. But this is a rare combination.

Academic institutions that pay relatively high salaries to their faculties have better students than those that pay lower salaries, largely because higher salaries, by attracting better faculties, raise an institution's reputation (decomposition coefficient of reputation, .34). The remainder of the simple correlation between salaries and student abilities (row 4 in Table 6.2) is spurious, owing to the influence of size (.27).[13] When other conditions are controlled, the beta weight is negative ($-.16$), and though it is not quite twice its standard error (falling short by .03), it is close enough to invite speculation about the reason for such a possible negative connection between faculty salaries and student aptitudes. A reciprocal effect might be responsible.

The intrinsic rewards derived from teaching students with high aptitudes may reduce the extrinsic rewards in the form of salaries required to recruit equally good faculties, in accordance with the suggestion made earlier that better students attract better faculty members. The question arises why faculty salaries have a *positive* influence on an institution's reputation among able students (Table 4.2), which was interpreted as the effect of differences in faculty quality reflected in salaries even when formal qualifications are controlled, while salaries are *negatively* related to the abilities of incoming students. The answer may well be that if the reputations of institutions as well as their faculties' formal qualifications are controlled, so are the differences in faculty quality reflected in salaries and affecting reputations, which strips salaries of their other implications and leaves only their significance as financial rewards, thereby disclosing the need to offer greater financial incentives for teaching poorer

[12] If teaching emphasis is added to the independent variables in Table 6.2, its direct effect on student aptitudes is negative but not significant ($b^* = -.12$, which is .02 less than twice its standard error; $r = -.26$), and the other beta weights are little altered.
[13] The indirect effects mediated by faculty qualifications (.24) and research emphasis ($-.21$) neutralize each other.

students. If this inference is correct, it implies that we need to raise salaries for teaching poorly prepared students from underprivileged groups if we want them to get a decent education.

The superior reputations of affluent academic institutions, which can afford the salaries to recruit better faculties, enable them to get better students. Most of the effect of affluence on student aptitudes is mediated by reputation (decomposition coefficient, .26).[14] The beta weight in row 2 of Table 6.2 indicates, however, that affluence also has a small direct positive effect on the abilities of incoming students when the institution's reputation and a number of other conditions are controlled. The most plausible interpretation of this residual effect of affluence on student aptitudes is that greater economic resources enable an institution not only to pay faculties higher salaries but also to offer students more and larger scholarships than can institutions with slim financial resources. The more luxurious facilities in affluent institutons may play a role too. Another possibility is that children of middle-class parents score better on aptitude tests and can more easily afford the higher tuitions in most affluent colleges than the sons and daughters of poorer parents. In any case, the affluence of a university or college increases its chances of success in the competition for the best students as well as in that for the best faculty members.

Large institutions of higher education have much better students than small ones, independent of other conditions, as the beta weight in row 3 of Table 6.2 shows. The pronounced influence of size on student aptitudes cannot reasonably be attributed to the superior quality of large universities, inasmuch as several indicators and known correlates of academic quality—though not all conceivable ones, of course—have been controlled. Neither is the large size of *public* universities, which charge lower tuition rates, responsible, because there is hardly any difference between public and private institutions in freshmen SAT scores ($r = .06$). The greater visibility of large academic institutions undoubtedly attracts disproportionate numbers of good students to them. A small college must achieve a considerably higher academic standing than a large university to become as well known. Furthermore, a large university probably is considered by bright students to be a more stimulating environment than a small college, as illustrated by the derogatory expression "jerkwater college." The location of many large institutions of higher

---

[14] Here again, the indirect effects of affluence on student aptitudes mediated by faculty qualifications (.17) and research emphasis (−.16) neutralize each other.

education in or near big cities is another factor likely to help them obtain good students.

But why does the large size of an academic institution, independent of other conditions, decrease its reputation among highly able students (Table 4.2) and still increase the number of able students entering it (Table 6.2)? There are both methodological and substantive grounds for this difference. The index of reputation is the number of choices received by an academic institution from National Merit Scholars *divided by the size of its freshmen class*. Since an indicator of institutional size is in the denominator, the index refers to an academic institution's reputation *relative* to its visibility and capacity, which depend on its size. Although this index of reputation does not hold institutional size constant, as its zero-order correlation with size shows (.26), it seems to control enough of the greater visibility of large institutions to reveal, when other conditions are controlled, the negative significance of the impersonal atmosphere in large institutions of higher education. Inasmuch as the average SAT scores do not control size at all, they fully reflect the greater visibility and drawing power of large academic institutions, supressing any negative influence of the greater impersonality accompanying large institutional size. Aside from this methodological factor, however, there may well be a substantive reason for the observed difference. National Merit Scholars are likely to be better informed about various colleges, more attuned to not readily apparent differences among them, and less influenced by the greater visibility of large institutions than are students who are very able but not quite so outstanding.

A final condition shown in Table 6.2 to influence the aptitudes of the freshmen entering a college is its location in the South (row 1). The lower reputations of Southern academic institutions account partly for the lower abilities of their undergraduates (decomposition coefficient, $-.21$), but Southern colleges have less able students independent of their reputations and other conditions (see the beta weight). The inferior quality of secondary education in the South is in all likelihood responsible for the lower abilities of Southern college students, given the inclination of the majority of students to attend colleges in the region where they have grown up.

In conclusion, the conditions influencing an academic institution's reputation among outstanding students (Table 4.2) are compared to those influencing the aptitudes of the students entering it (Table 6.2). Three conditions that enhance an institution's reputation also raise the abilities of its incoming freshmen, not only as a result of its higher reputation but in addition independently of its reputation; these are its location outside the South, its affluence, and the qualifications of its faculty. Eastern colleges have still better reputations than others in the

North—that is, those in the Midwest or West—and the abilities of their undergraduates are superior too, primarily because colleges in the Northeast have the best reputations, and the differences in student abilities disappear when reputations and other conditions are controlled.[15] Other influences on reputations and on freshmen aptitudes are not the same. The differences with respect to salaries and size have already been discussed. Three further conditions affect reputations without affecting the abilities of entering students.

Religious commitments appear to prompt many outstanding students to prefer denominational colleges and improve the reputation of these colleges among them, wiping out the differences in preferences the inferior quality of religious institutions otherwise would produce. The aptitude scores of freshmen reveal no similar influence of religious commitments compensating for the inferior quality of religious colleges. The reason probably is that the final selection of a college, as distinguished from verbal preferences, is affected by the lower tuition rates of public institutions, which together with the superior quality of private secular ones counteract and nullify the preferences for denominational colleges resulting from religious convictions.[16]

Many departments, creating a diversity of course programs in an academic institution, and few hierarchical levels, making its structure less bureaucratic, are two other conditions increasing the preferences of outstanding students for a college without influencing the aptitudes of the students actually going there.[17] Perhaps these differences reflect the more informed and sophisticated choices of National Merit Scholars, who may be more sensitive than other high school seniors to factors that are not widely known, as suggested earlier. The only factor influencing average

[15] The dummy variable, Northeast, has a simple correlation of .41 with mean SAT scores. If it is added to the variables in Table 6.2, the beta weight is only .03, less than one standard error; the decomposition coefficient of the mediating influence of reputation is .20.

[16] Religious affiliation has a correlation of $-.19$ with mean SAT scores, which is spurious $(b^* = -.07)$, owing to size $(-.21)$. Private secular control has a correlation of .29 with mean SAT scores, which is spurious $(b^* = .07)$, largely owing to reputation (.16), though its correlation with reputation (.30) is in turn spurious $(b^* = -.13)$, owing to Northeastern location (.15) and salaries (.14). The correlation of public control with mean SAT scores is inconsequential (.06), and so is the beta weight under control. In all cases, the beta weights and decomposition coefficients are those in the regression equation when the given independent variable is added to those in Tables 6.2 and 4.2, respectively; all beta weights are less than twice their standard errors.

[17] When departments and levels are added to the independent variables in Table 6.2, the regression analysis indicates that mean SAT scores are affected neither by the latter $(b^* = -.02; r = -.00)$ nor by the former $[b^* = -.02; r = .38,$ which is spurious, the decomposition coefficient of size (log) being .38].

SAT scores but not reputation (aside from reputation itself, of course) is an emphasis on publishing research, which affects the abilities of entering freshmen adversely.[18] One might speculate whether in the choices of the very best students—the National Merit Scholars—the advantage of a scholarly faculty oriented to research has greater weight than in the decisions of other undergraduates and thus neutralizes the disadvantage of research commitments that infringe on faculty teaching time.[19]

FACULTY-STUDENT CONTACTS

The importance of faculty contacts with students outside of class for effective education is often stressed. For example, Jacob notes that "teachers receptive to unhurried and relaxed conversation out of class" have more influence on students than others.[20] Research by Wright indicates that the frequency with which Ph.D. candidates have out-of-class contacts with faculty members is positively related to their chances of actually earning the Ph.D.[21] Some consequences of faculty contacts with students will be analyzed in Chapters Eight and Nine. Here conditions that influence the frequency of faculty interaction with students are examined. The faculty members interviewed were asked how many undergraduates and how many graduate students they meet outside of class for more than 10 minutes in the typical week. Inasmuch as the median number of undergraduate meetings is seven, one measure used is the proportion of individuals sampled in an academic institution who report conferences with seven or more undergraduates per week, and another is the proportion reporting that frequent conferences with graduate students. In the average academic institution, 64 per cent of the faculty members interviewed see at least seven undergraduates weekly in personal meetings, and 14 per cent have such meetings with seven or more graduate students. (Forty-four per cent report no contacts with

---

18 If research emphasis is added to the independent variables in Table 4.2, the regression analysis reveals it to have no direct effect on reputation ($b^* = .08$, less than twice its standard error). The correlation coefficient (.29) is spurious, owing to salaries (.26).
19 Although selectivity and mean freshmen SAT scores are correlated (.41), their association is spurious and disappears under the controls used in Table 6.2 ($b^* = .04$), mostly owing to reputation (.21). One would expect rejection rates to influence the aptitudes of incoming students, and why they do not remains unexplained.
20 Philip Jacob, *Changing Values in College*, New York: Harper and Row, 1957, p. 8.
21 Charles Wright, "Success or Failure in Earning Graduate Degrees," *Sociology of Education* 38 (1964), 73–97.

graduate students, presumably in most cases because they have no graduate students.)

A question raised in Chapter Four was whether many graduate students deprive undergraduates of faculty attention. The data suggest that this is the case in one sense though not in another. The frequencies of faculty contacts with graduate students and with undergraduates exhibit a surprisingly small negative correlation (−.23). Yet the same conditions that increase the contacts of faculty members with graduate students tend to decrease their contacts with undergraduates. These findings suggest that what reduces faculty attention to undergraduates in institutions giving graduate training is not the disproportionate amount of faculty time graduate students preempt but some underlying factor that concentrates faculty attention on graduate training. Actually, the amount of contact faculty members have with graduate students has no independent effect on their contacts with undergraduates when other conditions are controlled.[22] Since several conditions influence faculty interaction with graduate students and with undergraduates in complementary ways, it is convenient to discuss them together (see Tables 6.3 and 6.4).

Saying that graduate students do not take up disproportionate amounts of faculty time is not the same as saying that the proportion of them in an academic institution does not affect the way faculty members distribute their time between them and undergraduates. The larger the proportion of graduate students in an institution, and hence the smaller the proportion of its undergraduates, the more faculty members have many conferences with graduate students and the fewer of them have many with undergraduates, as the second rows in Tables 6.3 and 6.4 show. This finding does not necessarily mean that graduate students receive disproportionate faculty attention, because it would result if faculty time were allocated exactly in proportion to the numbers of graduate students and undergraduates. The data give no indication that there is much departure from such an equitable distribution of faculty time, though they are not precise enough to tell with certainty. Thus the partial *metric* regression coefficients of percentage of graduate students are nearly the same, .34 for Table 6.3 and −.35 for Table 6.4, which implies that for every 3 per cent increase in graduate students, 1 per cent more of the faculty spend much time with graduate students and 1 per cent fewer spend much time with undergraduates. Many graduate students

---

[22] If contact frequency with graduate students is added to the independent variables in Table 6.4, the beta weight with contacts with undergraduates is −.02; its difference from the simple correlation (−.23) results mostly from percentage of graduate students (−.10) and number of departments (−.08).

Table 6.3   Faculty Contacts with Graduate Students

	Beta Weight	Simple Correlation
1. Size	−.24	.23
2. Percentage of graduate students	.33**	.34
3. Departments	.40*	.29

$R^2 = .17$ $(\hat{R}^2 = .15)$; $n = 114$

* More than twice its standard error.
** More than three times its standard error.

Table 6.4   Faculty Contacts with Undergraduates

	Beta Weight	Simple Correlation
1. Size	.02	−.50
2. Percentage of graduate students	−.29**	−.43
3. Departments	−.28*	−.51
4. Teaching emphasis	.26**	.44
5. Federal support	.20*	−.04
6. Student aptitudes	−.28**	−.51

$R^2 = .51$ $(\hat{R}^2 = .48)$; $n = 114$

* More than twice its standard error.
** More than three times its standard error.

take up time that would otherwise be devoted to undergraduates, but seemingly not in excess to their numbers. Nor does university status exert an independent influence on faculty contacts with graduate students.[23] One would have suspected graduate work to absorb more of the interests and energies of faculty members, but perhaps the greater independence of graduate students counteracts the greater interest of faculty members in advanced training. Whereas in this case it is difficult to separate the influence of the nature of academic work from that of the ratio

[23] If university status is added to the independent variables in Table 6.3, its beta weight with contacts with graduate students is .13, less than two standard errors ($r = .27$, largely owing to many departments, which has a decomposition coefficient of .22). If university status is added to the independent variables in Table 6.4, its beta weight with contacts with undergraduates ($-.19$; $r = -.42$) is also less than twice its standard error, but only slightly (by .02). University faculties may have fewer contacts with undergraduates than college faculties independent of other conditions, though most of the difference between them is the result of other conditions.

of graduate students, and there is no evidence that advanced academic work has a distinctive effect, another aspect of the nature of academic work clearly affects faculty-student contacts.

Specialized academic work diverts faculty attention from undergraduate education to graduate training. A large number of departments, which is indicative of institutionalized specialization of academic disciplines, increases faculty contacts with graduate students and reduces them with undergraduates, as shown in the third rows of Tables 6.3 and 6.4. Specialists are less interested in the broader education of undergraduates and devote more of their time to training graduate students to become fellow specialists. The finding may also reflect another social process, however.

A large number of departments in an academic institution, with its size held constant, entails smaller as well as more specialized departmental groups. Inasmuch as genuine colleague relations require that specialized academic interests coincide with congenial personality attributes, the chances for the development of strong colleague relations depend on a fairly large number of fellow specialists, among whom most are likely to find some who are congenial. The small size of departmental groups, and the greater internal specialization often accompanying departmental specialization, reduce the likelihood that most faculty members find congenial fellow specialists on the faculty, which may well encourage working in closer contact with advanced graduate students and research assistants and treating them as colleagues and collaborators. This tendency is manifest in the more frequent contacts with graduate students of faculty members in institutions with more specialized and smaller departments. A high degree of academic specialization, which implies few colleagues with similar specialized interests on the faculty, makes senior graduate students the most suitable colleagues for faculty members and thus intensifies communication between them, which infringes on the time of faculty members and reduces their contacts with undergraduates.[24]

Academic specialization appears to diminish faculty involvement with undergraduate education, and so does the large size of academic institutions, primarily because there is more specialization in large universities

[24] Limited additional support for this interpretation is provided by the findings that the mean size of departments in an academic institution has a positive correlation, albeit a weak one, with contacts with graduate students (.16) and a substantial negative correlation with contacts with undergraduates ($-.39$). A possible reason for the weak positive correlation of average size of departments and faculty contacts with graduate students is that departments tend to be both larger and more specialized in large than in small academic institutions, which conceals the influence the interpretation assumes to be exerted on faculty involvement with graduate students by the *combination* of *much* specialization and relatively *small* departmental groups.

than in small colleges. Large institutional size increases faculty contacts with graduate students and decreases contacts with undergraduates, but these effects of size on faculty-student interaction are entirely indirect (compare the simple correlations and the beta weights in the first rows of Tables 6.3 and 6.4). Faculty members in large academic institutions are more likely than those in small institutions to have extensive contacts with graduate students because there are more graduate students (.14) and particularly because departments are more specialized (.33). When these two conditions are controlled, the beta weight of institutional size (which reflects, since number of departments is controlled, departmental size) is actually negative (−.24), and though it is less than twice its standard error (by .09), it gives a bit of support for the interpretation advanced that small departmental groups promote faculty interaction with graduate students. Faculty contacts with undergraduates are less frequent in large than in small academic institutions for the same reasons—more graduate students (−.12) and more specialized departments (−.24)—plus the lesser emphasis on teaching in large institutions (−.15). Since the beta weight is practically nil (.02), these intervening variables fully explain why undergraduates receive less faculty attention in large than in small institutions—because academic work is more specialized, teaching is less emphasized, and there are fewer undergraduates, though the last factor, in contrast to the first two, probably does not reduce the faculty contacts of any one undergraduate.[25]

An emphasis on teaching expands faculty communication with undergraduates in an institution of higher education, as row 4 in Table 6.4 indicates, without affecting the extent of faculty interaction with graduate students one way or the other.[26] An emphasis on research publications exerts no independent effect on contacts with either undergraduates or graduate students.[27] These findings accord with the interpretation

[25] Faculty members in private secular institutions have fewer contacts with graduate students (if this dummy variable is added to the independent variables in Table 6.3, $b* = −.28$; $r = −.27$) but not more with undergraduates (if added to Table 6.4, $b* = .13$, less than two standard errors; $r = .02$). No interpretation for these findings comes to mind.

[26] If teaching emphasis is added to the independent variables in Table 6.3, the beta weight is .06, less than one standard error ($r = −.08$).

[27] If research emphasis is added to Table 6.4, the beta weight is −.11, less than two standard errors [$r = .39$, the difference being largely due to departments (−.16) and teaching emphasis (−.13)], while the beta weight of teaching emphasis (.22) remains more than twice its standard error. If research emphasis is added to Table 6.3, the beta weight is −.03 [$r = .18$, the difference being due to departments (.23)].

that a balance of concern with teaching and concern with research is most appropriate for training graduate students, which was suggested in Chapter Five to explain the finding that the proportion of graduate students in an institution is the only factor discovered that has similar positive effects on both teaching and research orientations. The lack of influence on involvement with graduate students of both a predominant concern with teaching and a predominant concern with research may reflect this assumed need for a balance between the two for graduate training. Extensive involvement with undergraduates, however, does benefit from a preponderant orientation to teaching, although it does not seem to be impeded by a strong interest in research, unless research interests restrict those in teaching. Faculty contacts with undergraduates are less extensive in academic institutions that recruit better qualified faculty members than in others $(r = -.49)$, but only because conditions in the former, such as concentration on graduate work and departmental specialization, reduce these contacts. The formal qualifications of the faculty exert no independent influence on contacts with undergraduates, as becomes apparent when other conditions are controlled, nor do they affect contacts with graduate students.[28]

One might expect faculty members who are in institutions that attract the brightest students to have most interest in and contacts with undergraduates, but this does not appear to be the case. On the contrary, the higher the abilities of undergraduates, the less often do faculty members meet with them outside of class, as row 6 in Table 6.4 shows. Although this finding does not demonstrate that the worst *individual* students receive most faculty attention, which is doubtful, it does imply that the frequency of faculty conferences with undergraduates in an institution depends on the students' need for help in their academic work more than on how interesting their superior abilities make it to educate them. Less able students have more difficulties in college than bright undergraduates who can work more easily on their own, and the lower the abilities of students in a college, the more assistance does the faculty seem to give them. As mentioned, however, it may not be the individual students with the least aptitudes who get most attention from faculty members. Rather, the finding may reflect the prevailing customs in colleges that have the best undergraduates for students to seek less individual help and for faculty members to give less. This would mean that freshmen with average or lower aptitudes would get less faculty guidance if they went to a

---

[28] If faculty qualifications are added to Table 6.4, the beta weight is $-.08$; if added to Table 6.3, the beta weight is $-.08$ $(r = .16)$; either is less than one standard error.

college with mostly bright students than if they went to one in which the rest of the students have no higher abilities than they themselves.[29]

The amount of federal financial support a university or college receives influences the frequency of faculty contacts with undergraduates. The original assumptions were that the percentage of an institution's revenue from federal resources is largely indicative of research support for the faculty and that the consequent involvement of faculty members in large research projects limits the time they devote to conference with undergraduates. A number of findings seem to support these assumptions: federal financial support is strongly correlated with an orientation to research in an institution $(r=.56)$, and this emphasis on research is negatively correlated with faculty contacts with undergraduates $(-.39)$. Although the latter relationship disappears when teaching emphasis as well as other conditions are controlled, as has been mentioned, this does not prove that concerns with research do not diminish faculty contacts with undergraduates by reducing concerns with teaching. Indeed, the frequency of an *individual* faculty member's interaction with undergraduates is inversely related to his research involvement $(r=-.19)$ and specifically to his having received research support (from any source, since no information on its source is available; $r=-.19$).

Other students of higher education concur with the inferences about federal grants these data suggest. Kerr concludes from his experience as the president of a major university that federal support has a detrimental effect on undergraduate education.[30] In a study of 36 universities and colleges deliberately selected to represent great differences in federal support, Orlans reaches the conclusion that federal programs have contributed much to "scientific research and education at a few leading graduate and professional schools," but that they have "accelerated the long-standing depreciation of undergraduate education at large universities. . . ."[31] He finds that the universities that receive most federal support have larger classes than others and that their faculty members know fewer undergraduate majors or graduate students by name.[32]

[29] To study the effect of student climates on the educational progress of students would require a design similar to the one used in the preceding chapter to analyze the effect of the colleague climate among faculty members on their academic work. The data on individual students necessary for this purpose are not available. Mean SAT scores of undergraduates do not affect contacts with graduate students. If added to Table 6.3, the beta weight is $-.13$ $(r=.04)$, which is less than two standard errors.

[30] Clark Kerr, *The Uses of the University*, Cambridge: Harvard University Press, 1963, pp. 64–65.

[31] Harold Orlans, *The Effects of Federal Programs on Higher Education*, Washington: Brookings Institution, 1962, pp. 133–134.

[32] *Ibid.*, pp. 44–49.

The data analyzed here contradict the assumptions initially made by the author and the conclusions reached by others that federal grants have adverse effects on undergraduate education. As a matter of fact, extensive federal support apparently somewhat increases faculty contacts with undergraduates in an institution of higher education, as the beta weight in row 5 of Table 6.4 indicates, and although it has no positive effect on the educational progress of undergraduates, neither has it a negative effect on their progress.[33] The positive influence of federal grants on faculty contacts with undergraduates is evident only when other conditions producing a spurious negative association between the two are controlled; these conditions are departmental specialization $(-.12)$ and teaching emphasis $(-.09)$.[34] What led to the wrong prediction is the assumption that federal support primarily represents research grants to the faculty. Actually, the majority of the 3 billion dollars in federal grants to academic institutions in 1966 (55 per cent) was allocated to educational programs, not to research and development, most of it financed by the U.S. Office of Education for undergraduate facilities and fellowships. In addition, the proportion of federal funds for education has expanded and that for research has declined in recent years.[35] The finding implies that the increasing amounts of federal funds for educational programs have reversed any previous negative implications of federal grants for undergraduate teaching and that federal support now strengthens faculty involvement with undergraduates.

DILEMMAS OF HIGHER EDUCATION

The dilemmas that often confront us in social life are of interest not alone because their paradoxical character is intriguing but especially because the conflicting tendencies they reveal are harbingers of social change and signs of the dialectical social forces underlying this change. The analysis of institutions of higher education in the preceding chapters

[33] Its correlation with the measure of college completion is .06 and that with the measure of undergraduates' progress to graduate school is $-.00$. These measures will be discussed in Chapter Nine.

[34] On the other hand, faculty contacts with graduate students are, if anything, less frequent in universities receiving much federal support than in those receiving little. When percentage of revenue from federal sources is added to the independent variables in Table 6.4, the direct effect is negative, and though the beta weight $(-.16, r=.03)$ is not quite two standard errors, it is within .03 of this criterion.

[35] National Science Foundation, *Federal Support for Academic Science and Other Educational Activities in Universities and Colleges*, NSF 67–16, Washington: U.S.G.P.O., 1967, esp. p. vii.

disclosed several dilemmas. The organization of academic work discussed in Chapter Three poses a dilemma. The differentiation of the academic structure in large universities that permits their faculties to carry out highly specialized scientific and scholarly tasks, which are most likely to contribute to the advancement of knowledge, simultaneously creates administrative problems that tend to expand the administrative apparatus and lead to the development of a bureaucratic hierarchy.

Another academic dilemma, which also has its source in size and differentiation, is that of recruitment noted in Chapter Four. The conditions that facilitate the recruitment of good faculty and good students—for example, many diverse and specialized departments—require economic and intellectual resources available only in large universities, but the impersonality and bureaucratic structure characteristic of large academic institutions make it more difficult for them to attract the best students and faculty members. Whereas these conflicting forces are generated in the differentiated internal structure of academic institutions, the discussion in Chapter Five indicated conflicting tendencies resulting from the status differentiation in the larger stratification system that constitutes the external context of universities and colleges. The characteristics of individuals that are generally valued and raise their status, such as research competence, decrease their own commitments but increase those of others to their institution, because their having socially valued attributes simultaneously enhances their alternative opportunities and makes their presence an attraction for others.

Additional dilemmas are implicit in the analysis presented in this chapter. One is inherent in a tradition of academic excellence, or, for that matter, any tradition that makes objective achievements a positive value. How selective a college is in student admissions appears to depend on its academic tradition, which makes high scholastic standards an important social value. What is meant by a social tradition is not only that the members of an institution, or society, have been socialized to share certain values but also that their common values create strong bonds of solidarity among them. Achievement values, like those of an academic tradition, have necessarily contradictory consequences in a social structure, because the universalistic criteria of judgment and acceptance that the content of the values demands come into conflict with the particularistic allegiances that the sharing of values and a common tradition entail.[36] Inbreeding and its adverse effect on selectivity

---

[36] Talcott Parsons first introduced the dichotomy "universalism-particularism," a refinement of Toennies' famous pair of concepts, in 1939; this analysis is reprinted in his *Essays in Sociology,* Glencoe, Ill.: Free Press, 1949, pp. 185–199.

reflect the particularistic allegiances that are engendered by a common academic tradition, which contradict the stark impersonal commands of the universalistic values of academic achievement. A shared tradition involves common bonds of solidarity, and although the tradition may initially rest on a shared commitment to strictly academic merit, the emergent solidarity affects judgments and makes them depart from impersonal standards of merit.

The quality of the students a college attracts is governed by conditions that are incompatible, which creates dilemmas for student recruitment, as already mentioned. The well-qualified faculty and the variety of departmental offerings that appeal to outstanding students require resources available primarily in large universities, but the impersonal and bureaucratic conditions that tend to prevail in large institutions lessens their appeal to outstanding students. Moreover, the better qualified faculties that draw better students to a college are typically oriented more toward research than toward teaching, and such a research emphasis discourages better undergraduates from coming to an institution of higher education.

Faculty involvement in graduate work and in undergraduate education depend on opposite conditions in academic institutions. Indications are that what limits faculty contacts with undergraduates in institutions with many graduate students is not so much that the graduate students pre-empt faculty time as that the factors that promote interest in graduate training reduce interest in undergraduate teaching. A notable illustration is the institutionalized specialization of academic work produced by the institution's differentiation into many departments, which increases faculty members' involvement with graduate students and decreases their involvement with undergraduates. Thus the differentiation of the formal structure in various dimensions that develops in large academic institutions is apparently at the roots of several conflicting dialectical forces. It is necessary for specialized academic work, but it leads to the proliferation of administrative machinery. The many departments facilitate faculty and student recruitment in large academic institutions, whereas the several administrative levels impede it. Institutionalized specialization accentuates faculty participation in graduate training but attenuates faculty participation in undergraduate education.

The student protests that have occurred on many campuses in the last decade are expressions of the conflicting tendencies in modern institutions of higher education as well as of the conflicts and serious dislocations in the larger society, which have been greatly aggravated in the United States by the war in Vietnam. A brief comparison of the wave of student uprisings in 1968 with those that took place in 1970, in reaction to the invasion of Cambodia, is instructive in this connection. Political events outside the campus were important factors in the demonstrations at both periods. It will be remembered, however, that the demonstrations in 1968 often developed into conflicts of students with the administration and the faculty, whereas faculties and administrations, as well as the general public, had considerable sympathy for the student protests against the Cambodian invasion and the killings of students at Kent State and Jackson State Universities in 1970. Given these differences, one would not expect the same conditions in academic institutions to influence the demonstrations in 1968 and in 1970, and this expectation is borne out by the crude measures available of the demonstrations that occurred in both years.[37] The only factor that made demonstrations more likely at both times was the large size of an academic institution,[38] which conforms to the generalization advanced that the large size of universities engenders conflicting tendencies in them.

The existence of a formal system of ratings by students of the teaching in their classes, on the other hand, seems to have had opposite influences on student protests in 1968 and 1970, making protests less likely in 1968 but more likely in 1970.[39] A system of student ratings implies that students are given some voice, and thereby some influence, over the quality of their education, which is a demand frequently made by students. In terms of these assumptions, the findings suggest that acceding to reasonable demands of students and permitting them to exercise limited influence discourages protests directed against the university, as many of those

[37] The measure for 1968, which was collected in the original interviews with administrators, is described and analyzed in Peter M. Blau and Ellen L. Slaughter, "Institutional Conditions and Student Demonstrations," Social Problems 18 (1971), 475–487. The measure for 1970 is based on mail-back questionnaires sent to one administrator and the student editor of the college newspaper in each institution after the Cambodia invasion in 1970. So few student editors returned questionnaires, probably in part because final examinations were just starting, that only responses from administrators could be utilized. The measure used, which is close to the one for 1968, is the number of issues raised during the demonstration against the Cambodian invasion, with no demonstration being scored zero. Seven-tenths of the sampled institutions that returned questionnaires (72 of 105) had a student protest against the Cambodian invasion, about the same proportion as that of institutions that had a serious student uprising in 1968. The correlation between demonstrations in 1968 and in 1970, so measured, is .34, but when size (log) is controlled, the beta weight is only .19, barely twice its standard error.

[38] The correlation of size (log) with the 1968 measure is .45, and its correlation with the 1970 measure is .42.

[39] The beta weight of student ratings, with size (log) controlled, is $-.20$ with the 1968 measure $(r = -.25)$ and .19 with the 1970 measure of serious demonstrations $(r = .13)$; both are more than two standard errors.

in 1968 were, but gives students more strength to stage demonstrations not directed against their own institution, like those following the Cambodian invasion and the killings of students in 1970. An institution of higher education in a democracy has the obligation to prepare college students for their role as citizens and active participants in the political life of the nation by encouraging them to exercise responsibilities and some influence over their own destinies. By discharging this obligation and not keeping students under a paternalistic yoke, a college lessens internal conflict but increases the chances of student actions precipitating external conflict. For the freedom to make independent judgments enhances the likelihood of conflict with political authority—a dilemma a democracy must be capable of tolerating lest it be no longer a democracy.

The ultimate dilemma of higher education in a democratic society is how to allocate resources between students with high aptitudes, in order to take advantage of their potential for making outstanding contributions, and those with low aptitudes, in order to make up for the handicaps of their background and inferior high schools. "Thus far we have been assuming," Jencks and Riesman state, "that every institution's primary interest is in attracting better faculty and turning out more distinguished alumni." Instead of simply accepting this assumption, they go on, it may be questioned by asking "whether the 3,000th dollar spent on a talented undergraduate has more effect than the first (or perhaps the 500th) dollar spent on a mediocre one. Does an Ivy League college that spends $20 a day on able undergraduates really achieve five times as much as an overgrown teachers' college which spends $4 a day on less gifted young people?"[40]

With the waning of the conception of higher education as a commodity for sale to those who can afford it, the distribution of resources for educating various groups becomes a matter of public concern and policy. The academic value system creates predispositions to concentrate on those students whose early promise maximizes the chances that they will make original contributions to knowledge. The populist and anti-intellectual themes in the American culture produce opposite tendencies. The inclusion of professional and vocational training in universities and the spread of junior colleges reflect the populist value pattern, whereas the stress on academic scholarship and advanced students in the major universities reflects the concentration on an intellectual elite. One aspect of the Chinese cultural revolution apparently was an attempt to transform universities from institutions training an intellectual elite into

40 Jencks and Riesman, *op. cit.*, p. 128.

those furnishing a minimum of higher education to large numbers. The basic question is whether a society's viability depends most on the adequate training of large masses or on the great contributions only the best minds can make. We do not know. Surely it depends on both, but the fundamental dilemma is how to distribute resources between the two.

CHAPTER SEVEN

BUREAUCRATIC AND PROFESSIONAL AUTHORITY

Bureaucratic authority has its source in a superior official position, which bestows upon incumbents the power of command and puts at their disposal sanctions to enforce their commands. Professional authority has its source in expert knowledge, usually gained through prolonged training, which enables those possessing it to direct the endeavors of others to achieve certain ends. Superiors can use their sanctions to coerce, and experts can use their knowledge to persuade, but the exercise of authority implies that social norms largely obviate the need for doing so because they legitimate the superior's right to issue commands or certify that the expert's knowledge entitles him or her to give directives.

The distinction is an analytical one, and concrete cases manifest various admixtures of the pure types, particularly when professionals are employed in bureaucracies, where they are appointed to official positions on the basis of their expert knowledge, and their bureaucratic and professional authority reinforce each other. Nevertheless, it is usually possible to distinguish the predominantly bureaucratic authority exercised by persons in administrative positions, though they may be professionals, from the primarily professional authority exercised by specialists working in their field, though their official position may strengthen their influence. In universities and colleges, the authority of administrators is bureaucratic and that of the faculty is largely professional.

Although academics are not like professionals in every respect, they do share numerous characteristics with professionals, and some important shared attributes are embodied in the concept of professional authority. As pointed out in Chapter One, academics have in common with professionals the insistence on exclusive authority over their own work, the demand for self-regulation without administrative interference, and the claim that the colleague group alone may set standards of specialized competence and judge the performance of individuals. These claims to professional autonomy and self-regulation create potential conflicts with the bureaucratic authority of administrators, since administrative and professional considerations are often at variance, for example, when budgetary requirements conflict with optimum professional service to clients, or when administrative demands infringe upon the specialized responsibilities of experts.

The generally recognized differences in jurisdiction between bureaucratic and professional authority avert many potential conflicts. University administrators rarely if ever tell faculty members what topics to cover in their classes or how to conduct experiments, and faculty members acknowledge that class schedules must be coordinated by administrators, just as hospital administrators do not tell physicians how to perform operations, and physicians recognize the need of their schedules to be coordinated by administrators.[1] But jurisdictions cannot always be neatly separated, and conflicts arise when they cannot be. A typical illustration of such an area of overlapping jurisdictions in academic institutions is the appointment of faculty members, which involves budgetary commitments that are administrative responsibilities and judgments of specialized competence that are professional ones.

The distribution in decision making and influence between the administration and the faculty in an academic institution represents the extent to which bureaucratic or professional authority predominates. Although administration and faculty are not the only two groups in universities and colleges, the differences in authority between them among institutions tend to reflect similar differences between other groups. Variations in the power of trustees are associated with variations in that of administrators, and both are indicative of the degree of bureaucratic centralization of authority. Students have little influence, and the institutions in which they have some are largely those also characterized by decentralization of authority to the faculty. The focus of the analysis in this chapter is on the basic differences among academic institutions in the extent to which authority is centralized in a bureaucratic manner, either

---

[1] See Mary E. W. Goss, "Influence and Authority Among Physicians in an Outpatient Clinic," *American Sociological Review* 26 (1961), 39–50.

in the hands of trustees or in those of administrators, rather than decentralized to the faculty in accordance with the professional model. But the authority of the president, given its importance, is singled out for special attention.

The conditions in an academic institution affecting the centralization and decentralization of authority in two areas—educational policies and faculty appointments—are examined. These two areas are emphasized because the issue of bureaucratic versus professional authority is joined in them. This is not the case in such other areas as financial policies, over which faculties rarely claim jurisdiction, or conducting research, over which trustees and administrators rarely do. Top administrators naturally have much authority over many decisions in most universities and colleges, and this similarity may overshadow the important differences in faculty authority among institutions with regard to decisions of distinctive professional concern. Gross and Grambsch stress the similarity in the distribution of authority among the 68 American universities that produce most Ph.D.'s. "American universities are remarkably similar in their power structures. At almost all institutions, the president, vice-president, and regents are perceived as having a great deal of say in making big decisions, whereas alumni, students, citizens, and parents are perceived as having little or no say."[2] It should be noted, however, that the research by Gross and Grambsch is confined to major universities without religious affiliations, that they later add that there are considerable differences in the power of the faculty even among these, and that the degree of institutional variation in centralized authority depends on the nature of the decisions under consideration.

Concerning financial policies, for example, there is much agreement among the members of various academic institutions that authority is centralized. In more than half of the 114 institutions sampled in which faculty members were interviewed, 88 per cent of the respondents checked that the trustees exert substantial influence over financial policies, 99 per cent checked that the administration does, while only 7 per cent attributed influence over financial affairs to the senior and none to the junior faculty. Concerning educational policies and faculty appointments, however, there are great differences among institutions. The proportion of sampled faculty members who considered trustees to have much influence over general educational policies ranged from 0 to 83 per cent in the 114 institutions sampled. With respect to the administration's influence over faculty appointments, the range is between 6 and

[2] Edward Gross and Paul V. Grambsch, *University Goals and Academic Power*, Washington: American Council on Education, 1968, p. 97.

99 per cent, and the proportion checking that the senior faculty has in effect the authority to make the final decisions in faculty appointments has a range from 0 to 80 per cent in the unweighted sample of 114 institutions. The responses to these three questions provide the main measures of centralization and decentralization to be analyzed. Since faculty members participate hardly at all in financial decisions,[3] responsibilities for the allocation of funds are analyzed only in the section dealing with the president's authority.

CENTRALIZATION OF EDUCATIONAL MATTERS

Before turning to the investigation of the characteristics of universities and colleges that promote or impede bureaucratic centralization of educational decisions, a few remarks are in order to summarize the procedures used for selecting this and the other measures of centralization, which were described in Chapter Two. As noted there, much information pertaining to authority and influence in various areas was collected from administrators and faculty members, and a factor analysis with 119 of these items was performed. Exploratory analysis was carried out with factor scores, composite scores of items, and separate items, on the basis of which five items have been selected to be analyzed as dependent variables in this chapter (two more will be considered in subsequent chapters). These are: (1) the item with the highest loading on the strongest factor (accounting for most of the common variance), referring to educational centralization; (2) the item with the highest and (3) that with the highest negative loading on the second-strongest factor, referring to centralization of faculty appointments;[4] (4) the item with the highest loading on another factor, referring to the president's authority over funds; and (5) another item indicating the president's influence over faculty appointments.[5]

Educating students is the professional responsibility of the faculty, and the degree to which educational decisions are centralized in a university

[3] A survey of 970 academic institutions conducted by the American Association of University Professors in 1970 also indicates that faculty members participate least in financial decisions; Otway Pardee et al., "Report of the Survey Subcommittee of Committee T," *AAUP Bulletin* **57** (1971), 70.

[4] These three variables are the ones described in the last paragraph of the preceding section.

[5] For an analysis of several other measures of decentralization in these academic institutions, using the unweighted sample, see R. Danforth Ross, "Academic Decision-Making," Ph.D. dissertation, University of Chicago, 1971.

or college reflects its conformity to the bureaucratic rather than the professional model. The measure of centralization of educational affairs is the proportion of the faculty members interviewed in an institution who state that the board of trustees has a good deal of influence in formulating general educational policy. Since this item was chosen because it has the highest loading (.68) on the factor indicative of centralization of educational affairs, it represents more or less other items with high loadings on this factor, for example, that the faculty does not have substantial influence over educational policy ($-.65$). How centralized educational matters are in an academic institution is associated little with the degree of centralization in faculty appointments or with the president's authority. None of the correlations of the former with any of the latter measures exceeds .25. These are independent dimensions of the authority structure. Centralization is not a unidimensional attribute of academic institutions, nor is it of other organizations.[6]

The formulation of educational policies is no less centralized in large universities than in small colleges, which is surprising, since the faculties of major universities are widely assumed to have more influence than those of small colleges. The data here support this assumption with regard to other aspects of decentralization to the faculty, as we shall see, but not with regard to educational decentralization. The extent of centralization of educational responsibilities is one of the few characteristics of academic institutions that are not appreciably affected by their size ($r = -.06$), and neither is there less educational centralization in universities granting Ph.D.'s than in colleges ($r = .12$).[7] In Kerr's judgment, American faculties have been more interested in influencing faculty appointments than in educational policies. Since 1945, he writes, "there has been remarkably little faculty discussion of general educational policy. By contrast, there has been a great deal in England, particularly in the 'new universities,' where faculty discussion of educational policy has been very lively, and faculty influence, as a consequence, substantial."[8]

An inference that might be derived from Kerr's comments is that the stronger involvement in research than in teaching of the faculties of major universities diminishes their interest in shaping educational policies and thus counteracts the tendency for more responsibilities to be decentralized to these faculties than to those in small colleges, with the result

---

[6] See Peter M. Blau and Richard A. Schoenherr, *The Structure of Organizations,* New York: Basic Books, 1971, pp. 112–113.

[7] If these two variables are added to those in Table 7.1, the beta weight of size is $-.12$ and that of Ph.D. status is .11, both of which are less than two standard errors; none of the other beta weights are appreciably changed by these additions.

[8] Clark Kerr, *The Uses of the University,* Cambridge: Harvard University Press, 1964, p. 23.

that *educational* policies are no more decentralized in large universities than in small colleges. This interpretation implies that superior academic quality promotes centralization of educational responsibilities. But the data negate this hypothesis. There is no indication that the better faculties in better academic institutions are inclined to abdicate responsibility for formulating educational policies, to surrender the professional authority they can command, and thus to encourage by default centralized direction of educational affairs. On the contrary, the higher the quality of the faculty and of the institution, the more decentralized does the influence over educational matters tend to be.

Row 5 in Table 7.1 indicates that educational policies are *less* centralized in academic institutions with superior reputations than in others. Superior qualifications of the faculty also somewhat discourage centralization of educational responsibilities, as the simple correlation in row 4 suggests, though only indirectly (the beta weight is insignificant), by helping to raise the institution's reputation (decomposition coefficient, $-.20$). Not the formal qualifications of the faculty as such but their effective utilization to improve the institution's academic reputation seems to be the basis of the faculty's greater influence over educational policies and greater freedom from centralized control of educational activities. A faculty's academic achievements, which depend on its qualifications, earn it greater professional authority. To be sure, an academic institution's reputation among outstanding students and their counselors may primarily rest on the achievements not of its present faculty but of their predecessors. Differences in faculty quality among institutions tend to persist over long periods, however. Besides, the educational authority accruing to a faculty as the result of its academic achievements is likely to become institutionalized and perpetuated to future generations of faculty in the university or college. Indications of such institutionalization will be discussed shortly.

Is the less centralized control to which faculties in superior academic institutions are subject an institutional expression of *noblesse oblige*? A more plausible explanation of it can be given, inasmuch as the institution's superior reputation rests in considerable part on the academic abilities and achievements of its faculty. Faculty members capable of making substantial academic contributions are more important to their university or college than it is to them, because its academic standing depends on them, and because they have good opportunities elsewhere. This principle is manifest in the effects faculty qualifications have on the allegiances of faculty members to their local institutions, which were analyzed in Chapter Five. The same principle can account for the lesser restraints by centralized authority and the greater influence of faculty members whose superior qualifications enable them to contribute to the institution's academic standing. Their contributions to their present institution and the demand for them by others give them bargaining power they can use to increase their influence and decrease centralized control over their activities.

What discourages bureaucratic centralization of educational responsibilities most in a university or college is an institutionalized faculty government in which a large part of the faculty participates. Only two crude measures of a democratic faculty government could be collected in interviews with administrators. One is simply the proportion of the faculty who are members of the basic faculty governing body, which is usually called the senate. The percentage of faculty members on the senate is, as one would expect, smaller in large than in small institutions $(r = -.39;$ with size in logarithmic transformation, $r = -.52)$. Size should therefore normally be controlled when using this measure of faculty government, but this is not necessary in this case, since size is unrelated to educational centralization and controlling it makes no difference. The second measure of democratic faculty government is the proportion of elected rather than appointed or ex officio members on the most important faculty committee, which is the senate or its council in a quarter of the institutions sampled and a committee concerned with educational policy in the majority of the rest.

Crude though the two indicators of a democratic faculty government are, both exert independent effects reducing bureaucratic centralization in the formulation of educational policies, as the last two rows in Table 7.1 show. An institutionalized faculty government is not mere window dressing but an effective mechanism for restricting centralized control over educational programs, in accordance with the professional demands of the faculty. Formal institutionalization of faculty authority fortifies it. Wide participation of faculty members in the senate as well as democratic procedures for selecting those serving on important committees enhance faculty influence in educational matters. The majority of small colleges do not elect a senate but include all faculty members in it. Lawry advocates that small colleges substitute senates composed of faculty representatives for those consisting of the entire faculty, which he calls faculty meetings, arguing that such meetings of the total faculty are dominated by administrators whereas a senate is organized by the faculty and thus strengthens faculty influence.[9] The data here do not support

[9] J. S. Lawry, "A Faculty Senate at a Small College: Why?" *AAUP Bulletin* **57** (1971), 377–380.

Table 7.1   Centralization of Educational Matters

	Beta Weight	Simple Correlation
1. South	−.12	.30
2. Affluence	−.14	−.23
3. Administration/faculty	.38**	.23
4. Faculty qualifications	.14	−.18
5. Reputation	−.35**	−.44
6. Percentage of faculty on senate	−.42**	−.34
7. Percentage elected on committee	−.31**	−.34

$R^2 = .46$ ($\hat{R}^2 = .42$); $n = 114$

** More than three times its standard error.

this argument. The finding that the percentage of faculty members on the senate is inversely related to centralization of educational policies implies that faculties all of whose members are on the senate (whatever its name) tend to be less dominated by centralized educational policies, according to their own reports, than those with fewer participants in senate deliberations.

Row 3 in Table 7.1 indicates that a high ratio of administrators to faculty members in an academic institution promotes centralization of the decisions governing educational policies. The faculty's obligations to teaching and research limit their involvement in formulating policies and participating in the governing of the university or college. Their academic obligations and their interest in faculty self-government put faculty members under cross-pressure, which is a source of ambivalence about sharing responsibility for the management of the academic institution. Many jokes about deans and disparaging remarks about faculty members who accept administrative positions reflect this ambivalence. So do the contradictory attitudes faculty members often express when pleading, on the one hand, for more democratic procedures and complaining, on the other, about too much committee work and too many administrative duties. But committee work and administrative duties are the means by which democratic participation in running the institution is accomplished.[10]

Administrators do not experience this cross-pressure, because administrative responsibilities are their primary obligations. Or perhaps it would

[10] Talcott Parsons, in a personal communication, suggested the idea that the dislike of faculty members for administrative and committee work limits their effective demands for democratic participation in university government.

be more accurate to say that, since most are former faculty members, they have resolved the conflict in favor of the rewards administration brings. They can relieve faculty members of administrative duties and the conflicting demands these duties and their academic commitments make on them. The larger the number of administrators relative to that of faculty members, the easier and more tempting it is for faculty members to divest themselves of administrative burdens to free more time for teaching and research, and the result is greater centralization of educational matters in the institution. An interest in educational policy is one of the incentives for becoming an academic administrator, and a large administrative staff in an academic institution tends to concentrate decisions about educational policies in its own hands and to serve as a communication channel for the board of trustees, increasing its influence over decisions. Research on government bureaus discloses that a large administrative staff promotes centralization of authority there,[11] just as it appears to do in universities and colleges.

Two other conditions indirectly affect the degree of centralization of educational matters. Affluent academic institutions are somewhat less centralized than those with fewer economic resources (see the simple correlation in row 2 of Table 7.1) mostly because they have higher academic standing (decomposition coefficient of reputation, $-.18$). Educational affairs are more centralized in Southern academic institutions than in those in other regions, but this difference disappears when other conditions are controlled (compare the positive simple correction with the beta weight in row 1 of the table). What accounts for the greater centralization of educational authority in Southern than in other universities and colleges is that Southern institutions have less democratic faculty governments (decomposition coefficient for both indicators together, .19) and that they have lower reputations (.14).

In sum, the conditions discovered to have most impact on centralization of educational policies in universities and colleges are a high administration-faculty ratio, a low reputation, and a weak faculty government. Although a large administrative apparatus promotes bureaucratic centralization of educational affairs, it is questionable whether this implies a failure to conform to professional standards, as initially assumed. The expert training and competence of academics, on which their claim to professional authority and self-regulation rests, are not in education but in their specialized scholarly disciplines. Faculty members generally have no more basic knowledge about educational principles, and possibly less, than administrators. Hence the influence of the administration-faculty ratio on educational authority reflects not only

[11] Blau and Schoenherr, *op. cit.*, p. 129.

the significance of a bureaucratic apparatus for centralized control but also the disjunction between the faculty's expert knowledge, which is in their specialized subjects, and much if not most of their work, which is teaching these subjects. The difference in this respect between major universities and undergraduate colleges poses a paradox. Faculties of colleges that are not renowned for scholarly research devote more of their time and energy to teaching than those in major universities. Their consequent greater understanding of teaching should give these faculties a stronger professional claim to influencing educational policies than that of the research faculties in institutions with high academic reputations, yet the negative relationship between reputation and educational centralization indicates that the former have less influence over education than the latter. Factors other than relevant professional competence apparently govern faculty influence over educational matters.

APPOINTMENT POWER

Faculty appointments squarely pose the issue between the administrative requirements of bureaucratic authority and the academic requirements of professional authority. According to academic professional standards, only fellow experts may decide what new faculty specialists are needed and whom to appoint. But budgetary considerations dictate that the commitment of the institution's financial resources made by appointing faculty members be decided upon by administrators responsible for the budget. To resolve this issue, a distinction is usually made between the administrative responsibility for deciding which positions or slots are available and the faculty responsibility for judging the competence of candidates to fill these positions. Notwithstanding this distinction, however, the relative influence of administration and faculty over appointments remains an area of potential conflict, and there are great differences in their respective appointment power among academic institutions. Given the importance of responsibility for faculty appointments, the conditions affecting two indications of it are examined—the centralized influence of the administration over appointments and the decentralization of the authority to make final appointment decisions to the senior faculty.[12] The two measures and the procedure for selecting them were

---

[12] The difference in wording—"influencing" versus "making formal decisions"—was intended by Talcott Parsons and Gerald M. Platt, whose survey is used for these measures, to distinguish influence from authority. The analysis here focuses more on the process through which influence becomes institutionalized as authority than on this difference in question wording.

Table 7.2   Administration's Influence in Appointments

	Beta Weight	Simple Correlation
1. Size (log)	−.51**	−.69
2. Salaries	−.23*	−.66
3. Clerks/faculty	−.15*	−.41
4. Faculty qualifications	−.04	−.52
5. Research emphasis	−.18*	−.60
6. Computer use	.23**	−.24

$R^2 = .64$ $(\hat{R}^2 = .62)$; $n = 114$

* More than twice its standard error.
** More than three times its standard error.

described earlier. Although these two variables are inversely correlated (−.62), the conditions affecting them are sufficiently different to justify analyzing both.[13]

The superior quality of the faculty in a university or college reduces the influence of the administration over faculty appointments. Three manifestations of faculty quality indicate this (their combined effect is substantial, though no single beta coefficient is large). If the faculty commands high salaries, which tends to reflect greater academic abilities and achievements, as previously pointed out, influence over appointments is less centralized in an academic institution than if the faculty commands lower salaries. Although the pronounced negative correlation between salaries and centralization is partly spurious, owing to their common dependence on size (decomposition coefficient, −.32), salaries also have a direct negative effect on centralization (see the beta weight in row 2 of Table 7.2), plus an indirect effect mediated by the stronger orientation to research of faculties commanding higher salaries (−.10). An emphasis on research among the faculty has an independent effect reducing centralization, as row 5 reveals. Dressel and his colleagues obtained a parallel result in their study of individual departments: "the greater the emphasis upon basic research in the department, the more likely it was that decision making would be delegated for recruitment and selection of new faculty. . . ."[14] The qualifications of an institution's faculty are also

[13] Every independent variable included in one table but not in the other (Tables 7.2 and 7.3) has been shown in separate regression analyses not to influence that other dependent variable, which is why it has been excluded from the table.
[14] Paul L. Dressel et al., *The Confidence Crisis*, San Francisco: Jossey-Bass, 1970, pp. 74–75. The passage cited goes on to indicate that decentralization in various other respects is also most likely in departments emphasizing research.

inversely associated with centralized control of appointments, but their effect is entirely indirect (see row 4). Part of the negative simple correlation between qualifications and centralization is the spurious result of the effects of size on both $(-.21)$, and the rest is produced by the higher salaries better qualified faculties command $(-.17)$ and by their stronger orientation to research $(-.11)$. These findings support the interpretation advanced in the preceding section.

It is not the mere possession of formal qualifications but their effective utilization in academic pursuits that increases the faculty's power relative to that of the administration, as suggested earlier, and as implied by the present finding that formal qualifications attenuate centralized administrative controls only to the extent to which they strengthen the research concerns of faculty members and raise the salaries their academic achievements command. A faculty interested in research and capable of making research contributions has bargaining power that enables it to demand freedom from domination by centralized authority and to command greater influence in academic affairs as well as higher salaries. The academic accomplishments and prestige that enhance the faculty's power in relations with the administration depend, of course, not on formal qualifications alone, and the direct negative effects of salaries and research emphasis on centralization reflect this. Predominant concern with research also discourages administrative interference with appointment decisions for another reason. Research competence in an academic field evidently must be judged by experts in that field, whereas the same is not true for teaching competence, not merely because teaching skills are less highly specialized but particularly because academic faculties have no special expertness in teaching. Administrators' judgments about teaching may well be as good as physicists' or poets', but their judgments about physics or poetry surely are not.

It is possible to test the assumption made in this discussion that actual research accomplishments increase faculty influence and restrict administrative control over appointments. The average research productivity of the faculty in an institution is a rough indication of its scholarly accomplishment, and though it ignores the quality of the publications, its visibility makes it undoubtedly important in the evaluations of faculty achievements.[15] Whereas this variable has been placed last in the causal sequence, in order to use it as an effect criterion for the various characteristics of academic institutions, it is now taken out of this sequence to test the implications of the assumption that faculty publication output reduces administrative centralization and accounts, at least partly, for

---

[15] The measure is the number of papers plus five times the number of books a faculty member reports to have authored or coauthored, averaged for the faculty members in an institution sampled.

the negative effects of the three indicators of faculty quality on central-ization. If average faculty research productivity is added to the inde-pendent variables in Table 7.2 in a new regression analysis, it is seen to have a negative direct effect on administrative centralization of ap-pointment decisions ($b^* = -.24$, more than twice its standard error; $r = -.68$). Furthermore, the research productivity of the faculty mediates a good part—more than any other intervening variable—of the negative effects on centralization of research emphasis ($-.15$), faculty qualifica-tions ($-.13$), and salaries ($-.15$).[16] These data support the assumption that visible research accomplishments promote the faculty's independence from centralized bureaucratic controls and their power to select their own colleagues in an academic institution.

Since administrative centralization of appointment decisions is an attribute of the academic institution, not of individual faculty members (even though responses from these individuals are used to measure it), the findings imply that the research achievements of an institution's faculty improve the independence and influence of individual faculty members regardless of their own scholarly contributions. This is not to say that an individual's outstanding academic contributions and standing do not enhance his personal influence in the institution, only that the research accomplishments of the institution's faculty as a whole, by dis-couraging bureaucratic centralization, enhance the freedom and power of individuals independent of their own research achievements. Some evidence of this is provided by examining the responses of *individual* faculty members to the question of how much influence the administra-tion has over faculty appointments (a five-point score). Answers to this question by 2348 individual faculty members exhibit little correlation with their own research productivity ($-.05$) but a substantial negative correlation with the average research productivity in their institution ($-.37$). This indicates that the reports of faculty members about the administration's appointment power in their institution are little dis-torted by their academic standing. It also implies that the freedom from bureaucratic controls and the influence of individual faculty members depend to a considerable extent on their *colleagues'* research standing,[17] an implication that will be further tested later.

16 The beta weights of all the independent variables in this regression analysis of administration's influence on appointments are: size (log), $-.46^{**}$; salaries, $-.15$; clerical-faculty ratio, -11; faculty qualifications, $-.04$; research emphasis, $-.10$; com-puter use, $.20^*$; faculty research productivity, $-.24^*$.

17 The negative relationship between colleagues' research productivity and individual's report on the administration's influence over appointments persists in a regression analysis of these reports of 2348 individuals in which their own research productivity as well as the independent variables in Table 7.2 are controlled. The beta weight of colleagues' research productivity is $-.12$, more than three times its standard error.

Returning to Table 7.2, row 3 indicates that a high ratio of clerks to faculty members slightly decreases administrative influence over faculty appointments. In the preceding section, we saw that the administration-faculty ratio promotes *centralization* in one area, and now we see that the clerical-faculty ration promotes *decentralization* in another. This difference parallels differences in the conditions that affect the two ratios, which were discussed in Chapter Three. The analysis there showed that differentiation in the two main dimensions of the institution's structure —into several schools and colleges and into a multilevel hierarchy— increases the ratio of administrators (Table 3.6), whereas differentiation into structural subunits—into many departments—increases the clerical ratio (Table 3.7). The data suggest that many clerks work in and for departments, particularly if large numbers of them are available in an institution. A large clerical staff relieves faculty members of administrative detail, freeing their time to work on personnel committees and participate in appointment decisions, thereby limiting the administration's influence on appointments. To be sure, the argument was advanced before that administrators too relieve faculty of administrative duties. There is an important difference in the nature of the administrative work involved, however. The faculty's administrative duties that senior administrators are willing to assume are responsibilities through which influence is wielded, whereas the administrative routines that can be assigned to clerks do not deprive faculty members of academic influence but free their time to exercise it.

The use of computers for administrative purposes in institutions of higher education has an effect on centralization opposite to that of the use of computers in government bureaus. The beta weight in row 6 of Table 7.2 indicates that extensive administrative use of computers, excluding their use in scientific research and teaching, promotes centralization of appointment decisions. This is concealed in the negative simple correlation, which is spurious, produced by the effects of size (decomposition coefficient, $-.28$) and a combination of other conditions. The employment of computers to automate operations in government agencies, by contrast, has been found to foster decentralization of personnel and other responsibilities.[18] Leavitt and Whisler predicted in an early paper that computers would centralize control in the hands of management by improving information feedback.[19] The research on employment

[18] Blau and Schoenherr, *op. cit.*, pp. 124–128.
[19] Harold J. Leavitt and Thomas L. Whisler, "Management in the 1980's," *Harvard Business Review* 36 (1958), 36, 41–48. See also Thomas L. Whisler, *The Impact of Computers on Organizations*, New York: Praeger, 1970.

security agencies contradicts this prediction, but that on universities and colleges supports it. The reason for the difference probably lies in the way computers are utilized. In the government agencies studied, computers were used largely for routine tasks that had been performed previously by clerks. Computers in this capacity serve as an impersonal mechanism of control that substitutes in part for directives from top management and thus encourages delegation of responsibilities to middle managers. In academic institutions, computers are often put to more sophisticated use and provide the central administration with helpful information, as Leavitt and Whisler predicted, thereby strengthening the administration's influence in the selection of faculty members. A powerful position enables persons to take advantage of technological improvements to obtain knowledge that further enhances their power.

The characteristic of academic institutions that limits the administration's influence over faculty appointments most is their large size, as the top row in Table 7.2 shows. The simple correlation indicates that differences in size alone account for nearly one-half of the variation among institutions in the degree of centralization of appointment decisions. Part of the negative effect of size on centralization is indirect, mediated by the more research-oriented faculties recruited with the higher salaries of larger institutions (salaries and research emphasis together, $-.25$), though the more extensive administrative use of computers in larger institutions somewhat counteracts this negative effect ($.13$). But most of the impact of large size reducing centralized control of faculty appointments is direct (see the beta weight). Bureaucratic authority over faculty selection is more pronounced in small than in large academic institutions, contrary to the stereotype of the bureaucratization of large universities. In a small college, the number of new faculty members to be hired every year is small enough for the president and academic dean to become involved in their selection, and they typically wield much influence when they do become involved. The number of faculty appointments made every year in a large university is too great to make this possible, nor can other administrators participate as actively in the selection process in large as in small institutions, since their ratio to faculty members is lower in large ones. The sheer pressure of the large volume of work entailed by recruitment as well as other administrative responsibilities in large institutions restricts the administration's involvement and power in faculty appointments.

The large size of an academic institution greatly increases the senior faculty's authority to make appointment decisions, as shown in row 4 of

Table 7.3, which is the counterpart of the reduction large size effects in the administration's influence over appointments. The better qualified faculties in large institutions, who are more interested in research than in teaching, account in part for the greater decentralization of appointment procedures there than in small institutions (decomposition coefficient of qualifications and teaching emphasis together, .18). But size also has a substantial direct effect on the appointment power of the senior faculty, which probably reflects the pressure to decentralize recruitment generated by the extensive recruitment activities required and by the voluminous other responsibilities of administrators in large universities. Another complementary finding is evident in the table's fifth row. A high ratio of clerical personnel to faculty members slightly strengthens the faculty's control over appointments, just as it weakens the administration's, which lends further support to the interpretation that an insufficient clerical staff, by overburdening faculty members with clerical routines, infringes upon faculty participation in committee work and in recruitment, thereby diminishing the faculty's influence.

The more affluent an academic institution is, the more decisive is the voice of the senior faculty in personnel selection (row 3 in Table 7.3). Various conditions in affluent universities promote their greater decentralization of responsibilities; these include their faculties' better qualifications and lower involvement with teaching than research (together, .17). There remains a small direct effect of affluence on decentralization, however, when most of the conditions governing decentralization have

Table 7.3   Senior Faculty's Appointment Authority

	Beta Weight	Simple Correlation
1. West	.22**	.32
2. Religious	−.16*	−.56
3. Affluence	.12*	.50
4. Size (log)	.30**	.68
5. Clerks/faculty	.13*	.44
6. Inbreeding	−.14*	−.26
7. Faculty qualifications	.19**	.58
8. Teaching emphasis	−.17*	−.57
9. Percentage elected on committee	.22**	.27

$R^2 = .78$ $(\hat{R}^2 = .76)$; $n = 114$

* More than twice its standard error.
** More than three times its standard error.

been controlled. (It might be noted that three-quarters of the variation among institutions in the faculty's authority over appointments is accounted for by the independent variables in Table 7.3.) The economies necessitated by meager resources are likely to put restraints on faculty recruitment in several ways, in addition to failing to provide adequate clerical help to facilitate faculty recruitment (decomposition coefficient of clerical ratio, .06). In the extreme case, administrators may make most appointment decisions themselves for fear that those of the faculty would be too costly. Or they may veto faculty appointment decisions frequently on budgetary grounds. Or they may refuse funds for bringing candidates to the campus to be interviewed, which makes recruitment so frustrating that it discourages faculty participation in it.

Religious colleges and universities tend to be less affluent than secular ones, but this is not the main reason for the little influence their faculties have in the selection of fellow faculty members, indicated in row 2 of Table 7.3. The small size of most religious institutions is part of the reason for the weak authority of their senior faculties (decomposition coefficient, $-.15$), and so is the prevailing emphasis on teaching combined with the less qualified faculties in religious institutions (together, $-.13$). Independent of these and other conditions, faculties in denominational institutions still have somewhat less appointment power than those in others, as the beta weight shows. Religious orders often dominate Catholic colleges, sometimes in a high-handed manner, as the case of St. John's University a few years ago illustrates, and the domination of many fundamentalist Protestant colleges by religious boards of trustees is probably no less pronounced. Such domination is not likely in the best denominational universities and colleges, but these are far outnumbered by religious colleges of low quality. The situation of the faculty there is aptly described by Riesman: "In such institutions, the teachers are but hired hands, and their institutions are colleges only by the grace of semantic generosity."[20] Boards and administrators whose religious commitments justify their authoritarian conduct in their own eyes give hired hands little say.[21]

[20] David Riesman, *Constraints and Variety in American Education,* Lincoln: University of Nebraska Press, 1956, p. 49.

[21] The survey of the American Association of University Professors found faculty control to be weaker in public than in religious institutions (Pardee, *op. cit.,* p. 71). In the data here, public ownership exhibits a positive simple correlation with faculty's appointment authority, but when this dummy variable is added to the independent variable in Table 7.3, the regression analysis reveals that the faculty's appointment power in public institutions is low ($b^* = -.23$), though not as low as in religious ones ($b^* = -.27$). The last coefficient ($-.27$) indicates that the beta weight in Table 7.3 ($-.16$) underestimates the negative effect of religious affiliation on faculty power.

Whereas the institutionalized religious authoritarianism of many denominational colleges and universities restricts faculty control over appointments, the institutionalization of democratic faculty government expands it. We saw earlier that democracy in the governance of an academic institution, although it is often minimal, decreases centralization of educational responsibilities, and row 9 in Table 7.3 reveals that it also increases decentralization of appointment responsibilities. But in this case only one of the two indicators of institutionalized faculty government has such an effect. The democratic election of faculty representatives to committees enhances the appointment power of the *senior* faculty, whereas wide participation in the senate does not, perhaps because representation on committees is more likely to involve senior than junior faculty, for whom wide participation may be more important.[22]

Whether the frontier spirit of the West also fosters democratic tendencies is unknown. Impressionistic evidence could be cited for and against such a hypothesis. But the data do show that, whatever the reason, appointment authority is more decentralized to the faculty in Western than in other universities and colleges (see row 1).

Three factors pertaining to the recruitment of an institution's present faculty affect the power of its senior members in the recruitment of future faculty. The more inbreeding an academic institution exhibits by appointing its own graduates to the faculty, the less authority does the faculty have over the selection of colleagues, as shown in row 6 of Table 7.3. Although this relationship is weak, it has suggestive implications. The analysis in Chapter Five disclosed that inbreeding strengthens the allegiance of faculty members to their institution (Table 5.5). A faculty's strong commitment to the university or college may undermine its bargaining power in demanding a decisive voice over faculty appointments. Inbreeding implies that many faculty members have never tested what

[22] Junior faculty members may influence but rarely have formal authority to make decisions on faculty appointments. Only 8 per cent of the individual faculty members interviewed state that the junior faculty has such authority at their institution, whereas 33 per cent report that the senior faculty does. The dependent variable in Table 7.3, which is based on the latter responses, exhibits a correlation of .18 with the proportion of an institution's faculty members who are on the senate; if this proportion is added to the variables in Table 7.3, its beta weight with decentralization is .05, less than one standard error, the correlation being due to size (log; decomposition coefficient, .17).

alternative opportunities are open to them, which weakens their bargaining power. Besides, the paternalism reflected in hiring one's own probably finds also expression in the inclination of top administrators to treat the faculty paternalistically and give it little independence. There may be a reverse effect as well and faculty control over appointments may reduce inbreeding, on the assumption that faculty members base their judgments on objective criteria of merit more than administrators do. But the interests of faculty members in their own best graduates make this a questionable assumption, and findings that cast doubt on it will be discussed in Chapter Nine. Two other factors revealed in Table 5.5 to increase the allegiance of faculty members to their institution also decrease faculty authority over appointments—an emphasis on teaching and *low* formal qualifications.

Row 8 in Table 7.3 shows that an emphasis on teaching in an academic institution has a small adverse effect on the faculty's control over recruitment. Research faculties command more power than teaching faculties in selecting their colleagues. This negative effect of a prevailing teaching orientation on the decentralization of personnel decisions to the senior faculty corresponds to the previously observed negative effect of a research orientation on the centralization of personnel decisions in the hands of the administration. But an emphasis on research reveals no independent effect on the decentralization measure in Table 7.3, and an emphasis on teaching reveals none on the centralization measure in Table 7.2.[23] The difference may well be fortuitous, though it is possible that the superior status of researchers is most relevant for protecting their prerogatives to choose their own colleagues from administrative interference, whereas the main significance of a teaching emphasis may be that the specialized academic rather than pedagogical expertness of faculty members does not furnish strong grounds for giving them an authoritative voice in the selection of teachers. Row 7 in Table 7.3 indicates that superior formal qualifications of the faculty promote decentralization of appointment responsibilities, just as they were seen earlier to reduce administrative centralization in appointments, except that they have some direct effect on decentralization.

Although three factors related to recruitment—inbreeding, emphasis on teaching, and faculty qualifications—have opposite effects on the allegiance of faculty members to their own institution and on their power to make appointment decisions, allegiance itself does not affect that

---

[23] If research emphasis is substituted for teaching emphasis in Table 7.3, its beta weight is .03 ($r = .56$); if teaching emphasis is substituted for research emphasis in Table 7.2, its beta weight is nil ($r = .43$).

power.[24] The loyalty of faculty members to their institution does not lessen their authority in it. However, the same conditions that weaken the faculty's bargaining power in the academic market both increase their commitments to their present institution and undermine their bargaining power and authority in it.

Does the greater appointment authority of faculties with superior qualifications and research potentials actually mean, as has been assumed, that even persons who do not have such attributes commanding academic prestige exert more influence over appointments if they are among colleagues who do than if their colleagues also lack these attributes? To answer this question, let us briefly examine the results of a regression analysis of the responses of 2332 *individual* faculty members interviewed as to how much influence "you personally have in appointing faculty at this institution." Some of the conditions affecting the dependent variable in Table 7.3 affect these responses as well, but this is not the case for all, because the individual responses refer to influence, not formal decisions, of particular individuals regardless of rank, not of the entire senior faculty, and also because there are inherent differences between the power of a collectivity and that of the individuals composing it. (Institutional conditions discovered to affect the responses are controlled in the regression analysis.[25]) The impact of size illustrates these differences.

The large size of an academic institution greatly increases the control over appointments of the faculty as a collective body, as we have seen, but it reduces the influence of individual members $(b^* = -.13)$.[26] The explanation is simple: although the faculty has more power in large than in small institutions, this power is divided among more individuals in large ones. But it is not shared equally. The individual's influence depends on his or her academic position and formal qualifications. Tenured faculty members have substantially more say than nontenured ones in the selection of their colleagues $(b^* = .29)$. The individual's formal qualifications $(b^* = .16)$ further increase his or her influence over

[24] If the proportion of faculty members with strong allegiance to an institution is added to the independent variables in Table 7.3, its beta weight with faculty decisions in appointments is $-.09$, less than two standard errors $[r = -.52,$ which is spurious, mostly owing to size $(-.15)$ and the three factors just discussed (together, $-.15)]$.

[25] Religious affiliation, size (log), inbreeding, faculty qualifications, and election to faculty committees do affect individual's influence; West, affluence, clerical-faculty ratio, and teaching emphasis do not.

[26] All the beta weight in this regression equation (with correlations in parentheses) are: religious, $-.09^{**}$ $(-.06)$; size (log), $-.13^{**}$ $(.03)$; inbreeding, $.06^*$ $(-.06)$; percentage elected on committee, $.08^{**}$ $(.09)$; colleagues' qualifications, $.11^{**}$ $(.13)$; own qualifications, $.16^{**}$ $(.24)$; tenure, $.29^{**}$ $(.33)$.

appointments, and they also have some indirect effect due to the greater likelihood of fully qualified faculty members to have tenure (decomposition coefficient, .06).

Superior formal qualifications of the other faculty members in an academic institution enhance an individual's influence over appointments regardless of his own qualifications and rank $(b* = .11)$. Whereas this independent effect of the proportion of colleagues with advanced degrees on a faculty member's personal influence is not large, it is appreciable—greater than most effects of other institutional conditions on the individual's influence (see footnote 26) —and it is observable when these conditions as well as two characteristics of the individual are controlled. The power the academic standing of an institution's faculty commands tends to become institutionalized in the collective body of the faculty and consequently to affect the individual member's power independent of his own standing.

THE PRESIDENT'S AUTHORITY

The president of a university or college is without question a dominant figure in the conduct of its affairs. Gross and Grambsch conclude from their research on the 68 American universities granting most Ph.D.'s that the president has most power in nearly all of them (with a power score of 4.6), substantially more than the vice-president (4.1), the deans (3.6), and the faculty (3.3), let alone the students (2.4), and being approximated only by the power of the board (4.4).[27] Clark stresses the crucial role the president played in his study of the creation or transformation of Reed, Antioch, and Swarthmore. At Reed: "Foster personally hired the faculty and for a few critical years personally selected the students. For a time all echelons in the organization were a direct expression of his will." At Antioch: "The charismatic leader [Morgan] brought new purpose and sought to specify that purpose in new programs and new forms of organization. Many persons inside and outside the organization subscribed to the man and his ideas and became followers, encouraged by his convincing forcefulness and dedication." At Swarthmore: "When the battle was joined with the defenders of the *status quo*, he [Aydelotte] was able to fall back on much personal devotion. At a crucial time in his attempt to change Swarthmore, he crowned his leadership with success by bringing to the college from the foundations and a few private

[27] Gross and Grambsch, *op. cit.*, p. 76.

donors, *on the basis of faith in him,* such major resources that he could not be denied."[28]

The personal qualities of the president can decisively influence the fate of an academic institution, for better or for worse, and they have much to do with how he exercises his authority and how much authority he has to exercise.[29] But conditions in the institution also affect his authority. It is in the nature of the present inquiry that the analysis be confined to the institutional conditions affecting the president's power and neglect the bearing his personal traits have on his power. This neglect is undoubtedly responsible for the fact that much less of the variation in presidential authority than of that in most institutional characteristics examined can be explained.

The conditions affecting two aspects of the president's authority—his influence over faculty appointments and the discretion he exercises in allocating unexpended funds—are analyzed. Although the administration's influence in faculty appointments has already been investigated, the administration, particularly in large universities, includes many officals besides the president, whose control over appointments deserves special attention, since it neither is affected by the same conditions nor has the same implications for the work of the faculty as that of the administration generally, as we shall see. The measure is the rating of the president's influence in faculty appointments, on a five-point scale, provided by himself or his deputy in a personal interview.

To obtain indications of the president's financial authority, he (or his deputy) was asked who has discretion to redistribute unexpended funds for tenured faculty, as well as for other budget items. The authority to reallocate unexpended funds is an unequivocal sign of control over financial resources, whereas the amount of discretionary power derived from authority over the general budget, with its many items committed for specific purposes, is ambiguous. Responses were coded to score the president's sole authority over unexpended funds highest (seven points), their return to the general institutional funds lower (five), and the authorization of departmental chairmen to use them lowest (one), with intermediate scores being given to various administrators and their combinations, depending on their rank. Thus the score directs attention to

---

[28] Burton R. Clark, *The Distinctive College,* Chicago: Aldine, 1970, pp. 242–244 (italics in original).

[29] For the sake of readability, and with apologies to the women presidents of academic institutions, I shall dispense with the phrase "he or she" and refer to the president by the masculine pronoun.

the degree of centralization of financial authority in the hands of the president, and this is why a lower rank is assigned to return of unexpended to general institutional funds, which may raise the authority of trustees at the expense of the president's. Control over the redistribution of unexpended funds for tenured faculty is exercised by the president, either alone or together with a vice-president, in one-third of the institutions sampled, and in a larger proportion of those in the universe (because it includes a larger proportion of small institutions than the sample).

The presidents of large academic institutions exert less influence on faculty appointments than those of small ones, as the simple correlation in the first row of Table 7.4 shows. This finding corresponds to the lesser centralization and greater decentralization of faculty appointments in large than in small institutions observed in Tables 7.2 and 7.3. But the negative effect of large institutional size on the president's appointment power is weak and largely indirect (note the beta weight), with most of it being due to the multiple administrative levels in large institutions ($-.09$). For a multilevel hierarchy in an institution of higher education reduces the president's influence in faculty recruitment, as indicated in row 2 of Table 7.4.

The pressure of a heavy load of administrative responsibilities in large universities leads to the development of multilevel hierarchies, as we saw in Chapter Three (Table 3.3), with vice-presidents and deans being interposed between the president and the department chairmen. These middle-level administrators assume some of the administrative responsibilities that are exercised by the president in a small college, including some authority over faculty appointments, thereby reducing the president's influence. A multilevel hierarchy decreases the president's appointment power not by increasing the faculty's but by enhancing that of

Table 7.4   President's Influence in Appointments

	Beta Weight	Simple Correlation
1. Size	$-.05$	$-.21$
2. Levels	$-.25*$	$-.32$
3. Last president's tenure	$.34**$	$.38$
$R^2=.22$ $(\hat{R}^2=.20)$; $n=112$		

* More than twice its standard error.
** More than three times its standard error.

deans.[30] Interestingly enough, a multilevel hierarchy also promotes delegation of personnel responsibilities to middle managers in government bureaus.[31] A hierarchical structure that removes the top administrator from the bulk of the personnel in an organization creates constraints to decentralize personnel selection to officials on middle levels, who are in closer touch with personnel requirements, whether the organization is a university or a government bureaucracy.

The institutional condition that has most effect on the appointment authority of the president is the length of tenure of his predecessor. Row 3 in Table 7.4 shows that the longer the last president had been in office, the greater is the influence his successor wields over faculty appointments. But is it correct to consider this the influence of an institutional condition? Does it not rather reflect the fact that strong presidents who are charismatic leaders remain in office longer and command more authority? It does undoubtedly in part, but this interpretation does not explain why the *former* president's years in office affect the *current* president's influence, particularly since the latter's own length of tenure does not appreciably increase his influence over faculty appointments $(r=.10)$. To explain this finding requires reference to both personal and institutional factors. Presidents who remain in office for many years probably do so because their leadership is successful, and they are likely to consolidate their power in the course of their long tenure in the office of president. These results of the leadership qualities of a president often become institutionalized. The power a successful president accumulates in many years typically leaves a residue of institutionalized authority in the office of president, which strengthens the influence of his successor.

The persistent exercise of influence in an academic community, which is usually attributable to the personal qualities and accomplishments of those exercising it, tends to become institutionalized and transformed into socially accepted authority attached to certain positions, which gives the incumbents influence that is no longer dependent on their personal qualities and accomplishments. Three instances of such institu-

---

[30] When number of levels is added to the independent variables in Table 7.3 in a regression analysis of faculty's appointment authority, the beta weight is negative $(-.12; r=.17)$, and though very small, it is twice its standard error. A five-point score of dean's appointment authority, in contrast, exhibits a substantial positive correlation with number of levels (.39), and a considerable positive beta weight of levels remains (.32, more than three standard errors) in a regression analysis of the dean's authority that controls its only discovered antecedents—South $(b^*=.21^*; r=.39)$, private secular control $(-.13; r=-.28)$, and mean student aptitudes $(-.23^*; r=-.36)$.

[31] Blau and Schoenherr, *op. cit.*, pp. 128–129.

tionalization of authority have been revealed by the analysis in this chapter. First, the academic status of the faculty in a university or college enhances its authority as a collective body, thereby strengthening the influence of individual members independent of their own status. Second, an institutionalized faculty government limits bureaucratic authority over faculty members and contributes to their authority. And now we see, third, that presidential leadership of long duration expands the institutional authority of the presidency and thus the influence of the next incumbent of this office. Moreover, such consolidation of presidential authority seems to inhibit the development of democratic institutions of faculty government, as suggested by the negative correlation between the length of tenure of the previous president and the proportion of elected faculty members on the most important committee (−.36).[32]

The theoretical assumption that a long period of presidential leadership leaves a residue of generalized authority in the institution of the presidency that enlarges the power of the next president receives some additional support from the finding, shown in row 4 of Table 7.5, that his predecessor's length of tenure also increases the current president's authority to reallocate funds.[33] To be sure, an alternative interpretation of both findings would be that some academic institutions consistently appoint better leaders to the presidency, who remain in office longer, and who have more power. But this alternative assumption implies that the length of tenure of the *current* president is positively related to his power, whereas his own tenure is appreciably correlated neither with his influence over appointments, as noted, nor with his control of funds (.06). This does not prove the assumption that the power of successful presidents becomes entrenched in the office and endures as authority beyond their retirement, of course, but it lends it some probability. The findings have another implication as well. The fact that the last president has been in office for a long period in an academic institution indicates that the rate of presidential succession has been low. Gouldner's case study of a gypsum plant suggests that a high rate of succession of top execu-

[32] The current president's length of tenure exhibits virtually no correlation with the proportion of elected members on the most important faculty committee (−.03).
[33] The correlation between the two measures of the president's authority—over appointments and over unexpended funds—is .35, which is not so large as to make it highly likely that the same antecedents are associated with both. Adding president's authority over funds to the independent variables in Table 7.4 hardly reduces the beta weights. They are: size, −.02; levels, −.22*, last president's tenure, .29**; authority over funds, .21*.

Table 7.5   President's Authority over Funds

	Beta Weight	Simple Correlation
1. West	−.25*	−.28
2. Religious	−.35**	−.20
3. Size	−.30**	−.22
4. Last president's tenure	.19*	.26

$R^2 = .26$ ($\hat{R}^2 = .23$); $n = 112$

* More than twice its standard error.
** More than three times its standard error.

tives fosters bureaucratic centralization. [34] The data on universities and colleges point to the opposite conclusion. In academic institutions, a *low* rate of succession of top administrators appears to promote centralization of authority in the office of the president and to curb the development of democratic procedures of faculty government.

The presidents of large academic institutions have less control over the distribution of funds than those of small ones, as can be seen in row 3 of Table 7.5. In this case, the influence of size is direct and considerable, and multiple levels exert no influence.[35] The reason that a multilevel hierarchy reduces the president's authority in faculty recruitment but not in financial matters may be that recruitment decisions require closer contact with the faculty than budgetary decisions, and multiple levels restrict the president's contact with the faculty. The negative effect of institutional size on centralized authority over unexpended funds is one further indication of the pressure to delegate responsibilities generated by a large scale of operations and the consequent heavy load of administrative work.

Although religious academic institutions are on the average smaller than secular ones, the authority of their presidents to reallocate funds is more limited (see row 2 in Table 7.5). How can the finding that the presidents of denominational institutions have less financial authority than other academic presidents be reconciled with the earlier finding (in Table 7.3) that the faculties in religious institutions have less authority than secular faculties? It is hardly plausible to infer that authority over

[34] Alvin W. Gouldner, *Patterns of Industrial Bureaucracy*, Glencoe, Ill.: Free Press, 1954, pp. 59–101, esp. pp. 69, 96–99.
[35] If number of levels is added to the independent variables in Table 7.5, its beta weight (−.15; $r = -.23$) is less, whereas that of size (−.24) remains more, than two standard errors.

financial affairs, which is generally more centralized than authority in other matters, is more decentralized in the otherwise more centralized religious than in secular academic institutions. Aside from the president and a few top administrators, the only persons who have substantial control over financial resources are the trustees. In two-fifths of the universities and colleges sampled, unexpended funds are returned to the general institutional funds, which means that they are again at the disposal of the board of trustees, particularly if board members rather than the president play the dominant role in budgetary decisions. The reason that presidents of religious institutions have little discretion over funds is in all likelihood that financial responsibilities are more centralized in the board of trustees, not that they are more decentralized to deans and chairmen, just as other responsibilities are more centralized in religious than in secular institutions.

Finally, row 1 in Table 7.5 indicates that the presidents of institutions of higher education in the West exercise less discretion in the distribution of funds than do academic presidents in other parts of the United States. One might think that the reason is that many academic institutions in the West, notably in California, are part of larger systems of numerous universities and colleges and that the financial authority of the institution's president is limited by that of the chancellor or president of the system. But this is not the reason; controlling whether an institution is part of a larger system does not alter the picture.[36] Inasmuch as appointment authority is more decentralized to the faculty in the West than elsewhere (see Table 7.3), the lesser discretion over funds of academic presidents in the West probably also implies more decentralization of financial responsibilities in the academic institutions of that region. But why Western universities and colleges should be more decentralized than those in the rest of the country is not clear, unless there is some validity to the speculation that the democratic spirit of the Western frontier is still alive.

ACADEMIC STANDING AND DECENTRALIZATION

American universities and colleges differ substantially in their authority structure. Some of them conform to the bureaucratic model, with author-

---

[36] If the dummy variable, whether the institution is part of a system of universities or colleges, is added to the variables in Table 7.5, it has virtually no relationship with president's authority over funds ($b^* = .04$; $r = .07$); the effect of location in the West remains essentially the same ($b^* = -.26$), and so does that of the other independent variables.

ity over academic affairs being centralized at the top, while others conform to the professional model, with much authority over faculty appointments as well as educational matters being decentralized to the faculty. Most of these differences result from conditions that contradict the bureaucratic stereotype. To be sure, not all do—after all, stereotypes are not entirely devoid of any connection with reality. The findings that a large administrative apparatus and the extensive use of impersonal computers in administration foster bureaucratic centralization are in agreement with the prevailing conception of bureaucracy. But in other respects, the distribution of responsibilities for academic decisions conflicts with the usual notions of bureaucratic centralization. The impact of institutional size is a good example.

Large universities are often criticized for being bureaucratic and dominated by administrators, whereas small colleges are idealized as communities of scholars that democratically govern themselves. Contrary to this stereotype, however, large universities not only have a relatively small administrative apparatus, as the analysis in Chapter Three showed, but academic authority is also much more decentralized in them than in small colleges. Only in one respect can large academic institutions be considered to be more bureaucratic than small ones: their hierarchical structure consists of more levels. On the other hand, the large size of an academic institution exerts more pronounced and pervasive effects on decentralization of authority than anything else. Other conditions affecting the distribution of academic authority violate the bureaucratic stereotype too. A multilevel hierarchy, a large clerical apparatus, and a high rate of succession of top administrators are generally thought of as bureaucratic attributes, yet all three promote decentralization of authority in institutions of higher education. What appears to encourage centralized control in academic institutions is a paternalistic orientation of the trustees and top administrators, not an impersonal bureaucratic orientation, as illustrated by the greater centralization in religious colleges and in those that appoint their own graduates to the faculty. And what strengthens the faculty's authority seems to be not so much mere acceptance of professional norms as its bargaining power and an institutionalized faculty government.

In the study of government agencies, two theoretical assumptions were introduced to explain what conditions foster decentralization of authority to middle managers there.[37] The first is that certain conditions put pressure on top management to delegate responsibilities. The most important of these is the large volume of administrative responsibilities in

[37] Blau and Schoenherr, *op cit.,* pp. 131–137.

large organizations, and two others are multilevel hierarchies that remove top management from operations and a small administrative staff that limits the staff assistance available to top management. The same three conditions promote decentralization in academic institutions—large size, multiple levels, and a relatively small staff of administrators. On the other hand, a small *clerical* staff has the opposite effect, since insufficient clerical personnel overloads faculty members with administrative detail while an insufficient staff of administrators overloads the president.

The second assumption does not fare as well as the first when applied to the data on universities and colleges. It is that conditions that increase the reliability of operations and thus reduce the risk management incurs in delegating authority encourage its delegation. This principle helped explain the paradoxical finding that government agencies tend to be more decentralized the more bureaucratized their procedures, especially their personnel procedures, are, because formalized and standardized procedures make operations more reliable. It also served to explain the greater decentralization in these agencies resulting from the use of computers to automate operations and from superior qualifications of employees, both of which also make operations more reliable. In academic institutions, however, bureaucratic procedures, such as faculty regulations, standardized salary raises, and mechanical teaching aids, do not affect the distribution of authority, and the administrative use of computers increases centralization, not decentralization. Although superior qualifications of the faculty do increase decentralization, this is best explained in other terms than reliability of performance and risk education, particularly since the other evidence indicates that the principle that decentralization depends on conditions that regulate performance and make it more reliable does not apply to academic institutions.[38]

The most important conditions for the decentralization of authority in an academic institution are its size and the academic standing of its faculty as well as its own. The pronounced effect of the large size of a university on decentralization supports the inference derived from the study of government bureaus that the heavy load of administrative responsibilities in large organizations creates pressures to decentralize decisions. Numerous factors affecting the academic standing of its faculty

[38] Indeed, we might claim to have somewhat anticipated this by stating (*ibid.*, p. 137) "that the emphasis on reliable performance and the low tolerance for variability... make very large organizations not ideally suited for professional and scientific work, at least, not unless special arrangements succeed in combining tolerance for ambiguity with effective administration. This is, of course, the problem faced by large universities."

and indicative of that of the institution itself also promote decentralization of authority. The reputation of a university or college, its affluence, the salaries it pays to recruit faculty, the formal qualifications of its faculty, the emphasis on research rather than on teaching, and the faculty's research productivity—all these are associated with more decentralized control of academic affairs. Since the academic qualifications and performance of the faculty play a crucial role in this syndrome, one might be tempted to claim that these findings confirm the assumption that reliable performance contributes to decentralization. This would be sophistry, however, since it would distort the original meaning of the phrase "reliable performance," which was intended to refer to faithful performance of duties in accordance with established procedures. Scholarly achievements and reputations do not rest on such faithful adherence to established practice but on endeavors to depart from it in search for new ideas, a search that must be carried out in a variety of directions by many men and women for a very few of them to succeed in making significant contributions to knowledge.

Not the reliable performance of duties but the power acquired in social exchange by faculties who have superior academic standing is the source of their authority within their university or college. Scientists and scholars who command wide respect among colleagues in their discipline achieve influential positions outside their own academic institution, are sought after by other institutons, and are needed by their own, since its academic standing depends on them. Research has more prestige than teaching in academic circles, and research faculties consequently have more influence in their institution than teaching faculties. To be sure, academic standards, like professional standards generally, demand faculty autonomy and self-regulation, but these demands are not met unless faculties have the academic standing and bargaining power to implement them, as implied by the centralized control the data reveal to be exercised over faculties who lack such standing and power. Similarly, the need for freedom from bureaucratic restraints to carry out good academic work does not suffice to bring about decentralization without sufficient faculty strength to command authority, inasmuch as this need is unquestionably also experienced by faculties who are subject to centralized bureaucratic control. High academic standing earns faculty members alternative opportunities outside their institution, which empowers them to enforce their demands inside and to realize their collective objectives of self-regulation and freedom from centralized controls. The adverse effect of inbreeding on decentralization illustrates that conditions that restrict alternative opportunities jeopardize these objectives. Whether superior academic prestige rests on solid scholarly contributions or successful deception—impression management, as Goffman calls it[39]—does not affect these considerations.

The influence that accrues to a university faculty with high academic standing becomes institutionalized in the form of faculty authority, which enhances the influence of individual faculty members independent of their personal academic standing. His or her colleagues' academic status therefore affects the influence an individual faculty member has in an academic institution. By the same token, an institutionalized faculty government reduces centralized control and strengthens the authority of the faculty in a university or college. The power a successful president accumulates during a long tenure becomes institutionalized in a complementary manner in greater authority of the presidential office, which strengthens the control of the next president. Another illustration of the significance of institutionalized authority—in this case, the authority legitimated by religious values—is the centralized control that prevails in religious universities and colleges. Power institutionalized in the form of authority endures and becomes independent of the original source of power.

In the major universities, which have renowned faculties, authority over appointments as well as educational matters is largely decentralized to the faculty. Does this mean that the trustees and presidents of major universities have little power and only those of small colleges or second-rate universities exercise much authority? It does imply that academic affairs are much more likely to be dominated by trustees and top administrators in smaller colleges and institutions of low quality than in the best universities. But it does not indicate that the board of trustees and the central administration of major universities are powerless. Control over the allocation of economic resources lies largely in the hands of the board and the central administration. The great financial resources of big universities give those controlling them much power. Short of military force, control over the allocation of economic resources is the ultimate source of power in an institution. Hence the basic power in major universities, too, is exercised by the board of trustees and the central administration, notwithstanding the extensive decentralization of authority over academic affairs to the faculty.

[39] Erving Goffman, *The Presentation of Self in Everyday Life*, Garden City, N.Y.: Doubleday Anchor, 1959, pp. 208–237.

CHAPTER EIGHT

INSTITUTIONAL INNOVATION

The highest academic rewards are earned for scholarly research that is judged to help advance knowledge. The academic standing of institutions of higher education as well as that of individual faculty members depends on their contributions to specialized research and scholarship. A university cannot be among the best unless its faculty members concentrate their efforts on furthering the advancement of knowledge both through their own research and by training future scholars and scientists.

The academic reputations of individuals do not accurately reflect their contributions to the advancement of knowledge, however, because the true judgments about how much a body of research contributed to scientific progress or scholarly developments can be made only after the fact by the next generation or in the next century, and these future judgments often do not validate those contemporaries had made. Human judgments of the future import and relevance of creative academic work on the frontiers of knowledge are necessarily fallible. Academic freedom —the freedom to pursue lines of inquiry that are generally disapproved— protects scientific progress somewhat from our fallible judgments, and so does the apparent—but only apparent—waste of having thousands of persons engaged in research that is widely recognized as inconsequential. For the work that fails to win the approval and recognition of contemporaries may prove to be that of greatest future significance in the realm of creative endeavors to provide new insights.

It is the paradoxical responsibility of a university to find ways to institutionalize creative scholarship and research. Of course, only human beings can have original insights and make contributions to knowledge, and the creative imagination needed for original scholarship cannot be readily harnessed by bureaucratic procedures. Nevertheless, mobilizing scientific and scholarly creativity is a basic challenge confronting a major university, which meets this challenge by instituting conditions that stimulate and facilitate original research and scholarship at the frontiers of knowledge. Of special importance in this respect is the establishment of departments in new academic specialties. Without keeping up with developments in various fields by creating new departments, a university is handicapped in recruiting the best specialists, and it fails to furnish those it has with the colleague environment most conducive for carrying out scientific or scholarly work in the most advanced branches of their disciplines. The establishment of departments in new fields is an institutional innovation through which a university promotes innovative research capable of making original contributions to knowledge. It institutionalizes academic creativity.

SPECIALIZATION

Some characteristics of universities are surrounded by myths that remain alive in the face of contrary evidence. Size is one, specialization another. Universities are always warned about getting too large, since large universities are stultifying places, whereas small academic institutions are intellectually stimulating communities of scholars who democratically govern themselves—though only in this land of academic mythology, not in reality, as we have seen. Similarly, as Berelson sardonically notes, "specialization is always 'undue.' "[1] The assumption is that specialists are narrow technicians, not genuine scholars, who are sages with broad knowledge in many fields. But this is largely the prejudice of the layman, which better describes the dilettante than the modern scholar. A person who has some knowledge in many areas has, with rare exceptions, not much knowledge in any of them. The jack-of-all-trades is the master of none. A high degree of specialization characterizes advanced academic

[1] Bernard Berelson, *Graduate Education in the United States*, New York: McGraw-Hill, 1960, p. 116.

work today not alone in the sciences but even in philosophy, the discipline originally named for its members' love of general wisdom. To be sure, scientists and other scholars are interested in general knowledge in their field, that is, in theories that can explain a variety of particular events, but such general theoretical knowledge in a discipline tends to be highly specialized at the same time. It requires expertness in an academic specialty, not broad wisdom.

The tremendous growth of science during this century in the world generally and in this country particularly, which was alluded to in the first chapter, has been accompanied by increasing specialization in the various disciplines. Many specialized fields today did not exist a century ago. One example is nuclear physics, which has many specialties within it; linguistics is another, which is quite different from the earlier philology; statistics was not a separate discipline, though a few individuals were interested in statistics as early as the seventeenth century; psychology has become a discipline only since the middle of the last century, and sociology is younger still. The development of science is intimately bound up with increasing specialization. As science expands, men and women work in more specialized areas, and their specialized work advances scientific knowledge. For scientific progress to occur, academics must have opportunities to work in specialized fields and incentives to move into them. To furnish these opportunities and incentives, universities must be flexible enough to adapt their existing structure to changing scientific developments and establish departments in new fields, which provide faculty members with occupational positions and with a basis for identifying with new specialized roles. They are now no longer anthropologists with a special interest in linguistics, for instance, but linguists whose distinct role is defined by the formal structure and by their social relations with colleagues and students that are shaped by the structure. The flexibility of universities to make these innovations, in turn, depends on the larger academic system in the society of which individual universities are part.

Ben-David attributes scientific progress in a country to a decentralized system of universities and the consequent competition among independent academic institutions. This conclusion is based on his analysis of the dominant position in the medical sciences Germany achieved in the nineteenth century and the United States did in the twentieth, as well as on developments in other disciplines. He summarizes the trends in medical discoveries since 1800 in these words: "French supremacy in the beginning of the century with Britain a close second gave way to an overwhelming preponderance of German discoveries through the second half of the last century. The American share was rapidly increasing from the 1880's and became the largest by 1910–1919."[2] After rejecting alternative explanations of these developments by showing that in terms of interest in medical research "Britain had most of the advantages over the United States [at the end of the nineteenth century], similar to those possessed by France over Germany at the beginning,"[3] he concludes that "decentralization seems to have been the decisive factor in determining the differences in scientific creativity between the two countries [in either case]."[4]

Since Germany did not become a unified nation until the nineteenth century, there existed 19 independent universities maintained by the various states in Germany proper, and there were additional German-language universities in Switzerland, Austria, and some provinces. "At the same time the French boasted a unified academic system, most of it situated in Paris."[5] Hence German-speaking medical scientists interested in a new specialty, like physiology, could bargain for an appointment in this specialty with numerous universities, whereas no such opportunities existed in France.

> All of this led to a complete transformation of the scientific career in Germany. In spite of the strictures against narrowness and of the continuing lip-service paid to the image of the scientist who works because of devotion, science became a specialized and regularized occupation.[6]

> Academic appointments [in France, by contrast,] were regarded as honors rather than careers, and turning science into an occupation would have seemed something like a sacrilege. A corollary, in this amateur stage of science, was the absence of specialization.[7]

> "Competition" in this paper refers to the general conditions underlying all the processes described above: it is a situation in which no single institution is able to lay down standards for the system of institutions within which people (in this case students and teachers) are relatively free to move from one place to another. Under such circumstances university administrators required neither exceptional boldness nor foresight for continually expanding facilities and training, and for creating new scientific jobs. There was little if any need for fateful individual decisions. Improvements and innovations had to be made from time to time in order to attract famous men or keep them from leaving.[8]

---

[2] Joseph Ben-David, "Scientific Productivity and Academic Organization in Nineteenth Century Medicine," *American Sociological Review* **25** (1960), 830.
[3] *Ibid.*, p. 840.
[4] *Ibid.*, p. 835.
[5] *Ibid.*
[6] *Ibid.*, p. 838.
[7] *Ibid.*, p. 836.
[8] *Ibid.*, p. 840.

The growth of science in the United States during the last century, which has made it the leading nation in science, provides another illustration of Ben-David's thesis that scientific progress depends on the constraints to institutionalize new specialties experienced by independent universities in a decentralized system that strengthens the bargaining power of faculty members. He notes that the academic system in the United States "was far more decentralized than in Germany. There different states competed with each other. In the United States the state universities not only competed among themselves; they also had to compete with the private universities."[9] The bargaining power of professional scientists in this decentralized system often forces bureaucratic administrators to accede to their wishes, for the sake of maintaining the university's academic standing, and to institute innovations that permit more specialized research and further scientific progress. To clarify the underlying social processes, it is necessary to examine the rewards that govern academic pursuits and the crucial intervening factor that connects the decentralized system of independent universities and the rewards for specialized academic work, namely, a flexible departmental structure.

In a trenchant analysis of the battles that often rage over priorities in scientific discoveries, Merton points out that these conflicts have their source in the great significance respect from colleagues for original contributions to knowledge has for scientists. "Recognition for originality becomes socially validated testimony that one has successfully lived up to the most exacting requirements of one's role as a scientist."[10] The most important and distinctive reward in the scientific community is a scientist's reputation among his peers for having made original discoveries that constitute major advances in the field. By sharing his or her discoveries with colleagues, a scientist contributes to their knowledge and earns their respect for his or her valuable contributions in exchange.

This exchange of recognition and prestige in the scientific community for contributing to knowledge in the field is so important for the process of scientific creation, Storer suggests, because new discoveries derive their significance from being meaningful to fellow experts and thus

[9] Joseph Ben-David, "The Universities and the Growth of Science in Germany and the United States," *Minerva* **7** (2) (1968/69), 19.
[10] Robert K. Merton, "Priorities in Scientific Discovery," *American Sociological Review* **22** (1957), 640.

must be validated by the acknowledgment of colleagues that they are valuable.[11] Hagstrom sums up several forms this recognition takes: "An individual establishes his status as a scientist by having his research contributions accepted by a reputable journal; he achieves prestige as a scientist by having his work cited and emulated by others; and he achieves elite status by receiving collective honors."[12] A position in one's specialty at a major university not only is a reward in its own right but also greatly enhances the individual's chances of making the scholarly contributions that bring these other rewards.

The distinctive departmental structure of American universities makes it relatively easy to offer positions to specialists in new fields who work at the frontiers of knowledge, at first within departments and later, as the specialty grows, by establishing a separate department for it. When graduate studies were introduced into American higher education about 100 years ago, the model adopted was presumably that of the German university, but it underwent basic changes as it was transplanted across the Atlantic, as Ben-David shows.[13] The structure of German universities consisted essentially of chairs, to which research institutes were attached, and the full professors occupying the chairs dominated individually their research institutes and collectively the university. The vested interests of these professors, who were a small minority of the academic staff, in maintaining their oligarchy made them resistant to establishing positions in new fields. The departmental structure that developed in American universities is fundamentally different.

Appointments to positions in new specialties are a threat to the existing power structure in German but not in American universities with their departmental organization, where appointing specialists in new fields often strengthens the position of a chairman or dean. Hence the *structural* reason for opposition to new specialties existing in German universities are not present in the United States, though professional jealousies causing such opposition exist, of course, in both countries. "The size of the American department and the presence of a number of professors in it made possible the growth of the department, and within the department . . . the introduction of relatively independent subspecialities,"[14] fostering the emergence of new academic roles and new professional careers. An illustration Ben-David cites is statistics, which

11 Norman W. Storer, *The Social System of Science,* New York: Holt, Rinehart and Winston, 1966, pp. 57–74.
12 Warren O. Hagstrom, *The Scientific Community,* New York: Basic Books, 1965, p. 28.
13 Ben-David, *op. cit.,* pp. 1–35.
14 *Ibid.,* pp. 20–21.

had been more advanced in Europe, most recently in England, but which became a separate discipline first in the United States, because flexible departmental structures facilitated appointing statisticians initially in other departments, enabling them to develop a professional identity and association, and creating eventually separate departments of statistics.[15]

The greater opportunity for professional roles in specialized academic fields to crystallize in the United States "is intimately connected with mobility of American scientists [*sic*], which is in its turn the most important element in the adaptiveness of American universities to new possibilities in research and training." Another factor Ben-David considers to be related to the specialized academic roles and the faculty's mobility in the United States is that American "scientists have become less identified with their universities than with their discipline. . . . There exists a *professional community* of scientists or scholars in each field, and one's standing in this community is a more important matter than in other countries. One of the tangible manifestations of the importance of the professional community is the relatively greater importance of professional-scientific associations in the United States than in continental Europe."[16]

The strong orientation of American scientists and scholars to their specialized discipline and its association has much bearing on their relations with colleagues in their own universities and on the developments of new departments. When a new specialty first emerges, most academics interested in it work in different departments, since there are as yet few departments if any in this specialty. These persons have few professional interests in common with others in their department, making them particularly prone to be oriented to fellow specialists outside, which further reduces their integration in their own department. A large department in a major university is likely to have a number of members with divergent specialized scientific concerns. Hagstrom points out that this situation creates conflicts over faculty appointments, student requirements, and teaching curricula, as well as competition for the best students and research assistants. "In rebellious specialties, professors are more likely to take the side of their students against requirements that they take courses in the central areas of the discipline."[17] If a new specialty is represented by several members of a department, notably if they include one or more with outstanding reputations, concessions are frequently made, in order to adapt to these conflicts, by granting the spe-

15 *Ibid.*, pp. 14–18.
16 *Ibid.*, pp. 24–25 (italics in original).
17 Hagstrom, *op. cit.*, p. 201.

cialists autonomy in instructing their own students and possibly by assigning them a quota of faculty appointments. While these adaptations permit "specialists with rather different goals to coexist in harmony in the same departments,"[18] they further deepen the divisions among departmental subgroups.

Once a specialty gets strong enough, it usually seeks greater autonomy in faculty and student recruitment and in degree programs by attempting to set up its own department. Hagstrom suggests that this is unlikely to be successful in weak institutions. "Structural changes are usually made first by leading universities and followed later by others."[19] He notes that a claim to establish a separate department tends to encounter resistance, not only from chairmen and others whose vested interest it may threaten, but also from administrators who are reluctant to make the enduring commitments a new department involves. In the meantime, a compromise may be reached by creating a separate research institute or committee of instruction for the emerging specialty, which gives its members more autonomy than a departmental subgroup has and yet entails less enduring commitments on the part of the university than a new department does. At the University of Chicago, for example, such committees usually start with a small program of specialized courses, which may soon be abandoned or may progress to grant their own degrees and appoint their own faculties, when they generally are accredited as departments. For a new specialty to become institutionalized, it must succeed in establishing its own departments at various academic institutions.

Let us extract from this discussion the main propositions and those implications that can be tested, if only indirectly, with the data on universities and colleges. Progress in science depends on specialized research at the frontiers of a discipline. Scientists are unlikely to concentrate on specialized work unless they can achieve recognition from fellow experts for their discoveries that make original contributions to the specialty. The existence of a reliable network of experts qualified to supply social recognition for original discoveries in a specialty is contingent on the professionalization of the specialty, which means that specialized work is carried out in professional roles that entail occupational careers and not as an avocation of amateurs. Thus the institutionalization of a specialty has a decisive impact on the quality of accomplishments, for professional-

18 *Ibid.*, p. 202.
19 *Ibid.*, p. 220.

ization—whether in baseball or in microbiology—requires that formal positions in institutions provide opportunities for performing the specialized tasks as part of occupational careers.

Flexible departmental structures of universities facilitate the institutionalization of new specialties in several ways, and the chances that flexible internal structures exist are greater in a decentralized academic system with many independent institutions than in either a centralized system (like the French) or one dominated by one or two universities (like the English). The flexibility of departments helps in the initial institutionalization of a new specialty with as yet few practitioners by making it easy and advantageous to offer a single position, for example, to a statistician in a department of agriculture or biology whose members conduct much quantitative research. Such early appointments have repercussions that promote the further institutionalization of specialties. They expand the size of departments, increase their heterogeneity, and precipitate conflicts between faculty members in different specialties. As long as a department has only one member in a specialty, he or she is constrained to seek colleague support and stimulation outside in association with fellow specialists. Even later, when there are several specialists, the heterogeneity of academic interests and conflicts in large departments tend to maintain these cosmopolitan orientations. The orientations to outside colleagues as reference groups in heterogeneous departments are likely to intensify conflicts and strengthen the determination of specialists to try to establish a separate department or, if this fails, to seek an appointment in another university that has a department in their specialty. The mobility of faculty members, which is fostered by their cosmopolitan orientations, in turn keeps the institutional structures flexible, because universities are constrained to find positions for available specialists to replace the faculty members they recurrently lose.

The central significance of structural flexibility and the institutionalization of departments in new fields determined the choice of the measures to be analyzed in the next two sections. The main measure refers to the existence of departments in a selected number of new fields in an academic institution. Two supplementary measures indicate the recent creation of a new and abolishment of an old department, respectively.

Although Ben-David's analysis compares academic *systems* in different countries, inferences can be derived from it concerning the influences of conditions in an academic *institution* on innovation. If centralization inhibits departmental innovation, one would expect that (1) academic institutions that are part of larger systems are less innovative than those that are independent, and (2) decentralization within an academic institution promotes innovation. Ben-David also suggests that (3) the large size of an academic institution and of its departments fosters innovation, and one may infer from his comparison of the old European with the relatively young American universities, which are more flexible, that (4) within the United States too the older academic institutions are less innovative than the newer ones. His emphasis on the significance the prevailing American orientation to fellow specialists outside one's institution has for specialization implies that (5) such a cosmopolitan orientation to outside reference groups increases the likelihood that new departments become established. Both the influence of large size and that of a cosmopolitan orientation on innovation are also implicit in Hagstrom's discussion. Hagstrom also advances the additional hypothesis that (6) leading universities institute structural innovations earlier than academic institutions with lower reputations. An inference derivable from his observation that the conflicts preceding the creation of a new department often unite faculty members with graduate students is that (7) frequent faculty contacts with graduate students characterize emerging specialties.

INSTITUTIONALIZING NEW DISCIPLINES

By establishing departments in new specialties, an academic institution keeps abreast of recent scientific and scholarly developments and institutionalizes the pursuit of new knowledge. To indicate this tendency to institutionalize academic innovation, a list of nine specialties was selected from a larger impressionistic list of new fields on the basis of the criterion that the proportion of academic institutions that had a department in a given field in 1928 was less than half the proportion that had it in 1968. Since the number of institutions has nearly doubled in this period, the large majority of the departments in any specialty defined as new did not exist when faculty members retiring now did their graduate work. The list includes a few applied fields, several outside the natural sciences, and some such as anthropology that have a fairly long history but have only recently been introduced in colleges, in a deliberate attempt not to confine the indicator to disciplines represented only in major universities. The nine new specialties are anthropology, biochemistry, biophysics, journalism, linguistics, microbiology, nursing education, statistics, and urban studies. The measure is the ratio of departments in these fields to other departments in a university or college.[20]

[20] The attempt not to confine the measure to Ph.D.-granting universities was successful. The dummy variable, university status, has a correlation with the ratio of departments in new fields of only .26, and when size is controlled, the beta weight is a mere .06, less than one standard error.

The assumption made in using this index as a dependent variable is that it reflects the continuing tendencies of academic institutions to add departments in new specialties, tendencies that, though measured by past innovations, are expected to be manifest in current innovations as well. This assumption is required to infer from the following analysis the conditions in academic institutions that influence departmental innovation. Some of the main conclusions are corroborated by the other measures, which require no such assumption.

Gellard finds in a study of government finance bureaus that administrative innovations occurred more often if the top executive had been recently appointed than if he was an oldtimer.[21] In universities and colleges the opposite seems to be the case, as indicated in row 8 of Table 8.1. Departmental innovations in an academic institution are more likely if the president is an oldtimer than if he has occupied his position for only a short period. The beta weights show that the president's length of tenure exhibits a stronger direct relationship than any other factor with innovative departments. This difference in findings immediately raises suspicions about the assumption made above, inasmuch as some of the departments in new fields had undoubtedly been established before the current president took office. The long tenure of an academic president might not be the cause but the consequence of innovation, because the vitality of an institution that readily moves into new specialties may encourage the president to remain in office longer. However, the length of tenure of the *previous* president exhibits an independent positive relationship with departmental innovation (see row 6). Since this predecessor of the current president was appointed 20 years ago in the average institution, many if not most of the departments in new disciplines are likely to have been created after he became president, which provides some justification for reverting to the original assumption that innovation is the dependent variable. The finding that the length of tenure of the last and that of the current president have parallel effects on departmental innovation suggests that the underlying factor is the rate of presidential turnover, which implies that a high rate of presidential succession (the inverse of long tenure) discourages departmental innovation. This conclusion still must be reconciled with Gellard's contrary finding. The reason for the difference may be that the innovations he observed in government bureaus and those we are examining in academic institutions are quite different in nature.

Given the importance and authority of the president of a university

---

[21] Jacques Gellard, "Determinants and Consequences of Executive Succession in Government Finance Agencies," M.A. thesis, University of Chicago, 1967.

Table 8.1   Departments in New Fields

	Beta Weight	Simple Correlation
1. Age	−.23**	−.06
2. Size	.28**	.38
3. Revenue spent on books	−.15*	−.22
4. Student aptitudes	.23*	.29
5. Graduate student contacts	.21*	.23
6. Last president's tenure	.25**	.18
7. Percentage of faculty on senate	.28**	.00
8. President's tenure	.38**	.30
9. Centralized initiative	−.23**	−.20
10. Centralized salary influence	−.22*	−.18

$R^2 = .51$ $(\hat{R}^2 = .46)$; $n = 112$

* More than twice its standard error.
** More than three times its standard error.

or college, frequent turnover of presidents constitutes major administrative changes in the institution. Besides, a new academic president tends to make additional administrative changes. He usually reorganizes the team of top administrators under his direction, not only by making new appointments but also by changing the structure of positions, perhaps abolishing the provost and creating a new post of executive vice-president. In short, new top executives are likely to make administrative innovations in academic institutions, just as they do in government bureaus. These administrative changes tend to occupy much of the attention of the new president, and they require adaptations by other administrators, those who have remained in their positions as well as the new ones, and adjustments by the faculty.

Times of great administrative change are not opportune for starting academic innovations and establishing new departments. The preoccupation of the new president and his top administrators with reorganizing the administration probably discourages groups of faculty specialists from proposing a new department, and so does their own need to adjust to the new administration. Moreover, the novice president must adapt to his recently acquired position and responsibilities, making it difficult for him to devote the considerable efforts necessary to decide whether a department in a new specialty should be instituted. After the president has been in office for some time and things have settled down, the time is propitious for initiating innovations in departmental structure. These conjectures—and they are mere conjectures—can help explain why high rates of presidential succession inhibit departmental innovation and why they reduce presidential authority, as findings in Chapter Seven indicated. They suggest that the recurrent administrative changes entailed by high rates of presidential turnover create immediate problems of adjustment that do not leave sufficient time and energy for such long-range concerns as consolidating presidential authority and organizing new academic specialties.

It has been implicitly assumed in this discussion that the creation of departments in new fields tends to occur on the initiative of the faculty to which the president reacts. This assumption corresponds to the hypothesis suggested by Hagstrom's discussion, inferred from Ben-David's analysis, and explicitly stated by Clark that "the more decentralized the decision-making structure, the more innovative the organization," referring to institutions of higher education.[22] Other authors have expressed the opposite opinion. Hutchins, speaking of the faculty, states that "the academic body is likely to be favorable to accepted doctrine and routine performance."[23] Kerr agrees: "In a very real sense, the faculty is the university . . . Yet when change comes it is rarely at the instigation of this group of partners in a collective body."[24]

The data fail to confirm the opinion of these two university presidents of the lack of faculty initiative, at least with respect to innovating departments, and they support the decentralization hypothesis of innovation. Row 9 in Table 8.1 shows that the chances that an academic institution has numerous departments in new fields are less if the initiative to establish new departments is centralized than if it is decentralized to the faculty, as indicated by whose initiative was responsible for the creation of the *last* new department.[25] Although we do not know where the initiative for establishing the various departments in new specialties

---

[22] Terry N. Clark, "Institutionalization of Innovation in Higher Education," *Administrative Science Quarterly* 13 (1968), p. 21.

[23] Robert M. Hutchins, *The Learning Society*, New York: Praeger, 1968, p. 115.

[24] Clark Kerr, *The Uses of the University*, Cambridge: Harvard University Press, 1964, p. 100.

[25] The measure is the level in the academic hierarchy from which the initiative came. In the unweighted sample, it came most frequently from the faculty (44 per cent; together with chairmen, 54 per cent), though the proportion of cases with faculty initiative is lower in the universe, which includes more smaller institutions, where faculty initiative is less prevalent.

came from, the finding does suggest that faculty initiative in proposing new departments increases the likelihood that new specialties have become institutionalized as departments. Still, these data may simply indicate that departmental subgroups are sometimes successful in advocating a separate department for their specialty despite opposition from the rest of the faculty, which would be in agreement with Kerr's view that faculties collectively are prone to resist change. But the data do not support this either. The president or his deputy reports active opposition to the creation of the last new department by chairmen in only 6 and by other faculty bodies in only 13 per cent of the cases (in the unweighted sample). Moreover, two general indicators of decentralization are also positively related to innovation.

The larger the proportion of faculty members on the senate, controlling the institution's size, the greater is the number of innovative departments in the university or college, as revealed by row 7 in Table 8.1. Large-scale participation of the faculty in the institution's governing body apparently increases the likelihood of departmental innovation. In addition, decentralized authority over faculty raises has an independent positive effect on the creation of departments in new specialties. Row 10 shows that the higher the level of the official who has most influence over faculty raises, the smaller is the number of departments in new fields. (In about one-half of the unweighted sample, this official is the chairman —most often—or dean or both rather than a member of the central administration.[26]) There is no indication that the power of chairmen or the wide participation of the faculty in decisions governing the institution inhibits innovative changes in departmental structure. These findings contradict the assumption frequently made that innovations in the institutional structure of a university or college require the intervention of top administrators because the faculty, with vested interests in the status quo, is opposed to such changes. But the findings do not imply that academic faculties selflessly support innovations for the sake of the advancement of knowledge in disregard of their own interests, since departmental innovations often are in the faculty's interest.

The conflicts Hagstrom describes in departments with faculty members in one or more deviant specialties are a source of strain, deplete faculty energies, and make the department a less suitable environment for serious academic work. The separation of the deviant specialists into a new

---

[26] In the universe, the proportion of institutions in which chairmen or deans influence faculty raises most is less than one-half, since this influence is less decentralized in small institutions, which are underrepresented in the unweighted sample.

department, possibly together with similar specialists from other departments, alleviates these problems and improves social integration in the
old department, or departments, as well as in the new. The chairman of
the old department can command more authority in the absence of opposition from the members of the new specialty who have little respect for
what they consider an old-fashioned approach. The other members of
the old department can perform their academic responsibilities without
having continually to dispute how this work should be performed with
colleagues who apply the standards of a different specialty. These advantages for the faculty and chairmen directly concerned may account for
the greater likelihood of departments in pioneering fields to be instituted
if faculty participates widely in decision making and authority is decentralized. The specialists in the new field are particularly interested in
founding their own department, and they are undoubtedly the ones who
often take the initiative to have it established. The budgetary commitments required by new departments create problems for administrators
who are responsible for the budget, which may be another reason why
administrative centralization decreases the likelihood of new departments
being formed. The conclusion implied by the findings on decentralization that faculty interests promote the development of more specialized
departments supports the assumption made in Chapter Three that the
inherent advantages of specialization generate a progressive division of
labor even when it does not routinize jobs and effect economies in which
management is interested.

Two inferences were derived from Ben-David's decentralization-
innovation hypothesis: (1) academic institutions that are part of a system of universities or colleges are less innovative than independent
institutions; and (2) the decentralization of authority within an institution promotes innovation. The research results just reported corroborate
the second inference. The principle that decentralization is important
for academic innovation, which Ben-David derives from analyzing the
external system among universities in a country, applies to the internal
structure within academic institutions. The first inference is negated by
the data, however. The fact that a university or college is part of a
larger system exhibits a slight *positive* correlation with departments in
new fields (.20), which becomes inconsequential but remains positive if
size is controlled.[27] Of course, American universities and colleges that
are part of systems must compete with others in the country for fac-

---

[27] The beta weight of the dummy variable, being part of a larger system, with size
controlled, is .12, which is less than two standard errors.

ulty and students, but the restraints the system puts on their competition with one another do not seem to inhibit institutional academic innovation.

The sheer probability that a sufficient number of faculty members are interested in a new specialty to mobilize enough strength to succeed in forming their own department is greater in large than in small academic institutions. Accordingly, both Hagstrom and Ben-David hypothesize that large size fosters departmental innovation. The data in row 2 of Table 8.1 confirm this hypothesis. But the discussions of these authors suggest specifically that the large size of departments, rather than that of the total academic institution, leads to specialization and heterogeneity within them, and sometimes ultimately to one subgroup's breaking off, perhaps combining with faculty members in other departments, and creating a department of their own. If the average size of an institution's departments is substituted for its total size in a regression analysis with otherwise the same variables as those in Table 8.1, the results indicate that institutions with large departments are more likely than those with small departments to establish additional ones in new fields. The effect of average departmental size on innovation ($b^* = .26$; $r = .30$) is not much less than that of total institutional size.[28] There is good reason to consider the size of the entire academic institution more important for departmental innovation, however, aside from the possibly spurious statistical result that it has a slightly more pronounced relationship with innovation than mean departmental size. New departments are often composed of faculty members who had been in two or more different departments,[29] and total institutional size (number of faculty members) takes into account the probability that a considerable number with interests in the same new specialty are found either in one or in several departments of an academic institution.

Students as well as faculty members appear to play a role in the development of institutional specialization. Hagstrom's discussion of the con-

[28] This substitution does not change any of the other beta weights by more than .03, and all remain more than twice their standard error. The same is true for the rest of the beta weights if both total size and average department size are included in the regression equation, but the influence on innovative departments is split between these two variables, and neither beta weight is twice its standard error, with that of total size being slightly larger (.18) than that of average departmental size (.15).

[29] See Hagstrom, *op. cit.*, p. 224.

flicts in heterogeneous departments, in which specialists in emerging disciplines often side with their graduate students in disputes about requirements with colleagues, implies that faculty relations with graduate students are closer in emerging than in other disciplines, as noted in the last hypothesis outlined above. Row 5 in Table 8.1 reveals that faculty contacts with graduate students are indeed positively related to the existence of a number of departments in new disciplines. In this case, it is plausible to consider departments in new specialties the cause, not the effect. Faculty members in highly specialized new fields may be more inclined than others to have extensive contacts with graduate students. This conclusion accords with the surmise in Chapter Six that a high degree of specialization prompts faculty members, because there are few with the same specialized interests on the faculty, to treat graduate students as colleagues and to interact with them frequently, which was suggested to explain why number of departments, with institutional size constant, increases faculty contacts with graduate students (Table 6.3). A related finding, shown in row 4 of Table 8.1, is that high aptitudes of incoming students, which are probably also indicative of high aptitudes of advanced students, have an independent positive relationship with departments in new fields. A possible interpretation, which again considers innovative departments the cause, is that institutions of higher education that pioneer in new disciplines attract the brightest students. The two findings together, however, can also be interpreted in terms of the original assumption that departmental innovation is the dependent variable.

Frequent contacts with bright advanced students both require and motivate the faculty to keep abreast of new developments and become acquainted with the latest specialties emerging in the discipline. As a result, some faculty members may themselves acquire an interest in a new specialty, and others are likely to become aware of the need to hire specialists in new areas of the discipline lest the department become obsolete. These processes stimulated by highly able students and extensive contacts with graduate students may ultimately lead to the establishment of departments in new specialties. Academic institutions in which frequent contacts with bright advanced students put pressure on the faculty to keep up with developments in their disciplines probably have a tendency to pioneer in new fields of scientific and scholarly endeavor.

A leading university with a secure reputation should find it easier to venture into new fields than one that has low academic standing. This is one of Hagstrom's hypotheses (numbered 6 in the foregoing list); it is also hypothesized by Clark ("leading graduate schools . . . are very open to experimentation and innovations that contribute to the goals of advancing research or teaching . . ."[30]) ; and it agrees with the impression many of us in academic life have. But this impression is wrong, shaped by our experience in a few selected institutions, and perhaps further distorted by wishful thinking and academic snobbery. In any case, the data negate the hypothesis. An academic institution's reputation is essentially unrelated to its departments in pioneering fields ($r = .05$) ; so are the qualifications of its faculty ($.09$) ; and the association between the proportion of outstanding and the ratio of pioneering departments is spurious and becomes trivial if size is controlled.[31] Once we have learned that, we may well remember how conservative many famous universities are— notable examples being Harvard, Oxford, Cambridge, and the Sorbonne.

These are not only famous universities but also old ones with an academic tradition of several centuries, which suggests that the weight of tradition in older universities dampens the innovative spirit. The hypothesis that older academic institutions are less inclined than younger ones to create innovative departments (number 4 in the foregoing list) has been inferred as well from Ben-David's contrast between universities in Europe, which are older and less innovative, and those in the United States, which are newer and more likely to move into new academic specialties. It is noted by Clark too: "Very new institutions are often the most aggressively innovative."[32] The negative beta weight in the top row of Table 8.1 confirms this hypothesis.

The traditionalism of older academic institutions apparently inhibits the tendency to pioneer by establishing departments in novel specialties (though various conditions in older institutions counteract this effect and conceal it in the zero-order correlation). The assumption that academic traditionalism is the reason that an institution's age discourages instituting departments in new fields can be tested by examining the influence on innovative departments of the proportion of revenue spent on books for the library, which has been previously considered an indication of an institution's academic traditionalism (see the discussions of Tables 6.1 and 2.1). Row 3 in Table 8.1 shows that the share of an institution's financial resources spent on books exhibits a small inverse relationship with innovative departments, independent of other condi-

---

30 Clark, *op. cit.*, p. 17.
31 The correlation between the proportion of departments rated by Cartter as among the top 20 in the field and the ratio of departments in new disciplines is .26, and the beta weight, with size controlled, is .07, less than two standard errors. The correlation between faculty research productivity and the ratio of innovative departments is .30, and the beta weight (.12) is again less than two standard errors if size is controlled.
32 Clark, *op. cit.*, p. 18.

tions, which supports the assumption. Research in most traditional academic disciplines depends on extensive libraries more than research in many new specialties does, which undoubtedly accounts in part for the finding. But the independent negative effects of this indicator of traditionalism and of age also suggest that a strong academic tradition in a university or college discourages the institutional innovations that are important for the progress of science and scholarship.

How long ago a university or college was founded affects its present departmental structure. Stinchcombe observes that the historical period in which an industry originated exerts a similar influence on its structure and that of the firms composing it. "For economic organizations . . . , structural characteristics of a type of organization tend to persist, and consequently there is a strong correlation between the age at which industries were developed and their structure at the present time."[33] This does not mean that institutions never change, only that the constraints of the existing institutional structure limit the changes that occur. As Stinchcombe notes, "organizational types generally originate rapidly in a relatively short historical period, to grow and change slowly after that period."[34] Even if growth is not slow, change is. The ossification of institutional structure that sets in with increasing age is especially dangerous in academia, because scientific progress is retarded unless universities recurrently modify their structure and institutionalize new fields of endeavor.

CREATING AND ABOLISHING DEPARTMENTS

A flexible departmental structure is of great significance for academic institutions. It enables universities to pioneer in the arts and sciences by institutionalizing new specialties; it is required for colleges to keep up with these developments; and it mitigates the dead hand of tradition and the power of vested interests that tend to evolve in institutional structures and deflect academic pursuits from their true course. Jencks and Riesman comment on the proposal sometimes made that departments should be abolished by stating that such formal subgroups are necessary in a large academic institution, though at any moment a reorganization would be advantageous, "simply because the new units would be less hallowed by tradition. . . . Abolishing old departments and establishing

[33] Arthur L. Stinchcombe, "Social Structure and Organizations," in James March, *Handbook of Organizations*, Chicago, Rand McNally, 1965, p. 159.
[34] *Ibid.*, p. 168.

new ones must, therefore, be a continuing process, like Jefferson's revolution every twenty years."[35]

The first measure of the flexibility of an academic institution to be analyzed in this section is how recently (in which year) the last new department was established. American universities and colleges generally have flexible departmental structures. In the average institution, the last department was created only a little more than two years before 1968, the year when administrators were interviewed. The standard deviation is 2.2 years, which implies that in five-sixths of all four-year institutions of higher education at least one new department was formed between the fall of 1963 and the spring of 1968. Its limited range means this variable is not a sensitive indicator of innovation, which may be the reason why less of its variation can be accounted for than that of the dependent variable just analyzed. The second indicator of flexibility is whether any department (or departmental major) has been abolished in the five years preceding the interview, which did occur in 53 per cent of the academic institutions. Since this is a dichotomous factor, no regression analysis of it is presented, but the antecedent conditions exhibiting substantial correlations with it are noted. These two variables are essentially uncorrelated (−.01), and the ratio of departments in new fields exhibits little correlation with either the first (.13) or the second (.10). The three can be considered independent measures of departmental flexibility. The assumption made in order to treat the ratio of departments in new fields as a dependent variable—that earlier innovative tendencies are indicative of later ones—is not necessary with respect to the two variables now under investigation, since the creation and abolishment of departments actually took place quite recently in the great majority of institutions.

The larger an academic institution is, the higher is the rate of formation of new departments. Row 1 in Table 8.2 indicates that large academic institutions have established a new department more recently than small ones, which implies that the largest universities tend to create new departments practically every year. This parallels the earlier finding that large academic institutions have more departments in new fields than do small institutions. The larger the number of faculty members in an institution, the greater are the chances that subgroups with common academic interests will emerge, perhaps starting by teaching some interdisciplinary courses or engaging in joint research projects. Most of these subgroups do not develop beyond this stage. But the larger number of such subgroups

---

[35] Christopher Jencks and David Riesman, *The Academic Revolution*, Garden City, N.Y.: Doubleday Anchor, 1969, p. 525.

in large universities increases the probability that some of them will grow and endure, and that a few of them will ultimately seek to form their own department, whether in one of the newest specialties or in an older discipline that previously had no separate department. The theoretical generalization discussed in Chapter Three that large size *generates* structural differentiation, which was inferred from the correlation of size with number of departments, as well as with number of other subunits, receives support from the finding that large size actually promotes the *creation* of new departments.

Some academic institutions have schedules that stipulate regular salary increments for faculty members, whereas in others salary raises are not standardized but based on recommendations. A schedule of standardized salary increments enhances the likelihood that new departments will be frequently established, as row 2 in Table 8.2 shows. Clues for interpreting this finding are provided in a study by Glaser of scientists in research organizations, about one-half of whom worked under a system in which they were regularly considered for advancement, while the other half had to be specially recommended by the supervisor for promotion.[36] Glaser found that scientists who had to be recommended for advancements were more likely than those under the standardized system to state that they frequently observed cases of two colleagues with equal competence and ability who were in different salary grades. In accordance with these judgments of undeserved advancements, those who had to be recommended were more dissatisfied with the promotion system; the juniors who had not yet received professional recognition were also more dissatisfied with chances for advancements, while the seniors with professional recognition were no more satisfied with promotion chances under the recommendation than under the standardized system. In short, advancements based on recommendations are often perceived, rightly or wrongly, as unfair, engender criticism of the system, and make scientists with lower reputations more discontent with opportunities without making scientists with higher reputations more content. The implication is that standardized salary raises remove one source of distrust, envy, and competition among faculty members, which enhances the likelihood that those with common academic interests cooperate and sometimes join in endeavors to set up new departments.

Conditions within the academic institution may facilitate cooperation among faculty subgroups who share scholarly interests, but the impetus for changing the departmental structure tends to come from outside.

[36] Barney G. Glaser, *Organizational Scientists*, New York: Bobbs-Merrill, 1964, pp. 31–40.

Table 8.2   Recency of Creation of Last Department

	Beta Weight	Simple Correlation
1. Size (log)	.29*	.29
2. Standardized salaries	.25**	.24
3. Local allegiance	−.23*	−.30
4. Percentage of faculty on senate	.35**	.02
5. Centralized salary influence	−.35**	−.36

$R^2 = .34$ $(\hat{R}^2 = .31)$; $n = 102$

* More than twice its standard error.
** More than three times its standard error.

Faculty members primarily oriented to their own university or college become enmeshed in its institutional structure and are unlikely to be active proponents of modifications in that structure. A cosmopolitan orientation to the discipline outside keeps faculty members informed about recent developments and provides a stimulus for altering departmental arrangements in accordance with these developments. The discussions of both Ben-David and Hagstrom suggest the hypothesis (number 5 in the list presented earlier) that a cosmopolitan orientation encourages and local allegiance to one's own institution discourages departmental innovation. Row 3 in Table 8.2 indicates that a high proportion of faculty members with strong allegiance to their local institution does indeed make the creation of new departments less frequent. Since superior faculty qualifications reduce local allegiance (see Tables 5.3 and 5.5), they would be expected to exhibit a corresponding positive relationship with departmental innovation, but this is not the case. The correlation between faculty qualifications and how recently the last department was established is trivial (.04).[37] Though the leadership of a scientist or scholar of renown may greatly improve the chances that a new department will be set up,[38] the formal qualifications of faculty members in general are apparently not what stimulates their interest in

[37] Faculty qualifications, if added to the independent variables in Table 8.2, have a beta weight of −.16; if added to the independent variables in Table 8.1, the beta weight is −.15 $(r = .09)$. Both beta weights are less than two standard errors, though the one with recency of last new departments is close to meeting this criterion (within .03), which may signify that not fully trained, probably younger faculty members have been most active in recent departmental innovations. If local allegiance is added to Table 8.1, the beta weight is .14 $(r = .12)$, less than two standard errors.
[38] Hagstrom stresses the importance of such leadership; *op. cit.*, pp. 216–219.

new departmental arrangements.[39] What does is their involvement with outside reference groups in their disciplines and their complementary lack of involvement with the existing institutional structure.

The previous conclusion that decentralization of authority within a university or college promotes departmental innovation is confirmed by the results obtained with the independent measure of such innovation now under consideration, as the last two rows in Table 8.2 disclose. The wider the participation of faculty members on the academic senate, which is indicative of institutionalized faculty authority, the more likely it is that a new department has come into existence within the last year or two. (This influence is concealed in the simple correlation and becomes apparent only when size is controlled.) In addition, centralization of influence over faculty raises exerts an independent effect decreasing the rate at which new departments are created. Faculty members have a greater interest in and awareness of new academic developments than administrators, and they are most affected by the intradepartmental conflicts the divergent orientations of different specialists engender. The interests of faculty members in new specialties and in reestablishing departmental integration by formally separating specialists who have little in common apparently override any vested interests they have in the existing institutional structure. The more decentralized authority is to the faculty, therefore, the more frequently do new departments become established.

The abolishment of departments that have become obsolete probably furnishes a more severe test of the flexibility of the institutional structure than does the creation of new ones, because the elimination of departments directly conflicts with vested interests. Unfortunately, the crude measure available—simply whether any department has been eliminated in the past five years—is not sensitive enough to discern many conditions that affect this aspect of flexibility. It is worth noting, however, that the size of an academic institution is unrelated to the likelihood that departments will be abolished $(r = -.04)$. The greater flexibility exhibited by large institutions in creating new departments is not accompanied by

---

[39] This finding answers a question raised in Chapter Four. The interpretation was suggested there that the effect of number of departments on faculty qualifications, with size and salaries constant (Table 4.1), implies that specialized academic work attracts qualified faculty, because they prefer it, and enables an institution to recruit better faculty than its salaries would otherwise make possible. But it was noted that an alternative interpretation would be that better qualified faculties encourage the development of new specialized departments. The findings that faculty qualifications are not positively related to either of two measures of the creation of new departments negates the alternative interpretation and thus supports the original one.

greater flexibility in abolishing old ones, but neither do the innovative tendencies of large universities occur at the expense of maintaining obsolete departments in disproportionate numbers. Only two conditions that affect the elimination of old departments could be discovered. Southern academic institutions are less inclined than those in the rest of the country to abolish departments $(r = -.34)$. One might interpret this in terms of the greater conservatism and traditionalism of the South, were it not for the findings that Southern institutions are not appreciably less likely than others to have created departments in new fields $(-.09)$ or very recently $(-.09)$. The more centralized authority over the expenditure of funds is in the hands of the president, the less likely it is that old departments have been recently abolished $(r = -.28)$, and this negative influence of centralization on departmental elimination is independent of that of Southern location.[40]

The theorem that decentralization in an academic institution promotes structural flexibility is dramatically supported by the last finding. The innovation of departments in new specialties and the creation of new departments generally serve the interest of some faculty members in an institution, though they may hurt the vested interests of others. The strong interests of some faculty members to see the new department established are likely to outweigh the weaker interests of others to prevent its establishment, particularly since the others have reason to support the proponents of the new department in exchange for future support when they themselves may need it for their proposal to change departmental arrangements or for some other proposal of theirs.[41] But there are few faculty members who have a strong interest in abolishing a department, and several who have a strong interest in opposing its abolition. The intervention of a strong president is therefore generally held to be necessary to eliminate obsolete or weak departments. The finding that centralized presidential authority decreases the chances that departments will be abolished contradicts this notion and corroborates once more the principle that structural flexibility depends on decentralization.

[40] The dummy variable, South, and presidential authority over unexpended funds are hardly correlated (.06). If a regression analysis of the dummy variable, departmental elimination, on both these independent variables is performed (ignoring for the moment the procedural decision not to use dummy dependent variables in regression), the beta weight of Southern location is $-.32$ and that of centralized authority over funds is $-.26$, both being more than three standard errors.

[41] On the significance of such political exchanges for decision making in collective bodies, see James S. Coleman, "Foundations for a Theory of Collective Decisions," *American Journal of Sociology* **71** (1966), 615–627; and "Collective Decisions," in Herman Turk and Richard L. Simpson, *Institutions and Social Exchange*, Indianapolis: Bobbs-Merrill, 1971, pp. 272–286.

Let us briefly list those results of the preceding section that were replicated by the analysis in this section, which did not require the somewhat tenuous assumption that the past innovative tendencies of academic institutions are indicative of their current ones. The finding that institutional innovation in the form of establishing new departments is more prevalent in large than in small academic institutions has been confirmed. The conclusion that academic traditionalism inhibits innovation has not been. But an institution's age is without question a condition antecedent to the formation of departments in new fields, whenever this may have occurred, validating the assumption that such innovation is the dependent variable. The difference in findings suggests that an academic tradition of long standing discourages only the creation of departments in pioneering specialties—"newfangled ideas"—but not that in other disciplines. The conclusions that high presidential turnover inhibits and frequent faculty contacts with bright graduate students stimulate the establishment of new departments have not been confirmed and must consequently be considered tentative. Also tentative are the findings that standardized salary raises encourage and strong commitments to the local institution discourage the creation of new departments, which have been obtained only with the second measure and not with the first. The proposition that has received the firmest support is that decentralization promotes the structural flexibiliy of academic institutions on which institutional innovation and ultimately the progress of science depend.

DILEMMAS OF SCIENTIFIC ADVANCEMENT

The advancement of human knowledge entails distinctive dilemmas. But on closer inspection some of these are found to be not entirely dissimilar to dilemmas encountered in other areas of social life. This is the case for the dilemma underlying the topic of this chapter, the university's responsibility for institutionalizing scholarly creativity and scientific progress. To institutionalize as yet unforseeable future developments, which seems to be a contradiction in terms, is not the unique problem of academic institutions. It is precisely the problem democratic institutions are designed to solve. Social systems contain the seeds of their own destruction, to paraphrase Marx, and democracy has the purpose of forestalling the revolutions that would otherwise bring about the needed transformations by institutionalizing procedures through which the members of society can continually destroy and recreate their institutions in as yet unanticipated ways. The dilemma comes to the fore when people committed to democratic institutions are confronted by demagogues bent on destroying democracy, compelling them to choose between living under this threat and abrogating democratic procedures to avert it. An analogy in academic institutions occurs when commitments to scholarship and the freedom to pursue it are tested by secret military research; faculties then must choose between tolerating such misuse of the university or suppressing their colleagues' academic freedom to prevent it.

By instituting positions and departments in new specialties at the frontier of knowledge, universities create the institutional conditions that foster creative research and help advance knowledge. One important condition for the development of pioneering specialties in a university is large size. A large number of scientists and scholars in diverse disciplines is a fertile soil for social contacts and exchanges of ideas that stimulate fresh ideas, and it increases the chances that most find congenial colleagues with common academic interests. Some of the subgroups that form eventually become departments in new specialties. The large size of a university does not merely increase the *number* of departments in new specialties, which would simply reflect the greater probability that among many persons there are a few with a given interest, but also their *ratio* to old departments, which probably reflects the additional influence of communication among persons with common interests in an emerging specialty. Moreover, the large size of an academic institution promotes decentralization of authority to the faculty, and both large size itself and the decentralization to which it gives rise encourage the institutionalization of new specialties. For new specialties are more likely to evolve and to attain departmental status in academic institutions in which faculties have much authority and autonomy than in those in which authority is centralized in the hands of administrators.

Faculty autonomy poses dilemmas, however, for the academic institution and for individuals, as freedom and independence always do. One of them is the problem of the weak department that has not been successful in upgrading itself. Should the administration and the rest of the faculty intervene to improve the department, at the cost of departmental autonomy, or not interfere to protect faculty autonomy, at the cost of lowered academic standing? In Chapter Nine we shall see that limited administrative intervention seems to improve faculty quality, but this does not resolve the dilemma, of course. Another dilemma is that of the individual scientist or scholar, whose ultimate reward for his endeavors is to win lasting fame for his great contributions to knowledge, but whose responsibility demands that he train students so well that they can surpass him and make his own work obsolete. The incentives provided by fame and tenure operate in incongruous ways. Tenure and, generally, academic freedom supply many scientists and scholars with rewards that enable a very few to make greater contributions to knowledge than they could without such protection. Fame, in contrast, is a high reward very few will attain but whose promise serves as incentive to spur the efforts of many.

The extensive specialization that is essential for scientific progress and the social integration that is essential for the university to remain an academic community pose a dilemma. In other organizations, the differentiation of the common task into interdependent functions creates simultaneously a basis for integration, because the interdependence of parts requires them to cohere and helps integrate them. But the academic specialties in a university are not directly interdependent.[42] The members of each can pursue their research and teaching independently of the work of others, and the high degree of specialization makes communication between different fields difficult.[43] The fact—assuming it is a fact—that integration is more problematical in universities than in other organizations is ironical, since the very term "university" implies an integrated whole, deriving as it does from *unus verus*, turned into one.[44]

There is one source of interdependence among the specialties in a university, however, and that is their responsibility for higher education, notably undergraduate education in the liberal arts. Inasmuch as students must be educated in a variety of subjects, specialists could not perform their teaching role without the presence of different specialists. The conflicts between research and teaching might lead one to propose that research and graduate training be separated from undergraduate education, but this would deprive the various specialties of the main basis for cohering together in a large and diverse university, which constitutes the stimulating academic environment that benefits specialized research, as we have seen in this chapter, and undergraduate education

---

[42] See Hagstrom, *op. cit.*, 244–245.

[43] Notwithstanding Durkheim's emphasis on the integrative function of the division of labor in society, I think that modern societies are in this respect more similar to academic institutions than to other organizations, and that the lack of direct interdependence among segments in contemporary societies is at the roots of the severe problems of integration and of the anomie pervading Western societies today.

[44] The importance of social integration in a university is rightly emphasized by Hutchins, though his one-sided advocacy of integrating scholarship blinds him against realizing the importance of specialization (*op. cit.*, p. 108). "The aim of the university is to tame the pretensions and excesses of experts and specialists by drawing them into the academic circle and subjecting them to the criticism of other disciplines." Nothing is said about subjecting broadly ranging philosophers, like Hutchins, to the criticisms of specialists, or about the need for specialized expertness to make significant contributions to scholarship or science.

to boot, as we shall see in the next. The obstacles to communication among different specialties would pull them apart were it not for the common purpose provided by education in the liberal arts, which keeps them together. The dilemmas posed by the conflicting demands of specialized research and undergraduate education cannot be escaped, for general undergraduate education is the cohesive force that unites heterogeneous specialties in an institution and thereby makes possible the large and diverse universities that are, paradoxically, most conducive to the development of increasing specialization.

A final dilemma of scientific pursuits is posed by the need of the academic community to be responsive to the urgent problems of society and produce knowledge to solve them, on the one hand, and its need to remain sufficiently detached from the exigencies of daily life to advance the general scientific knowledge that may ultimately contribute most to society, on the other. Society has a right to demand that the scientists and scholars whom it supports not completely withdraw into ivory towers and ignore threats to its very existence while they are preoccupied with abstract issues. At the same time, scientific progress demands that scientists do withdraw from the problems of everyday life into the ivory towers of their laboratories or studies to seek solutions to abstract theoretical problems. These are, of course, contradictory demands, which is precisely why they create a dilemma.

CHAPTER NINE

ACADEMIC PERFORMANCE

The inquiry in this book has centered attention on the institutional structure of universities and colleges in the United States and the organization of academic work in them. A study of the academic performance of individual faculty members and students would require a different research design. To find out which students drop out of college, which teachers have most impact on students, or which scholars accomplish most in their research, one would have to investigate the influences of such factors as individual abilities, socialization, motivation, training, relations with fellow students or colleagues, and career choices, not primarily the institutional conditions that have been examined here. But a comparison of differences in academic performance *among institutions* can help round out the analysis of the organization of academic work presented. After having traced the interrelations among conditions that compose the academic structure, we would like to know the significance of various conditions for actual academic performance. Three indicators of academic performance are employed in this chapter as effect criteria to evaluate how different ways of organizing academic work influence what this work accomplishes.

The two basic responsibilities of academic institutions are education and scholarly research. Accordingly, the analysis presented here uses two measures of the educational progress of students, which are indicative of both student performance and faculty's teaching performance, and one measure of faculty research accomplishments. Since the primary concern in utilizing these output criteria is to appraise the significance of *institutional* conditions for academic performance, it is necessary to control input, that is, student quality in the first two cases and faculty quality in the third.[1] Differences in both student and faculty quality are controlled in the analysis. Extensive controls somewhat compensate for the crude measures of academic performance that have to be employed, because a measure of an underlying concept that is distorted by some other factors—correlated biases—is improved if these factors are controlled, as noted in Chapter Two. For example, student progress is an impure measure of teaching effectiveness, because its indications of that effectiveness are distorted by the better and more highly motivated students in very selective colleges, but holding constant incoming students' aptitudes and institution's selectivity corrects these biases of the measure.

The index of college completion or low dropout rates is the number of students who received their college degree in an institution in 1967 divided by total number of its undergraduates. However, this proportion is not only affected by students who failed to complete their college education within four years, having dropped out temporarily or permanently, but also by increases in enrollments during the four years. Expansion therefore must be controlled when this measure is used. Although only data on the expansion of the faculty are available, the growth in faculty appears to correspond rather closely to that in students. In the average American institution of higher education, the faculty increased nearly 7 per cent in 1967–68, which implies a growth rate of close to 100 per cent in 10 years, and that is just slightly less than the growth rate in student enrollment in the 1960s.[2] If there were neither expansion nor dropouts, the proportion of graduating seniors would be 25 per cent of all undergraduates. Actually, the proportion in the average college is 15 per cent. About one-half of the difference of 10 per cent reflects

[1] Alexander W. Astin, as previously noted, stresses the importance of controlling input quality in the study of the influences of conditions in colleges on educational outcomes; "The Methodology of Research on College Impact," *Sociology of Education* 43 (1970), 223–251.

[2] "Enrollments grew from 2,660,000 in fall 1955 ... to 6,928,000 in fall 1968, which is more than a 100 per cent growth rate in ten years," states Joseph Ben-David, citing a report from the American Council of Education as his source; *American Higher Education*, New York: McGraw-Hill, 1972, p. 1.

expansion, and the other half dropout (including students who failed so many courses or took so few that they could not graduate within four years).

The second indicator of educational performance is a continuation rate, specifically, the proportion of graduating seniors in 1967 expected to continue in graduate or professional schools. The source is a questionnaire sent to each institution by the American Council of Education. The figures represent estimates by administrators based undoubtedly on requests for the transcripts of their grades students need to enter graduate schools, which should make these estimates quite reliable.[3] A check on their reliability can be made. The proportion of graduating seniors in 1967 expected to go to graduate school in the average institution yielded by these data is 39 per cent. The national figure of the proportion of graduating seniors in the preceding year who entered graduate school in 1965 was 41 per cent,[4] and though the national percentage might have increased some by 1967, the index would still furnish rather accurate estimates.

The measure of faculty research productivity is the score derived from the faculty survey by Parsons and Platt previously described. Each faculty member sampled was asked how many articles and how many books "you authored or coauthored," and the score is the number of articles plus five times the number of books, averaged for the respondents from a given institution. This is merely a rough indication of research performance. It not only ignores quality but probably also includes unpublished reports, since the score per faculty member in the average institution is seven, which is suspiciously high for publications. However, unpublished drafts of papers and monographs are frequently included in bibliographies and considered in evaluating faculty members, and the sheer volume of research output often assumes considerable significance in academic evaluations (as adumbrated in Chapter Five), regrettable as this may be.

Unpublished papers are more likely to be reported by persons who have few than those who have many published papers, which creates a conservative bias that reduces and makes it more difficult to observe differences, and hence strengthens confidence in those that have been observed. Moreover, Cole and Cole demonstrate that there is a fairly

[3] These data were coded from Otis A. Singletary, *American Universities and Colleges*, Washington: American Council of Education, 1968, which supplies the information for only 89 of the 115 institutions in the sample.
[4] See Ben-David, *op. cit.*, p. 2.

high correlation between the quantity of a scientist's research output and its quality, as reflected in the frequency with which the scientist's publications are cited by others.[5] Aggregating the scores of individual respondents into an institutional index is likely to produced more reliable indications of production quantity by reducing the significance of the idiosyncratic responses of braggarts, but it is unlikely to improve the score's reliability as an indication of research quality, because institutional pressures probably create institution-wide tendencies to sacrifice research quality in order to raise its quantity. In sum, the measure probably reveals differences in research productivity among institutions quite accurately but differences in research quality less well.[6]

COLLEGE DROPOUT

Do students in small colleges have a better chance to complete their degrees in four years while those in large universities often take longer or drop out? The answer is, no. The size of an institution of higher education makes no difference in the likelihood of speedy college completion $(r = -.02)$, despite the fact that large institutions tend to have larger classes than small ones,[7] and there is no appreciable difference in this likelihood between universities granting Ph.D.'s and colleges that do not $(-.09)$. As a matter of fact, the chances of college students to

[5] Stephen Cole and Jonathan R. Cole, "Scientific Output and Recognition," *American Sociological Review* 32 (1967), 377–390. The correlation for the sample of 120 physicists in their study is .72. For several studies finding similar associations in other fields see the references cited in their footnote 1.

[6] It should be noted that any bias resulting from quality differences, just as that owing to overreporting of unpublished papers, probably creates a conservative bias that attenuates relationships and thus does not make those observed questionable. Besides, controlling reputation should reduce the effect of such bias. A measure of scholarly performance that takes quality into account is the number of departments in an institution rated among the top 20 in the discipline by Allan M. Cartter, *An Assessment of Quality in Graduate Education*, Washington: American Council of Education, 1966. But this measure is not useful in a study that includes colleges as well as universities, since the large majority of academic institutions in the universe have not a single department rated by Cartter. Whether the number or the proportion of Cartter-rated departments is used as a measure, the effects of size (with proportion, $r = .50$) and affluence (.57) are so great that the influences of other factors are inconsequential once these two are controlled.

[7] See Donald J. Reichard, *Campus Size*, Atlanta: Southern Regional Education Board, 1971, p. 9.

obtain their degrees within four years seem to be neither diminished by an emphasis on research in the institution $(r = -.02)$ nor significantly improved by an emphasis on teaching (.09). This lack of differences, however, conceals counteracting influences exerted on the progress of undergraduates by the various conditions in universities that offer much graduate work, compared to those in colleges where faculty members have more opportunity for personal contacts with undergraduates. The implications for the education of college students of the stimulating academic atmosphere in a diverse university are not the same as those of the primary emphasis on research that tends to prevail or those of the bureaucratization that tends to develop in large complex institutions. In the analysis of the various influences on educational performance, the aptitudes of incoming freshmen, which improve their performance, and the expansion of the institution, which artificially lowers the index of performance, are controlled (see rows 9 and 1 in Table 9.1).

The factor that has the strongest effect on the educational progress of undergraduates is the proportion of graduate students in the academic institution. Row 2 in Table 9.1 shows that undergraduates earn their degrees at higher rates in universities with many graduate students than in colleges with few. One might have thought that many graduate students impede undergraduate education by diverting faculty attention from undergraduates, and we saw that the proportion of graduate students in an institution actually reduces the contacts of faculty members with undergraduates (Table 6.4) and increases those with graduate students (Table 6.3). But the analysis of these findings in Chapter Six suggested that they imply simply that faculty members distribute their time between graduate students and undergraduatees in proportion to their numbers and that there is no indication that graduate students preempt disproportionate amounts of faculty time. The finding that many graduate students further rather than hinder the education of undergraduates supports this interpretation, since the progress of undergraduates would be expected to suffer if many graduate students took up excessive amounts of faculty time. The fact that an institution has not only many M.A. students but is a university granting Ph.D.'s has a small additional positive effect on the rates of college completion, as becomes evident when other conditions are controlled (see the beta weight in row 3).

The stimulating academic atmosphere in a university with many graduate students benefits the education of undergraduates. Ben-David notes: "An institution merely concerned with teaching can hardly compete with the college of a large university in terms of intellectual stimulation and

Table 9.1   Rate of College Completion (Low Dropout)

	Beta Weight	Simple Correlation
1. Expansion	−.12*	−.30
2. Percentage of graduate students	.42**	.46
3. University	.17*	−.09
4. Student-faculty ratio	−.26**	−.44
5. Standardized salaries	.19**	.43
6. Levels	−.17*	−.40
7. Faculty qualifications	.30**	.37
8. Research emphasis	−.36**	−.02
9. Student aptitudes	.18*	.20
10. Undergraduate contacts	.23**	−.05
11. Mechanical teaching aids	−.18*	−.43
12. Percentage elected on committee	−.20**	−.20

$R^2 = .74$ $(\hat{R}^2 = .71)$; $n = 114$

* More than twice its standard error.
** More than three times its standard error.

scholarly competence."[8] The classes of undergraduates are more interesting if they include graduate students, who frequently raise issues and start discussions, and contacts with graduate students in extracurricular activities and informal gatherings provide additional opportunities for invigorating intellectual discussions. Graduate students also furnish role models for undergraduates. The larger the proportion of graduate students in an institution, the more undergraduates can find an appropriate role model whose commitment to academic work is likely to strengthen their interest in academic studies. Graduate students are more suitable role models for college students than are faculty members; they are closer in age, interests, and social position, and thus are more likely to participate in common social activities. In these social gatherings, debates of intellectual issues and discussions of academic subjects are integrated with various other activities, which makes academic matters part of the common subculture, whereas academic pursuits otherwise tend to be segregated in the classroom and kept distinct from the social life of undergraduates. Graduate students have good reason to engage in social

[8] Ben-David, *op. cit.*, p. 45.

intercourse with undergraduates, because such interaction gives them opportunities to demonstrate their superior academic knowledge and experience and earn the respect of undergraduates in exchange. The intellectual benefits college students derive in return for their social acknowledgment of the superior status of advanced students in intercourse with them are manifest in their educational progress, which surpasses that of undergraduates who do not have occasion for social interaction with graduate students.

A practical implication of this finding is that it would be detrimental for undergraduate education to separate it from graduate education and research in universities and consign it exclusively to undergraduate colleges, as is sometimes recommended.[9] Despite the conflicts between specialized research and undergraduate teaching—and we shall shortly encounter evidence of this conflict—their underlying relationship is symbiotic. As noted at the end of Chapter Eight, undergraduate education is the common bond that keeps diverse specialities together in large, complex universities, which is the most conducive environment for specialized research, and which is now found to be also the best environment for undergraduate education.

The finding also has implications for two other conclusions reached earlier. The proportion of graduate students in an academic institution was observed in Chapter Five to strengthen both teaching and research concerns, the only factor discovered to have parallel effects on these usually divergent orientations (see Table 5.1 and footnote 11 in Chapter Five). The conjecture advanced there that teaching as well as research suffers in purely undergraduate colleges is confirmed by the finding that the educational progress of undergraduates is more rapid the higher the proportion of graduate students in an institution. In Chapter Four, we saw that the preferences of outstanding students were *not* influenced by the proportion of graduate students in an institution or by whether it is a university; the question was then raised whether the dispositions of these students to discount the advantages of universities with many graduate students, presumably because undergraduates are fearful of receiving less attention there, are realistic. The finding that undergraduates make more progress, not less, in universities with many graduate students suggests that these preferences and the fears probably inspiring them are unrealistic. But we shall see that in several re-

[9] But Ben-David concludes wisely (*ibid.*) that "it is intellectually advantageous for an institution to combine liberal undergraduate education with a graduate school in the arts and sciences."

spects the college choices of good seniors in high school reveal amazing astuteness.

This interpretation of the lower college dropout rates in universities with many graduate students than in colleges with few or none, in terms of the intellectual atmosphere in universities and the role of graduate students, implicitly assumes that other differences between these two kinds of institutions of higher education, such as differences in the quality of their faculties, do not account for the findings. The assumption is justified because other differences have been controlled in the analysis. Faculty members naturally play an important part in the education of undergraduates. We all can remember some impressive teachers we had, who may have decisively affected our education and our careers. Although the distinctive styles of great teachers are not captured by the research design, even its gross indicators reflect the significance of teachers for undergraduate education. Row 7 in Table 9.1 shows that superior qualifications of the faculty contribute to the educational progress of students.

In addition to qualifications, the time the faculty is able and willing to devote to undergraduates affects their educational progress. Large numbers of students and heavy teaching loads that overburden the faculty have detrimental effects on teaching quality and student performance, as implied by the negative coefficient of the student-faculty ratio in row 4 of Table 9.1.[10] Besides, the more frequently undergraduates have individual conferences with faculty members, the better is their educational progress (row 10). Face-to-face contacts with teachers improve the chances of students to complete their college education, independent of their abilities when they enter college, which justifies the stress many educators place on personal contacts with students outside the classroom. The positive influence of faculty-student contacts on educational performance is concealed in the simple correlation by the counteracting effects of percentage of graduate students ($-.18$) and undergraduate aptitudes ($-.09$), because teachers spend less time with undergraduates, as Table 6.4 showed, the smaller their number relative to that of graduate students and the higher their aptitudes. The abilities of students influence their educational performance (row 9 in Table 9.1), but the advantages of students with high aptitudes are much reduced by the extra help undergraduates

[10] If student enrollment is substituted for the student-faculty ratio in Table 9.1, it also has a negative effect ($b^* = -.27$, more than three standard errors; $r = -.31$). Thus, if size is measured by student body rather than total faculty, it has a negative effect on educational performance, but since the important factor is the student-faculty ratio, the table revealing its negative effect is presented. The R^2 is very slightly lower when enrollment is substituted for student-faculty ratio (.71; $\hat{R}^2 = .68$).

with low aptitudes tend to get from faculty members (decomposition coefficient of faculty-undergraduate contacts, −.12).[11]

Whereas most of the conditions characteristic of major universities benefit undergraduate education, not all do. Row 8 in Table 9.1 indicates that a strong emphasis on research and publications in an academic institution makes it less likely for undergraduates to complete their degree requirements within four years. A prevailing concern among the faculty with scholarly research apparently encroaches on the time and effort they devote to teaching and reduces their effectiveness as teachers. This negative influence of research emphasis on education is not evident in the simple correlation, since it is counteracted by the positive effects of both faculty qualifications (.18) and proportion of graduate students (.16). Nevertheless, able applicants to colleges seem to be aware of the disadvantage of strong research emphasis for undergraduate education, as well as of the advantage of superior faculty qualifications for it, and they reflect both in their choices of colleges as shown in Tables 4.2 and 6.2.

The favorable academic climate for undergraduate education in universities (beta weight in row 3 of Table 9.1) is neutralized by the greater research emphasis in universities (decomposition coefficient, −.23), which is the reason that the simple correlation reveals no appreciable difference in rates of degree completion between universities and colleges. However, the proportion of graduate students has both a gross and a net effect greatly increasing the rates of college graduation (see row 2), testifying to the significance of advanced academic work generally and the role of graduate students specifically for stimulating undergraduates and improving their educational performance. The contribution to undergraduate education of faculties with superior qualifications (beta weight in row 7) is contingent on their not being fully immersed in research (decomposition coefficient of research emphasis, −.22), and their teaching is most likely to be successful if it is made challenging by the presence of graduate students (.18) and the high aptitudes of undergraduates (.09).

[11] The beta weight in row 9 indicates the better chances of college completion of students in colleges with high average aptitudes *independent* of the reduction in these advantages resulting from less faculty help. The simple correlation is spurious, mostly due to the effect of faculty qualifications on both mean aptitudes of undergraduates and college completion rates (.16). This implies that the average abilities of students in a college, as distinguished from their relative abilities within the college, have no influence on their chances of college completion. One reason undoubtedly is that academic standards in colleges with better students tend to be higher. Another reason will become apparent in the next section when the influence of institution's reputation on the rates of going to graduate school are discussed.

Bureaucratization is an impediment to education, which shows that stereotypes are not always wrong, although much of the time they are. Two indications of bureaucratization have independent detrimental effects on the progress students make in college, and while each effect is small the two are cumulative. A multilevel administrative hierarchy, previously considered to be an expression of a bureaucratic structure, reduces the rate at which college students obtain their degrees, as indicated in row 6 of Table 9.1. This finding suggests that outstanding students are quite realistic when they refrain from choosing institutions of higher education that have bureaucratic structures with multiple levels (see Table 4.2). It seems that the ill effects of multilevel hierarchies on education are somehow conveyed to outstanding high school students, though perhaps only in the form of the negative stereotype of bureaucracy, and affect their preferences, just as the implications of a research emphasis and of faculty qualifications for education seem to be transmitted to them. A bureaucratic hierarchy that removes the president and the central administration from students and faculty creates obstacles to communication, and the consequent difficulties of integrating the various parts of the educational enterprise may well be detrimental to its success.

An expression of the bureaucratization of the educational process itself is illustrated by resort to mechanical teaching aids, such as television, language laboratories, programmed learning machines, and computers. Row 11 in Table 9.1 shows that the use of such mechanized teaching procedures is disadvantageous for the educational progress of students. Mechanical teaching devices are no adequate substitute for face-to-face contacts between teachers and students. Does this mean that technological innovations have no place in education? Not necessarily, provided they are introduced in the proper context, to avert rather than intensify bureaucratized teaching procedures. In large lecture classes, contact between teacher and students is so minimal that utilization of mechanical teaching aids may be a preferable substitute. A review of many studies comparing conventional with televised lectures concludes that "one-way television instruction [is] not demonstrably inferior to face-to-face teaching."[12] This conclusion is rather misleading, however, since it applies only if there is no discussion in either case or some face-to-face discussion in both, whereas two-way television, designed to substitute for personal

[12] Robert Dubin and R. Alan Hedley, *The Medium May Be Related to the Message,* Eugene: University of Oregon, Center for Advanced Study in Educational Administration, 1969, p. 16.

class discussion, is manifestly inferior, as the data demonstrate.[13] Huge lectures amplified by loudspeakers may well benefit from adding television screens, and various mechanical aids can improve education that is essentially based on face-to-face discussion groups.

Generally, what impedes effective education is not so much the use of technical devices as the mechanical and bureaucratic orientation to education their extensive and unthinking use signifies and fosters. Such a bureaucratic approach to education can develop easily if huge numbers of students and heavy teaching loads make an institution of higher education into a teaching factory, as implied by the previously mentioned adverse effect on education of a high student-faculty ratio (row 4).

Not all bureaucratic procedures are disadvantageous for higher education, and not all consequences of democratic procedures are advantageous for it, as much as we would like to think they are. The standardization of faculty salary raises on the basis of a regular schedule is a bureaucratic procedure. Yet we saw in Chapter Eight that standardized faculty salaries encourage institutional innovation in the form of creating new departments (Table 8.2), and row 5 in Table 9.1 indicates that such standardization also somewhat improves educational performance. The interpretation of the first finding in the last chapter drew on a study of scientists by Glaser that suggests that salary advancements based on recommendations, compared with a standardized system, engender dissatisfaction, invidious comparisons, and distrust. Such tendencies may inhibit the cooperative efforts of faculty members that are necessary to initiate the establishment of new departments. The lesser jealousies and distrust of faculty members under a standardized system of salary increments might also increase their tendency to cooperate in discharging their educational responsibilities, and their cooperation probably helps integrate course offerings, strengthen educational programs, and enhance teaching effectiveness. A more direct effect of standardized salaries is that they make salary increments, though not promotions in rank, independent of the recommendations of chairmen and deans. Faculty members who are less dependent on their chairman and dean are likely to be freer and more relaxed than others in the classroom and in interaction with students, readier to explore new educational approaches and deal with subjects closest to their academic interests. Their greater independence and freedom may well raise the respect of their students for them and, for this and other reasons, make them better teachers.

Democratic decision making entails costs in time and effort, and these

---

[13] *Ibid.*, pp. 1–29, esp. pp. 10–14.

seem to infringe on educational activities in academic institutions. Row 12 in Table 9.1 reveals that democratic procedures of faculty government —specifically, elected faculty representatives on important committees— are negatively related to the rates at which undergraduates complete their college education. A possible reason is that elected faculty committees are inclined to set particularly high academic standards, which make it more difficult for students to earn their bachelor degrees. But this interpretation implies that decentralization of educational policies to the faculty also makes it more difficult for undergraduates to complete their degree requirements, which is not the case.[14] Another possibility is that the relationship is spurious, produced by some undiscovered common correlate of the two variables. A final possibility that cannot be excluded, however, is that faculty involvement on committees takes time and effort that are diverted from the performance of educational duties, and the less effective teaching that results may be the price of democratic faculty government. This is sheer speculation, but if it is correct, it implies that students pay the price of democracy in faculty government.

CONTINUATION RATES

The two measures of educational performance are correlated. The higher the rate at which students entering a college graduate from it, the higher is the rate at which these graduates continue their education beyond college $(r = .40)$. This association is largely the result of the fact that some conditions in academic institutions exert parallel influences on both aspects of educational performance.[15] However, most of the conditions influencing these two rates are not the same. Actually, only three of the antecedents discovered in each case are common to both. In the analysis of the rates of continuing to graduate (or professional) schools, the initial quality of students is controlled through two variables, the college's reputation and its selectivity in admissions, rather than through the aptitudes of entering students, because the latter has no independent effect on continuation rates when other conditions are controlled.[16]

[14] When the measure of centralization of educational matters is added to the variables in Table 9.1, the beta weight is $-.06$ $(r = -.23)$, less than two standard errors.

[15] When the continuation rate is added to the variables in Table 9.1, the beta weight is .00. When the college completion rate is added to the variables in Table 9.2, the beta weight is .07, less than one standard error. None of the other beta weights in either table are appreciably changed (by as much as .03).

[16] If student aptitudes are added to the variables in Table 9.2, the beta weight is $-.05$, less than one standard error. The simple correlation of .29 is spurious, mostly owing to the influences of faculty qualifications (.12) and Southern location (.11).

Although larger proportions of students go to graduate school in some fields (e.g., physics) than in others (e.g., engineering or education), it is hoped that the exclusion of all specialized colleges and the extensive controls prevent this fact from distorting the research results.

Row 1 of Table 9.2 shows that graduates of Southern colleges are less likely than those of colleges in the rest of the United States to expect to continue in graduate school. This is not due to the lower academic standing of Southern institutions of higher education, since the institution's reputation is controlled in the analysis. Neither is it due to the lower abilities of Southern students, since adding the measure of average student aptitudes—which exerts no independent effect on continuation rates, as just mentioned—does not alter the difference in plans for further education between Southern and other college graduates. What may be responsible for this difference is that a firm academic tradition of advanced education has not taken root in the South, at least not a tradition of graduate training for large numbers of professionals and academics rather than a select elite. The weak Southern tradition of a broadly based advanced education undoubtedly has its source in turn in the poverty of the South and the consequent limited opportunities for professionals, scientists, and scholars. This difference in academic tradition between the South and the North is manifest in the fact that nearly twice as many Northerners as Southerners have been to graduate school,[17] and it is already apparent in the plans of college freshmen. A survey by the American Council of Education found that more than one-quarter of the freshmen in the rest of the country but only one-fifth of those in the South plan to get a Ph.D. or professional degree.[18]

If a tradition of academic scholarship encourages students to continue their education beyond the bachelor's degree, older universities and colleges, which have a tradition of long standing, should send more of their students to graduate school than do younger institutions. Row 2 in Table 9.2 indicates that this is the case. Although part of the influence of age on plans for graduate work is produced by the better qualified faculties in older institutions of higher education (decomposition coefficient, .11), most of it is direct, probably reflecting the significance of a scholarly tradition that has been perpetuated over many generations and become entrenched in the institution. In previous discussions of academic traditionalism, the financial resources devoted to the library as well as age

[17] Among American men 20–64 years of age in 1962, 3.3 per cent in the South and 6.1 per cent in the North (rest of the country) had gone to graduate school; computed from Peter M. Blau and Otis Dudley Duncan, *The American Occupational Structure,* New York: Wiley, 1967, pp. 508, 480.
[18] Estimates derived from the figures (which do not permit precise computation) in "The American Freshman," *ACE Research Reports* 6 (6) (1971), 25, 49.

Table 9.2   Rate of Continuing Education in Graduate School

	Beta Weight	Simple Correlation
1. South	−.24*	−.34
2. Age	.24**	.35
3. Public	−.31**	−.33
4. Percentage of graduate students	.26**	.48
5. Faculty qualifications	.22*	.38
6. Reputation	−.25*	.30
7. Local allegiance	−.17*	−.17
8. Selectivity	.21*	.29
9. Mechanical teaching aids	−.15*	−.29
10. Department eliminated	.23**	.36

$R^2 = .62 \ (\hat{R}^2 = .57); \ n = 89$

* More than twice its standard error.
** More than three times its standard error.

were used as indicators of it, and the two were seen to have parallel effects. The proportion of revenue spent on books, however, does not affect the rates of continuing to graduate school ($r = .04$). The likely reason is that devoting substantial resources to the library rather than to alternative facilities such as laboratories is indicative of traditionalism in the sense of an emphasis on traditional fields of scholarship, whereas what stimulates students to continue their education is a lively tradition of advanced academic pursuits, not a traditionalistic adherence to classical disciplines. An academic tradition must not become traditionalism but remain vigorous and alive to arouse student interests in graduate work.

Much advanced academic work in an institution tends to maintain a vigorous and up-to-date tradition of scholarly and scientific endeavors, which furnishes to undergraduates continual evidence of the value of graduate education. The larger the proportion of graduate students in an institution, accordingly, the greater is the likelihood that undergraduates make plans to go to graduate school, as shown in row 4 of Table 9.2. This finding conforms to the earlier interpretation that graduate students become role models for undergraduates and thereby strengthen their interest in further education—in obtaining higher degrees as well as in completing college (Table 9.1).[19] Graduate students play an important part in the transmission and perpetuation of a university tradition of

[19] The effects of percentage of graduate students on the two rates are independent; see footnote 15 above.

advanced academic work. They demonstrate and communicate to under-graduates the social value and importance of science and scholarship, stimulating them to pursue academic or professional training, which produces new cohorts of graduate students, who in their turn will trans-mit these academic values to future generations.

Undergraduates are encouraged to proceed to graduate school not only by the specific role graduate students play as communication links but also by the prevailing emphasis on advanced academic work that the presence of many graduate students in a university manifests. A tradition of advanced academic work depends on a well-qualified faculty, and we saw in Table 4.1 that both the long academic tradition of an institution (age) and its concentration of advanced work (percentage of graduate students) lead to the recruitment of better qualified faculty members. The superior qualifications of the faculty exert an independent effect, which reinforces that of the institution's age and proportion of graduate students, increasing the chances that undergraduates plan to go to grad-uate school (see row 5 of Table 9.2), just as they improve the perform-ance of undergraduates while in college (shown in Table 9.1). The reasons for the two influences may not be identical, however. The better teaching by faculty members with superior qualifications—unless their research completely distracts their attention—is probably what contrib-utes to the progress of undergraduates in college, whereas their greater involvement in advanced academic work is likely to be what stimulates students' interest in graduate work.

The orientation of an institution's faculty members to fellow special-ists outside their own institutions helps keep alive a flourishing tradition of advanced academic work. The analysis in Chapter Five indicated that superior qualifications promote involvement in research and that both these qualifications and this involvement incline faculty members to be oriented more toward outside reference groups of fellow specialists than to the local group at their institution (Tables 5.2, 5.3, and 5.5). The less local allegiance faculty members express, the higher are the rates of college graduates who expect to continue their education in graduate school, though the relationship is weak (row 7, Table 9.2). It appears paradoxical that the loyalty of faculty members to a college makes them less effective as teachers who can arouse an interest in advanced educa-tion. The reason for the paradox is that the most inspiring scholars and scientists are not typically the faculty members with the strongest local commitments. To kindle the scientific curiosity of students and whet their appetite for scholarship requires faculty members who, if not themselves engaged in research, sustain an active concern with developments in their fields by keeping in contact with the larger discipline instead of limiting their horizons to their own institution. Such a cosmopolitan orientation to the discipline may be particularly important for good teachers in small colleges, who lack the facilities to conduct major research. The orientations of faculty members to their various specialized fields reflected in their lower commitment to the local institution make them provocative teachers who can stir students' interest in advanced learning.

A tradition that emphasizes the importance of advanced education should also find expression in high academic standards. We observed in Chapter Six that an institution's age and some other indication of an academic tradition raise admission standards, that is, increase its selectivity in admitting applicants (Table 6.1). The more selective an academic institution is in admitting freshmen, the greater is the proportion of its college graduates who proceed to graduate school, as revealed in row 8 of Table 9.2. It is quite plausible that the high admission standards made possible by a large pool of applicants make those finally accepted better students and thus more promising candidates for graduate schools. But this plausible argument implies that the influence of selectivity on the likelihood of students to go to graduate school is mediated by the higher aptitudes of incoming freshmen, which is not the case. Freshmen aptitudes exert no independent influence on the rates of continuing to graduate school when selectivity and other conditions are controlled, whereas selectivity exerts such an influence when freshmen aptitudes and the other factors in Table 9.2 are controlled. A possible interpretation, which is clearly ad hoc, is that admission officers and selection committees take motivations and potentials into account, which produces better predictions of future academic success than aptitude scores alone.

In sum, the chances of college students to continue their education in graduate school are strongly affected by the academic climate and tradition in an institution. The analysis has disclosed that these chances are independently affected by the following five conditions reflecting various aspects of an institution's tradition of advanced academic pursuits: (1) the age of the university or college, revealing an academic tradition of long standing; (2) the proportion of graduate students, manifesting concentration on advanced academic work; (3) the qualifications of the faculty; (4) weak faculty commitments to the local institution, assumed to be indicative of orientations to the wider academic community; and (5) selectivity in admissions, denoting high academic standards. Note that all five factors influence the rates of continuing beyond college, but only two of them (numbers 2 and 3) influence the rates of college completion. It appears that a tradition that emphasizes the importance of advanced scholarship has its primary impact on plans to pursue graduate training and only much more indirect significance for undergraduate education.

If an emphasis on advanced academic work and high academic standards make it more likely for an institution's college graduates to go on to graduate school, one would expect that the students of the best institutions with the highest reputations are most likely to continue their education after graduating from college. Moreover, an institution's reputation is strongly associated with the aptitudes of its entering freshmen (see Table 6.2). The decision to control reputation in the analysis of continuation rates as a means of controlling the input of student abilities rested on the assumption that it has a positive effect on continuation rates. Contrary to anticipation, however, the superior reputation of an academic institution actually reduces the chances that its graduates plan to proceed to graduate school, as indicated by the beta weight in row 6 of Table 9.2. Although the simple correlation is positive, it is produced by a number of conditions associated with reputation that influence continuation rates, such as faculty qualifications (.13), location outside the South (.10), and a combination of others. Thus more graduates of institutions with superior reputations than of others go to graduate school, but the institution's superior reputation itself, independent of the conditions associated with it, diminishes the likelihood that its graduates plan to do graduate work.

This surprising finding can be interpreted in terms of the "frog-pond effect" of colleges with different standing, which was originally observed by Davis.[20] The high academic standards and many excellent students in the best colleges make those whose academic abilities are considerable but not outstanding look poor by comparison, discouraging them from thinking of themselves as qualified for advanced academic work. Students with the same abilities who go to a college of lower standing, where the achievements of most fellow students do not surpass theirs, are induced by their social environment to form a self-conception as promising candidates for academic or professional careers, encouraging them to go to graduate school.

This effect of reference-group comparisons in colleges differing in reputation may well be reinforced by differences in the amount of personal help students receive from faculty members. The finding in Chapter Six that the high average aptitudes of students in a college decrease the frequency of faculty conferences with them (Table 6.4) led to the inference that little individual faculty guidance of undergraduates becomes the prevailing practice in the best institutions with very bright

---

[20] James A. Davis, "The Campus as a Frog Pond." *American Journal of Sociology* **72** (1966), 17–31. See also David E. Drew and Alexander W. Astin, "Undergraduate Aspirations," *American Journal of Sociology* **77** (1972), 1151–1164.

students, so that even students who need personal help from the faculty are less likely to get it there than they would in poorer colleges with few very bright students. An implication of this speculative inference is that the educational prospects of students who go to the best colleges, where they receive less faculty attention, are somewhat handicapped; their lower chances of going to graduate school are indicative of such a handicap and thus lend credence to the inference.[21] Still another factor that may contribute to the lower continuation rates of the graduates from institutions with the best reputations is that the colleges with the highest prestige are attended by students from the wealthiest families, many of whom plan to go into business or industry and have little interest in advanced academic work. Astin suggests this interpretation for the parallel finding of his mentioned previously that the Eastern colleges with the highest prestige are found, when proper controls are introduced, to produce fewer graduates who later earn Ph.D.'s than colleges with much lower academic reputations.[22]

Whereas students from wealthy families may not be interested in graduate education because they have better career opportunities than it can offer, students from poor families are unlikely to be able to afford to continue their education beyond college. To be sure, students who have demonstrated outstanding academic abilities in college can get fellowships to do graduate work, and those with very strong motivations are willing to work and be supported by spouses in order to go to graduate school. But for most students whose parents cannot help support them, the direct cost of graduate education plus its indirect cost in lost earnings are prohibitive. This is undoubtedly the reason why graduates of public colleges, which have lower tuition rates and therefore disproportionate numbers of students from less prosperous homes, are considerably less likely to go to graduate school than those of private colleges,

---

[21] If the measure of student aptitudes is *substituted* for the reputation index in a regression analysis with otherwise the same variables (instead of being added, as was done in the regression reported in footnote 16), its beta weight is also negative (−.15), but less than two standard errors (.05 short). Why do student aptitudes have, in contrast, a positive direct effect on college completion rates? Partly because faculty contacts with undergraduates are controlled in Table 9.1, thus holding constant the disadvantage of getting less faculty help in colleges with brighter students. The high aptitudes of college students have not only a direct effect increasing the chances of completing college but also an indirect one reducing these chances, which is mediated by the less frequent conferences with faculty members there (decomposition coefficient, −.12), as mentioned earlier in the text and in footnote 11.

[22] Alexander W. Astin, "'Productivity' of Undergraduate Institutions," *Science* **136** (1962), 134.

as shown in row 3 of Table 9.2. Thus the finding reflects the influence of the financial resources of students on graduate education (and this influence is therefore partly, though not entirely, controlled in the analysis). Alternatively, one might think that the finding can be attributed to the lower reputations or the less selective admission policies of public institutions of higher education, but these conditions cannot account for it, since they have been controlled. What might contribute to the lower rates of continuing education of public institutions, however, is that students from disadvantaged families are less likely than those reared in the middle class to have gone to good primary and secondary schools, to have been freed from the need to work part-time, and to have consequently performed well in college.

The bureaucratization of education reduces the chances of students to advance to graduate training, and a flexible academic structure increases these chances. Extensive use of mechanical teaching aids in a college slightly depresses the rates at which its graduates continue their education in graduate school, which is shown in row 9 of Table 9.2, just as it depresses their rates of progress in college, which was shown in Table 9.1. There is no reason to assume on the basis of these results that technological innovations cannot be used intelligently to improve instruction. An illustration is the imaginative utilization of the computer at Dartmouth to teach undergraduates how to analyze sociological data.[23] The problem is that technical educational devices are most likely to be used in situations that invite a mechanical approach to teaching even without their use—where large classes and heavy teaching loads overburden a harassed faculty with mediocre qualifications—and that their availability creates the temptation to rely on them to save teaching personnel, engendering further bureaucratization of the educational process.[24] The mechanical approach to teaching that resort to mechanized teaching aids often implies is probably what affects educational performance adversely.

A flexible departmental structure appears to improve the education provided in an academic institution. Universities and colleges that exhibit flexible institutional structures by having eliminated departments

---

[23] James A. Davis and Joanna H. Sternick, *The Impress Primer*, Dartmouth College, lithographed, 1971.

[24] The three conditions discovered to exert an influence on the use of mechanical teaching aids are the large size of an academic institution, its high student-faculty ratio, and the small proportion of faculty members with advanced degrees. The beta weights in a regression analysis of use of mechanical teaching aids on these independent variables (with the simple correlations in parentheses) are: size (log), .50** (.44); student-faculty ratio, .20* (.27); faculty qualifications, −.16 (.00). The last beta weight is .02 less than twice its standard error.

in recent years are more likely than others to succeed in preparing and interesting many of their students to go to graduate school (see row 10 in Table 9.2). Since the majority of the departments that have been eliminated were in professional or technical fields rather than the natural sciences, social sciences, or humanities, one implication of the finding is that concentration on the strictly academic disciplines in the arts and sciences provides the undergraduate education most likely to lead to advanced training either in professional or in other graduate schools. But the finding may also be interpreted in more general terms to indicate that a rigid institutional structure that does not adjust to changing conditions is detrimental to education.

In conclusion, the question is raised how much change in the various independent variables in Table 9.2 is necessary to produce a 1 per cent increase in the proportion of college graduates expected to go to graduate school. This question is meaningful only for the five independent variables that are neither dichotomies (like those in rows 1, 3, and 10) nor arbitrary scores (like those in rows 6 and 9). To answer it, the partial *metric* regression coefficients (b's) are examined. Independent of other conditions, every eight-year increase in the age of an institution of higher education ($b = .13$), and thus of the duration of its academic tradition, produces an increase of 1 per cent in the rate of its graduates who plan to go to graduate school. These rates of continuing education in graduate school also increase by 1 per cent for every $3\frac{1}{2}$ per cent increase in the proportion of graduate students in the institution ($b = .28$); for every 3 per cent increase in the proportion of its faculty members with advanced degrees ($b = .30$); for every $4\frac{1}{2}$ per cent decrease in the proportion of its faculty with strong local allegiances ($b = -.22$), which implies a corresponding increase in the proportion with a cosmopolitan orientation; and for every $4\frac{1}{2}$ per cent increase in the proportion of applicants for college admission who are not accepted ($b = .22$), which indicates greater selectivity.[25]

[25] The same procedure may be applied to the analysis of college dropout in Table 9.1. The proportion of students who do not drop out but receive their degrees increases 1 per cent for every 6 per cent increase in the graduate students at the institution ($b = .17$); every decrease of five and one-half students per faculty member ($b = -.18$); an average decrease of .7 levels ($b = -1.41$); every 9 percent increase in the proportion of faculty members with advanced degrees ($b = .11$); every 10 per cent decrease in the proportion of the faculty who state publishing research is a faculty obligation ($b = -.10$); every 13 per cent increase in the proportion of the faculty who see more than seven students weekly ($b = .08$); and every 33 per cent decrease in the proportion of elected faculty members on the most important committee ($b = -.03$). To put the figures in perspective, it must be remembered that the dependent variable refers to the proportion of the total student body who graduate, not to the proportion of the cohort who graduate, which is at least four, and probably five or six, times as large.

FACULTY RESEARCH PRODUCTIVITY

The reputation of an academic institution is, of course, strongly correlated with the research productivity of its faculty, as is evident in row 5 of Table 9.3. Were this not the case, the two measures would be suspect. By the same token, the pronounced association between the two increases confidence in both measures, justifying the use of student preferences as an index of the reputations of academic institutions, and also implying that the faculty productivity score, crude as it is, does supply some indication of the research contributions of the faculty.[26] A plausible substantive interpretation of the correlation is that an academic institution's reputation depends in large degree on its faculty's scholarly contributions. According to this interpretation, the faculty's research productivity should have been treated as an independent variable affecting the institution's reputation. But doing so would have put the cart before the horse.

A university's reputation rests for the most part on the contributions of its past rather than its present faculty, and its superior reputation helps it to recruit a productive faculty, whose scholarly work sustains its reputation. The beta weight in row 5 reflects largely the pull of the institution's reputation for faculty members able to make research contributions. By controlling reputation, and faculty qualifications as well, the influences of conditions within academic institutions on faculty research productivity can be isolated from this process of selection in which the better faculties, which give the institution a superior reputation, attract better new faculty members, who make scholarly contributions. This does not mean, however, that all factors influencing scholarly output through selection have been taken into account. Concern is with the influences of institutional conditions on research productivity whether this influence results from successful recruitment of better faculties— that is, selection—or providing a better research climate for those already in residence.

Money buys a lot of things, and it helps in getting others that cannot be bought for money. Scholarly productivity is an example. The first row in Table 9.3 shows that affluent universities have more productive faculties than others. One might suspect that affluent institutions use the better salaries they can afford to hire faculty members who have already published much, but this does not seem to be the case. If it were, salaries

---

[26] The measure of faculty research productivity is also substantially correlated with both the number (.47) and the proportion (.43) of the departments in the institution rated among the top 20 in the report by Cartter.

Table 9.3   Faculty Research Productivity

	Beta Weight	Simple Correlation
1. Affluence	.08	.49
2. Size	.12	.57
3. University	.26**	.60
4. Faculty qualifications	−.06	.54
5. Reputation	.30**	.52
6. Research emphasis	.18*	.63
7. Administration's appointment power	−.25**	−.68
8. President's appointment power	.23**	.11

$R^2 = .69$ $(\hat{R}^2 = .67)$; $n = 114$

* More than twice its standard error.
** More than three times its standard error.

would have a direct effect on faculty productivity, which they do not.[27] The influence of financial resources on research is more indirect, producing conditions that improve the recruitment of faculty members with high research potentials and helping them to realize these potentials once they are there. The most important of these conditions is the institution's superior reputation (decomposition coefficient, .15), which in turn has been produced partly by the better salaries and facilities that attracted qualified faculties to affluent institutions in the past, and which subsequently attracts research faculties and thus creates a colleague climate encouraging research. A combination of other conditions also raises scholarly standards in recruitment and consequently the faculty's publication output in affluent institutions, notably the fact that more of them are Ph.D.-granting universities (.09), the greater research emphasis in them (.08), and the lesser power of their administrations to intervene in faculty appointments (.09).[28] The difference in faculty publications between richer and poorer institutions is largely accounted for by these factors, as the inconsequential beta weight discloses.

[27] If salaries is added to the variables in Table 9.3, their beta weight is .05 $(r = .64)$, less than one standard error.
[28] Some of the indirect effects mediated by certain intervening variables mentioned here and elsewhere, because they combine to produce a substantial gross effect, are individually too small to have been included in the earlier analysis of these intervening as dependent variables, since the beta weights did not meet the criterion of being twice their standard error.

The size of an academic institution is also highly correlated with the research productivity of its faculty (see row 2 in Table 9.3). Previous investigators have observed the strong association between size and faculty contributions and stressed its significance.[29] But they relate departmental size to the renown or output of the entire department, which makes a substantial correlation between the two virtually inevitable, since even a random distribution of faculty members would raise the output of departments and of institutions having many of them. These strictures do not apply to the measure used here, which is research productivity *per faculty member*. Yet the size of an academic institution does have a pronounced effect on the average research output of its faculty, though this effect is largely indirect. The research productivity of individual faculty members tends to be greater in large than in small academic institutions because they are more likely to be Ph.D.-granting universities (.15), research is more emphasized in them (.11), and their administrations have less influence in appointment decisions, (.15), all of which improve the recruitment of faculties with scholarly promise and thus the scholarly climate at the institution. It should be kept in mind that the effects of affluence and size on the research output of faculty members are real, not spurious, though they are indirect. Affluence and large size help produce conditions in academic institutions that facilitate recruiting a productive faculty.

University faculties publish much more than college faculties, as row 3 in Table 9.3 indicates, and a substantial difference in faculty productivity between universities and colleges persists when other conditions are controlled. Only a small part of the simple correlation is spurious, owing to the affluence and size of universities (together, .10). One-half of the difference university status makes in the faculty's research productivity is indirect, resulting from the stronger research emphasis (.12) and the lesser administrative centralization of appointment authority (.15) in universities, and the other half is direct (see the beta weight).[30] The analysis in Chapter Five provides clues for interpreting this difference. We saw there that universities put considerably more weight than colleges on research in faculty appointments, which increases the obli-

[29] See, for example, Warren G. Hagstrom, "Inputs, Outputs, and the Prestige of University Science Departments," *Sociology of Education* 44 (1971), 375–397; and Lauren G. Wispe, "The Bigger the Better," *American Psychologist* 24 (1969), 662–668.

[30] The findings that university status does and size does not have a direct effect on faculty research productivity correspond to the earlier findings that only the former has a direct effect on research emphasis (Table 5.2), though research emphasis is controlled in Table 9.3. The reason in both cases is that size as such does not affect the criteria of faculty selection, whereas university status does.

gation to publish, and that university status affects the research involvement of individual faculty members, in part directly but in large part indirectly through the climate of research-oriented colleagues who have been appointed in universities.

Thus university appointment policies select faculties on the basis of their research abilities (see the last two columns of Table 5.2). Universities also furnish better opportunities to carry out research, such as lower teaching loads and superior facilities of all sorts, encouraging research independent of appointment policies (footnote 19 in Chapter Five). And the resulting climate of research-oriented colleagues in universities further stimulates individuals and puts pressure on them to become involved in research, as the analysis in Chapter Five also showed. The incentives presumably created by making promotion to tenure contingent on research seem to play no role. These findings suggest that the research contributions of university faculties are the product of appointment procedures that select faculty members on the basis of research qualifications, conditions that facilitate research, and a colleague climate that encourages research activities, none of which are found in most undergraduate colleges.

The qualifications of the faculty in an academic institution have been included in the regression analysis primarily to control this aspect of input quality in ascertaining the influence of institutional conditions on research output. But row 4 in Table 9.3 reveals that the formal qualifications of the faculty exert no appreciable direct effect on research productivity, although there is a substantial simple correlation between the two. Part of this correlation is spurious, because institutions that are affluent, large, and universities recruit faculties who have both better formal qualifications and superior publication records or potentials than do poor small colleges (decomposition coefficient of the three antecedents together, .20). Some of the effect of qualifications on productivity is mediated by a relatively weak influence of the administration in faculty appointments (.13), to be discussed shortly. But the most important factor responsible for the association between a faculty's formal training and its scholarly productivity is the institution's reputation (.17), and another intervening variable is the research emphasis in the institution (.11). These findings suggest one important way in which a tradition of academic scholarship that contributes to knowledge is sustained in an institution, complementing the analysis of graduate students in the preceding section.

A position in a university with a high reputation in which research is emphasized acts as a catalyst that fructifies the scholarly potentials acquired in advanced academic training, whereas these potentials are likely to wither and die in the climate of an institution of low academic standing whose members are not oriented to scholarly research and may even belittle its significance. The large amount of research conducted by the faculties at major universities creates an academic climate that stimulates and facilitates the research involvement of new faculty members, at the same time putting normative pressures on them to engage in research, as we saw in Chapter Five, and the result is actually higher research productivity, as we see now. Thus qualified faculty members who are attracted to and can obtain positions at universities with high reputations probably become more productive scholars than they otherwise would be and thereby help perpetuate the university's tradition of scholarship and preserve its reputation, which was built by earlier generations of productive scholars.

It is implicit in these considerations that an emphasis on research in an academic institution and among its faculty increases research productivity, as row 6 in Table 9.3 shows. The simple correlation is partly spurious, mostly because university faculties are more oriented to research and publish more than college faculties (decomposition coefficient of university status, .16). Some of the effect of research emphasis on research output is mediated, as many other factors are, by a comparatively weak appointment power of the administration (.15). The direct effect manifest in the beta weight is not large, perhaps because it is attenuated by the indirect processes that bring it about (notwithstanding its appearing as a *direct* effect statistically, which simply means that the intervening processes are not captured by the research design). Much emphasis on research will induce many faculty members, though not all, to become involved in research; only a portion of those engaged in research will succeed in obtaining results worth reporting; and not all of these will actually write a paper or a book. The process goes on beyond this point: some of the reports written will never be published, and a mere fraction of the published papers will later be found to have made original contributions to knowledge. Yet it takes large numbers of scientists and scholars who are engaged in research for a minute fraction of them significantly to advance scientific progress and human understanding.

The consequences of the faculty appointment power in an academic institution for research productivity, shown in the last two rows of Table 9.3, are paradoxical if not downright inconsistent. The more influence in faculty appointments the administration generally has, according to statements of faculty members, the *lower* is the publication rate, as has been implicit in the earlier references to the mediating effects of decentralized appointments on research productivity. In contrast, the more influence the president personally has in faculty appointments, according to his or her own statement, the *higher* is the publication rate. Both effects are considerable, although part of the very strong negative simple correlation between administrative centralization and productivity is the spurious result of common antecedents.

Several possible explanations of this apparent inconsistency must be considered. The strange result may have been produced by methodological defects, either by unreliability of the measures or by wrong causal assumptions. It is improbable, though not impossible, that the findings are attributable to measurement error, inasmuch as parallel results are obtained when using a different measure (a factor score instead of the item of administration's influence in appointments). With respect to causal assumptions, the postulated causal sequence can be plausibly reversed by assuming that greater research contributions of the faculty strengthen its influence and weaken the administration's, as was actually suggested in Chapter Seven. However, this interpretation cannot account for the finding that the president's influence is *positively* related to the faculty's research accomplishment. The assumption made is that administrative decentralization and faculty research productivity mutually affect each other, which means that the pattern observed in the table cannot be dismissed on methodological grounds but requires substantive explanation, speculative as this explanation may have to be.

Faculty research output is high if the president says he has ample appointment power and faculty members say the administration does not have too much, thereby implying that their power is not too much infringed upon. One possible inference of reading the findings in these terms is that the research of faculty members benefits from increases in both their own power and the president's, because power is not a zero-sum game. However, the proposition that power is not a zero-sum game rests on premises that are not applicable. It may refer to the greater power accruing to all members of an organization or group as the collectivity's power expands, or it may refer to the reciprocal influences group members exert on one another, which increase the controlling power of each though not their relative power. Neither premise applies to the relative power of various parties within an academic institution over faculty appointments, which *is* a zero-sum game. Another inference that can be derived is that conditions in an academic institution are conducive to productive research if there is little dissatisfaction with the distribution of power—if the president is satisfied with his and faculty members are satisfied with theirs. Although this may well be true, it begs the question. Unless one assumes that *false* perceptions of power are responsible for the differences found, the question remains what power constellation satisfies both and thus improves the faculty's publication records. The interpretation advanced is that the existence of a productive faculty in a university depends on opposite forces that create checks and balances.

The administration of an institution of higher education comprises vice-presidents, deans, and other administrators as well as the president. Hence the findings that research productivity is inversely related to the administration's but not to the president's appointment power suggest that it is the power of administrators in intermediate positions that has a detrimental effect on faculty research output. This interpretation is analogous to Simmel's principle that the power of a ruler is more compatible with considerable power of the populace and the legal equality of all subjects than with a powerful aristocracy. He states, for instance, that a strong ruler "favors the efforts of the lower classes which are directed toward legal equality with these intermediate powers."[31] Indeed, the data indicate that substantial authority over faculty appointment of deans affects research productivity adversely.[32]

The faculty's decisive voice in selecting new faculty members without unwarranted interference from administrators raises the scholarly output at an academic institution for various reasons, but it recurrently leads to poor appointment decisions that might lower this output. Faculty members are better qualified than administrators to judge the abilities of specialists in their fields and are thus more likely to appoint candidates capable of making research contributions. Their knowledge of experts in the field who might be available for appointments or who can recommend promising young candidates is not taken advantage of if faculty members have little say in recruitment. Faculty members prize their autonomy, resent domination by administrators, and object to being saddled by administrative fiat with incompetent or undesirable colleagues; the most productive among them, who have the opportunities, are likely to leave under these conditions. The continual frustrations of having to deal with a centralized administration in all probability also have deleterious effects on the scholarly research of the faculty members

[31] Georg Simmel, *The Sociology of Georg Simmel*, Glencoe, Ill.: Free Press, 1950, p. 199.
[32] The measure is the president's (or his deputy's) five-point rating of the influence of deans in faculty appointment decisions. It has a correlation of $-.21$ with faculty research productivity. If added to the variables in Table 9.3, its beta weight is $-.13$, more than two standard errors. This variable is used only to test an inference and not in the basic research, because the reliability of the estimate of a superior of the influence of subordinates is questionable.

who remain at the institution. In short, the great influence of administrators on faculty appointments is assumed to be detrimental for the scholarly productivity at an academic institution because it results in the appointment of less productive faculty members, in the resignation of the most productive ones who are there, and in frustrations and dissatisfactions that inhibit the scholarly research of those who stay.

But faculty members are human and thus are, like all human beings, affected in their decisions by their own interests and value orientations. They tend to have preferences for their former students, who would carry on their research tradition. Their academic life is bound up with a certain orientation in their discipline, making them look askance at very different approaches and unfavorably disposed to candidates for appointments trained in other schools of thought, which creates the danger that a department is narrowly restricted to one academic viewpoint and excludes alternative perspectives in the discipline. It is also to be expected that some faculty members will be apprehensive about appointing candidates who would trespass on what they consider their domain of research facilities and students, or one who threatens by his or her brilliance to outshine them. Such fears obviously lead to poor selection. Hutchins comments that "departments and selection committees and individual professors seem often moved by fear of competition on the one hand and by affection for their disciples on the other."[33] An outside check on these and similar tendencies is necessary for optimum appointment decisions that maintain a faculty of productive scholars at an academic institution. The president's authority to veto faculty appointments appears to provide this external check, not because he is less biased than faculty members, but because he does not share their biases.

A careful balance must be struck between the need for faculty autonomy in making appointments and the need for an external check on their appointment decisions. A number of reasons for the importance of both have been suggested. Deans and other middle-level administrators who have much appointment authority are likely to exercise it by becoming involved in the selection process, which undermines faculty autonomy and tips the balance, with the result that scholarly productivity suffers. A president who has much appointment authority, being farther removed, is more likely to exercise it by vetoing some recommendations than by participating actively in the selection of candidates. This is less subversive of faculty autonomy and can provide the independent check on faculty appointment decisions that contributes to good selection and high research productivity.

33 Robert M. Hutchins, *The Learning Society*, New York: Praeger, 1968, p. 115.

EDUCATION AND SCHOLARSHIP

In conclusion, a brief comparison is presented between the conditions in academic institutions that influence educational performance and those influencing the performance of scholarly research. It should be noted that there is very little relationship between the two indicators of effective teaching and the indicator of effective scholarship. The correlation of faculty research productivity with the rate of college completion is nil (.00), and its correlation with the rate of continuing to graduate school is slight (.14). These data clearly show that good teaching and productive scholarship are not incompatible, though they simultaneously show that the two do not go hand in hand. After comparing the influences governing education and research, those governing departmental innovation will be added to the comparison.

Some characteristics of academic institutions further both the educational progress of students and the scholarly productivity of the faculty. Centers of graduate training with well-qualified faculties are better academic environments not only for faculty research but also for undergraduate teaching than are undergraduate colleges with many faculty members who never completed advanced training in their fields. The proportion of an institution's faculty who have advanced degrees, though it appears to be a superficial indication of faculty qualifications, is the only specific factor discovered that has positive effects on all three measures of academic perfomance—on the educational progress of undergraduates, their chances of going to graduate school, and the faculty's research productivity. A well-trained faculty tends to create a climate of lively research and scholarship in an academic institution, without which even individuals with advanced training are unlikely to be stimulated to engage in productive scholarship, and which is a challenging educational environment for students.

Undergraduate colleges have disadvantages for good education as well as for productive scholarship, but different aspects of graduate universities benefit the two. Many graduate students improve the educational performance of undergraduates, since graduate students serve as role models, as communication links between undergraduates and faculty, and also as links transmitting a tradition of advanced education from generation to generation. The most advanced graduate training indicated by the granting of Ph.D.'s rather than the proportion of graduate students is important for the scholarly productivity of the faculty, probably because only at this stage are appointments really made contingent on scholarly publications or potentials, and perhaps also because large numbers of M.A. students infringe on time for research.

Two attributes of academic institutions have opposite effects on teaching and research. It is noteworthy that only two factors with such conflicting influences were discovered among scores of variables examined, though between 57 and 71 per cent of the variations in the three performance measures are accounted for. The two are the institution's emphasis on publishing research and its reputation. An emphasis on the obligation to publish selects faculty members primarily oriented to research, which has the expected result of channeling their energies and making them more successful researchers than teachers. The high academic reputation of an institution, built in large part by the scholarly contributions of previous generations of its faculty, helps to recruit productive scientists and scholars, which illustrates how institutional reputations and traditions of scholarly research are perpetuated. But independent of the quality of its faculty and students, an academic institution's high reputation depresses the chances of college graduates to proceed to graduate school, probably because they develop less favorable self-conceptions of their academic abilities and get less help from the faculty than students in institutions with lower reputations and fewer outstanding fellow students.

A variety of conditions in universities and colleges do not have opposite effects on education and scholarship but have significance for only one of the two. The research productivity in an academic institution benefits from an appointment procedure that gives the faculty much autonomy unimpeded by administrative intervention in the selection process yet also provides an outside check on faculty decisions in the form of the president's power to veto recommendations for appointments. None of the indicators of centralization or decentralization affect either measure of educational performance. On the other hand, several indications of bureaucratization have detrimental effects on teaching without exerting any influence on research, perhaps because research undertakings, if other conditions are favorable, can be removed from the institution's administrative machinery, whereas the educational enterprise is inextricably interwoven with it. Mechanical teaching has adverse effects on both measures of educational performance; undergraduate progress is also adversely affected by a bureaucratic structure of multiple levels, a high student-faculty ratio, and the impersonal atmosphere manifest in few faculty-student contacts; and progress to graduate school is adversely affected by an inflexible institutional structure. If the conclusion is correct that bureaucratization harms teaching much but research little, it is a danger sign, for it implies that the most influential faculty members, whose primary interest tends to be scholarly research, have few incentives to oppose the bureaucratic tendencies that are harmful to education.

How do the conditions that promote institutional innovation in a university or college, which were discussed in Chapter Eight, compare with those that benefit scholarship and education? Two factors exert such crucial impact on both departmental innovation and scholarly research that one might consider them virtually institutional prerequisites of productive research in advanced specialities. A university can hardly maintain a leading position in advancing knowledge in new fields unless it is large and unless authority in it is decentralized, except for some veto power of the president over appointments. Several factors contribute to both institutional innovation and educational performance: a faculty not so strongly committed to the local institution that they lose contact with fellow specialists elsewhere and new developments in their fields; bright students who challenge faculty members; and standardized salary raises, which seem to reduce distrust and encourage cooperation among faculty members. Only one condition with opposite effects on innovation and education was discovered. The academic tradition that has developed over many generations in old academic institutions inhibits innovation, on the one hand, and increases the chances of students to go to graduate school, on the other. There is also an indirect indication of such conflicting influences. Democratic faculty government promotes innovation, but possibly at some cost to effective teaching, though it should be noted that different measures of faculty government have these contrasting effects.

While there is some conflict between research and teaching in institutions of higher education, it is largely indirect. The educational performance in an academic institution is essentially independent of the productive scholarship of its faculty. As a matter of fact, successful teaching and research productivity depend in part on similar conditions, notably the superior qualifications of the faculty and the serious academic atmosphere pervading the daily life in a university with many graduate students. There are also conditions that have opposite effects on education and scholarship, like an institution's reputation and the emphasis on research in it. The coexistence of some conditions that have opposite and some that have parallel effects on the two functions is the source of the teaching-research dilemma, because it shows that the conflicts between the two cannot be resolved without depriving either of important benefits by simply separating them into different institutions —undergraduate colleges and graduate centers.

The factors that have adverse effects on teaching without affecting research one way or the other are of special significance, for they are indicative not of dilemmas that must be lived with but of problems that could be solved yet show no signs of being solved. Several bureaucratic tendencies fall into this category: a mechanical and impersonal approach to teaching, a bureaucratic structure that has excessive administrative ranks and is inflexible, and a simplistic managerial conception of education as an output that can be produced more efficiently by increasing students per paid man-hour. Scholarly productivity appears to be immune from the deleterious consequences such bureaucratization has for education, which implies that the academic interests of the most influential scientists and scholars in an institution are not directly involved in fighting against bureaucratic processes that damage the educational enterprise.

CHAPTER TEN

DIMENSIONS OF ACADEMIC
DIFFERENTIATION

This chapter is devoted to a review of main findings and a discussion of some of their theoretical implications. The summary of the research findings views them from a new perspective. The original analysis focused attention on a given characteristic of American universities and colleges and traced antecedent conditions that affect it directly or indirectly. The review of results starts with a given condition in academic institutions and examines its various influences that have been discovered. The antecedent conditions that exert most influence, to which the discussion is confined, can all be conceptualized as resources, broadly defined to encompass human and institutional as well as financial assets. After summarizing the effects of various resources, differentiation in academia is explored in theoretical terms.

Social differentiation is of central significance in the conceptual framework of sociology; hence many of the inquiry's implications of theoretical interest to sociologists pertain to differentiation in academic life. Inasmuch as the core of sociology is the study of social structure, and inasmuch as social structure denotes that people belong to various subgroups and differ in status, these socially produced differences and how they come about are of prime theoretical concern. Care must be taken not to confound several ways the concept of differentiation is applied. First, the social system or structure to which it refers must be specified.

The differentiation of a society's academic system, which means that it comprises many diverse universities and colleges, is of course not the same as the differentiation of a university, which means that it consists of many diverse departments, and still another matter is the differentiation of a department, which means that many specialties are represented in it. A second distinction that should be kept in mind is that between the degree of differentiation existing in social structures and the process in which they become more, or possibly less, differentiated. In other words, differentiation may indicate either a static or a dynamic attribute of social structures. Third, differentiation occurs along several dimensions. Although groups of all kinds are often socially ranked in the larger social structure, there is a fundamental contrast between differentiation that is not directly based on a rank order, such as that among academic disciplines, and differentiation of status in terms of a ranking criterion—or social stratification—such as that among universities varying in academic standing.

The discussion of theoretical topics is divided into two sections, one dealing with the extent of differentiation in the structure of academic institutions and the other with the academic stratification system. In the former section, the major concern is exploring the principles that govern differentiation, disregarding for the moment whether or not differences in power or prestige accompany it, with special emphasis on the progressive division of academic labor and increasing specialization. Both the degree of differentiation and the process through which it becomes more pronounced in academic institutions are analyzed to test and refine some theoretical assumptions derived earlier from research on other kinds of organizations. The analysis of the academic stratification system includes a discussion of dilemmas, since status hierarchies create dilemmas, and since the social change engendered by dilemmas depends on the status structure. The concluding section returns briefly to the problem posed in the first chapter of the implications of bureaucracy for scholarship.

EFFECTS OF VARIOUS RESOURCES

Various resources are needed to maintain a good university. Material assets are not sufficient; it takes human and institutional resources too. Economic resources are important, however, because they help supply the requisite intellectual human resources. Besides, their having done so in the past built the foundation of the present institution's academic tradition and climate, which also are significant resources.

Affluent institutions pay better salaries than poor ones,[1] which makes them more successful in competing for the best qualified faculties who are most committed to scholarly research, and they can recruit larger faculties, which enables them to establish more departments in specialized fields. Hence affluent academic institutions have the highest reputations, the best students, and the most productive faculties with the highest records of scholarly publications. They also provide more clerical help than poor institutions. Affluent universities that have high academic standing tend to be decentralized with respect to educational affairs and faculty appointments, quite possibly because the need to economize fosters tighter administrative reins. Disproportionate numbers of their faculty members have been reared in the middle class, which suggests some class bias in recruitment. The overall impression is that of an elite university.

Investing financial assets in high faculty salaries bears interest, as it were. Comparatively high salaries enable an academic institution to recruit a faculty with superior qualifications, who are oriented to research, strengthen the institution's reputation, and attract able students. High salaries have more impact than any other factor on attracting well-qualified faculties, not because income is necessarily more important than the intrinsic rewards of academic work, but because better qualified academics have the bargaining power to obtain both—good salaries in universities that have favorable conditions for rewarding academic work.

High salaries appear to be particularly salient for upwardly mobile faculty members from poorer homes, who nevertheless get on the average lower salaries than those reared in the upper-middle class, probably as the result of subtle discrimination against them in the institutions with the best reputations and highest salaries. Whereas the better qualified faculties recruited with better salaries attract better students, higher salaries seem to be required to obtain equally good faculty members to teach mediocre students than to teach bright ones. In institutions that pay high faculty salaries, authority over faculty appointments is usually not centralized in the hands of administrators. Generally, then, low salaries go together with other disadvantageous conditions in institutions of higher education, which furnishes an institutional source of academic status consistency or crystallization,[2] since it makes the position of faculty members who get low salaries worse with respect to power and prestige as well.

[1] Every relationship mentioned in this section refers to a finding, which can be looked up in the table in which the dependent variable under discussion is analyzed or, in the case of indirect effects, in the accompanying text.
[2] See Gerhard Lenski, "Status Crystallization," *American Sociological Review* **19** (1954), 405–413.

The number of faculty members in an academic institution is indicative of the quantity of its human resources. The size of an institution's faculty affects nearly all its other characteristics.[3] It appears in 25 of the 30 tables in this book, because it influences all these dependent variables directly, indirectly, or both, and it is substantially correlated with several additional factors not analyzed as dependent variables, including affluence (.31), proportion of graduate students (.41), and university status (.60; in logarithmic transformation, .66). To be sure, large universities differ from small colleges in many ways beside size, and one might suspect that these other factors are responsible for the pervasive associations of size with other characteristics. After all, institutional size exhibits correlations of more than .60 with the number of departments and the number of schools and colleges; with university status, salaries paid, emphasis on research rather than teaching, and concentration of appointment power in the hands of faculty members instead of administrators. Yet even when all relevant conditions are controlled, size has a direct effect on 19 of 28 institutional characteristics analyzed as dependent variables (excluding those in Tables 5.2 and 5.5, which are characteristics of individuals, not institutions). The only five factors not affected by institutional size are the class background of the faculty, selectivity in student admissions, centralization of educational matters, undergraduate progress, and rate of continuing to graduate school. It is noteworthy that size affects neither of the two indicators of educational performance.

The size of an academic institution unquestionably has a predominant effect on its character, and the same is the case in other types of organizations.[4] The reason is that institutional size comprises several elements, though numerous correlates of it have been controlled. It refers to both economic and manpower resources (even if affluence per student is controlled), an impersonal atmosphere, a large administrative work load, and the statistical probability of finding colleagues with common interests.

The 21 direct effects of the size of academic institutions can be classified under these categories.[5] They are schematically presented in Table 10.1, together with the main indirect effects they mediate. It takes large

[3] Edward Gross and Paul V. Grambsch report that among *universities,* size exerts little influence on goals, except that there is more emphasis on research, new ideas, and keeping up to date; *University Goals and Academic Power,* Washington: American Council on Education, 1968, pp. 43–44.

[4] See Peter M. Blau and Richard A. Schoenherr, *The Structure of Organizations,* New York: Basic Books, 1971, pp. 56–57.

[5] The 21 direct effects include 19 in the tables presented plus the effects of large size on percentage of graduate students and university status.

Table 10.1   Effects of Large Size[a]

Economic and Manpower Resources
1. Many graduate students
2. Ph.D.-granting university; mediated by it, high research productivity
3. High salaries; mediated by it, superior faculty qualifications
4. Many specialized departments; mediated by it, superior reputation, high clerical-faculty ratio, more contacts with graduate students, and fewer with undergraduates
5. Several schools and colleges; mediated by it, high administration-faculty ratio and greater interest in outside faculty
6. Emphasis on research
7. High student aptitudes

Impersonality
8. Lower faculty qualifications
9. Lower attraction to good students
10. Less allegiance to local institution

Administrative Load
11. More administrative levels; mediated by it, narrower span of control of the president, also of vice-presidents, and less influence of the president over appointments
12. Wide span of control of the president
13. Wide span of control of vice-presidents
14. Low administration-faculty ratio (economy of scale)
15. Low clerical-faculty ratio (economy of scale)
16. Less interest in outside faculty
17. Less appointment power of administration
18. More appointment power of faculty
19. Less financial authority of president

Chances of Common Interests
20. More departments in new fields
21. Frequent creation of departments

---

[a] Each dependent variable is mentioned only once, unless size has effects in opposite directions on it. If additive indirect effects of size are mediated by several intervening variables, only the strongest is noted.

manpower resources for an institution of higher education to train many graduate students and to become a Ph.D.-granting university, because a large faculty is required to have many departments in diverse specialties, to maintain several professional schools, and to attract students with high aptitudes. The financial assets of large institutions make it possible to pay adequate faculty salaries and recruit a faculty oriented to scholarly research. But the impersonal atmosphere in multiuniversities, independent of other conditions, appears to make them less attractive for the best students as well as faculty members and to weaken faculty allegiance to the institution. Thus, whereas large manpower and economic resources are assets, the impersonal atmosphere in large universities is a liability.

The heavy load of administrative work in large institution increases the absolute number of administrative personnel, though it reduces the relative number of both administrators and clerks, and it engenders a differentiated administrative structure with more hierarchical ranks and a wider span of control of the president and the officials reporting to him. The pressure of a large volume of administrative work also seems to discourage efforts to recruit outside faculty and, particularly, to encourage decentralization, decreasing the administration's and increasing the faculty's influence in appointments and fostering delegation of the authority over the expenditure of funds. The greater decentralization in large multiuniversities conflicts with the common stereotype. Finally, the fact that the sheer chance that faculty members find congenial colleagues with whom they share specialized academic interests increases with increasing size makes it most likely in large institutions for departments in new fields and new departments generally to be formed.

In addition to these direct influences, the large size of an academic institution has numerous indirect effects, and sometimes its indirect and direct effects are in opposite directions. The more advanced and specialized academic work in large institutions, as well as their higher salaries, facilitate the recruitment of well-qualified faculties, who are oriented toward research, attract outstanding students, and contribute to the institution's academic reputation. These positive indirect effects of institutional size on faculty quality outweigh its negative direct effect. Faculty members of large academic institutions spend more time with graduate students and less with undergraduates than do those of small colleges, because there are more graduate students, the specialized interests of the faculty are best suited for graduate training, and the high abilities of undergraduates reduce their need for faculty help. Large institutional size, by giving rise to a more highly differentiated administrative structure, has a number of indirect effects that counteract its direct ones. The multilevel hierarchies in large institutions narrow the span of control of top administrators; their complex differentiated structure enlarges the administration-faculty ratio; and their numerous schools and colleges strengthen interest in outside faculty. All of these indirect effects of size are opposite to its direct effects, but multiple levels also reduce the president's appointment power, which parallels the direct influences of size on decentralization. Finally, faculty research productivity in large universities is higher than in small colleges, since university appointment policies emphasize research and large institutions are less centralized.

An indication of the quality of an academic institution's human resources is the proportion of its faculty who have completed advanced training and thus all formal qualifications for scholarship in their field. When most members of a faculty have finished their formal training, the prevailing orientations among them tend to be toward scholarly research and toward fellow specialists outside their institution, which curtails their commitment to the local institution; such a cosmopolitan orientation to the larger academic community beyond the walls of the campus also characterizes top administrators of institutions with well-qualified faculties. Superior qualifications of the faculty raise an institution's reputation and attract the best students to it, for good reasons, since the high qualifications of the faculty improve both the educational performance of undergraduates in college and their chances of going to graduate school. Authority tends to be more decentralized in institutions that have better qualified faculties, inasmuch as the research involvement and productivity of such faculties help enhance the institution's reputation and their own, and consequently strengthen their bargaining power.

Other aspects of the quality of human resources are the orientation of the faculty, the institution's reputation, and the aptitudes of its students. An orientation to research in an institution and among its faculty increases research productivity and limits the administration's influence in faculty appointments, but it is detrimental for undergraduate teaching and disinclines able students, quite realistically, from coming to the college. A faculty of "locals" committed to and entrenched in an institution is less likely than one oriented to outside reference groups in their discipline to contribute to educational progress in their institution either as active agents in the creation of new departments or as teachers inspiring undergraduates to take up graduate work. Thus involvement in the local institutional structure, though it tends to be accompanied by an orientation to teaching, seems to impede education as well as innovation.

The superior quantity and quality of faculty manpower are essential ingredients of a major university of high repute that attracts the best students. The greater the reputation of an academic institution, the higher are the aptitudes of its students, and the larger is the proportion of its undergraduates who proceed to graduate school. But when other conditions are controlled, a high reputation is seen to depress the rate of continuing to graduate school, probably because high academic standards, unfavorable comparison with exceptional fellow students, and less personal communication with the faculty discourage plans for graduate work in the best colleges. The relative academic standing of an institution tends to be perpetuated through its faculty's scholarly productivity, which is substantially correlated with the institution's reputation. Universities and colleges with good reputations also have more middle-class faculties, which implies some class bias in recruitment, and educational affairs are less centralized in them than in other institutions.

The effect of the average aptitudes of freshmen on their progress in colleges is not as straightforward as one would expect. (*Nota bene* that institutional averages are under discussion, not individual differences within institutions.) The positive simple correlation between the abilities of the freshmen class and speedy college completion must be considered spurious, resulting largely from the dependence of both the abilities of entering freshmen and their progress in college on the qualifications of the faculty. The aptitudes of the freshmen class do have a direct effect increasing the proportion of them who receive college degrees within four years, other conditions being equal. Other conditions alter the situation, however, because faculties in colleges that have students with relatively low aptitudes give more help in personal conferences, which reduces the handicaps of the less able student cohorts enough to make the difference in college completion between them and others inconsequential. The high ability of the students in an institution and frequent contacts with advanced students appear to keep the faculty alert and attuned to new developments in science, which is reflected in the greater likelihood that departments in new fields become instituted.

An academic tradition that has developed over many generations and advanced academic work that sustains the tradition's vigor and keeps it from turning into sterile traditionalism may be considered institutional resources of a university. The long tradition of an academic institution promotes high standards of scholarship, though it inhibits innovation. Older academic institutions have higher standards for faculty recruitment and for student admission than do newer institutions, which they maintain by offering sufficiently high salaries to employ better qualified faculty members and by rejecting larger proportions of student applicants. The scholarly tradition of older institutions encourages disproportionate numbers of their undergraduates to continue their education in graduate school. But the conservative traditionalism that often accompanies a long history creates a reluctance in older institutions of higher education to establish departments in new fields.

Advanced scholarship and research keep a flourishing academic tradition alive and continually invigorate it. Universities with many graduate students attract faculties with the best qualifications and the strongest interest in research; faculty members have the opportunity there to work with graduate students, which is more challenging for researchers than teaching only undergraduates. The stimulating academic atmosphere in a university with much graduate work and the role graduate students play as links between undergraduates and faculty improve the likelihood that undergraduates complete their college education and that they proceed to graduate schools. Universities have a more complex structure than colleges, with a larger number of more specialized departments, several schools and colleges, and a multilevel hierarchy. The greater specialization makes jobs at universities more inviting for well-qualified faculty members, and it expands the clerical staff universities need for their many specialized departments. Appointment policies in universities emphasize research competence and the obligation to publish, there is more interest in hiring outside faculty than in colleges, and the faculty's research productivity is higher.

The departmental structure of a university or college is the institutional embodiment of the academic division of labor in the form of specialized official subgroupings. The academic specialization and diversity manifest in many departments attract both qualified faculty and outstanding undergraduates to an institution, even though such specialization diverts faculty attention from undergraduates to graduate students. An indication of the significance of the formal division of academic labor as an institutional resource is that many specialized departments raise a university's reputation. Many departments tend to become organized into separate schools and colleges, and they enlarge the clerical personnel required in an institution. The complex structure that differentiation in various dimensions generates has implications for administration and education, which will be discussed presently. It suffices to note now that a pronounced division of academic labor benefits an academic institution, whereas a multilevel hierarchy harms it, especially with regard to recruitment of good faculty and students. But these two aspects of differentiation tend to occur together, since both increase with increasing institutional size.

Another institutional resource is the academic climate in a university or college, that is, the predominant orientation to academic work among colleagues. The utilization of economic resources to offer sufficient salaries to recruit good faculties has a "snowball effect" on the scholarly research being carried out in an academic institution, and so do university appointment policies that stress research capabilities. Both not only raise the scholarly quality of individual faculty members but thereby also create an academic climate in the institution that spurs research efforts. The scholarly research of individual faculty members depends to a considerable extent on the colleague climate in their institution. To be sure, by the time a person joins a faculty, his ability to make contributions to knowledge has been largely formed. But whether his or her scholarly potentials are stimulated and realized or stultified and dissipated hinges in large part on the colleague climate at the institution.

Even as superficial an indicator of the academic environment as the proportion of colleagues on the faculty with advanced degrees exerts nearly as much influence on the likelihood that an individual is engaged in research as his or her own completion of advanced training. The qualifications of colleagues have a structural effect on research involvement at an institution, which supplements the effect of the individual's own qualifications. Hence high salaries and university policies making appointments contingent on research increase scholarly research in two ways, by selecting faculty members qualified for and oriented to research and by consequently creating an institutional climate in which colleague pressures further enhance research involvement. University procedures requiring publications for promotion do not seem to serve as effective incentives motivating individuals to engage in research, yet they are effective in intensifying research activities through selection and through producing a research climate.

THE PROCESS OF DIFFERENTIATION

The American system of higher education comprises hundreds of universities and colleges, and additional hundreds of separate professional schools and junior colleges. Some of these institutions are part of state systems, but most are independent. Of those offering four-year degrees in the liberal arts, which are the ones that have been studied, three-quarters are independent. These institutions of higher education compete for academic standing, promising students, capable faculty members, and benevolent donors. Ben-David considers the rapid scientific progress in the United States during this century to be the result of the competition among many independent universities and colleges. He also suggests that the process of competition encourages further differentiation among institutions, since those that cannot compete with the best in overall standing seek to succeed by making distinctive contributions in one special area or another.[6] And just as the differences among academic institutions beget more external differentiation, so too with the internal dif-

---

[6] Joseph Ben-David, *American Higher Education*, New York: McGraw-Hill, 1972, p. 41.

ferentiation within a university, not only today but already in the Middle Ages. "The intellectual division of labor arising from the location of different kinds of existing studies within one corporate organization also stimulated the further differentiation which gave the natural sciences their place at the universities. . . . Even though these activities were not institutionalized, the mere size and internal differentiation of the universities permitted enough interested persons to find each other."[7]

The differences among American universities and colleges have been analyzed at length in this book, and the internal differentiation within them has received particular attention in Chapters Three and Eight. But the focus of the discussion was not the same in the two places. Chapter Three dealt with the *extent* of differentiation in academic institutions, whereas Chapter Eight was concerned with the *process* of differentiation indicated by the addition of new departmental specialities, which makes the academic division of labor more pronounced. In short, the statics of differentiation was analyzed in the one and its dynamics in the other chapter. The objective now is to bring these results together and examine their implications for the theory of differentiation in organizations developed earlier on the basis of research on government bureaus.[8] The data on universities and colleges furnish an especially good test case of the theory, because academic pursuits and institutions are so different from the government activities and agencies studied, and because the new data include information about the process of differentiation, whereas previously this process had to be inferred.

The basic empirical propositions can be subsumed—in more concise form than in Chapter Three—under three theorems:

1. Increasing organizational size generates differentiation at declining rates.

---

[7] Joseph Ben-David, "The Scientific Role," *Minerva* 4 (1) (1965), 21.

[8] Since the theory was originally published in 1970 (in virtually the same form as in Blau and Schoenherr, *op. cit.*, pp. 300–320), several authors have attempted to put parts of it into mathematical or statistical form. See Norman P. Hummon, "A Mathematical Theory of Differentiation in Organizations," *American Sociological Review* 36 (1971), 297–303; Marshall W. Meyer, "Some Constraints in Analyzing Data on Organizational Structures," *ibid.*, pp. 294–297; Bruce H. Mayhew, Jr., et al., "System Size and Structural Differentiation in Military Organizations," *American Journal of Sociology* 77 (1972), 750–765; Bruce H. Mayhew, Jr., et al., "System Size and Structural Differentiation in Formal Organizations," *American Sociological Review* 37 (1972), 629–633. It is possible that the first theorem will turn out to conform to a statistical law of probability. Whether this would suffice to explain it or a substantive explanation of it in theoretical terms would still be required is a debatable issue. I take the latter position; for the former, see Anatol Rapoport, "Rank-Size Relations," *International Encyclopedia of the Social Sciences,* New York: Macmillan, 1968.

2. Increasing organizational size reduces administrative ratios at declining rates.

3. Structural differentiation in organizations enlarges administrative ratios.

The last theorem can explain parts of the other two, on the assumption that the managements of organizations seek to minimize administrative costs. If differentiation increases the need for costly administrative personnel, one may infer that increasing differentiation engenders growing resistance to further differentiation, which can explain why the impact of size on differentiation declines as it produces more differentiation. Similarly, the greater need for administrative personnel produced by pronounced differentiation, which tends to accompany large organizational size, counteracts the economy of scale in administration, which may explain why the impact of size on reducing the administrative ratio (the administrative economy of scale) declines as size, and with it differentiation, increase. Structural differentiation creates problems of communication and coordination in an organization that raise administrative costs. Feedback processes resulting from this cost of differentiation attenuate the effects of size on both differentiation and administrative ratios, according to the theory, which is reflected in the declining strength of these effects.

But what explains the two influences of size themselves? The theory was elaborated to suggest hypotheses to explain why the expanding size of organizations promotes differentiation and reduces the proportion of administrative personnel,[9] and the data on academic institutions help test these hypotheses and discriminate among them. The first hypothesis derives from Durkheim's principle that the social solidarity that transforms a large number of individuals into a society or other integrated collectivity rests either on distinctive common values that unify them or on the division of labor into complementary activities that make them interdependent.[10] Inasmuch as the employees of an organization do not share distinctive profound values that set them apart from the rest of the community, their integration as an organized collectivity is rooted in their interdependence, produced by the division of labor among individuals and among structural components of the organization along crosscutting lines, such as functional subdivisions and administrative levels. Thus one theoretical assumption introduced is that large organizations

[9] Peter M. Blau, "Interdependence and Hierarchy in Organizations," *Social Science Research* 1 (1972), 1–24.

[10] Emile Durkheim, *The Division of Labor in Society*, New York: Macmillan, 1933.

require much differentiation to create the interdependence that integrates many employees in a common enterprise.

The need to integrate large numbers of employees in a common endeavor may produce extensive differentiation of large organizations into many subunits for another reason. Individuals cannot directly relate themselves to an entire society or any other large collectivity, but their integration in it is always mediated by small groups in which frequent face-to-face contacts occur. The process of social integration depends on regular personal communications in which individuals are socialized and receive social support. The family illustrates this. Intimate contacts in small families make it possible for children to be socialized and acquire the common language and cultural values that make them integral members of the society. Organizations are not composed of families, but they too must provide opportunities for face-to-face contacts in small groups for new members to become socialized and integrated, and for old members to obtain social support and remain integrated. The differentiation of organizations into departments and work groups creates the substitutes for families in which daily social interaction socializes newcomers, acquaints them with informal as well as formal procedures, supplies both them and oldtimers with advice and social support, and thereby effects social integration. Accordingly, the second theoretical assumption is that organizations become increasingly differentiated the larger they are in order to produce sufficiently small subgroups for the regular personal contacts that are essential for social integration.

The differentiation of work within an organization also has instrumental advantages, however, and these rather than its implications for social integration may be responsible for its development as far as the organization's size permits. The division of labor separates tasks into more homogeneous duties of organizational subunits and individuals, which typically range from quite routine to highly specialized jobs. Since routine jobs can be filled with less skilled personnel and highly specialized ones require and make possible greater expert skills, the division of labor enables an organization to discharge more complex responsibilities with less skilled personnel. These are compelling reasons for a management interested in maximizing performance and minimizing labor cost to make the administrative decisions that produce as much subdivision of work as is feasible given the size of the organization. This third interpretation of why differentiation progresses with the expanding size of organizations contains several assumptions that should be distinguished. One question is whether the improved performance specialization makes possible suffices to generate increasing subdivision of work, independent of immediate economic benefits, or whether the reduction in labor cost routinization effects is necessary for this purpose. Another assumption made that requires testing is that the differentiation of work in organizations depends on the initiative of a management responsible for and interested in efficiency.

Since several theoretical hypotheses have been suggested to explain one empirical proposition—the influence of organizational size on differentiation—the question remains which of these principles furnish the explanation that is probably valid. If the data on academic institutions allow us to discard some of the five theoretical assumptions made, they would strengthen confidence in the remaining theoretical principles. The five assumptions are: (1) differentiation creates the interdependence necessary to integrate large numbers of employees in a common enterprise; (2) it produces the small groups essential for the process of social integration of individuals; (3) it entails specialization, which has inherent (noneconomic) advantages; (4) it reduces labor cost through routinization; (5) its development is contingent on the intervention of management prompted by an interest in economic efficiency.

Differentiation in all three dimensions for which indicators are available increases at declining rates with increasing size in academic institutions, as it does in other types of organizations. Moreover, the larger an academic institution, the greater is the frequency with which new departments are added to it. These findings confirm the first theorem in both static and dynamic terms. The dynamic formulation of the first theorem —that large size *generates* differentiation—was originally a mere inference from cross-sectional data showing strong correlations between organizational size and various aspects of differentiation. This inference is supported by the positive associations of the size of academic institutions not only with the *existence* of differentiation but also with the *process* of increasing differentiation. Meyer's research based on longitudinal data also confirms the dynamic inference that large size produces greater differentiation.[11]

Another implication of these findings on universities and colleges is that the fourth assumption listed above is not tenable. A pronounced academic division of labor generally, and the formation of departments

---

[11] His data on government finance departments show that organizational size at an earlier period, controlling differentiation then, is associated with differentiation at a later period; Marshall W. Meyer, "Size and the Structure of Organizations," *American Sociological Review* **37** (1972), 434–440.

in new specialties particularly, by no means make the jobs of faculty members more routine, nor do they reduce labor cost for the specialized scientists and scholars. The advancing division of labor with expanding organizational size cannot be explained in terms of its routinizing effect that lowers labor cost, because if this were the explanation the academic division of labor, which does not have this effect, would not advance with expanding institutional size, while it does.

The two factors that have most influence on the process of differentiation in academic institutions manifest in the addition of new departments are the institution's size and decentralization of authority to the faculty in it. Faculty members are more likely than administrators to take the initiative to form new departments in large academic institutions, in which new departments are most frequently created, and such faculty initiative increases the likelihood that departments in new fields become established. Various other indications of decentralized authority also enhance the frequency with which new departments are instituted. The fifth assumption is contradicted by these findings.

The process of progressive differentiation and specialization clearly does not hinge on the initiative of top administrators who are interested in the improvements in efficiency that differentiation realizes. To be sure, major structural changes in most organizations can be instituted only by top management, and this applies to the establishment of new divisions or departments, that is, to increasing differentiation. Even in universities, where the faculty has considerable authority, the formation of departments requires presidential approval, and high turnover of presidents inhibits the establishment of departments in new fields, because recently appointed presidents still adjusting to their new responsibilities cannot easily devote the time and effort required to decide whether the commitment of resources entailed by a new department is justified. To say that structural changes depend on the decisions of top administrators empowered to make them, however, is not the same as claiming that the interests of top administrators are the driving force producing these changes. The data indicate that faculty initiative and influence make new departments and thus increasing differentiation and specialization in academic institutions most likely. This conflicts with the fifth assumption and requires discarding it.

Specialization appears to have intrinsic advantages that set in motion social forces generating the division of labor as far as other conditions permit, size being a major condition limiting it, the state of the technology being another. The division of labor is more pronounced in large than in small societies—at least, when the stage of their technology is held constant—and in large than in small organizations. Often the advancing division of labor improves economic efficiency, which is the immediate stimulus for its development in profit-making enterprises and government bureaus charged with maximizing productivity within the limitations of an imposed budget. But the data on universities and colleges reveal that the division of labor also progresses when it does not raise short-run efficiency measurable in economic terms. This implies that the noneconomic advantages of specialization suffice to generate differentiation of work, which supports the third theoretical assumption.

The hypothesis that the dynamics of specialization is rooted in structural forces and instrumental advantages that are not dependent on the intervention of managers prompted by an interest in profit or efficiency is not intended to mean, however, that these social forces are independent of the actions of human beings or of their interests. Only individuals can initiate and implement plans to institute new departments, or other changes intensifying differentiation, but social conditions are what constrain individuals to take such action by making it in their interest to do so. Not all interests of individuals, or of organizations, are purely economic; people are also interested in power and prestige. Specialized scientific or scholarly work is most likely to enhance the academic standing of individuals and institutions, which strengthens their power in the academic community and raises their income. The differentiation of work is intimately bound up with the interests of individuals and organizations, even in situations where it does not produce direct economic benefits for them, which exerts social constraints on them to further its progress.

Does social integration have any bearing on the differentiation of formal organizations into structural components? Two hypotheses why it may do so have been suggested, one referring to the interdependence among subunits performing complementary responsibilities, and the other focusing on the significance of recurrent face-to-face contacts in small groups. With regard to the first, the specialized departments in an academic institution are not directly dependent in the performance of their work on one another, in contrast, for example, to the various parts of an assembly line, or to the sections in an employment agency collecting unemployment taxes, distributing unemployment benefits, and providing employment service to the unemployed. As a matter of fact, the more highly specialized the departments of a university are, the more difficult it is for their members to communicate about scholarly matters and find a common ground for social integration. To be sure, these very problems of communication among differentiated specialties create a need for integration lest the university fall apart, or at least no longer constitute a coherent academic community. But to postulate that a need for integration must give rise to ways of meeting that need by improving integration would be to commit the fundamental fallacy of functional analysis. The differentiation of academic institutions into specialized departments, far from integrating them by making them highly interdependent, weakens their integration by creating obstacles to communication among them. This conclusion negates the first assumption in the foregoing list.

Yet differentiation probably does contribute to social integration, though in another manner. Formalizing the differences among academic specialties by instituting separate departments for them increases the homogeneity of departmental groups, which in all likelihood enhances the social integration of their members. Hagstrom's observations on the conflicts in departments with faculty members from diverse specialties were summarized in Chapter Eight.[12] He notes that adjustments to conflicts may be made by granting different specialties considerable autonomy, but doing so merely affirms the lack of cohesive unity of the department. These conflicts and divisions, which often involve differences between a new specialty and the older discipline from which it emerged, encourage attempts to form new departments. Success in these attempts requires extensive collaboration among faculty members in a specialty, possibly from several departments. Envy and distrust inhibit such cooperation, which may be the reason why new departments are more frequently created in institutions with standardized salary increments than in those in which faculty members compete for salary raises. The chances for institutionalizing a new specialty as a department are also improved if the faculty members, who are most attuned to new academic developments in their fields, exercise much influence in the institution and if the president, who must commit the institution's resources to a new department, has been in office long enough to be no longer preoccupied with administrative adjustments and thus to have the time and energy to be responsive to the academic concerns of the faculty. The disruptive conflicts between the members of the new specialty and the old-timers in the department make both parties interested in a separation. The establishment of a separate department for the emerging specialty restores good relations and improves social integration in the old department by removing dissident elements as well as in the new one.

[12] Warren O. Hagstrom, *The Scientific Community*, New York: Basic Books, 1965, pp. 195–226.

Thus differentiation reduces the size and heterogeneity of departments and thereby furthers social integration, in conformity with the second theoretical assumption advanced. The larger an academic institution, the more differentiated its structure must become for its departments to be relatively small and homogeneous, and the same is true for other types of organizations. If large size were not to promote differentiation and the largest universities had no more departments than the average number, which is 25, their departments would have, on the average, close to 200 faculty members, which is far too many for a primary group in which face-to-face contacts prevail. The existence of small groups within a large collectivity may be considered a prerequisite of the social integration of its members, which necessitates regular face-to-face communication that socializes newcomers and provides social support to both them and old-timers. These primary groups emerge spontaneously when no formal provisions are made for them, as illustrated by the street corner gangs in city slums. In formal organizations, in which most matters are regulated by explicit procedures, formal provisions exist that make all members part of small colleague groups, and differentiation is the mechanism effecting this.

In sum, the research on universities and colleges negates three of five theoretical assumptions that could explain the impact of size on differentiation, which consequently should be dismissed; it corroborates the other two (those numbered 2 and 3 in the list) and adds to their probable validity. Inasmuch as small groups that permit recurrent face-to-face social interaction are essential for social integration, the increasing size of organizations must be accompanied by differentiation into increasing numbers of subunits. And inasmuch as specialization has compelling advantages for performance, independent of its immediate economic benefits, work tends to be subdivided in organizations as far as their size permits. Parsimony would make it preferable to end up with one theoretical premise instead of two from which the theorem that organizational size generates differentiation follows, but neither of these two has yet been falsified. It is conceivable that both assumptions are correct, and that the small subunits needed for social integration are produced in work organizations by the division of labor because specialization has compelling instrumental advantages.

The *insufficient* size of departments, or other work groups, also inhibits social integration and effective performance, however, which tends to limit the division of labor in organizations. A colleague group must be small enough for all members to know one another well and for their frequent personal contacts to create the network of social relations that attains and sustains social integration. But if it is too small, it lacks the coherence and spirit of a group with a structure of social relations. Although friendship pairs and triads furnish social support, they cannot make individuals integral parts of a colleague group. When differentiation proceeds to the point at which work is utterly fragmented and so are social relations, as it does in assembly-line factories, both social integration and task performance suffer. A critical mass of departmental members is needed to offer a diversified academic program, to provide each with stimulating and congenial colleagues, and to foster the development of a cohesive network of integrative social relations. The increasing differentiation at declining rates with increasing institutional size gives large universities several advantages over small colleges. For it has the result that the departments in large universities are more specialized, are sufficiently small and homogeneous for integrative social interaction, but are larger than those in small colleges. The larger specialized departments in large universities, unless they grow too large, provide each member with a range of colleagues for academic discussions and sociable companionship, which creates a favorable environment for academic work as well as social integration.

The opposite effects of size and structural differentiation on the proportion of administrative personnel in an organization can be explained by a single theoretical assumption. Administration is conceptualized as the responsibility for organizing, in the broadest sense, the work of others. Organizing work entails large initial investments and comparatively small subsequent expenditures of time and effort. Employees must be recruited, resources mobilized, facilities purchased, and procedures designed. These administrative investments are not much greater if the volume of work being organized is large than if it is small. The work involved in establishing a new professional school is hardly less if it remains small and lasts for only a few years than if it expands and endures for centuries. Once a computer program has been developed, it can be used for a few computations or thousands of the same kind. Accordingly, the assumption is that the administrative investments required for organizing work are *relatively* independent of the volume of fairly *homogeneous* work being organized. This theoretical assumption is intended to explain why the proportion of administrative personnel declines with increasing organizational size, since administrative investments can be distributed over a larger volume of work in large than in small organizations, and also why the number of administrative personnel expands with increasing differentiation,[13] since the greater heterogeneity of subunits implicit in differentiation requires additional administrative investments.

It may be objected that there is a simpler alternative explanation of why the large size of organizations reduces and their complex structure enlarges the proportion of administrative personnel. The high degree of differentiation in large organizations suggests that work there is usually fragmented into simple routines. Simple jobs require less supervision than complex jobs,[14] which can account for the negative effect of size on the administrative ratio, and the interdependence of fragmented work requires much coordination, which can account for the positive effect of differentiation on this ratio. The data on universities and colleges conflict with this alternative interpretation, however. Large size decreases and differentiation increases the ratios of administrative personnel in academic institutions, just as in other organizations, although academic administrators do not supervise faculty, the work of specialized scientists and scholars is not simpler than that in less differentiated institutions, and the performance in various academic specialties is not greatly interdependent. But this low degree of interdependence in universities and colleges raises another question. If there is little interdependence among subunits, why does differentiation into many of them enlarge the amount of administrative work and personnel? The answer is precisely because there is little interdependence.

Whereas we have examined how faculty members become integrated into departments in some detail, a still unresolved question is how the diverse departments and schools and colleges become integrated into the university. The lack of direct interdependence among them makes their integration into an academic community problematical. Differentiation, by increasing specialization that creates obstacles to intellectual communication, makes it more problematical. Interdisciplinary groups and institutes tie different subunits together and mitigate the situation some-

---

[13] On the basis of his longitudinal data, Meyer (*op. cit.*) casts doubt on the proposition that structural differentiation expands the administrative apparatus. But since he does not control indicators of both vertical and horizontal differentiation simultaneously, but only one at a time, and uses a different measure of administrative apparatus (raw number rather than proportion of administrative personnel), his regression analysis for a single time period would not duplicate ours (Blau and Schoenherr, *op. cit.*, pp. 90–92, 334–335, and esp. 194–195). Hence the discrepancy between his findings and ours does not result from the use of longitudinal data but from the use of different procedures.

[14] The larger an organization, the wider is the average span of control of supervisors; see Blau, *op. cit.*, p. 9.

what, but the interlocking of subunits is probably more pervasive in other kinds of organizations than in academic institutions. There is a fundamental reason for the specialized structural components to stay together, of course, and that is the common educational enterprise. Undergraduate education in the liberal arts necessitates that different academic disciplines be part of a single institution, and specialized research and graduate training, despite the fact that specialization pulls fields apart, also benefit from their remaining together in a university. The faculty is the productive labor force in an institution of higher education. Its members are occupied with teaching their various subjects and carrying out research. The responsibility for maintaining the educational enterprise is the administration's. This involves above all keeping its various parts together, which is more difficult, requiring greater administrative investments and manpower, the more specialized and diverse these parts are.

The administrative structure of universities and colleges is amazingly homologous to that of other types of organizations. The interrelations of size, differentiation, and administrative apparatus in academic institutions closely parallel those in other organizations, and so does the inverse relationship between vertical and horizontal differentiation in the structure. Other influences on differentiation are probably also similar, though the evidence in these cases is inferential.

Independent of size, universities have more differentiated structures than colleges in all three respects, which suggests that complex tasks foster the development of a complex structure. These findings correspond to the thesis of Lawrence and Lorsch that the complex demands made by a diverse environment give rise to differentiated structures in organizations—in their study, private firms.[15] An implication of this thesis is that extensive communication with a diverse and demanding environment promotes the process of differentiation, which is indirectly supported by data on academic institutions. Specifically, the establishment of new departments, which manifests differentiation in process, is more likely if the faculty is not so committed to the local institution that they lose touch with colleagues in their various disciplines outside and if they have much contact with bright graduate students, who may be considered a demanding environment. Traditionalism inhibits the formation of departments in new fields, with the result that the age of an academic institution is reflected in its departmental structure today, which Stinchcombe discovered to be the case for the institutional structure of private firms

---

[15] Paul R. Lawrence and Jay W. Lorsch, *Organization and Environment*, Boston: Graduate School of Business Administration, Harvard University, 1967, esp. pp. 156–158.

as well.[16] In short, fundamental social forces appear to govern the development of the formal structure of organizations regardless of their type. The same structural arrangements, however, do not necessarily have identical implications for responsibilities that are so different as those of government bureaus, private firms, and academic institutions.

ACADEMIC DILEMMAS AND STRATIFICATION

The concept of social differentiation refers to differences among groups and among positions of individuals based on a variety of social criteria, not necessarily a status hierarchy. But most social differences that are not originally based on a hierarchy of ranks become associated with variations in resources, prestige, and power and thus intertwined with the stratification system. The division of labor is an example. Though it is in principle independent of hierarchical status and distinguishes merely occupational roles, occupational positions are a main source of power, prestige, and economic benefits. A status hierarchy engenders dilemmas, because ranked positions have contradictory implications for incumbents and for others. The outcome of dilemmas in which the interests of various groups conflict, in turn, tends to be determined by the distribution of resources and power in the stratification system. A review of dilemmas of academic life indicates their connections with the academic system of stratification.

A dilemma has two horns, which distinguishes it from a problem. If the end is given and the question is only one of the means to achieve it, we have a problem, and if the means are not known or not at our disposal, we cannot solve the problem. But if the means are known and available, a problem can be solved, whereas a dilemma cannot be. The simplest form of a dilemma occurs when the accomplishment of two or more ends depends on the same scarce means, since the more one end is attained the more the other must be sacrificed, and the choice how to distribute the means poses a dilemma. One illustration is the dilemma of the allocation of educational resources, how much of them should be devoted to the brightest students who promise to make the greatest contributions to human knowledge and welfare, and how much to the average or weaker students to enable them to lead a better life and raise the contributions they can make to the commonweal. A second illustration

[16] Arthur R. Stinchcombe, "Social Structure and Organizations," in James March, *Handbook of Organizations,* Chicago: Rand-McNally, 1965, pp. 153–169.

is the dilemma of the distribution of scientific manpower and effort between applied research that can solve urgent social problems and theoretical research that advances knowledge but does not directly supply solutions for practical problems. A third illustration is the reasearch-teaching dilemma.

To put this last dilemma in perspective, it must be emphasized at the outset that good teaching and good research are not incompatible, that effective undergraduate education at an institution and faculty research productivity are not inversely related, and that some conditions improve both teaching and research. Specifically, universities are not only superior to undergraduate colleges with regard to faculty research and publications, but the academic atmosphere in universities with many graduate students, combined with the significance of graduate students as role models, also enhances the educational progress of undergraduates. In addition, superior qualifications of faculty members, presumably by making them more stimulating teachers and colleagues, improve the educational performance of their students and the research performance of their colleagues, as well as their own.

Yet there are conflicts between teaching and research. Faculty members with superior qualifications tend to be oriented to research more than to teaching, and while their good qualifications hasten the educational progress of undergraduates and attract able students to the institution, their focus on research slows the educational progress of undergraduates and makes the institution less attractive to able students. In addition, highly specialized academic work, which helps to raise an institution's reputation and intensifies faculty involvement with graduate students, reduces the contacts of faculty members with undergraduates. The simultaneous existence of some conditions that benefit both research and teaching and others that benefit the one at the expense of the other is what causes a dilemma, because it indicates that the conflicts between undergraduate teaching and research cannot be solved by creating separate institutions for the two without harming them. The emphasis on research in the best and richest institutions exemplifies how the stratification system governs the outcome of dilemmas.

A somewhat different source of dilemmas is that an objective of an institution, though not in conflict with another, depends on several conditions that are incompatible, because individuals have conflicting desires or ends. The dilemma faculty and student recruitment poses for the size of an academic institution is an example. To recruit good students, an academic institution must have a good faculty, and to recruit a good faculty, it must offer sufficient salaries to compete successfully for the most promising candidates. High academic standing also facilitates recruitment of both faculty and students, and so do many departments, since specialized advanced academic work appeals to qualified faculty members, and since a diverse program of course offerings appeals to able students. An institution must be large to have the resources to pay high salaries, to offer specialized and advanced academic work in a large variety of departments, and to attain high academic standing. But the impersonality of large academic institutions makes them less attractive to both good faculty and good students, as does the bureaucratic structure that tends to develop in large institutions.

Note that there is no conflict between the organizational objectives of recruiting a good faculty and recruiting good students, for the two groups are largely attracted by the same features of academic institutions. The conditions that facilitate their recruitment are incompatible, however, because both groups want some features primarily found in large universities and others hardly ever found there. The dilemma of institutional size is rooted, not in conflicts between ends of the institution, but in conflicting ends of individuals, who prefer, to use the most dramatic illustration, small institutions with many diverse and specialized departments.

Faculty recruitment illustrates the dilemma created by incompatible requirements for the achievement of given ends in another respect. To recruit and keep a good faculty, authority over appointments must be decentralized to the faculty, who have the specialized competence to judge candidates, and whose best members with the greatest opportunities will leave if colleagues are imposed on them against their will. However, inherent biases in the recruitment choices of faculty members require appointment decisions to be made by outsiders for optimum selection. The data suggest that the most productive faculties exist if the administration generally does not encroach on faculty appointment power but the president does exercise veto power over faculty recommendations. This is a practical compromise. In actual life dilemmas must always be solved one way or another, through checks and balances or through suppression of one of the interests, yet the practical solutions do not eradicate the dilemma or the countervailing forces underlying it, and the recurrent conflict between administration and faculty over appointment power is a manifestation of these forces. Implicit in the right of a group to make the decisions to uphold certain standards there is always the possibility that the decisions will threaten these standards. In its most profound form, this is the dilemma of democracy: freedom of speech may be used to abrogate freedom of speech; democratic procedures can be used to abrogate democratic procedures. The dilemma is that protecting democratic liberties in these instances entails curtailing them.

The purest type of dilemma occurs when the very process of attaining a goal has by-products that impede its attainment.[17] Although the line of distinction is not sharp and some of the foregoing dilemmas may be considered results of such by-products, universalistic social values are a more clear-cut illustration of this type. Social values are embedded in a matrix of social relations through which they are supported and enforced. In contrast to personal preferences, social values are rooted in a collectivity with a social structure and some social cohesion. Universalistic values set criteria that are independent of any particular social relations, but the group cohesion that sustains these social values, as any others, engenders particularistic preferences for the ingroup.[18]

A tradition of universalistic academic standards of merit in a university or college rests on the shared values of its members, which unite them and strengthen the social solidarity of the academic community. The merit criteria of the shared tradition and the ingroup loyalty fostered by its being shared create the dilemma of having to choose in faculty appointments between candidates who are best qualified and those who belong to the ingroup, having been educated at the institution and perhaps already teaching there. The pressure of the ingroup loyalties accompanying high academic standards in an institution is reflected in Berelson's findings that the 12 best American universities have much more inbred faculties than other academic institutions,[19] though they have the resources to compete successfully for faculty nationally, and though the data here imply that inbreeding has at least as adverse effects on faculty quality in the best as in other academic institutions.

The loyalty of the faculty to their university or college poses several dilemmas. Let us assume for a moment that faculty loyalty is the only desideratum. Even with this unrealistically restrictive assumption, institutions would be confronted by a dilemma in faculty recruitment. For faculty members who have superior qualifications and are greatly involved in research are less committed to their local institution than others, but their presence at the institution strengthens the local commitments of the rest of the faculty. Correspondingly, faculty members who

[17] This is a case of unanticipated consequences of social actions, which Robert K. Merton analyzed in his discussion of latent function and dysfunction, and to which he had called attention already in one of his earliest papers; see "The Unanticipated Consequences of Purposive Social Action," *American Sociological Review* 1 (1936), 894–904.

[18] One of Talcott Parsons' many definitions of universalism and particularism is in *The Social System*, Glencoe, Ill.: Free Press, 1951, p. 62.

[19] Bernard Berelson, *Graduate Education in the United States*, New York: McGraw-Hill, 1960, p. 115.

are oriented to teaching and have much contact with undergraduates are more loyal to their institution than others, but their presence weakens the loyalty of the rest of the faculty. A university or college is therefore confronted by the choice of hiring and promoting either faculty members whose scholarly concerns reduce their own commitment to the local institution or those whose lack of research interests makes the institution less appealing to others on the faculty. Paradoxically, by appointing less loyal faculty members an institution enhances faculty loyalty.

Faculty allegiance is not the sole objective of institutions of higher education, of course. The characteristics of faculty members that diminish their local allegience—superior qualifications and involvement in research—are the qualities most likely to contribute to the institution's academic standing. Besides, the local commitments themselves, which restrict stimulating contacts with colleagues in the field outside, do not benefit academic work. The more committed the faculty is to an institution, the less frequently are new departments created, and the fewer of its undergraduates proceed to graduate school. Furthermore, a number of conditions that increase the faculty's allegiance to an institution— low qualifications, inbreeding, and teaching emphasis—simultaneously decrease their authority in it. This implies that the dilemmas of loyalty are rooted in the academic stratification system.

The paradox that faculty commitments to an institution are enhanced by appointing faculty members with weak institutional commitments results from the influence of academic status on local commitments. High academic status creates a great demand for a person, by other academic institutions to raise their reputation and attract good students, by his own for the same reasons, and by faculty members as a stimulating and influential colleague. A man or woman who is much sought after tends to be less committed to a particular place than one who has nowhere else to go. Teachers are not as well known in their discipline as researchers who publish and give papers. Hence teachers are less likely than researchers to have alternative job opportunities, which is one reason for their greater commitment to their present institution. Another reason is that good teachers derive their gratification from teaching the students at their institution, whereas good researchers derive theirs more from contacts with colleagues in the discipline. The generally superior status of researchers not only gives them greater alternative opportunities and reduces their exclusive allegiance to their present institution, but it also makes them more desirable colleagues than those who only teach and consequently increases faculty allegiance to institutions that have many researchers and few teachers.

Social status in a stratification system is necessarily relative to the status of others, and status attributes therefore have opposite implications for ego and alter, which is the source of the loyalty dilemmas, and which is also the cause of the paradox of relative deprivation. The promotion of a soldier and the promotion of many of his fellow soldiers in the company have opposite effects on his attitudes toward promotions,[20] because his own promotion raises and theirs lowers his status relative to theirs. A similar phenomenon is observed in academic institutions. Controlling other conditions, graduates of colleges with superior reputations and highly able students are less likely to plan on graduate work than those of less good colleges, partly because their lower relative standing among classmates lowers their self-appraisals as students.

A fundamental characteristic of the academic stratification system is that research has higher standing than teaching. This is often lamented and sometimes lauded, but there is little disagreement about its being true. The universities with the greatest reputations are those whose faculties make research contributions. Affluent institutions take advantage of their superior resources to recruit researchers. Successful researchers command higher salaries, greater authority, and more prestige than successful teachers. The functional explanation of this difference in status is that research is of greataer importance for the society and requires more training and talent than teaching.[21] It is tempting for those of us who are engaged in research to accept this functional interpretation and adduce arguments in its favor. After all, researchers make the contributions to knowledge teachers need to teach; more researchers than teachers have completed advanced training; and the best researchers unquestionably have exceptional talents. That persons with superior abilities often achieve positions that command high status, however, does not prove that these positions *require* greater abilities than others. Much research does not necessitate outstanding skills, and really good teaching does. Who knows what great contributions higher education could make to

[20] Samuel A. Stouffer et al., *The American Soldier*, Princeton: Princeton University Press, 1949, Vol. I., pp. 244–258.
[21] The basic statement of the functional theory of stratification is in Kingsley Davis and Wilbert E. Moore, "Some Principles of Stratification," *American Sociological Review* 10 (1945), 242–249. A summary and evaluation of some of the many criticisms of the theory is presented in George A. Huaco, "The Functionalist Theory of Stratification," *Inquiry* (Oslo, Norway), 9 (1966), 215–240.

the commonweal if the rewards of undergraduate teaching were high enough to prompt the best academic minds to concentrate their attention on it? There was a time when surgeons had low status, little skill, and scant success in curing people, and as the status of surgeons rose, so have their abilities and their accomplishments. How much training and talent are *needed* for a *position* is not a meaningful question that can be answered, because the services provided and thus the qualifications needed are not fixed but depend on the status rewards offered to fill the position. Hence the functional theory of stratification must rest on the axiom that the functional importance of a position determines its hierarchical status, but this axiom casts grave doubts on the theory.

The social worth or functional importance of services cannot be separated from the rewards others willingly offer in exchange for these services. If more people pay more money to listen to Elvis Presley than Jascha Heifetz, making Presley richer, more famous, and more influential, the difference expresses the greater social worth of Presley's contributions for most people, notwithstanding the disagreement of the minority of music connoisseurs. In other words, the differential distribution of social rewards among positions is the empirical indication of the comparative social worth of these positions, that is, of their functional importance as empirically manifest in the community. But this means that the basic premise of the functional theory of stratification is tautological. The social rewards offered by others for a certain service are the operational criterion that defines its functional importance, which therefore cannot be an independent cause of these rewards. To be sure, not all status differences are the result of variations in rewards others freely offer in return for benefits, which calls attention to another questionable assumption of the functional theory.

Social rewards are resources for obtaining additional rewards. Valued contributions earn social rewards in the form of respect, influence, and income, and thereby in the form of status in the stratification system. But prestige, power, and wealth are simultaneously resources, and each helps to acquire more of the others. Scholars of wide renown have more authority and get higher salaries than others. Power commands respect and can be used to achieve wealth. And wealth is a major source of power as well as prestige. Status crystallization, which refers to the tendency of high status in one respect to be associated with high status in another, illustrates this interdependence. If status incentives for making important contributions alone were operative, one would expect the relationships between status attributes to be negative, not positive, since positions that offer people much of one kind of incentive should require less of another kind to fill them properly. The axiom of functional theory that the distribution of social rewards in the stratification system is determined by the functional importance of positions implicitly assumes that resources have no effect on the ability to obtain rewards, which is patently false. The status hierarchy does not accurately reflect comparative social worth, because status-bestowing rewards, even if they initially express the social worth of services, are resources that come to exert an independent effect on the chances of getting rewards, notably in the cases of wealth, which can be inherited, and power, which often becomes institutionalized. The research on universities and colleges provides some illustrations.

The regular exercise of power in an academic community, or any other collectivity, tends to become institutionalized in the form of authority vested in official positions, with the result that the subsequent exercise of power is no longer directly dependent on its original source. The power the superior academic standing of a university faculty commands becomes institutionalized as collective authority, which gives individual faculty members more influence independent of their own academic standing. This means that even if the academic reputations of individuals were initially perfect replicas of the worth of their work, the positions in various institutions they obtain add to or detract from their power, thus necessarily creating discrepancies between the status of individuals and the value of their contributions. An institutionalized democratic faculty government is another illustration of the formalization of influence that broadens faculty control. By the same token, the successful leadership of a university or college president for many years leaves a residue of strengthened institutionalized authority in the office of president, which enhances the power of its next incumbent.

One major source of power is institutionalized authority, which has been made independent of services rendered by being vested in *positions*; another is control over economic resources, which can be inherited and consequently becomes also independent of services. These forms of power may be less significant in academia than in society at large, since academic status depends primarily on social recognition for valued contributions, which implies that the academic stratification system probably conforms more closely to the model of functional theory than society's class structure. However, institutionalized authority rooted in official positions, such as senior positions in major universities, plays a substantial role in academic life too, as has just been exemplified, and so does control of economic resources. The last statement at first sight does not seem to be true. In the largest and best universities, which exercise dominant influence in the national academic system, much decision making is decentralized to the faculty, whose status and influence do not rest on economic control. This does not mean, however, that faculty members exercise most power over academic affairs and that the presidents and trustees of the most influential universities are powerless figureheads, and neither does it mean that economic power has little significance in academic life.

In academic institutions no less than in other organizations, the most important decisions concern the allocation of economic resources. All significant changes require the commitment of financial resources, and the allocation of economic resources determines the structure of the university and the academic work being carried out in it. The president and the board of trustees set financial policies, and he and other top administrators make the main budgetary decisions. The analysis of faculty authority was confined to educational and appointment decisions and excluded financial responsibilities, because faculties have very little if any influence in financial matters. Nor is this an issue creating conflict, because the academic interests of faculty members—especially the outstanding scholars and scientists at the best universities who have most influence—make them uninterested in diverting time from their important academic pursuits to the financial affairs of the university. To use an extreme example, why should a Fermi want to take time out from his vital scientific work to help in distributing the budget at the University of Chicago? The faculty members whose renown gives them most authority are probably the ones most absorbed in their scholarly work and least interested in taking on financial responsibilities.

The allocation of economic resources is the undisputed prerogative of the board of trustees and the president in big universities as well as small colleges. In many small colleges, the administration keeps a close reign on the faculty. In major universities, the faculty has much freedom and influence, including the authority to decide whom to appoint to a vacancy in electrical engineering or in statistics, for instance. But their ability to make this decision depends on a prior one, namely, whether the university has established an engineering school or a statistics department. This type of decision entailing the allocation of resources is reserved for the trustees and the president, who therefore exercise the basic controlling power in the institution. Whereas the power of individuals in academia rests largely on their reputations, organizational power, here as elsewhere, rests on control over economic resources. The control the president and the board of a major university exercise through the allocation of economic resources leaves faculty members much freedom and much influence, yet it is the ultimate source of power at the institution, for it determines the shape of the university and the direction in which it is moving.

BUREAUCRACY AND SCHOLARSHIP

In conclusion, let us briefly return to the issue of bureaucracy and scholarship, which was raised in Chapter One. It was pointed out there that the concept of bureaucracy is too loose and must be dissected into its various elements to ascertain what the implications of different elements are for academic work. The analysis showed that universities and colleges have administrative structures that are similar to those of other bureaucracies. It also revealed that various elements of bureaucracy have different and sometimes contradictory implications in academic institutions, some that conflict with the prevailing stereotype of bureaucracy, and others that conform to it. Moreover, although the administrative structures of academic institutions are homologous to those of other kinds of organizations, the same structural features do not have the same significance for scholarship and for other kinds of work. For example, multilevel hierarchies have adverse effects on academic work but none that could be discovered on work in government bureaus, and the administrative use of computers tends to centralize authority in academic institutions but decentralize it in government agencies. Academic institutions have the difficult responsibility of providing an administrative framework for creative scholarship, which makes them particularly susceptible to the ill effects of bureaucratic rigidity.

A number of findings contradict the common notion of bureaucracy. The large multiuniversity is generally criticized for being bureaucratized, but large academic institutions are in most respects less bureaucratic than small ones. Large institutions tend to have a disproportionately small administrative apparatus, authority in them is much less centralized than in small institutions, and they are more likely to pioneer in new academic fields by establishing departments for them. Other organizational traits usually associated with bureaucracy also promote decentralization, not bureaucratic centralization; these include an administrative hierarchy with several levels, a large clerical apparatus, and a high rate of presidential succession. A paternalistic rather than an impersonal bureaucratic administration is most likely to exercise centralized control over the faculty, as illustrated by the centralization of religious colleges, small ones, and those that exhibit paternalism by appointing many of their own graduates to the faculty. Whereas one would expect bureaucratic standardization to inhibit innovation and impede academic performance, the standardization of faculty salaries fosters the creation of new departments and improves educational performance, probably because it encourages cooperation among faculty members by removing a source of conflict. The main conclusions are that large academic institutions tend to be less bureaucratic than small institutions and that several so-called bureaucratic characteristics reduce centralization of authority.

Not all observed relationships negate the prevailing conception of bureaucracy, however. In agreement with this conception, some bureaucratic traits increase centralization, and several have detrimental effects on academic performance. A large administrative apparatus strengthens centralized authority, and so does the mechanization of human relations implicit in the extensive administrative use of computers. Large academic institutions develop bureaucratic hierarchies with multiple levels, and these bureaucratic structures make it more difficult to recruit good faculty and good students. Students have sound reasons for preferring institutions without bureaucratic hierarchies, because their chances of completing college are better there than in institutions in which the president is removed from faculty and students by several levels of administrators. The progress of undergraduates is also adversely affected by a bureaucratic and impersonal orientation to teaching, whether manifest in a faculty overloaded with too many students by an efficiency-conscious administration, or in a faculty lacking interest in maintaining personal contacts with undergraduates. The extensive use of mechanical teaching aids is inversely related to both completing college and continuing education beyond it, probably because a mechanical approach to teaching kills interest in learning. Still another bureaucratic attribute that impedes educational performance is an inflexible institutional structure in which departments are practically permanent fixtures and are very rarely abolished.

Bureaucracy does come into conflict with scholarship. Several bureaucratic features of academic institutions have deleterious consequences for educational performance, but none of these, and no others that could be discovered, have negative effects on research performance, perhaps because research can be separated from an institution's administrative machinery while education is intricately enmeshed in it. This is a bad omen for the future of higher education. As increasing numbers of students go to college, the danger of bureaucratization grows, since bureaucratic procedures, though not inevitable in large institutions, are the easiest and cheapest way to give a semblance of higher education to huge numbers. For the sake of scholarship, the threat of bureaucratization must be fought, and the faculty would be expected to wage this fight. Yet if research is insulated from the bureaucratic machinery, the most influential faculty members, whose primary concern is research, have no immediate interest in shouldering the great burden of combating the process of academic bureaucratization that impairs education.

APPENDIX A

SAMPLING AND WEIGHTING PROCEDURE

The sample of American universities and colleges used is the same as that chosen for the study of faculty members by Talcott Parsons and Gerald M. Platt, in order to take advantage of their generous offer to let me use their data on faculty members. Since the sample was designed to represent individual faculty members rather than academic institutions, a weighting procedure was employed in the analysis to make the results representative of the universe of American academic institutions. This universe comprises the 1006 liberal arts colleges and universities in the United States in the early 1960s. It was obtained from the 1964 edition of *American Universities and Colleges*,[1] excluding from the nearly 1200 four-year institutions described there those that do not offer an education in the liberal arts, notably music and art schools, seminaries, technical institutes, and teachers colleges.

A stratified sample was selected by dividing the population of 1006 institutions of higher education into nine categories on the basis of two criteria, a rough indication of quality and size. Information on three factors known to be associated with institutional quality was available: the faculty-student ratio, the proportion of faculty members with doc-

[1] Allan M. Cartter, *American Universities and Colleges*, Washington: American Council of Education, 1964.

torates, and the educational and general expenses per student. (The number of students and the number of faculty members were adjusted by substrating one-half of those being part-time.) Institutions were divided on each of the three measures into high, medium, and low. Those high on two and either high or medium on the third measure were defined as high quality; those low on two and either low or medium on the third measure were considered low quality; and the rest were classified as medium quality. The second criterion of the sampling frame consists of three size classes, based on the adjusted number of faculty members in the liberal arts. This adjusted size is the total number of faculty members at the institution, minus the faculty in professional schools, plus one-half the estimated number of part-time liberal arts faculty. Cross-classification of the three quality and the three size classes yields the nine strata from which the sample was drawn at unequal rates.

The probability that an academic institution would be included in the sample was made proportionate to its size, except that the institutions classified as high quality were sampled at higher and those in the low-quality category were sampled at lower rates. The sampling ratios in the nine subgroups are shown in Table A.1, together with the two numbers on which these fractions are based (in parentheses): the number of institutions in the sample, and that in the universe. It is evident that high-quality institutions are represented at three times the rate of medium-quality institutions, which in turn are represented at a higher rate than low-quality institutions. In addition, the three measures on which the quality classification is based are correlated with size, and within each stratum the probability of an institution's selection was made proportionate to its size. As a result, the sampling ratio for the many

Table A.1   Sampling Ratios in Nine Subgroups

Quality	Size						Total	
	Large		Medium		Small			
High	.85		.60		.22		.45	
		(11;13)		(12;20)		(8;36)		(31;69)
Medium	.42		.18		.06		.15	
		(25;60)		(10;56)		(12;192)		(47;308)
Low	.39		.08		.04		.06	
		(10;26)		(11;130)		(16;473)		(37;629)
Total	.46		.16		.05		.11	
		(46;99)		(33;206)		(36;701)		(115;1006)

small and poor colleges in the lower right cell is less than one-twentieth that of the major universities in the upper left cell of the table. The actual sampling within each of the nine cells was done to assure that the four major geographical regions be represented.

A weighting procedure was employed to make the results obtained with this stratified sample representative of American four-year institutions of higher education in the liberal arts.[2] The procedure assumes that within strata cases are selected with equal probability but that selection among strata is with unequal probability, which is a fair approximation, though not an exact replica, of the sampling design. There are nine strata, and for each the number of cases in the universe, N_i, and the number in the sample, n_i, are known. Hence the total number of universities and colleges in the universe, N, is $\sum_{i=1}^{9} N_i$.

Within each stratum, the mean of a variable for the stratum is estimated by

$$\overline{X}_i = \frac{\sum_{j=1}^{n_i} X_{ij}}{n_i}$$

which is the sum of the observations in the stratum divided by the number of these observations. The within-stratum variances and covariances are calculated by the usual estimating method. The estimate of the variance of X is computed as

$$S_x^2{}_{(i)} = \frac{\sum_{j=1}^{n_i} (X_{ij} - \overline{X}_i)^2}{n_i - 1}$$

which is the sum of the squared deviations from the mean divided by $n_i - 1$. Similarly, the within-stratum covariance of X and Y is estimated as

$$S_{xy(i)} = \frac{\sum_{j=1}^{n_i} (X_{ij} - \overline{X}_i)(Y_{ij} - \overline{Y}_i)}{n_i - 1}$$

which is the sum of the products of the deviations from the respective means divided by $n_i - 1$. These values are computed for all nine strata.

[2] I am grateful to William H. Kruskall for suggesting the weighting procedure, to Francis Kinley Larntz for designing it, and to Robert Fay for programming it for the computer.

The mean of every variable for the total universe of academic institutions is estimated as

$$\bar{X} = \sum_{i=1}^{9} \frac{N_i \bar{X}_i}{N}$$

which is the stratum mean multiplied by the fractional part of all institutions in that stratum, summed for the nine strata. The variance of variable X for the universe is estimated by weighting the within-sample variances and also adding a term that takes into account the difference between the stratum means and the overall weighted mean. The formula is

$$s_x^2 = \frac{\sum_{i=1}^{9} (N_i - 1)s_x^2{}_{(i)} + \left[\sum_{i=1}^{9} N_i(\bar{X}_i - \bar{X})^2 - \sum_{i=1}^{9} [N_i s_x^2{}_{(i)}/n_i](1 - f_i)(1 - W_i) \right]}{N - 1}$$

where $f_i = n_i/N_i$ and $W_i = N_i/N$. The covariances of X and Y for the universe is, correspondingly,

$$s_{xy} = \frac{\sum_{i=1}^{9} (N_i - 1)s_{xy(i)} +}{N - 1}$$

$$\frac{\left[\sum_{i=1}^{9} N_i(\bar{X}_i - \bar{X})(\bar{Y}_i - \bar{Y}) - \sum_{i=1}^{9} [N_i s_{xy(i)}/n_i](1 - f_i)(1 - W_i) \right]}{N - 1}$$

For missing data, the within-stratum mean is substituted. This procedure produces a positive definite covariance matrix, and the matrix of weighted simple correlations in Appendix C is based on it.

APPENDIX B

VARIABLE DEFINITIONS,
BASIC STATISTICS,
AND SOURCES

This appendix furnishes the operational definitions of the 57 institutional characteristics that are analyzed in the tables. In addition, it gives the weighted mean and the standard deviation for every variable, and the number of cases on which these data are based. Since dummy variables are scored 1 and 0, the mean in these cases indicates the proportion of all institutions having the given attribute (for example, being located in the Northeastern regions of the country, as defined by the U.S. Bureau of the Census). The letters at the end of the descriptions refer in each case to the source from which the variable or the data used in computing it were obtained, and the key for the letters specifying the sources is at the end of this appendix.

	Mean	Standard Deviation	n
1. *Northeast*. Dummy variable that institution is in one of the following states: N.H., Vt., Me., Mass., Conn., N.Y., N.J., Pa.	.289	.458	115
2. *South*. Dummy variable that institution is in one of the following states: Del., Md., Va., W. Va., N.C., S.C., Ga., Fla., Ala., Miss., Ky., Tenn., Ark., La., Okla., Tex., D.C.	.270	.448	115

	Mean	Standard Deviation	n
3. *West.* Dummy variable that institution is in one of the following states: Mont., Wyo., Colo., N. Mex., Ariz., Utah, Calif., Nev., Ida., Ore., Wash., Alaska, Hawaii.	.113	.319	115
4. *Age.* Year the institution was founded, subtracted from 1968.[H]	85.8	41.9	112
5. *Public Control.* Dummy variable that institution is under state or municipal control.[S]	.291	.458	115
6. *Religious.* Dummy variable that institution is affiliated with religious denomination.[S]	.494	.504	115
7. *Private Secular.* Dummy variable that institution is private and nonsectarian.[S]	.214	.414	115
8. *Affluence.* Total revenue in dollars divided by total enrollment of both undergraduates and graduate students.[S]	2186	1794	105
9. *Size.* Total number of faculty, both full-time and part-time.[S]	304.2	499.9	115
10. *Size* (log). Logarithm to the base 10 of total number of faculty.[S]	2186	1794	105
11. *Enrollment* (log). Logarithm to the base 10 of total enrollment of both undergraduate and graduate students.[S]	3.360	.528	115
12. *Expansion.* Number of faculty hired minus number leaving, divided by the total number of faculty, in 1967–68.[A]	6.79	6.28	79
13. *Percentage of Graduate Students.* Number of graduate students divided by total enrollment.[S]	11.0	14.7	115
14. *University.* Dummy variable that institution offers doctorate degrees in any field.[G]	.222	.418	115
15. *Student-Faculty Ratio.* Ratio of total enrollment to total number of faculty.	17.12	8.72	115
16. *Salaries.* Average annual salary of full-time faculty in 1967–68.[AAUP]	10,721	1616	88
17. *Standardized Salaries.* Salary increments are based on standard schedule (scored 3), individual cases (1), or both (2).[P]	1.598	.761	115
18. *Departments.* Total number of departments in arts and sciences and in professional schools.[S]	24.63	19.04	113
19. *Schools and Colleges.* Number of schools and colleges in the institution.[S]	3.09	3.78	115

	Mean	Standard Deviation	n
20. *Levels.* Number of hierarchical levels with the president and the faculty (other than chairmen) being counted as the two extreme levels.[A]	4.346	.726	115
21. *President's Span of Control.* The number of officials reporting directly to the president.[A]	7.61	7.80	115
22. *Mean Span of Control of Officials Reporting to the President.* The number of officials two levels divided by the number one level below the president's.[A]	5.99	4.33	107
23. *Administration-Faculty Ratio.* Number of professional administrators divided by the total number of faculty.[A]	.250	.171	103
24. *Clerical-Faculty Ratio.* The number of clerical and other support personnel divided by the total number of faculty.[A]	1.357	.934	98
25. *Inbreeding.* Number of faculty with any degree from the institution hired in 1967–68, divided by the total number of faculty hired that year.[S]	.140	.125	72
26. *Faculty Qualifications.* The percentage of the total faculty with Ph.D.'s or professional degrees.[S]	38.39	15.91	104
27. *Reputation among Able Students.* The number of received college choices by semifinalists and recipients of letters of commendation from the 1961 National Merit Scholarship program, divided by the number of freshmen admitted.[AWA]	51.43	8.99	108
28. *Social Origins of Faculty.* Percentage of the fathers of faculty members who graduated from college.[F]	21.60	14.25	114
29. *Teaching Emphasis.* Percentage of faculty responding that teaching ability is important for senior appointments in their departments.[F]	58.07	18.34	114
30. *Research Emphasis.* Percentage of faculty responding that it is a faculty obligation at the institution to publish research.[F]	24.12	22.73	114
31. *Local Allegiance.* Percentage of the faculty stating that their allegiance to the institution is very strong.[F]	69.60	17.14	114
32. *Importance of Outside Faculty.* Top adminis-			

	Mean	Standard Deviation	n
trator's rating, from 1 to 5, of the importance of attracting outstanding researchers and scholars from other institutions.[P]	2.37	1.32	112
33. *Federal Support*. Percentage of the total revenue from federal government sources.[NSF]	11.81	10.40	104
34. *Revenue Spent on Books*. Percentage of total revenue spent on books and periodicals for the library in 1964–67.[S]	1.241	.504	104
35. *Selectivity*. Number of applicants rejected for admission divided by the number of applications received.[A]	30.69	20.20	113
36. *Student Aptitudes*. Mean mathematical SAT score of entering freshmen.[S]	517.0	85.6	81
37. *Graduate Student Contact*. Percentage of faculty who see more than seven graduate students per week outside of class.[F]	13.95	15.14	114
38. *Undergraduate Contact*. Percentage of faculty who see more than seven undergraduates per week outside of class.[F]	64.10	17.83	114
39. *Computer Use*. Sophistication of computer use in student affairs, financial affairs, use of physical plant, and general policy planning, each scored from 0 to 4, and the four scores summed.[A]	5.30	3.37	104
40. *Mechanical Teaching Aids*. Use of TV or videotapes (scored 1); also language labs (2); programmed learning machines and one of preceding (3); teaching with computers plus one of preceding (4).[A]	2.22	1.11	115
41. *Last President's Tenure*. Number of years previous president held office.[P]	13.22	7.52	99
42. *Percentage in Senate*. Number on faculty in decision-making body divided by total number of faculty.[P]	62.07	44.35	107
43. *President's Tenure*. Number of years the current president (1968) has been in office.[P]	7.48	6.84	111
44. *Percentage Elected*. Proportion of elected members on the most important faculty committee.[P]	40.64	42.30	110
45. *Centralization of Educational Matters*. Percentage of the faculty responding that the board of trustees has substantial influence in formulating general educational policy.[F]	34.77	18.48	114

	Mean	Standard Deviation	n
46. *Administration's Influence in Appointments.* Percentage of the faculty responding that the administration has substantial influence in appointing faculty.[F]	72.28	23.19	114
47. *Senior Faculty's Appointment Authority.* Percentage of the faculty responding that the senior faculty makes the formal decisions on faculty appointments.[F]	17.60	16.72	114
48. *President's Influence in Appointments.* President's influence in making appointments to tenured faculty positions. (Scored 1–5.)[P]	3.68	1.21	112
49. *President's Authority over Funds.* Discretion to redistribute unexpended funds for tenured faculty (scored 7 for president alone; 6 for president shared; 5 for vice-president or return to general institutional funds; 4 for same shared; 3 for dean; 2 for dean and chairman shared; 1 for chairman).	5.58	1.40	112
50. *Centralization of Initiative.* Who initiated the proposal to establish the most recent new department (scored 6 for trustees, 5 for president, 4 for vice-presidents, 3 for deans, 2 for chairmen, 1 for faculty).[P]	2.86	1.37	98
51. *Centralized Salary Influence.* Who initiates recommendations for raises in faculty salaries? (Scored same as number 49.)[P]	3.64	1.98	106
52. *Departments in New Fields.* The number of departments in nine new fields (anthropology, biochemistry, biophysics, journalism, linguistics, microbiology, nursing education, statistics, urban studies), divided by the number of other departments.[S]	.019	.028	112
53. *Recency of Creation of Last Department.* Year (last two digits) the most recent department was created.[P]	65.73	2.23	102
54. *Department Eliminated.* Dummy variable that at least one department or major was eliminated in the past five years.[P]	.532	.496	113
55. *Rate of College Completion.* Number of bachelor degrees granted in 1967–68, divided by undergraduate enrollment.[S]	15.39	6.11	114
56. *Rate of Continuing Education in Graduate*			

	Mean	Standard Deviation	n
School. Percentage of graduates expected to continue their education in graduate school.[S]	39.01	21.73	89
57. *Faculty Research Productivity.* Number of articles plus five times the number of books authored or coauthored by faculty members, averaged for the respondents in the institution.[F]	7.12	4.44	114

Major Sources

P: Interview with the president or his or her deputy.

A: Interview with an assistant to the president.

F: Faculty questionnaire from Parsons-Platt study (variables based on sampled faculty in institution).

S: Otis A. Singletary, *American Universities and Colleges,* Washington: American Council of Education, 1968.

Other Sources

AAUP: American Association of University Professors, "The Annual Report on the Economic Status of the Profession, 1967–68," *AAUP Bulletin* **54** (1968), 208–241 (column 4A).

AWA: Alexander W. Astin, *Who Goes Where to College?* Chicago: Science Research Associates, 1965, pp. 57–83 (column 6).

G: Jane Graham, *A Guide to Graduate Study,* Washington: American Council of Education, 1965.

H: G. R. Hawes, *New American Guide to Colleges,* New York: Columbia University Press, 1966.

NSF: National Science Foundation, *Federal Support for Academic Science and Other Educational Activities in Universities and Colleges,* NSF 67–14, Washington, U.S.G.P.O., 1967, pp. 110–136 (Table B-21, column 1).

APPENDIX C

MATRIX OF SIMPLE CORRELATIONS

TABLE C-1 ....

	NORTH EAST 1	SOUTH 2	WEST 3	AGE 4	PUBLIC CNTRL 5	RELIGI OUS 6	PRIV S ECULAR 7	AFFLUE NCE 8	SIZE 9	SIZE (LOG) 10	ENRLMT (LOG) 11	EXPANS ION 12	% GRAD STU 13	UNIVER SITY 14	STUFFA CULTY 15
1 NORTH EAST	1.000														
2 SOUTH	-0.387	1.000													
3 WEST	-0.227	-0.217	1.000												
4 AGE	-0.058	0.206	-0.149	1.000											
5 PUBLIC CNTRL	-0.113	0.165	0.128	-0.053	1.000										
6 RELIGIOUS	-0.231	-0.092	-0.030	-0.008	-0.534	1.000									
7 PRIV SECULAR	0.443	-0.116	-0.116	0.264	-0.333	-0.517	1.000								
8 AFFLUENCE	0.192	-0.064	0.061	0.230	0.200	-0.257	0.313	1.000							
9 SIZE	-0.115	-0.068	0.128	0.133	0.263	-0.362	0.151	0.309	1.000						
10 SIZE (LOG)	-0.185	-0.047	0.073	0.109	0.442	-0.518	0.141	0.257	0.824	1.000					
11 ENRLMT (LOG)	-0.160	-0.035	-0.126	0.096	0.243	-0.434	-0.001	0.052	0.714	0.936	1.000				
12 EXPANSION	-0.030	0.187	-0.053	0.180	0.096	-0.189	-0.018	0.184	0.037	0.002	0.045	1.000			
13 % GRAD STU	-0.350	-0.245	-0.158	0.005	0.377	0.056	-0.018	0.335	-0.021	0.316	0.245	0.028	1.000		
14 UNIVERSITY	-0.354	-0.054	-0.124	0.157	0.180	-0.189	0.056	-0.409	0.410	0.658	0.593	-0.062	0.724	1.000	
15 STU/FACULTY	-0.087	-0.169	-0.197	0.367	0.089	0.133	-0.018	0.184	-0.357	0.620	0.458	0.078	0.345	-0.036	1.000
16 SALARIES	0.137	0.031	-0.105	-0.128	0.339	-0.111	0.340	-0.115	-0.167	-0.054	0.390	-0.152	0.380	0.459	0.281
17 ST'D SALARY	-0.333	-0.104	-0.096	-0.076	-0.010	-0.169	-0.070	0.294	0.501	0.458	0.710	-0.250	-0.103	-0.358	-0.159
18 DEPARTMENTS	-0.201	-0.029	-0.069	0.062	0.036	-0.335	-0.268	-0.243	0.504	-0.270	0.758	-0.029	0.261	0.639	-0.095
19 SCH & COLL	-0.263	0.031	-0.128	0.131	0.284	-0.334	-0.018	-0.008	0.834	0.793	0.588	0.080	-0.029	-0.036	-0.327
20 LEVELS	0.109	0.206	0.131	0.059	0.311	-0.111	-0.092	0.231	0.808	0.823	0.514	0.074	0.380	-0.358	-0.188
21 PRES' SPAN	-0.099	-0.113	-0.002	0.178	0.194	-0.227	-0.206	-0.019	0.367	0.758	0.024	-0.096	-0.014	0.024	-0.103
22 VP'S SPAN	-0.134	-0.144	0.178	-0.115	-0.314	-0.194	0.347	0.144	0.083	0.514	0.007	-0.066	-0.066	-0.027	-0.237
23 ADMIN/FAC	-0.062	-0.090	-0.090	0.062	0.163	-0.245	0.049	-0.459	-0.025	0.112	-0.369	-0.208	-0.158	-0.046	-0.244
24 CLERKS/FAC	0.055	0.095	0.053	-0.005	-0.012	-0.274	-0.030	-0.107	-0.171	-0.279	0.180	-0.040	0.192	0.131	-0.361
25 INBREEDING	-0.134	-0.118	-0.082	0.528	0.010	-0.251	0.154	0.519	0.304	-0.288	0.102	0.098	0.426	0.440	-0.032
26 FAC QUALIF	0.036	-0.064	-0.129	0.224	0.238	-0.189	-0.293	0.510	0.071	0.061	0.278	-0.162	0.213	0.146	-0.225
27 REPUTATION	0.338	-0.409	-0.137	0.135	-0.120	-0.033	0.220	0.422	0.443	0.422	0.121	-0.262	0.092	0.247	-0.130
28 SOC ORIG FAC	0.351	-0.142	0.135	0.107	0.472	-0.387	0.304	0.263	0.265	0.289	0.117	-0.103	-0.123	-0.636	-0.254
29 TEACH EMPH	-0.217	0.187	0.038	-0.238	-0.057	-0.514	0.432	-0.390	0.263	0.290	0.542	-0.156	0.381	0.644	-0.036
30 RESRCH EMPH	-0.385	-0.204	-0.003	0.288	0.131	-0.336	-0.093	-0.422	-0.581	-0.595	0.447	0.040	-0.232	-0.325	-0.003
31 LOCAL ALLGNC	-0.355	-0.142	0.125	-0.101	-0.090	-0.113	0.164	-0.187	0.635	0.586	-0.546	-0.002	-0.325	0.497	-0.071
32 IMP OUTS FAC	0.347	0.209	-0.067	0.192	0.103	-0.351	-0.187	0.090	-0.450	-0.559	0.349	0.050	0.349	-0.110	-0.103
33 FED SUPPORT	-0.113	-0.246	-0.202	0.146	-0.127	-0.201	-0.113	0.306	0.292	0.347	0.217	0.039	0.497	-0.025	0.036
34 % ON BOOKS	-0.295	-0.064	-0.004	0.151	0.244	0.005	0.019	-0.128	0.421	0.347	-0.075	-0.046	-0.009	0.471	0.111
35 SELECTIVITY	0.576	0.246	-0.064	0.162	-0.138	-0.195	-0.267	0.252	-0.156	-0.283	0.137	-0.154	0.016	-0.110	0.223
36 MEAN S.A.T.	0.406	-0.438	-0.118	0.181	0.435	-0.093	-0.209	0.062	0.349	0.453	0.342	-0.193	0.338	0.271	0.273
37 GR STU CNTCT	-0.271	-0.128	0.143	-0.003	0.199	-0.414	0.471	0.428	0.122	0.256	0.210	-0.087	0.171	-0.424	0.100
38 UNDRGR CNTCT	-0.141	0.022	-0.128	-0.114	0.181	-0.389	0.252	-0.292	0.230	0.444	-0.449	0.073	-0.429	0.445	-0.201
39 COMPUTER	0.140	0.031	-0.021	-0.112	0.342	0.103	0.062	0.141	0.486	0.557	0.596	0.169	-0.093	-0.047	0.126
40 MECH TC4 AID	0.131	0.041	0.105	-0.026	0.210	-0.317	0.020	-0.082	0.277	-0.228	0.488	0.226	-0.156	0.100	-0.002
41 LAST PRS TEN	-0.243	-0.289	-0.153	-0.091	-0.090	-0.127	0.095	-0.134	-0.176	-0.521	-0.166	-0.172	-0.131	-0.350	0.185
42 % ON SENATE	-0.322	-0.165	-0.216	0.064	0.103	-0.088	-0.018	0.064	-0.387	0.087	-0.556	-0.131	-0.104	-0.201	-0.198
43 PRES' TENURE	-0.352	-0.037	0.159	0.140	0.392	-0.003	0.244	-0.003	0.084	0.154	0.087	-0.241	0.001	-0.044	0.202
44 % ELECTED	-0.216	-0.305	-0.127	-0.039	-0.060	-0.006	-0.138	-0.039	0.142	-0.001	0.114	-0.018	-0.055	-0.063	-0.198
45 CNTRLZ OF ED	-0.350	0.110	-0.029	-0.067	0.231	-0.389	0.435	-0.233	-0.057	0.096	0.096	-0.004	0.377	0.123	-0.096
46 ADM APP AUTH	-0.150	-0.133	-0.168	-0.155	-0.270	-0.556	0.199	0.501	-0.605	-0.690	-0.539	-0.060	-0.150	0.185	0.088
47 FAC APP AUTH	-0.243	0.010	-0.320	-0.106	0.131	-0.199	0.181	-0.372	-0.623	-0.623	-0.534	-0.098	0.333	0.458	-0.131
48 PRES AP AUTH	-0.156	0.064	-0.307	-0.186	-0.219	0.435	0.073	-0.031	-0.207	-0.203	-0.209	0.106	-0.286	-0.198	-0.096
49 PR FUND AUTH	-0.322	-0.279	-0.186	-0.084	-0.079	0.181	0.014	0.014	-0.221	-0.204	-0.155	-0.029	-0.201	-0.155	0.088
50 CNTRLZ INITV	-0.063	-0.057	-0.015	-0.202	-0.337	-0.014	-0.077	-0.077	-0.288	-0.385	-0.399	-0.029	-0.261	-0.131	-0.131

TABLE C-1 . . . .

	NORTH EAST 1	SOUTH 2	WEST 3	AGE 4	PUBLIC CNTRL 5	RELIGI OUS 6	PRIV S ECULAR 7	AFFLUE NCE 8	SIZE 9	SIZE (LOG) 10	ENRLMT (LOG) 11	EXPANS ION 12	% GRAD STJ 13	UNIVER SITY 14	STUFFA CULTY 15
51 CNTRLZ SALRY	-0.021	0.051	-0.035	0.027	-0.238	0.181	0.043	-0.006	-0.235	-0.349	-0.380	0.157	-0.055	-0.171	-0.152
52 DEPT WE4 FLD	-0.064	-0.091	0.107	-0.064	-0.167	-0.133	-0.023	0.113	0.378	0.375	0.370	-0.010	0.134	0.256	0.102
53 CR LAST DEPT	3.200	-0.088	-0.109	0.004	-0.170	-0.163	0.011	0.059	0.177	0.294	0.284	-0.104	-0.020	0.168	0.038
54 ABOLSH DEPTS	-0.030	-0.338	0.270	-0.121	-0.186	0.235	-0.081	0.049	-0.035	-0.124	-0.171	-0.099	-0.170	-0.094	-0.172
55 COLL CMPLTN	-0.253	-0.165	0.136	0.146	-0.103	0.084	0.012	0.245	-0.025	-0.170	-0.314	-0.297	0.455	-0.094	-0.443
56 CONT GR SCH	0.191	-0.335	-0.014	0.351	-0.332	0.198	0.127	0.184	0.112	-0.054	-0.070	-0.119	0.481	0.003	-0.006
57 FAC RES PROD	0.393	0.009	0.107	0.147	0.046	-0.286	0.297	0.486	0.567	0.562	0.396	-0.033	0.321	0.601	-0.253

TABLE C-1 ....

Correlation matrix (variables 16–30):

#	Variable	16 SALARIES	17 ST'D SALARY	18 DEPARTMENTS	19 SCH & COLL	20 LEVELS	21 PRES' SPAN	22 VP'S SPAN	23 ADMIN/ FAC	24 CLERKS /FAC	25 INBREE DING	26 FAC QUALIF	27 REPUTA TION	28 SOC OR IG FAC	29 TEACH EMPH	30 RESRCH EMPH
16	SALARIES	1.000														
17	ST'D SALARY	-0.253	1.000													
18	DEPARTMENTS	0.553	-0.198	1.000												
19	SCH & COLL	0.477	-0.237	0.803	1.000											
20	LEVELS	0.188	-0.222	0.442	0.481	1.000										
21	PRES' SPAN	0.220	-0.052	0.103	0.059	-0.147	1.000									
22	VP'S SPAN	-0.255	-0.019	-0.066	-0.084	-0.359	-0.147	1.000								
23	ADMIN/FAC	-0.151	-0.135	-0.249	-0.039	0.127	-0.193	-0.096	1.000							
24	CLERKS/FAC	0.406	-0.158	0.444	0.371	0.109	-0.158	-0.052	-0.041	1.000						
25	INBREEDING	-0.130	0.090	0.087	0.135	0.052	0.193	-0.184	-0.086	-0.125	1.000					
26	FAC QUALIF	0.731	-0.058	0.448	0.401	-0.155	0.221	-0.123	-0.121	0.362	-0.134	1.000				
27	REPUTATION	0.551	-0.060	0.283	0.177	-0.004	0.282	-0.096	-0.042	0.297	-0.173	0.581	1.000			
28	SOC ORIG FAC	0.436	-0.059	0.271	0.262	-0.314	0.157	-0.175	0.007	0.245	-0.174	0.383	0.552	1.000		
29	TEACH EMPH	-0.473	-0.233	-0.355	-0.594	0.204	-0.013	-0.125	0.093	-0.340	-0.135	-0.453	-0.453	-0.465	1.000	
30	RESRCH EMPH	0.561	-0.147	0.564	0.555	-0.205	-0.095	-0.041	0.029	0.300	-0.052	0.616	0.291	0.243	-0.591	1.000
31	LOCAL ALLGNC	-0.437	0.165	-0.392	-0.381	0.309	-0.059	-0.193	0.297	-0.318	0.162	-0.337	-0.343	-0.257	-0.437	-0.223
32	IMP OUTS FAC	0.241	-0.068	0.293	0.445	0.107	-0.033	-0.253	-0.154	0.210	0.051	0.453	-0.027	-0.031	-0.320	0.453
33	FED SUPPORT	0.259	0.035	0.424	0.423	0.145	0.050	-0.307	-0.030	0.219	0.143	0.296	-0.011	0.111	-0.352	0.562
34	% ON BOOKS	0.004	0.153	-0.123	-0.090	0.060	-0.120	-0.163	-0.011	-0.194	0.111	0.109	0.154	0.153	0.026	-0.104
35	SELECTIVITY	0.342	-0.017	0.075	0.056	-0.001	0.255	-0.130	-0.159	0.277	-0.072	0.280	0.407	0.373	-0.112	0.071
36	MEAN S.A.T.	0.533	-0.091	0.381	0.295	0.094	-0.001	-0.307	-0.304	0.277	-0.287	0.522	0.773	0.526	-0.269	0.170
37	GR STU CNTCT	-0.062	-0.067	0.286	0.231	-0.280	-0.073	-0.059	-0.036	0.378	0.055	0.161	0.047	-0.069	0.082	0.185
38	UNDRGR CNTCT	-0.536	-0.118	-0.502	-0.442	0.503	-0.280	-0.021	0.143	-0.224	0.054	-0.487	-0.471	-0.421	0.444	-0.391
39	COMPUTER CNTCT	-0.306	-0.118	-0.118	-0.152	0.254	-0.013	-0.119	0.202	0.235	0.162	0.276	0.027	0.175	0.578	0.361
40	MECH TCH AID	0.184	-0.287	-0.284	-0.324	-0.132	-0.029	-0.171	-0.031	-0.180	-0.006	-0.002	-0.096	-0.223	-0.375	-0.250
41	LAST PRS TEN	-0.256	0.141	-0.140	-0.163	-0.354	-0.003	-0.027	-0.047	-0.112	-0.055	-0.337	-0.267	-0.188	-0.044	-0.086
42	% ON SENATE	-0.172	0.211	-0.354	-0.373	-0.029	-0.009	-0.159	0.218	-0.144	-0.129	-0.017	0.069	-0.054	-0.163	-0.219
43	PRES' TENURE	0.392	0.011	0.126	0.083	0.043	-0.002	-0.115	-0.062	-0.007	0.058	-0.059	-0.065	-0.065	-0.074	-0.060
44	% ELECTED	-0.222	-0.161	0.105	0.073	0.142	-0.160	-0.129	0.034	0.017	-0.090	0.004	-0.047	-0.080	-0.131	-0.015
45	CNTRLZ OF ED	-0.307	-0.093	-0.120	0.095	-0.218	0.142	-0.160	0.234	-0.146	-0.153	-0.186	-0.436	-0.118	-0.087	-0.037
46	ADM APP AUTH	-0.565	-0.223	-0.502	-0.601	0.167	-0.242	0.085	0.166	-0.406	-0.051	-0.522	-0.522	-0.254	-0.430	-0.595
47	FAC APP AUTH	0.718	-0.176	0.570	0.623	-0.316	0.318	-0.052	-0.121	0.445	-0.259	0.578	0.481	0.516	-0.571	0.560
48	PRES AP AUTH	-0.111	0.096	-0.108	-0.192	-0.227	0.194	0.154	-0.233	-0.042	-0.042	-0.095	-0.050	-0.118	0.151	-0.081
49	PR FUND AUTH	-0.215	0.149	-0.227	-0.188	-0.198	0.063	0.025	-0.000	-0.057	-0.017	-0.226	-0.098	-0.025	-0.050	-0.145
50	CNTRLZ INITV	-0.205	-0.102	-0.198	-0.190	-0.186	-0.077	-0.144	0.093	-0.022	-0.044	-0.258	-0.019	0.025	-0.245	-0.297
51	CNTRLZ SALRY	-0.270	-0.079	-0.252	-0.223	0.042	-0.006	-0.241	-0.210	-0.289	-0.203	0.063	-0.090	-0.172	-0.216	-0.083
52	DEPT NEW FLD	0.190	-0.036	0.347	0.343	0.084	0.105	0.061	-0.216	0.008	0.024	0.089	-0.053	0.201	-0.302	-0.210
53	CR LAST DEPT	0.190	0.242	0.240	0.246	-0.006	0.058	0.148	-0.153	0.089	0.115	0.042	0.229	0.280	-0.293	-0.090
54	ABOLSH DEPTS	0.336	-0.056	-0.016	-0.005	-0.395	-0.115	-0.108	0.209	-0.158	-0.008	-0.086	0.081	0.016	0.078	-0.147
55	COLL CMPLTN	0.203	0.426	-0.076	-0.063	-0.067	0.116	0.044	-0.154	0.138	-0.035	0.373	0.230	0.112	0.087	-0.019
56	CONT GR SCH	0.334	0.165	-0.032	0.051	0.134	0.046	-0.289	-0.127	0.109	-0.124	0.384	0.302	0.133	0.009	0.054
57	FAC RES PROD	0.341	-0.191	0.550	0.539	0.134	0.203	-0.320	-0.099	0.432	-0.094	0.540	0.522	0.383	-0.415	0.633

TABLE C-1 ....

	LOCAL ALLGNC 31	IMP OUTS FAC 32	FED SUPPORT 33	% ON BOOKS 34	SELECT IVITY 35	MEAN S.A.T. 36	GR STU CNTCT 37	UNDRGR CNTCT 38	COMPUT ER 39	MECH T CH AID 40	LAST P RS TEN 41	% ON SENATE 42	PRES' TENURE 43	% ELEC TED 44	CNTRLZ OF ED 45
31 LOCAL ALLGNC	1.000														
32 IMP OUTS FAC	-0.239	1.000													
33 FED SUPPORT	-0.080	0.257	1.000												
34 % ON BOOKS	0.398	-0.233	-0.300	1.000											
35 SELECTIVITY	-0.272	0.155	0.054	0.315	1.000										
36 MEAN S.A.T.	-0.470	0.023	0.015	0.068	0.407	1.000									
37 GR STU CNTCT	-0.146	-0.168	-0.027	0.011	-0.102	0.035	1.000								
38 UNDRGR CNTCT	0.351	-0.136	-0.036	-0.100	-0.068	0.180	-0.226	1.000							
39 COMPUTER	-0.359	0.398	-0.202	0.116	0.190	0.141	-0.007	-0.258	1.000						
40 MECH TCH AID	-0.222	0.043	-0.128	-0.064	0.181	0.141	0.008	-0.101	0.361	1.000					
41 LAST PRS TEN	0.189	-0.036	-0.059	-0.170	-0.089	0.239	0.087	-0.157	-0.017	0.038	1.000				
42 % ON SENATE	0.336	-0.141	-0.233	0.275	0.145	-0.017	-0.108	0.120	-0.265	-0.215	0.067	1.000			
43 PRES. TENURE	0.087	-0.290	-0.009	-0.056	0.069	-0.205	-0.166	0.073	-0.183	0.196	0.026	0.112	1.000		
44 % ELECTED	-0.118	-0.052	-0.093	-0.032	-0.147	0.303	-0.077	-0.082	-0.101	-0.053	-0.360	-0.051	-0.027	1.000	
45 CNTRLZ OF ED	0.351	0.129	-0.013	-0.038	-0.322	-0.476	-0.080	0.085	0.053	-0.083	0.189	-0.339	-0.066	-0.342	1.000
46 ADM APP AUTH	0.453	-0.424	-0.396	-0.126	-0.171	-0.461	-0.246	-0.030	-0.233	-0.215	0.254	-0.329	0.062	-0.252	0.246
47 FAC APP AUTH	0.524	0.330	-0.292	-0.193	0.281	0.568	0.080	0.414	-0.476	-0.354	-0.193	-0.266	0.268	0.268	-0.178
48 PRES AP AUTH	0.242	-0.053	0.071	-0.138	-0.018	-0.064	-0.143	0.219	-0.101	0.074	0.384	0.126	0.095	-0.179	-0.032
49 PR FUND AUTH	0.020	-0.164	-0.021	-0.021	-0.013	-0.090	-0.199	0.270	0.039	0.192	0.265	0.013	0.062	-0.064	0.243
50 CNTRLZ INITV	0.318	-0.269	-0.151	-0.050	-0.097	-0.070	-0.144	0.194	-0.343	-0.152	0.134	0.232	0.189	0.061	0.134
51 CNTRLZ SALRY	0.205	0.094	-0.149	-0.066	-0.216	-0.208	0.084	0.243	-0.146	-0.255	0.106	0.452	0.198	0.036	-0.082
52 DEPT NEW FLD	-0.121	-0.070	-0.123	-0.225	-0.016	0.291	0.229	-0.212	0.189	0.284	0.184	0.002	0.295	-0.019	-0.182
53 CR LAST DEPT	-0.332	-0.088	-0.168	-0.035	0.186	0.328	-0.003	-0.240	0.114	0.270	0.019	-0.016	-0.025	-0.350	-0.085
54 ABOLISH DEPTS	0.080	-0.133	-0.023	-0.168	0.113	0.205	-0.155	-0.198	-0.121	-0.199	-0.100	-0.272	-0.040	-0.113	-0.249
55 COLL CMPLTN	-0.037	0.102	0.096	0.057	0.043	0.069	-0.052	-0.069	-0.139	-0.433	-0.060	0.296	-0.089	-0.197	-0.234
56 CONT GR SCH	-0.174	-0.052	-0.003	0.042	0.294	0.291	-0.067	-0.223	0.075	-0.288	-0.105	0.243	0.125	0.061	-0.284
57 FAC PRES PRDD	0.251	0.269	0.412	-0.179	0.146	0.407	0.171	-0.403	0.252	0.326	-0.081	-0.281	0.030	0.196	-0.201

TABLE C-1 . . . .

	ADM AP P AJTH 46	FAC AP P AJTH 47	PRES A P AUTH 48	PR FJN D AUTH 49	CNTRLZ INITV 50	CNTRLZ SALRY 51	DEPT N EW FLD 52	CR LAS T DEPT 53	ABOLSH DEPTS 54	COLL CMPLTN 55	CONT GR SCH 56	FAC RE S PROD 57
46 ADM APP AUTH	1.000											
47 FAC APP AUTH	-0.622	1.000										
48 PRES AP AUTH	0.114	-0.160	1.000									
49 PR FUND AUTH	0.278	-0.171	0.347	1.000								
50 CNTRLZ INITV	0.220	-0.237	0.352	0.346	1.000							
51 CNTRLZ SALRY	0.346	-0.158	0.149	-0.060	0.276	1.000						
52 DEPT NEW FLD	-0.218	0.307	0.034	-0.062	-0.196	-0.177	1.000					
53 CR LAST DEPT	-0.181	0.184	0.008	0.179	-0.028	-0.357	0.131	1.000				
54 ABOLSH DEPTS	-0.010	0.007	-0.395	-0.280	0.105	0.155	0.096	-0.007	1.000			
55 COLL CMPLTN	-0.093	0.097	0.025	-0.192	-0.049	0.124	-0.017	-0.041	0.174	1.000		
56 CONT GR SCH	-0.177	-0.120	-0.066	-0.191	-0.005	0.231	0.001	0.040	0.363	0.403	1.000	
57 FAC RES PROD	0.682	0.556	0.110	-0.082	-0.076	-0.070	0.299	0.084	-0.085	0.004	0.141	1.000

APPENDIX D

VARIABLES AND SIMPLE
CORRELATIONS FOR
INDIVIDUAL FACULTY MEMBERS

The units of analysis for the investigation of structural effects in Chapter Five are individual faculty members, not academic institutions as in the rest of the book. The data on individual faculty members are based on the survey of Talcott Parsons and Gerald M. Platt, complemented by the contextual characteristics of these individuals, that is, the characteristics of the academic institutions in which they work. This appendix briefly describes the sample of faculty members, presents the operational definitions of the 22 variables used in the analysis of individuals as well as the basic statistics for these variables, and supplies a matrix of simple correlations.

The sample of 2577 faculty members is confined to those in the liberal arts. The sampling procedure involves three steps. First, the likelihood that an academic institution is included in the sample was made proportionate to its size, as noted in Appendix A, except that institutions of superior quality were selected in disproportionate numbers. Second, the sampling of departments within an institution was designed to make the probability of inclusion proportionate to the size of departments, as determined by the 1966–67 catalogue. Departments with fewer than seven members were combined for sampling purposes. Departments were stratified into four major areas—humanities, natural sciences, social sciences, and vocational sciences. Six departments or combinations were selected from each institution, and the major areas to which these belonged were rotated. In a few very small institutions, all departments were sampled.

Third, the rates at which individuals within each department were selected are inversely proportionate to its size, so that a higher percentage of the members of small than those of large departments were sampled. Lists of faculty members in the selected departments were sent to their chairmen for updating. Graduate students were eliminated and part-time faculty members were given one-half of the weight of full-time faculty. Faculty members from 114 academic institutions cooperated with the survey. The number from a given institution that returned completed questionnaires ranged from 4 to 59, with a mean of 23 and a median of 21. The return rate was 65 per cent. Faculty members from better institutions are overrepresented in the sample.

Finally, a few remarks are necessary to explain the difference in the figures referring to the institutional context shown here and those referring to the same variables shown in Appendix B. For example, the mean for the dummy variable that a university or college is a public (not private) institution is .291 in Appendix B, whereas the mean for the same variable indicated below is .4691. This signifies that 29 per cent of the 1006 institutions in the universe are public, whereas 46 per cent of the 2577 faculty members in the sample are employed in public institutions, mostly because public academic institutions have a larger faculty than private ones. Similarly, 49 per cent of the institutions have religious affiliations, as Appendix B shows, but they are small, so that only 21 per cent of the sampled faculty members are in religious institutions, as shown below. Consequently, the simple correlations between two institutional characteristics based on the 2577 individual faculty members, which are presented here, are not identical with the correlations between the same characteristics based on the weighted sample of 115 institutions in Appendix C.

Variable Definitions and Basic Statistics

Institutional Context

1.	Northeast (see Var. 1, App. B).	.3232	.4678	2577
2.	Public control (see Var. 5, App. B).	.4641	.4988	2577
3.	Religious (see Var. 6, App. B).	.2115	.4084	2577
4.	Size (see Var. 9, App. B).	726.8	776.35	2577
5.	Size (log) (see Var. 10, App. B).	2.6048	.5020	2577
6.	Percentage of graduate students (see Var. 13, App. B).	18.569	15.520	2577
7.	University (see Var. 14, App. B).	.5359	.4988	2577

8. Salaries (see Var. 16, App. B). — 12,581 — 2,371 — 1967
9. Inbreeding (see Var. 25, App. B). — .1561 — .1398 — 1985
10. Percentage elected (see Var. 44, App. B). — 45.30 — 43.21 — 2523

Colleague Context

11. Percentage with advanced degrees: Fraction of the total faculty with Ph.D.'s. — .6461 — .2103 — 2577
12. Emphasis on teaching: Mean score (range, 1–5) that teaching ability is important for senior appointments in the department. — 3.9735 — .5263 — 2577
13. Weight of research: Mean score (range, 1–5) that it is difficult to achieve tenure at the institution for one not engaged in research. — 2.7921 — 1.2773 — 2577

Characteristics of Individuals

14. Advanced degree: Dummy variable that respondent has a Ph.D. — .6517 — .4765 — 2575
15. Natural scientist: Dummy variable that respondent's subject is in the natural sciences. — .2510 — .4337 — 2566
16. Emphasizes teaching: Five-point score on the importance of teaching ability for appointing senior faculty in the department. — 3.9713 — 1.1168 — 2473
17. Research weight: Five-point score on the difficulty of achieving tenure at the institution for one not engaged in research. — 2.8026 — 1.6926 — 2518
18. Research obligations: Five-point score on the obligation to publish one's research at the institution. — 3.3281 — 1.3648 — 2399
19. Research involvement: Five-point index with one point each for being engaged in research, carrying out research or creative activity, having had research support in the past three years, and expecting to publish the research. — 2.7932 — 1.4446 — 2432
20. Undergraduate contacts: Number of undergraduates seen more than 10 minutes outside of class in a typical week. — 8.7019 — 6.7268 — 2472
21. Tenure position: Dummy variable that respondent has tenure. — .5434 — .4982 — 2387
22. Allegiance to local institution: Five-point score that allegiance to present institution is very strong. — 3.5768 — 1.3012 — 2552

Matrix of Simple Correlation

	1 NORTHEAST	2 PUBLIC	3 RELIGIOUS	4 SIZE	5 LOG SIZE	6 % GRAD. STUD.	7 UNIVERSITY	8 SALARY	9 INBREEDING	10 ELECTED	11 % ADV. DEGREE	12 % EMPHAS TEACHING
1 NORTHEAST	1.00000											
2 PUBLIC	-0.42689	1.00000										
3 RELIGIOUS	-0.17304	-0.48195	1.00000									
4 SIZE	0.08107	0.14479	-0.31381	1.00000								
5 SIZE (LOG)	0.01714	0.34158	-0.42340	0.86831	1.00000							
6 % GRAD. STUDENTS	0.16901	-0.01288	-0.30720	0.60873	0.62164	1.00000						
7 UNIVERSITY	-0.11379	0.15514	-0.24782	0.55149	0.68604	0.49610	1.00000					
8 SALARIES	0.35677	-0.29945	-0.30269	0.59081	0.60375	0.66729	0.49864	1.00000				
9 INBREEDING	-0.10743	-0.20583	0.44483	0.04332	0.06923	-0.22483	0.06759	-0.23148	1.00000			
10 % ELECTED	0.20875	-0.18599	-0.03366	0.07947	0.02046	0.11425	-0.05746	0.22350	-0.35065	1.00000		
11 % ADVANCED DEGREES	0.14644	-0.04355	-0.27168	0.54628	0.63852	0.55176	0.59701	0.73320	-0.25606	0.17971	1.00000	
12 % EMPHASIZING TEACHING	0.02002	-0.28946	0.40776	-0.61508	-0.67625	-0.61582	-0.72329	-0.64341	-0.08067	0.04139	-0.63263	1.00000
13 % WEIGHT RESEARCH	0.13184	0.10260	-0.37248	0.58064	0.65010	0.66632	0.69881	0.80365	-0.22561	0.11538	0.72157	-0.82279
14 ADVANCED DEGREE	-0.06303	0.01950	-0.12002	0.24113	0.28193	0.24316	0.26374	0.31375	-0.11547	0.07948	0.44185	-0.27938
15 NATURAL SCIENCE	-0.00347	-0.02270	-0.03635	0.08164	0.09966	0.10985	0.14763	0.13460	-0.05628	0.02921	0.15938	-0.17793
16 EMPHASIZING TEACHING	0.00593	-0.13406	0.19179	-0.28954	-0.11933	-0.29123	-0.34201	-0.27363	0.03685	0.01530	-0.29955	0.47168
17 RESEARCH WEIGHT FOR TENURE	0.09551	-0.07478	-0.27863	0.43980	0.49354	0.50570	0.53233	0.57210	-0.18822	0.08597	0.54621	-0.55530
18 RESEARCH OBLIGATION	0.04191	0.08506	-0.12506	0.40319	0.46530	0.45246	0.51122	0.49973	-0.10468	0.06312	0.52211	-0.36240
19 RESEARCH INVOLVEMENT	0.10195	0.03484	-0.16830	0.28067	0.32466	0.27957	0.33676	0.42387	-0.11241	0.10303	0.48054	0.30409
20 UNDERGRADUATE CONTACT	-0.02551	-0.04013	0.08482	-0.25238	-0.27471	-0.29258	-0.28305	-0.26775	0.03005	-0.05233	-0.31563	-0.00306
21 TENURE POSITION	-0.02051	0.03404	-0.00495	0.00278	-0.00632	-0.00568	-0.03756	-0.01684	-0.02061	0.02070	-0.05138	0.12917
22 ALLEGIANCE	-0.02438	0.12254	0.17497	0.12890	-0.16553	-0.07962	-0.09295	-0.07644	0.15815	-0.01958	-0.13124	

TABLE D-1 ....

	13 % WT. RESEARCH	14 ADVANCED DEGREE	15 NATURAL SCIENCE	16 EMPHASIZ TEACHING	17 RESEARCH WEIGHT	18 RESEARCH OBLIGAT.	19 RESEARCH INVOLV.	20 UNDERGRD CONTACT	21 TENURE	22 ALLEGI- ANCE
13 % WEIGHT RESEARCH	1.00000									
14 ADVANCED DEGREE	0.31941	1.00000								
15 NATURAL SCIENCE	0.15551	0.22003	1.00000							
16 EMPHASIZING TEACHING	-0.38846	-0.14398	-0.15159	1.00000						
17 RESEARCH WEIGHT FOR TENURE	0.75682	0.22054	0.13881	-0.36205	1.00000					
18 RESEARCH OBLIGATION	0.62992	0.29413	0.16435	-0.26237	0.61908	1.00000				
19 RESEARCH INVOLVEMENT	0.41688	0.42285	0.16340	-0.24048	0.32162	0.33917	1.00000			
20 UNDERGRADUATE CONTACT	-0.31845	-0.15870	-0.13474	0.21115	-0.26007	-0.23695	-0.21451	1.00000		
21 TENURE POSITION	-0.00097	0.20551	0.05734	0.13318	-0.06957	0.00613	-0.00049	0.03358	1.00000	
22 ALLEGIANCE	-0.13551	-0.07779	-0.02907	0.27622	-0.12819	-0.05838	-0.17723	0.15283	0.30242	1.00000

AUTHOR INDEX

SUBJECT INDEX